The Jack Benny Times
1990-1995

*The newsletter of the
International Jack Benny Fan Club*

© Copyright 2001, Laura Leff

PREFACE

From "The Official History of the International Jack Benny Fan Club", February, 1987:

> The International Jack Benny Fan Club officially started on January 1, 1980. Laura Lee, aged ten years, was the sole founder and President. The first newsletters were individually typed and included copies of articles on Jack Benny and his colleagues. Four honorary members were soon added: George Burns, Irving Fein, Fred deCordova, and Itzhak Perlman. Membership grew slightly in the first years, but the club was still in obscurity. Because of constraints on Laura's time, the newsletters eventually fell out of publication and the club became dormant.
>
> In mid-1983, Laura discovered an article about a Jack Benny fan in Connecticut: Jay Hickerson. Laura contacted him about the small club and her desire for more members. Jay himself became a member and mentioned the club in his publication, Hello Again, named after Jack's immortal opening line. Laura received many letters of inquiry, and the small club began to expand. Seeing the renewed interest, in June of 1984 the newsletter was reinstated under the name The Jack Benny Times. In September of 1984, it became a bimonthly publication containing news and articles about Jack Benny, and information about gaining material on him such as tapes, books, and magazines. The fan club was then publicized in many other publications, as well as in radio interviews with Laura.
>
> In 1984, the word spread overseas about the club--with members in Europe, the club became international. In 1986, the Times was enlarged to encompass more articles...

And the years went by. When I restarted the Times in 1984, I was 15 years old. My enthusiasm was boundless, and I was determined to put whatever I could into the newsletter (and often did). The Times ran through the most eventful 11 consecutive years of my life: graduating high school; moving from my hometown of Grand Rapids, Michigan, to Fort Wayne, Indiana; getting my Bachelor's and Master's degrees; moving to California; starting a career; losing my mother; and getting married. I always had a difficult task of getting them out on time--which I usually didn't--but looking back, it's almost a miracle that they came out at all. I frequently commented, "It may not come out on time, but it *will* come out!"

It truly was the members that made it happen. People generously submitted stories, questions, xeroxes, and magazines, many of which are still waiting to be used. So often I would get busy, distracted, or discouraged; then a note would arrive saying, "I really enjoy the newsletter," making it all worthwhile. Even in 1994 when the entire year was one issue because of major personal changes, it was answered by an outpouring of support. And there were those who never said anything, but faithfully sent their checks for $6.39 every year.

There are some fantastic memories behind these articles: driving three hours to meet Phil Harris, pleading with a <u>Sugar Babies</u> stagehand for five minutes with Mickey Rooney, talking with Tony Butala at 3AM by a hotel swimming pool, cutting a Statistics class to interview Dennis Day, attending Jack's induction into the Television Academy Hall of Fame, and many others. I hope that the warmth and excitement of these occasions can come through the words, making you feel like you were there, experiencing it along with me.

I took a break in 1996, and the Vice President temporarily assumed day-to-day responsibilities. I returned in 2000, with the next issue of the <u>Times</u> coming out late that year. A few years from now, I look forward to the second volume of bound <u>Times</u>, with more information, interviews, and memories.

To Jack, for being Jack Benny.
To Jack's friends, for sharing their memories.
To Dan, for understanding.
To Joe, for his advice and support.
And to the members, for always being there.

Enjoy,

Laura Leff

Laura Leff
President, IJBFC

THE JACK BENNY TIMES

Volume X, Number 1 INTERNATIONAL DISTRIBUTION January-February 199

Mel Remembered

PRESIDENT'S MESSAGE

Jell-o again...guess what folks! On January 1, 1990, we officially celebrated our

TENTH ANNIVERSARY!!!

Do you believe it? It seems like only yesterday I was hand-delivering newsletters to members, putting them through the vents in lockers! We've come a long way, baby! As much as I would like to hand-deliver the newsletters to members all over America, Canada, England, Scotland, Egypt and Australia; I do not really have the funds at this time! (And I bet some of you don't have lockers.) In any event, my thanks to **YOU**, the members, who have made it all possible. Your letters; contributions of tapes, articles, photos, etc.; and other help has been **greatly appreciated**. I hope that the newsletters have maintained a quality worthy of your reading time (although perhaps not a timeliness in delivery...humblest apologies!). I hope that those of you obtaining 39 Forever and using the Jack Benny tape library have found these to be informative and enjoyable. Please know that if you ever have any questions, requests, comments, or suggestions, please feel free to write or call me: (219) 637-2287. Your opinions mean a great deal to me, and I want to be certain that the club is living up to your expectations. Once again, thank you to **all** of you. Here's to another ten years!

$6.39 DUE

BRUCE BAKER * STEVE BRENT * AL BRUTON, III * ROB COHEN * GEORGE C. COURTESIS * RICK CROUCHER * BILL GRAFF * RON GREGORY * ALAN GROSSMAN * SAREE KAMINSKY * THE LAKES * GLENN LAXTON * STEVEN LEWIS * JAMES A. LINK * FRANKLIN LOPSHIRE * TODDY MYERS * ROBERT OLSEN * STEPHEN OUALLINE * THE ROGERSES * JOHN SCHLAMP * KEVIN B. SHAFER * THE SPANGLERS * KEN WEIGEL * CHARLIE WILLER * DOUG WOOD

Have issues through June of this year waiting for you; am anxiously awaiting being able to send the other two to you! Please let me know when I may do so!

MEL BLANC REMEMBERED

Two recent additions to our family are Mary Lou Wallace and Walt Mitchell, who were personal friends of Mel Blanc. Mary Lou has written me a couple lovely letters which she has allowed me to transcribe. Thanks!

...As for Mel Blanc, Walt and I interviewed him in April 1978, for a nostalgia publication (The World of Yesterday) and it was apparent to Mel even at that point that we were more than just casual fans of his. We asked questions about all aspects of his career and made an effort to stay away from questions we figured he was tired of answering (e.g., "How did you create the voice of Bugs Bunny?") He happily answered our questions, but worked the conversation so that he told a lot of the stories that we thought we had spared him! He loved telling those stories, and he also loved going into any character (either cartoon or radio/television) that was being discussed. Anyway, Walt kept in touch with Mel while working on the article (which, with illustrations, came to about 50 pages--Mel was so pleased with the results that he wrote to the publishers and asked for two more copies!) and a wonderful friendship developed in the process! We visited him at his office in 1980, and visited him at his home in 1983, 1986 (three times during that trip), and 1987. In 1988, he came to see us in our hotel room in Hollywood (and took us to lunch, which he always did for us--always refusing to let us pay the check!) We also went to see his college talks in 1980, 1981 and 1982, and went to Washington, D.C. in 1984 to see him honored at the Smithsonian--Walt and I always joked that we were Mel's "groupies!"

I think that one of the reasons that Mel was so fond of us was because we were such fans of Jack Benny--Mel thought the world of Jack, and enjoyed recalling his friendship with him. Mel had had two clocks in his den that Jack had given him (Mel collected watches and clocks)--one was a wooden clock that I don't recall too well, and the other clock was a map of the world with a small clock in every time zone! Mel once told us that if we had known him while jack was alive, he would have introduced us to him. (This was no Hollywood baloney--Mel was a very sincere person.)

~~~~~~
3-19-90
[LL: Mel was made an honorary member of the fan club some time ago, but unfortunately we never received any response from him.]

I'm surprised that you never got any response from Mel. He seemed to be good about answering fan mail--from 1985 on he didn't write as many letters as he had because of his health. Because of his emphysema he tired easily, but always gave his all to his work, which he truly loved. His doctor told him not to talk continuously for more than half an hour at a time--from our experience and from what we heard from other people, it seems to be a safe bet that he broke that rule more often than not! I'll never forget that when we visited him in 1986, he had just had a surgical procedure to clear out his heart valve--this was similar to angioplasty (the balloon that clears out arteries) and Mel was one of the first five people in Southern California to have it done. At this point, he had to use oxygen all the time (eventually needing it less and less) and while we were taping a discussion with him (not knowing about the restriction, but still making sure we didn't put any strain on him) the subject of the Maxwell came up--before we could stop him, he went through the whole thing and apparently was none the worse for wear!

[LL: Want to insert this MJ anecdote here..."Only once did Mel worry about his own safety. He came into a regular reading and rehearsal on a Saturday and saw, to his dismay, that we had him doing the sound of the Maxwell's motor. He came to the writers and sheepishly said that he didn't know if he'd be able to do it Sunday. He was just getting over an attack of the flu and he still was suffering from a residual effect--a slight case of diarrhea. Therefore, he explained, coughing at that time wouldn't be the smartest thing he ever did. However on Sunday he was never better and he coughed loud enough to register eight on the Richter scale. We don't know how he did it--whether he was following the actor's credo, "The show must go on," or whether he had recovered enough to chance an accident, or whether he owed his perfect performance to liberal doses of Kaopectate."]

You are correct in your guess that Mel was a really terrific guy--I can't say enough about him. I still am amazed at times that Walt and I became such good friends of his (Noel write us that Mel considered us "cherished friends--almost like his own kids!") and that friendship is something that we'll always cherish! I assume that you have Mel's book (great stories about Jack!)--if so, take a look at the acknowledgements page, second paragraph. Walt and I knew for a long time that our names would be included, but we didn't think our names would be under "special thanks"--Mel sent each of us an autographed copy of the book. Mine reads "For my good friend Mary Lou--thanks for all your help. Love, Mel Blanc, 8/25/88." I can't remember exactly what Walt's says but it's something like "Thanks for your help--I couldn't have done it without you." I may have mentioned this in my other letters, but Mel used to say that we knew more about his career than he did! To our surprise, Noel says that we probably know more about Mel's career than anybody else--including himself!

I could go on about Mel because he was such a terrific person who we loved a lot and miss dearly (as I write this, it is six months since we lost him). Like Jack, Mel will live forever and, best of all, will be making people laugh forever.
~~~~~~
Please send all questions, comments, additions, corrections, etc. to:

Laura Lee, c/o International Jack Benny Fan Club Offices, 15430 Lost Valley Drive, Fort Wayne, Indiana 46845

Please friends, send no bombs.

(Source unknown. Sorry.)*

The Glorious Years with Jack Benny

Mel Blanc is quite literally a one-man stock company. With the possible exception of animated cartoons, I don't believe he ever found a more appropriate showcase in which to demonstrate the sheer vastness of his versatility, than in his performances with the late Jack Benny. From 1939 until Jack passed away, Mel worked with him extensively on radio and later on television. He also gave one of his funniest—yet one of his most dramatic!—performances in the entire history of his world of fantasy. It is only proper, therefore, that an extended portion of this article be devoted to this particular area.

For sort of an overall assessment from Mr. Blanc on the subject, I first asked him what it was like to work for and with the great comedian. "Well, I have worked with practically every star in the business, but **none** can compare with Jack Benny. He was a wonderful man. He wasn't only my boss, but he was my best friend, too. And Jack was very considerate; very liberal; just the opposite of what he was on the program, you know. And we never signed a contract. I never signed a contract with Jack. He just asked me at the end of the season, 'Say, you gonna be with me next year?' And I'd say, 'Well, if y' give me a raise an' buy me a drink! 'Well,' he says, 'C'mon, then. I'll buy you a drink!' That's the way we worked for years since 1939." Jack learned of Mel through Mel's work in animated cartoons. "He called me in and said (referring to his radio character and the script, 'I've got a bear down in my basement that's guarding my vault—he's already eaten the gas man!—but do you think you could do the growl of a bear?' And I thought for a moment; said, 'Yeah, I think I can.' He said, 'What would it sound like?' I said, 'Maybe like this:'" And at this point, Mel gave out with such a load roar that, even though Mary Lou and I were expecting it, we both gave a start! Naturally, Jack was impressed. "He said, 'Great! Great! You're on next week!' So for six months, all I did was the growl of a bear. Finally I said to him, 'You know, Mr. Benny, I can also talk?' Well, Jack fell down, pounded the table and said, 'Good! I'll have the writers write something in for you.'" And that was how this long and mutually rewarding association began.

Mr. Blanc continued, "So one of the first things they wrote in was the train caller at the Union Depot. You know, Jack always used to leave by train before planes were popular. And this train caller always said, 'Train leaving on Track Five for Anaheim, Azusa and Cuc------amonga!' Everybody beat me to 'Cucamonga!'" This last statement refers to the fact that when he made that announcement, he always paused in the middle when announcing "Cucamonga" and the pauses gradually got longer and longer. Finally on one broadcast, he stopped at "Cuc-" as usual and, following the script to the letter in this instance, waited for the rest of the cast to do about five minutes of dialog. The members of the studio audience knew they were deliberately being teased and they loved it, waiting patiently for Mel to finish the line. When, completely unrelated to what the rest of the cast was saying, he finally cut in with "-amonga," he virtually brought down the house!

The changing mood of the traveling public didn't faze Jack's writers in the slightest. One might have thought that the above joke format was doomed as train travel became less popular. "But even when planes came in," Mr. Blanc points out, "he had me as the plane caller on several programs. I was the guy who was supposed to be calling planes: 'Plane flying to Anaheim, Azusa....We don't stop at Cucamonga, so don't get off there!'"

"But then he had a parrot and he couldn't get that to come in on cue, so he said, 'Can you do a parrot?' I said, 'Yeah.'" At that point, he went into the whistling and squawking voice of Jack's parrot, ad-libbing "Benny's a cheapskate! Benny's a cheapskate!" as part of it! "Well, he almost kicked me out for sayin' that. But I was his parrot."

I asked Mr. Blanc if we could do the Mexican routine on the tape and he consented. This routine involved his aforementioned ability in the area of deadpan comedy. The Little Mexican (he had no name on the show) turned up every so often, and try as he might, Jack couldn't get more than single-syllable answers

*(Just before press time) Wait... I think this is

out of him whenever he saw him. I transported myself, via my imagination, to the local train station, and sure enough, there was the Little Mexican. I didn't have my watch with me, so I approached him:

"Excuse me...Sir?"
"Si."
"Is the train coming in on time?"
"Si."
"You're waiting for someone on the train?"
"Si."
"What's your name?"
"Sy."
"Sy?"
"Si."
"This person you're waiting for—is it a lady?"
"Si."
"A relative?"
"Your sister!"
"Si."
"What is her name?"
"Sue."
"Sue?"
"Si."
"Does your sister work for a living?"
"Si."
"What does she do?"
"Sew."
"Sew?"
"Si."

That was about all there was to that routine, although variations on it were done on the show from time to time. And as many times as they did it, Jack could never get through it with a straight face. That flat, almost woebegone expression of Mel's was just too much for the show's star. Mel commented, "Well, that's what used to break Jack up, you know. Jack would break up at every rehearsal, 'cause I'd keep a sober face no matter what happened. I'd **always** keep a sober face, and he would break up every time. Then he'd say, 'I'm **not** gonna break up on the show. I'm **not** gonna break up on the show.' Come the show, he'd break up every time! He just couldn't control himself; he got such a kick out of it."

Jack travelled around (in the scripts) in an ancient car known as a Maxwell. When Jack ordered Rochester to start the antique engine, it was heard to sputter, wheeze and gasp desperately before it finally turned over and started. This was not achieved with a mechanical sound effect device. It was Mel Blanc again, giving his all for the boss, and I **do** mean "all!" The subject did not come up in the course of the interview, but Mary Lou and I have seen Mr. Blanc performing this sound effect on television talk show guest shots. If you have also seen this, you can understand why it probably requires more physical effort on his part than any other voice or sound effect he does.

This came about quite by accident. There was a record on the turntable at the studio, containing the sound of an old car starting up, and this was ready to be used when the script called for it—almost! One day during a rehearsal involving that sound effect, Mel noticed within a minute or so of the required sound that the turntable was not plugged in! So when the sound effect cue came along in the script, Mel stepped up to the microphone and did the sound himself. He even made the sound funnier than the straight effect would have sounded, and the ad-lib was immediately added to his permanent repertoire. (Many years later, he used it as part of his voice for the title character of the SPEED BUGGY television cartoon show for Hanna-Barbera Productions.)

The writing staff of Jack's radio series played Mel's talent as a challenge. He says, "Milt Josefsberg—who wrote this book on the Jack Benny show, you know (**The Jack Benny Show**, Arlington House, 1977)—he was one of Jack's writers. And he tried to throw me once. He used to write into the script something I couldn't do. And we were visiting Epsom Downs in England, you know, where they have the horse races, and he writes into the script, 'Mel Blanc does an English horse whinny'— underlines 'English'! Now, how the heck can you tell the nationality of a horse? But I didn't say anything; I never say 'no'. When it came to the cue for an English horse whinny, I did it like this:." Mel's whinny was followed by an upper-crust Britisher's exclamation, "A-hawr!"

Another time, the sound cue read, "Mel Blanc makes the sound of a goldfish!" Again Mel wasn't fazed, but this time nobody else had any idea of what was coming. When Jack spoke to his goldfish and the goldfish was supposed to answer him, Mel walked up to the radio microphone, opened and closed his pursed lips the way a fish would—and the audience in the studio and at home heard absolutely nothing! That was, indeed, the sound of a goldfish! While we were discussing this, Mary Lou asked Mr. Blanc if he would assume the fish pose he had used, and let her take a picture. Amused at the request, he obliged— chuckling about it after the shutter whirred. This picture is reproduced in black and white with this article on page 12.

Behind the Scenes with Jack

Looking for more background information on how THE JACK BENNY SHOW was put together, I asked Mr. Blanc whether there was any difference between working on Jack Benny's radio show and working on other shows. He replied, "Uh, yeah, there was a world of difference. On the Benny show, we always used to do the rehearsals exactly as we were going to do the show, 'cause Jack would time it....and he would see whether the rest of the cast laughed at the jokes that were in the script. If they didn't, he would take that out or change it. He was quite an editor that way. And he had a marvellous sense of humor.... and great timing, which was so very important. And this was one of the things that Jack always did; whereas on the other shows—I used to do THE CISCO KID. We'd kid through the rehearsal just to time it. And I'd say, 'Ceesco, thee sheriff I theenk ees cuuumeeng!' You'd hear a lot of shots. And Cisco would say, 'Did he hitcha, Pancho?' I'd say, 'I dunno. Geeme a glassa water; I'll see eef I leeak!'" I was unaware that Mel had done that radio program. "Oh, sure," he said. "In Los Angeles I did that with Jack Mather for a good many years!"

Jack's insistence on sticking closely to the script seemed to preclude much chance of ad-libbing. But when I asked Mr. Blanc whether or not this was ever done, he replied, "Oh, yeah! I used to ad-lib all the time with Jack and usually at the rehearsal, and he would laugh and say, 'Keep it in!' 'Cause at rehearsal, that's how we got that English horse, you know. And he said, 'Oh, God! We've gotta keep that in the script!' So we did, and I did several things with Hack that I would ad-lib, the same as I do in the cartoons." But what about when the show was actually put on the air, I wanted to know? Did he ever ad-lib then? "Oh, yeah; once in a great while I'd throw in some crazy gag. Jack'd fall down laughing."

When I remarked that I understood that Jack was a great audience for other comedians, Mel acknowledged the fact: "He was. He was a marvellous audience." And at this point, Mr. Blanc added an unrelated but very important consideration: "You know, the joke was always pulled on Jack, and he was the brunt of all the jokes. But you'd say something to another listener; you'd say, 'Gee, I thought that was a very funny gag!' He'd say, 'Where did you hear it?' 'On THE JACK BENNY SHOW.' No matter who did it, it was always 'on THE JACK BENNY SHOW.'"

Professor LeBlanc

One of the best-remembered characters of all those which Mr. Blanc performed on THE JACK BENNY SHOW, was the role of Jack's long-suffering French violin teacher, Professor Le Blanc. Again for those readers who may be too young to have seen this character, I'll give a description. Professor LeBlanc (in the radio and television scripts) came to Jack's home every week to give him a violin lesson. After seventeen years, Jack's playing **still** had an effect on his listeners that was truly soul-stirring: The effect was the same as that which one feels when one hears a piece of new chalk squeaking its way across a blackboard!

(I should clarify two points here. One is that the violin lesson being a part of Jack's own weekly schedule was something his radio and television fans simply knew from occasional script references. The violin lesson sketches were not a part of the program each week. The other point is that Jack's terrible violin playing was entirely a fictional part of the character he played. Mr. Benny was actually one of the most skilled musicians on that instrument. In his later years, he would often help struggling symphony orchestras to raise capital, or raise money for different charities from time to time, by performing in serious classical concerts as special guest violinist with various orchestras. But on his program, he played the character of Jack Benny, would-be violinist, who **still** couldn't get the hang of it even after seventeen years of lessons. On very rare occasions, however, when he was not performing the story-line but was speaking to his audience in front of a curtain, he would step out of character when his guest for the week was noted for playing the violin, and he would play a perfectly-executed duet with the guest.)

Speaking of "executed," character Jack's playing so infuriated Professor LeBlanc that the teacher often thought along the lines of execution—either Jack's or his own! **Anything** to avoid the torture of the hour the weekly lesson took up! The character of Professor LeBlanc was a classic example of frustration comedy. The poor professor would often reach the point in a lesson where he could hardly stand the noise and would start screaming at Jack. After Jack calmed him down, the professor would apologize: "Forgive me, Monsieur Ben-nee! I lost my tempair....I wish it was my hearing!"

The professor's distain for Jack's playing wasn't exactly the world's best-kept secret! Audiences sized up the situation quite clearly as Jack sawed away at the famous eight-note beginner's exercise, while the professor marked time by singing such gems as:

Continued next issue!

FAN CLUB

15430 LOST VALLEY DRIVE
FORT WAYNE, IN 46845

Volume X, Number 2   INTERNATIONAL DISTRIBUTION   March-April 19

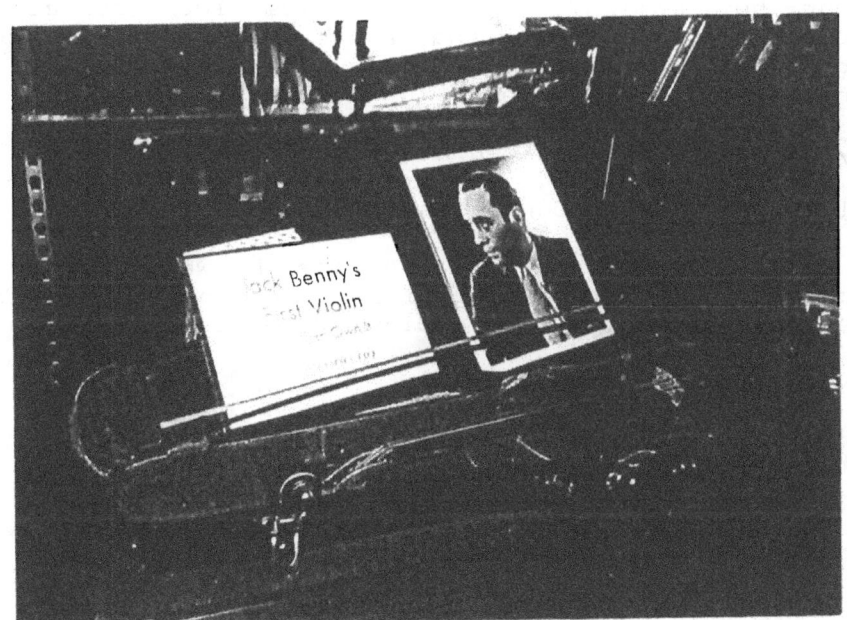

PRESIDENT'S MESSAGE

Jell-o again...welcome to another fun- and fact-filled (I hope) issue of the Times. Must note two movies that I saw recently, both on TNT (keep your eye on this network)! One I accidentally found in the middle; It's in the Air from 1935. Difficult to give a very accurate review when you do not know all the facets of the story, but I must say it was interesting. Flying at...what...150,000 feet in a hot-air balloon is not the first place you would think of for the character of Jack Benny! And doing a radio broadcast, too.

Also chanced upon one called What Price Hollywood? from 1932 with Constance Bennett, Lowell Sherman, and Gregory Ratoff. No, Jack was not in it. However, there was a black butler who had a minor, but comical, part. Am almost 100% certain that it was Eddie Anderson. Being that he did not debut on the Jack Benny Show until March 28, 1937, this is an interesting study of him early in his media career.

Jay Hickerson has revised his log of Jack Benny radio shows, and it is now available. For information, contact him at: Box 4321 (Blastoff), Hamden Connecticut 06514-0321.

Am still in need of data on the Maxwell Car Company. Have received some interesting items...anyone have ANYTHING else? Even references for information? Please let me know.

Now on with the show!

$6.39 DUE

JOHN MALONE * JEANETTE THOMAS
Have one more issue waiting for you folks!

WE MADE IT

Ladies and gentlemen, we have made it. I mean really made it. The International Jack Benny Fan Club is going to be part of the halls of immortality; 39 Forever has been special-ordered by the Smithsonian Institution. I am as surprised as you are! Tried to find a bindery locally to get it hard-bound, but was unsuccessful. In any event, sent the last copy from the second printing to them. My thanks goes out to all of you who helped "make it happen." A third printing will be obtained along with these newsletters; if you have not ordered your copy yet, please drop me a note if you are interested.

Copyright 1990, Laura Lee

JACK'S FIRST VIOLIN

Say, I received this great picture of (supposedly) Jack's first violin (see cover). Unfortunately, in my quest to raise the $20,000, I separated the letter from the photo. (Who was so kind as to send this to me? Sorry!) If memory serves, it is in Harrah's basement. The thing is...I have my doubts. Judging from the size of the violin in relation to the photo of Jack (which I assume is an 8 x 10), that would indicate that it is a full-size violin. I know that Jack's first violin was given to him on February 14, 1900, for his sixth birthday, and it was a half-size. Does anyone know anything about this? Will check into it, and let you know what I find.

JACK BENNY CLASSIFIED

LOOKING FOR: The Jack Benny Show with Ethel Merman playing a telephone operator (VHS), and other video items associated with Ethel Merman (especially Broadway-type videos). Have to trade: 1954 General Foods Salutes Rogers and Hammerstein with Jack in a long sketch, The Mouse that Jack Built direct transfer from 16mm, and Remember How Great from 1961. Skip Koenig, 1298 Wickapecko Drive, Ocean, New Jersey, 07712.

~~~~~~

WANT TO TRADE: Jack Benny TV shows and movies on VHS, or any other old radio stars and shows on tape (such as radio specials, NBC radio specials, CBS, etc.). Rob Cohen, 6635 Helm Avenue, Reynoldsburg, Ohio 43068. (Rob: I use Word Perfect and Q&A with an IBM system.)

~~~~~~

Radio-Historian/Author Charles Stumpf is selling off part of his vast collection of radio memorabilia (books, magazines, photos, scripts, etc.). Some items are for mail auction with bid deadline set at August 31, 1990. For free lists send SASE to: Charles Stumpf, 123 West Blaine Street, McAdoo, Pennsylvania 18237. And don't overbid me!

~~~~~~

LOOKING FOR: David R. Smith. Apparently contributed a handwritten itemization of Jack's TV career in the U.C.L.A. collection. If anyone knows his address, please send it to Laura Lee or Peter Tatchell, 40 Bambra Road, Caulfield, Victoria, Australia 3161.

THE TALE PIECE

Promised I would print your captions to the photo on the cover of September-October 1989 issue. These come from Joyce Shooks:

Jack: Say, Roch, the postal service is going to put me on a U.S. stamp!

Roch: Yeah, but it'll be on the 39 cent one!

OR...Jack: Laura thinks that the Mad Magnet vamoosed with the missing minutes of the 4-12-53 tape. Little does she know that I borrowed (ahem) them, and it'll cost her $39 to get them back!

Roch: Yeah, but what about the OTHER eighteen minutes of tape?

~~~~~~

Larry Adler commented in a recent letter that, "Jack was proud of [To Be or Not to Be] because, he told me, Lubitsch wanted him, and no one else, in the part.

~~~~~~

This favorite scene comes to us from Ken Weigel:

"Funniest Kubelsky I've heard in months was the 2-3-46 show, where Benny takes Mary to hear Isaac Stern in concert. Jack is complaining to Rochester that a comedian's pay is lousy compared to what a concert violinist earns. 'After all,' he says, 'I don't have much money.' 'I don't know,' says Rochester, 'Every time I turn your mattress over, Wall Street drops 3 points.'

"Later, from the cheap seats high above the concert stage, Benny spots the Colmans down below, and tries to get their attention. ('Oh Ronnie! Oh Ronnnnnnieeee!') He throws peanut shells down, and then throws the bag down, then hangs by his heels from the rail--and loses his toupee in Ronnie's lap. Ronnie knows it's Jack's toupee by the laundry mark: 'LSMFT.' A note sewn inside the lining asks the finder to watch the classified in the Beverly Hills papers--the owner will advertise for 'a missing cocker spaniel, with a part on the side.'"

ETHER ONE

How about a new column? In the spirit of "Radio is Alive and Well" from Jay Hickerson's newsletter, we introduce "Ether One" as a listing of stations playing Jack Benny programs. Dick Hill reports that KCMO radio in Kansas City, Missouri plays Jack's programs on Sunday morning. KMA of Shenandoah, Iowa played (assumedly still does) "early radio" on Sunday afternoons. Finally, KFAB in Omaha, Nebraska plays early radio in the evenings from 9:00 to 10:00.

If a station near you broadcasts Jack Benny (does WMT still do it?), drop me a line!

~~~~~~

Please send all questions, comments, additions, corrections, etc. to:

Laura Lee, c/o International Jack Benny Fan Club Offices, 15430 Lost Valley Drive, Fort Wayne, Indiana 46845

Please friends, send no bombs.

Continued from last issue!

"Make the notes a little thinner; I don't want to lose my dinner!"

Or: "My poor heart is nearly breaking; What an awful sound you're making!"

On one such episode in 1947, before the radio show moved to television, the professor arrived at Jack's house while Rochester was giving Jack a shave. With Rochester's cheery "Sit down, Professor; you're next!" the audience could hear Jack's valet going about the task at hand. All at once, Jack was heard to say:

"Ow! Rochester, you cut me!"

"It's about time you felt it; I did it a minute ago!"

"Well, why didn't ya tell me?"

"I was waitin' for y' t' bleed!"

"Don't be funny. Did you cut me bad?"

"Aw, it's nothin', Boss. I just snipped the stem off your Adam's apple!"

"Clumsy thing; now I'll have to buy a collar button! Well, wipe the soap off my face.... Thanks. Oh, Professor, I'll go put on a tie and then I'll come back for my lesson."

"Oui, Monsieur." When Jack closed the door and was out of earshot, Professor LeBlanc whispered to the valet.

"Rochestair, uh, the cut on Monsieur Ben-nee's throat—is it a bad one?"

"Naw, it's not deep at all. And it's all my fault."

"No-no, Rochestair. It was **my** fault. I didn't push your hand **hard** enough!"

Even the professor's exits were good for a laugh. One time, Jack said good-bye to him and he replied:

"But Monsieur Ben-nee! You have forgotten something: You have not paid me."

"Oh, yes. By the way, Professor, would you like some lunch?"

"No. I want the mon-ee this time!"

On another occasion, Professor LeBlanc declared wearily:

"That is enough for today. The lesson, she is ovair."

"Tut, tut, tut, Professor! The hour isn't up yet. Look at the clock. We still have 14 seconds to go!"

"14 seconds...and then you will give me back my pants?"

In still another example, at the close of the sketch the professor heads for the door, muttering to himself, "If I wasn't so hungry, I wouldn't come back!"

His Greatest Performance

Although it was destined to go for one more year on NBC, THE JACK BENNY SHOW was nearly ending its long run on CBS Television when a certain very special episode was filmed early in 1964. The Professor LeBlanc character, when featured in previous shows, was usually used in relatively short sketches, with the rest of the programs taken up with other matters to round out each of the episodes in which he appeared. But in this particular episode, the entire show centered around the character. There was a funny and yet highly dramatic aspect to the script which allowed Mr. Blanc to perform Professor LeBlanc in his usual hilarious manner on one level, while at the same time playing the character in a warmly sympathetic manner on another level. On top of that, this was one of the occasional instances where Mr. Blanc ad-libbed his role—this time without saying a word while he was ad-libbing! These factors combine to make this particular performance not only his very best interpretation of Professor LeBlanc, but (I believe most people would agree) surely his greatest performance of all time in all media. On Tuesday evening, August 23rd, 1977, CBS reran the show in prime time. (It was one of four shows chosen from 16 seasons of programs, so obviously CBS felt it was also one of the top programs of the series.)

I made reference to this particular episode, naturally, during the interview. Was a lot of fan mail received? You bet it was! When I asked Mr. Blanc about this, he immediately went into the Professor LeBlanc character to begin discussion of the show:

"Oui. We got loads of mail on that show. And he wore me out, being his violin teacher Professor LeBlanc. I worked with heem. I **slaved** with heem! Finally at the end of the lesson I would say, 'Please, Monsieur Ben-nee! Take the ball and chain off my foot! The lesson is ovair! Let me go home!' I would sing to him while he was playing, 'What a tune your fiddle brings on!/How I wish it had not strings on!' "

(My personal favorite of the couplets was the one which went something like, "Now please play it neic and classy!/Hold your tongue in; you're not Lassie!")

Dropping the characterization, Mr. Blanc continued. "Well, Jack loved that show, and he loved to work with me on that show, and I loved to work with him on it, too, because we...we actually characterized the two...as they should have been characterized. And when I got through with the show, Jack said, 'Mel, you're not only a comedian, you're a great actor!' I said, 'What did I do?' He says, 'You acted a beautiful part,' and I said to Jack, 'Jack, this is the best thing I ever saw you do, too, because you are actually a real bad violin player—which I thought you were!' " Jack must surely have cracked up at Mel's kiddingly outrageous insult. Obviously Mel wasn't about to let things get **too** mawkish! But I could tell from the way he spoke that he greatly appreciated Jack's sincere compliment.

The outline of the show, for those who may have missed it, is this: Some aspects of the series were very realistic, such as the fact that Jack played Jack Benny, a comedian who had his own television show. In the episode under discussion, he returned home from his broadcast very discouraged, but his attention was soon drawn away from this when he learned that his violin teacher was having a nervous breakdown and was in a local psychiatrist's office. Hurrying over to the office, Jack saw poor Professor LeBlanc sitting upright on the psychiatrist's couch, not saying a word, and staring blankly into space (or "Blanc-ly" into space, if you insist). His only movement was to absent-mindedly reach into a nearby box of tissues, take one out, put it into one or another of his pockets, and repeat this over and over and over, slowly. The psychiatrist doesn't know this, but the professor has finally cracked under the strain of being unable to teach Jack to be a good violinist even after giving him lessons weekly for seventeen years!

The psychiatrist asks Jack about his knowledge of the professor. Jack explains the situation and the scene dissolves into a series of flashbacks showing Jack at the various stages of his violin lessons with the professor. The further along the falshbacks go, the older the men get, but Jack's playing remains the same—terrible! The scene then shifts back to the psychiatrist's office. Understanding the circumstances, the psychiatrist suggests that Jack play his violin right there in the office, hoping the professor will hear the beautiful music and snap out of his condition.

Jack goes home and quickly returns with his instrument. He cautiously assumes his playing position and begins to play a song. The audience, of course, is expecting his usual off-key performance with scratchy noise thrown in for good measure. This time, however, (because the script calls for it) Jack plays the selection perfectly! As he plays, the professor begins to respond to the beautiful sound and by the song's end, he is back to normal. Realizing that Jack can finally play (at least once, anyway), the professor walks out of the psychiatrist's office a deliriously happy man, secure in the knowledge that he is not the failure he had thought he was.

While we were discussing this program, Mary Lou spoke up: "I want to ask a question concerning this particular episode. Now, in the psychiatrist's office when you're sitting there having your nervous breakdown, you sat there and you kept taking Kleenex out of the box and putting them in your pockets. Did you improvise that yourself?" "Yes, that was my own idea," he explained. "I saw a box of Kleenex there and I just kept takin' 'em out, kept takin' 'em out 'n' out 'n' out..." He chuckled at the recollection. I asked it that bit with the tissues was done during rehearsal. "No!" Mel exclaimed. "No, it **wasn't** done at rehearsal! It was during the show, right before the cameras! I saw the box of Kleenex there and I didn't just wanna sit there, so I kept takin' 'em out, puttin' 'em in my pocket!" He laughed again.

Meanwhile, I wanted to know if the flashbacks were real flashbacks taken from earlier programs, or if they were filmed at the same time as the rest of the episode, merely changing costumes to indicate different time periods. Mel answered, "We did them in different costumes; it was all done at the same time. We would put on different clothing, and in one spot I had a toupee and he had a toupee on, you know. We call 'em 'rugs!' And then my clothes would be torn." (The wardrobe department provided Mel with four or five tuxedos in graduated levels of decomposition to represent the passage of time. They were supposed to be the same tuxedo gradually wearing out!) "My shoes had holes in the bottom of 'em, an' everything, 'cause I wasn't makin' enough money to pay for new clothes. And finally it got to the point where I said, 'I can't live on what I'm making; I owe the bank; my wife, is gonna have a baby and I haveta have more money.' So he raised me....gave me a quarter more!"

Another of Mel's favorite gags from that show came at the point where, after a typically horrendous solo by Jack, Jack asked Professor LeBlanc, "Professor, how can I improve the tone quality of my playing?" "Pairhaps, Monsieur Ben-nee," suggested the professor, "eef you wehr to hold the violin upside down...?" "Upside down?" echoed Jack, puzzled. "But Professor, if I hold the violin upside down, the strings will be on the bottom! No music will come out!" With a shrug, the weary instructor replied, "We must try **any**theeng!"

Perhaps the fact that Mel Blanc can actually play the violin is not so well known due to the fact that he has rarely played the instrument publicly. Certainly he never gave Jack a demonstration of how the music should sound when they were performing the Professor LeBlanc sketches. Mel explains thus: "Well, when I was a kid I played violin just to practice playing the violin, you know. I took about eight years of lessons. I never was a **good** violinist but, uh, I played a number of tunes, so I **could** read music."

"Jack didn't know I played the violin," Mr. Blanc continued. "He was rehearsing a duet with Gisele MacKenzie and on this one show, I took the violin away from 'im and I played along with her. And Jack was flabbergasted! He says, 'Oh, my God! I didn't know you could play!....We're gonna keep that in the show!' So in the show, I came back with a buncha visitors, you know, and I walked up to him and I took the violin away from him and started playing with Gisele." As an afterthought, he added, "...and I had to join the union! I had belonged to the (musician's) union before, in Portland, Oregon, but I had to join the Los Angeles union to play on the show."

GROWING UP: America's median age will be 39 by 2010

The Associated Press

WASHINGTON — Thirty-nine, that magic age teetering between youth and maturity, will be the most typical age for Americans early in the next century, according to Census Bureau projections.

Historically a nation of youthful orientation, the United States is now thirty-something and heading upward, the Bureau reports.

Combining to increase the median age of the population are the maturing of the massive post-World War II Baby Boom and that generation's relatively low birth rates, which reduce the number of babies to pull down the numbers.

So if present trends continue, census officials expect that half of all Americans will be over the age of 39 by the year 2010, and half younger. The agency's most recent estimate of median age was 31.7 as of 1986.

Whether America will plateau at 39 — as did the late comedian Jack Benny — remains to be seen.

The median age of the country touched 30 for the first time in 1950, then slipped back as the Baby Boom produced a bouncing crop of youngsters.

It took until the 1980 census to hit 30 again, edged up to 31.7 as of 1986 and is expected to climb to 33 by 1990, 36.5 by 2000 and 39 by the year 2010, according to Census Bureau projections.

Michigan, which posted a median age of 31.1 for 1986, is expected to reach 38.3 by 2010.

Despite the aging of the population, however, the report anticipates that the so-called dependency ratio will decline.

That ratio is the number of people under 18 and over 65 compared to the number of people of working age in between. The younger and older groups are most likely to "depend" on those working.

The 1986 ratio of 62.2 dependents per 100 workers is expected to slip to 56.7 by the year 2010, with the low birth rate reducing the number of young dependents to a greater extent than aging adds to the older group.

While there have been reports of increases in the total number of births in the last few years, that is because the giant Baby Boom generation is largely in its prime childbearing years. The rate of births per 1,000 remains well below that of the post-World War II period.

The new census study also estimates that the nation's black population will increase

census study claims

to 13.7 percent by 2010. Blacks made up 11.8 percent of the population in 1980.

Nearly one in five Southerners will be black in 2010, 19.7 percent of the population. That will be up from 18.7 percent in 1980.

In the Northeast, blacks will increase from 10.1 percent to 13.2 percent. They will go from 9.1 percent to 11.9 percent in the Midwest and from 5.3 percent to 6.3 percent in the West.

The projections show the Northeast remaining the oldest section of the country, with the median age for that region increasing from 33.6 in 1986 to 40.3 in 2010.

 **FAN CLUB**

15430 LOST VALLEY DRIVE
FORT WAYNE, IN 46825

THE JACK BENNY TIMES

Volume X, Number 3   INTERNATIONAL DISTRIBUTION   May-June 19

PRESIDENT'S MESSAGE

Usually when I write about a person passing away, it is someone who worked directly on the Jack Benny Show: a performer, writer, etc. Or else it is someone who was a close friend of his; or someone rather indirectly linked with him such as, say, Parker Fennelly. However, this is a little different...but just as important.

Jack Bloom became a member of the International Jack Benny Fan Club on May 8th, 1986. In response to my lines about "No one is ever dead until they are forgotten...so Jack Benny shall never die" Jack wrote: "I'll agree with you. Jack Benny will not die. There is a constant flow of new material from and about the man. New radio shows, new television shows, new information in books, new information in magazines. If you haven't seen it or heard it or read it before--it's new. Right?" He also closed by saying, "By joining your club, I hope I can help in some small way. After all, my initials are JB, aren't they?"

Helping "in some small way" is one of the great understatements of the century. For quite some period of time, Jack and I wrote letters back and forth at a feverish pace. The correspondence I have from him is so voluminous that I put it in its own hanging folder, which is comparable to all letters from all members with last names H through K! I loved his letters; they always contained so much humor and vitality, and they helped me through some very difficult times. He even once asked me to call him "Uncle Jack," which I did.

Many times (another understatement) he would also send a book, tapes, a magazine, or some item associated with Jack or our other common loves, including George Gershwin and Al Jolson. Ah, those tapes. Actually, I would estimate that approximately 75% of our tape library was donated by Uncle Jack. He also did extensive research for 39 Forever, which was immensely helpful. He was one of three members that I granted free lifetime memberships for their great contributions to the club. Just musing here momentarily about all the items he sent over these few years; his sincere generosity was absolutely unparalleled by anyone I have ever known.

When I went out to Los Angeles in January of 1989, Uncle Jack was one of the most important people that I wanted to see. Unfortunately, he had a bad cold which he did not want to pass on to me; therefore, we relegated our conversation to the phone. Every morning, someone in the house where I was staying would awaken me with, "Uncle Jack is on the phone!" What a great way to wake up!

Copyright 1990, Laura Lee

Yet as you know, school often came between me and my duties to the club. It also did so for my correspondence with Uncle Jack. I always kicked myself that I had not written more often, but occasionally I would get out a three- or four-page letter to him. Broke another long silence a few months ago with a fairly sizable letter, but it seems that he had been in the hospital since early April. Kept in touch with his wife, Ayne, who was very kind to keep me posted on his condition. (Hope I was not too much bother.)

So that pretty much brings us to now. I got off the phone with Ayne about an hour ago; Uncle Jack passed away on June 24th. Obviously knew it was coming, but it is still rather "sinking in." We have not had rain in quite some time; but just minutes after I found out, I started hearing thunder and some rain. And it started me thinking...about a couple of things. Bob Hope said in Jack Benny's eulogy that, "I know it might sound corny, but there will be times from now on when the lightning will crackle with a special kind of sound, or thunder will peal with a special roar, and I'll think to myself that Cantor or Fields or Fred Allen must have just told Jack a joke." And also this:

> His life was gentle
> And the elements so mixed in him
> That nature might stand up and say to all the world:
> This was a man!

Thank you for indulging me in some reminiscing here; I will miss Jack even more than if he had truly been my Uncle.

Thank you, Uncle Jack, for everything.

~~~~~~

In recognition of Jack Bloom's contribution to the IJBFC, I am establishing the Jack Bloom-Pasadena Chapter, for members who have been active (receiving the newsletter) for four or more years. I am sure that most of you remember the running gag on Jack's show of the Jack Benny Fan Club, Pasadena chapter--hence the above name. Being that Uncle Jack's birthday was on July 2nd, and that the May-June issue (should) come out in July, each May-June issue will announce the induction of eligible members. Therefore, those eligible this year are:

>   JACK ABIZAID
>   **JACK BLOOM**
>   BRUCE BAKER
>   PHIL EVANS
>   ALAN GROSSMAN
>   JAY HICKERSON
>   TIM HOLLIS
>   SAREE KAMINSKY

LAURA LEE
GEORGE LILLIE
TOM MASTEL
BILL OLIVER
ROBERT OLSEN
JOHN SCHLAMP
JOYCE SHOOKS
DAVID SPANGLER
STEVE SZEJNA
BARBARA WATKINS
KEN WEIGEL
DOUG WOOD

NEW MEMBERS

Well, now that we have honored our established members, let us welcome our new members to the family!

****BOBB LYNES ****MARY LOU WALLACE ****WALT MITCHELL ****SCOTT BRICK ****DAVID M. ROGERS ****MEL SIMONS ****WILL JORDAN ****W. ROBERT SMITH ****KEITH LEE ****SANDRA WEBER ****BERNARD BECKERT ****JACK L. PALMER ****JEANETTE M. PALMER ****JOSEPH W. BAVETT, JR. ****ANDRE STOJKA ****JOHN W. CAIRNES, JR. ****CHARLES J. HUCK, JR. ****NANCY HUCK ****THOMAS SALOME ****JAMES ADAM ****RICH JONAS ****MIKE JONAS ****CHARLES FAIR ****CLIVE ROBERTS ****JACK GOOT ****ANN GOOT ****GEORGE SKARZYNSKI ****DARRYL E. HENLEY ****RICHARD HILL ****TOM KLEINSCHMIDT ****HERBERT SADOWSKY ****LORRAINE SADOWSKY ****LINDA SELSMAN-JONES ****ALEXANDRA SELSMAN ****PETER TATCHELL ****LINDA A. HARDING ****SACHA J. HARDING
*****TONY BUTALA

Many of these people are from the Al Jolson Society; a hearty welcome to people whose taste in comedy is just as good as their taste in music. Also would like to send our congratulations to Jack and Ann Goot, who celebrated their 60th wedding anniversary on June 6th. Welcome everyone!

SAM PERRIN: THE SEQUEL

As you remember from our last show, Sam and Peggy had just gone to the south of France with Jack and Mary. We now join our little foursome there...

S: So we're in the south of France, and Jack said to me, "Carlton Hotel." We were having dinner outside on the patio, it was just beautiful...just Jack, Mary, Peggy and me. But before we sat down, Jack said, "Listen, Mary doesn't want to go to the gambling casino, but if you bring it up, I think she will." So now we're having dinner, and I said, "Kind of a quiet night, isn't it Mary?" She said, "Oh, it's all right." I said, "You know, how about going to the gambling casino after dinner?" She said, "No, I don't want to go to the gambling casino." So I said, "Well, nothing else to do. I really would like to go out again." She said, "Sam, I don't want to go to the gambling casino." So I said, "Well Mary...," and Jack said, "Sam, what are you trying to do? Start a fight?"

L: Say, there was a bit on the show like that where Dennis came in and said something similar.

S: There was always something like that where someone would protect Jack, and Jack says "don't protect me."

L: Yeah, something like Dennis comes in, Mary answers the door, and he says, "I'm really gonna tell Jack off. I'm mad, and he's not paying me enough money." Then he goes in and says something very polite, and Mary says, "Dennis! Aren't you going to tell him off?" So Jack says, "What are you trying to do, Mary? Start a fight?"

S: Yeah. On the same trip when we first going to the south of France, we went by train. The worst possible train that you could be on. We got on a little late, and there was no dinner served. The staterooms were about like, if you had a shoehorn with you, you could get into them. Absolutely miserable. So Jack was saying, "Oh, this is terrible." We had two staterooms [for the four of us]...I was in the upper, Peggy was in the lower. We were just about to go to bed, and Jack said, "I'm going to take a sleeping pill." So Mary said, "Jack, give me one, too." Jack says, "Peggy, would you like a sleeping pill?" Peggy says, "Yeah." So he said to me, "Sam, would you like a sleeping pill?" I said, "Oh no, I wouldn't miss this trip for the world." And I never heard a man laugh like that. When he was in his upper bunk in the next room, he was pounding on the wall! He was easy to make laugh, but...he thought that was the funniest thing.

L: It was always the little things that made him laugh. George [Balzer] said something about when Jack wanted something "stronger" in the script, and George finally said, "Well, you could be right, since the four of us could be wrong." [Not necessarily direct quote; look it up in a back issue.]

S: I'll tell you a real story about Jack and his father [Meyer Kubelsky]. [Meyer] lived in Miami, and he went to the racetrack. Jack went down there to visit him, and they went to the racetrack. Jack would make the normal bet, because Jack was not a gambler--$2, $5. His father was writing. He said to his father, "Dad, what are you writing?" His father said, "I don't bet money. So I take a piece of paper, and I write down my selection, and I bet $2...and I put [$2] in [my coat pocket]. If

I win, I put it in [my right] pocket. If I lose, I put it in [my left] pocket." So Jack thought, "If the old man enjoys it, fine." So they play, and about in the fourth race, Jack comes back from making a bet, and he sees his father just sitting there. [Jack] says, "Aren't you betting on this next race?" He says, "Nope. No more racing." [Jack] says, "Why?" He says, "I spent all I had!"

L: That reminds me of the one where Jack's in Las Vegas and he hits the jackpot on the slot machine. The bellboy comes along, and he says "Mary," or "Don, you tip him. I don't have any change." In reference to the south of France, I know that Jack, Mary, Fred Allen and Portland were close friends. Did Fred Allen ever come with you on these vacations?

S: No, because he was in New York when he was on radio.

L: I just didn't know how much time they spent together. Just when one would visit the other coast, I assume.

S: Well, my present wife, Barbara and I had dinner with Portland at the Sunset Hotel.

L: Portland remarried, didn't she?

S: Well, she went with a man...but I can't remember his name. She never wore jewelry...but I never asked her why.

L: I once heard that Mary was kind of "into" jewelry.

S: I don't think so...no.

L: There was a thing where Hedda Hopper "crashed" one of their parties, was mad at them for some reason, and said that Mary had changed jewelry three times during the party.

S: Well, whatever Hedda Hopper said--that type--was nothing. I think everybody liked Mary. They were a little afraid of her, but they liked her.

~~~~~~
LOTS MORE TO COME!

Please send all questions, comments, additions, corrections, etc. to:

Laura Lee, c/o International Jack Benny Fan Club Offices, 15430 Lost Valley Drive, Fort Wayne, Indiana 46845

Please friends, send no bombs.

San Diego Union
Jan 19, 1989

Don Freeman
...Point of View

Let the names ring out: George Burns and Gracie Allen, Chet Huntley and David Brinkley, Red Skelton, David Susskind, David Wolper, Jack Benny. What names they are, names to fire the imagination, names to conjure with, names that embody the essence of television.

What emotions they have touched!

They have given us the gift of laughter; they have also enabled us to see the world and its happenings with clarity and to be moved emotionally by the catharsis inherent in drama and spectacle.

Certainly, in so many ways, our lives would not have been the same without them.

Consider them: a comedy team, a team of newsmen, two producers, two comics — all tapped for induction into the Television Academy Hall of Fame. The eight were honored at the annual black-tie ceremonies in Los Angeles a few weeks ago.

Now the two-hour festivities, on tape, will be aired Monday night at 8 on the Fox Network (locally on Channel 6).

I think back to a particularly memorable interview session with one of those honorees, a giant among comedians, the man from Waukegan — Jack Benny.

It was news to me, for instance, that Jack Benny was the first to introduce funny commercials on the air. But such nuggets of arcane information may be obtained when you interview a man who is sitting in a barber chair.

Jack Benny was at the barber shop at the Flamingo Hotel in Las Vegas, taking his ease as his locks were being trimmed.

"Canada Dry was our sponsor then, you see," Jack said, "and this was on our radio show in the 1930s. I told the audience the product, Canada Dry, was so *good* we had a salesman whose territory was the Sahara Desert.

"Well, the salesman ran into a *caravan* and the people in the caravan were *dying* of thirst."

Now he paused. "So the salesman gave each of them, these people dying of thirst on the *desert*, a bottle of Canada Dry Ginger Ale — *and not one of them said it was a bad drink!*"

Jack's blue eyes crinkled with laughter and then he quickly added: "Dammit, that's funny!"

A shake of the head and then: "But I was almost *fired* for my irreverence toward the product. That's how it was in those days — they were very *stuffy* about such things.

"Well, then came the reviews from across the country and the mail poured in, and a few weeks later the sponsor, Canada Dry, realized that funny commercials were a good idea."

Discussing the creation of his comic character, Jack said: "There is a lot of everybody, you see, in Jack Benny."

Five years of network radio exposure, by his own estimate, were required to establish the Jack Benny characterization firmly in the public consciousness.

But such a comic character can never be manufactured.

Jack said: "It has to develop naturally. You can't say, 'Let's *invent* this cheap, vain guy who drives a Maxwell, keeps his money in a vault, has a sassy butler named Rochester, and wears a toupee.

"Actually," Jack said, "it would be funnier if I really did wear a toupee, which I don't. But it all adds up to Jack Benny."

It added up as well to more than a half-century of laughter and a special kind of humor that created affection and warmth along with the laughs.

What Jack Benny created, along with his characterization of the lovable but petulant skinflint, was the enduring, understated, irrepressibly fresh comic spirit.

He was a rarity among funnymen, Jack Benny was, a comedian who never cracked a joke in public.

But merely the sight of him — his walk, his stare, his manner, the skillfully honed way he had of mirroring our own petty failings — all of this made us feel good. Jokes don't necessarily do this.

As a comedian, as a human being, as a gentleman, Jack Benny was a matchless piece of work, incomparable, and unique in our affections.

What a funny man he was, and how irreplaceable.

At 11:52 p.m. on Dec. 26, 1974, Jack Benny died.

He was 39.

Markets 7 Weddings

10-8-98

Good afternoon

Nation

ASSOCIATED PRESS

Jack Benny and Fred Allen, in the golden age of radio. WNBC went off the air yesterday after 62 years that included the first commercial, the comedy of Bob Hope and Benny, and the conducting of Arturo Toscanini. A sports-talk station took over the 660 spot on the AM dial from studios that inspired the name Radio City Music Hall.

FAN CLUB

15430 LOST VALLEY DRIVE
FORT WAYNE, IN 46845

THE JACK BENNY TIMES

Volume X, Number 4   INTERNATIONAL DISTRIBUTION   July-August 1990

FOUR–CARD STUD?

☺☺☺ **PRESIDENT'S MESSAGE** ☺☺☺

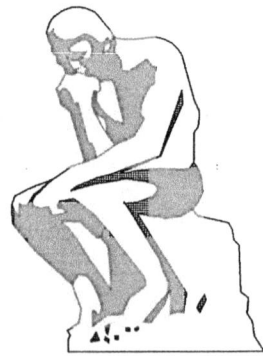

Jell-o again...notice anything different about this issue? Yeah! **IT'S ACTUALLY ON TIME!!!** In fact, I am typing this at 6:10 a.m. on July 23rd! Do you believe it? Well, am doing this for several reasons. One is that I am going (or I suppose have gone, by the time you are reading this) to Los Angeles for a few days in August, and will be busy with that work for a while. Another is that school starts up again at the end of August--right when the newsletter should be sent. So why not do it now, and have it out of the way? Hmmm...have given up telling you excuses of why the newsletter is late; am now giving excuses of why it is on time. My, how things change.

Speaking of change, you may also notice a few new doodads (see above), ruffles (see left), and flourishes (see cover). Also different print font (you're looking at it). Would like to express my sincere thanks to all involved for this (most of whom do not know that they are involved...apparatuses are at the college--ha ha!). If you are wondering (as I know some of you are), this is being printed on an HP Laserjet II printer in Tms Roman 10pt. (Use a "B" cartridge.) One name I **can** print is Syed M. Ali, who has been instrumental in the discovery of many of the doodads, etc. that come with WordPerfect. My infinite gratitude to him for everything.

Would like to take this opportunity to thank Rob Cohen for his donation to start a Jack Benny video tape library. Know that there are many of you that have expressed an interest in having such a service; if there is anyone who would like to purchase a VHS machine for me, I will be more than happy to comply. In the meantime, I remain a Beta baby. Do you have any suggestions for ways to start the ball rolling in this endeavor? If so, please let me know. As previously stated, I want this club to serve **your** wants and needs pertaining to Jack Benny collecting; if that entails a video library, let's find a way to do it!

Also would still like to plea for material on the Maxwell and Jack's houses. Will be doing some groundwork on both of these while in California, and can use absolutely anything that you have. You will also note that this is the issue for the annual tape trading list. Know that we have many new members who probably did not know about this; if you would like to be included, just drop a note to the address at the end of each and every issue. Plus, hope you know that if you have any questions, comments, or the like, please write or call: (219) 637-2287. If you get Jack on the answering machine, you have the right place.

One other thing just for those of you who really "take after" Jack in squeezing the penny until the "E Pluribus" laps over the "Unum." Did you ever realize that if you address a letter to either yourself (or a bogus address), put the intended receiver as a return address, and drop it in the mail without a stamp, it should theoretically reach its desired destination? You did not hear it here! ✼ ✼ ✼

© Copyright 1990, Laura Lee

£ ¥ ₨ ƒ **$6.39 DUE** £ ¥ ₨ ƒ

DON'T BE LATE!!!!

♪ ♪ WAYNE ENNIS ♪ ♪ LARRY GASSMAN ♪ ♪ DAVID HOWELL ♪ ♪ DANIEL L. PELLETIER ♪ ♪ JOEL RASMUSSEN ♪ ♪ CHRISTOPHER SNOWDEN ♪ ♪ CHARLES WRIGHT ♪ ♪

♠ ♣ TAPE TRADING LIST ♦ ♥

Ellen Barker, P.O. Box 1402, Reseda, California 91335

Hal Bogart, 2029 Aldersgate Drive, Lyndhurst, Ohio 44124

Yosef Braude, 25 Longhorn Road, Providence, RI 02906

Rob Cohen, 6635 Helm Ave., Reynoldsburg, Ohio 43068

The Everills, 1558 Knox Dr., New Haven, Indiana 46774

Andrew Haskell, 160 West 39th Ave., Vancouver, British Columbia V5Y 2P2, Canada

Mary Joyce, 1050 Locksley SW, Grand Rapids, Michigan 49509

Laura Lee, 15430 Lost Valley Dr., Fort Wayne, IN 46845

John Malone, Rural Route #2, Wee-Ma-Tuk, Cuba, IL 61427

Bill Oliver, 516 Third Street NE, Massillon, Ohio 44646

Lewis and Sedalia Pearson, 240 Ridge Drive, Marion, Iowa 52302

Michael Pointon, 11 Kings Court, Kings Road, London SW19 8QP, England

Keith Scott, 4 Bellbird Crescent, Forestville 2087, N.S.W. Australia

Joyce Shooks, P.O. Box 307, Sparta, Michigan 49345

Steve ♂ and Kim ♀ Smith, 1945 Coit NW, Grand Rapids, MI 49505

Steve Szejna, 3334 South 15th Street, Milwaukee, WI 53215

James E. Treacy, Jr., 5395 Petersburg Rd, Dundee, MI 48131

Is that everyone?

SAM PERRIN - THE INTERVIEW CONTINUES

L: This is something that has confused some people in the past; was Phil [Harris] actually the bandleader, and if he was, was Mahlon Merrick the musical director?

S: Well, they didn't use the band that much. The show would start [with them playing], and then Don Wilson would say "The Jack Benny Program!" So there wasn't much; I don't even remember now who directed it. Mahlon was the arranger...beautiful arranger. Officially, he was the musical arranger.

L: What do you think was the best show? Do you have any one that stands out in your mind?

S: I don't, because I don't recall Jack ever doing a "bad" show...Of course there are things, like the long walk. There was a sketch about the killers--it was a picture--Lancaster was in it, I think. A long walk...long walk...on sand, and then gravel, and then wood, and then steps...then they went into sort of a diner. Then there were five shots, and Jack says, "Ha ha! You missed me twice!"...

L:.....So what are you working on now?

S: Right now--do you know Fred Silverman?--his office has one of my shows. First, I wanted him to produce a play--a comedy. Almost went on, but my producer died. And I was told that it was the funniest play on paper. So I sent it to him, and he sent me a very nice letter back. He was not equipped for [a play], but he did say, "I am looking for a television series." So I think about ten [or more] years ago when I wrote this thing called My Son, the Doctor; and I sent it to NBC, and they called me and said they won't touch it. It was a Jewish mother. At that time, there was a little trouble with Israel. So I didn't know what to do about it; so Arthur Marx, Groucho's son, and Robert Fisher (sp?), they were doing Alice. So I asked them their advice. They said, "Why don't you let us read the script, and we'll talk about it." So they read the script, and they said, "Don't fight NBC...We'll get you Martha Raye, and make it a New Yorkish mother." So my producer said, "It's been submitted and turned down. They have a reason. Change the character, and don't make it Jewish." I called it Doctor Bracken, Call Your Mother, and I rewrote and rewrote and rewrote. And Pearl Bailey's manager read it, and he called and he said, "If you make it a black show, I'll give you Pearl Bailey." Great! So he's her manager; the William Morris Agency handles her. So they read it and called me and said, "We will spin it off the Bill Cosby show. So write it as a Bill Cosby show with this in it." Can't want anything better than that; he was much more popular then than he is now. So I wrote it, and I don't hear anything. So I called Irving Fein and said, "Irving, before I ask you to do something, I want you to read something. Then if you would like to do something, [great]...if you don't, [fine]." I sent him the script; and by himself, without even telling me, he sent it to the William Morris agency to Norman Brokaw, a very important man. Norman Brokaw handled Bill Cosby. Then he called me, and he told me what he did. I waited about a week and a half, I called Irving and said, "Irving, did you get any reaction from Norman Brokaw?" He said, "No...Call him." So I called him. Norman gets on and says, "Hey, Sam! How are you?" I said, "Norman, did you read the Bill Cosby script?" He said, "Sam, I'm going to tell you something. Bill Cosby has lawyers, highly-paid lawyers, and he had three spin-offs that were all bad. So his lawyer said, 'No more...and don't even read it, because you may get involved.' And he wouldn't read it." So when I talked to Norman he said, "Coincidentally, Cosby is out here now, and I'm having dinner with him tonight. I have other business to talk to him about, but I will talk to him about this. But I will tell you now: you don't tell Cosby what to do, or even argue with him." I said, "Okay." He couldn't move him. Then I received a very long letter from Marcy Carsey and Tom Werner--they are the company that does the Cosby show. And all the names were signed...except Cosby. So I figured, this is ridiculous. So I changed it back from <u>Dr. Bracken, Call Your Mother</u> to <u>My Son, the Doctor</u>, and then rewrote it. [Fred Silverman] has it now.

L: ...I've heard that Cosby is not much of a P.R. person.

S: ...People can make all the money they want; after all, they've gone through misery to reach that point, but I think [Cosby] is overdoing it.

L: ...He won't accept awards...he says he doesn't approve of competition.

S: Well, I think they could do something about that award business, too. I would hate to be nominated...I have been, rather my group of writers, at least seven times. We won twice. It's great when you win...so you're a loser if you don't? You're still a great writer. But I think there should be another way of doing it. He's right in that--there should be no competition.

[LL: Just can't let this opportunity slip by me. Aren't you tired of hearing all the people at, say, the Academy Awards smile and say that it's such an honor just being nominated, and that they don't care if they win or lose? Well, finally here is a straight answer on it. Rah rah rah!]

I would like the networks not to compete, but to give a listing of what's on tonight on **all** the stations. Even CBS [would] say, "At 7:00, on channel 4 is so-n-so, and on [NBC] is so-n-so." So it's like a restaurant row--you don't go in each restaurant, you go in **this** one. And then the next day, you may go into [another one]. I think it's a better idea than to compete.

♪♪♪♪♪♪♪♪♪♪♪♪♪♪♪♪♪♪♪♪♪♪♪♪♪♪♪♪♪♪♪♪♪

AND STILL MORE TO COME!

Please send all questions, comments, additions, corrections, etc. to:

Laura Lee, c/o International Jack Benny Fan Club Offices, 15430 Lost Valley Drive, Fort Wayne, Indiana 46845

Please friends, send no bombs.

Blanc

■ **Mel's message.** The late Mel Blanc, the voice of Porky Pig, Bugs Bunny and legions of other cartoon characters, put the same signature on his life as he did on his work, his son, Noel, said yesterday. "That's All Folks," reads the 5-foot white marble monument at the Beth-Olam Cemetery, near Hollywood's Paramount Studio. Those were "the last words he ever said on-camera or off-camera," Noel said. The headstone was set in time to mark the first anniversary of his father's death today.

"TRUTHFULLY, at this moment I have no television plans." It was Jack Benny answering a Radio-Television Life question, the first in a long list he had agreed to consider.

We asked him why no plans. He told us that he did not think television was going to kill radio right away and completely, the way many in radio predicted. So he will stick to radio for awhile, where the mass appeal still rests. But he adds, "Television is going to be the most important medium of entertainment at some time."

More important than movies? Yes, because people, so Jack Benny believes, will stay at home to watch video because staying home is following the line of least resistance. More important than radio? Yes, but not achieving its importance the way sound pictures absorbed silents, because sound improved all silent pictures whereas addition of sight to radio sound does not invariably make improvement enough to justify video supplanting all AM radio.

For now, however, Jack Benny says this: "I don't think bad TV can compete with good radio. It is physically impossible to do both television and radio shows and have

BENNY, COULD BE, has just seen the ghost of radio with television leering over AM's shoulder.

IN HIS VIDEO DEBUT, the Waukegan fiddler made more of a hit as a dead-pan hillbilly bow scraper than as an emcee.

Year of Decision

Jack Benny Knows That Television Is Breathing Heavily Down His Neck. It Is Not a Question of Whether He Will Do It, But When. This Article Throws Light on Uncertainty of His Position

By Evelyn Bigsby

them both good. If a performer has been lucky enough through the years to have built up a good show (on radio), his audience will expect him to deliver a good television show. Both radio and television would kill me. While I continue (weekly) in radio, I would like to do one important television show every two or three months and make it an event. If I were on television steady, then I would like to guest on radio now and then."

Benny admits he had "a lotta fun" doing his first TV show (it was the CBS inaugural). "Everybody seemed to like it," he commented, "and Mary, my severest critic, liked it. I relied mostly on what she said." He wasn't nervous . . . "television is practically what I used to do in vaudeville."

Why have trade papers come out all year, first stating Benny was going on TV right away, then saying he had decided to postpone his TV show until next season, then returning to the theme that he was hot again for video? Because he has not known himself what he wanted to do. He has been thinking it over. Yet he is as sure as death and taxes that he will have to do television. "I'll probably decide next year," he adds.

What kind of video show does Jack Benny think about for himself? (He discards any idea of a simulcast, radio and TV.) "I visualize my TV show as half and half, part television and part radio. I expect to keep my radio characterization intact. That goes for all my cast, too." And incidentally, Benny thinks all his regulars would be good on TV.

Would he like to film and edit his TV show or do it all live? It really doesn't matter, any more than it matters whether or not he tapes his radio broadcast. Only advantage of taping a radio show so far as Benny is concerned, is in case he wants to get away on a vacation, and only advantage of filming a TV show would be that he could do it from here.

What? Doesn't Jack Benny think the major portion of TV will come from Hollywood eventually? No, he isn't sure Hollywood is going to be the important center, although it *could* be on account of the actors here, and by "actors" Jack means supporting as well as stars. "We have the best here," he thinks, and having the best would naturally make a better show, although film or live, Benny considers the amount of work exactly the same and adds, "The fact you can improve a show after you've done it doesn't interest me. I don't think film makes too much difference. You should know whether or not you have a good show before you go on."

On radio now, Benny (and cast) handle about nineteen to twenty-two pages of script weekly during a half hour. Memorizing this much for video doesn't fluster the comedian. "I don't think it will be too tough." What will be tough for him is the production work involved in video, for he admits he fully expects to put the same passion for perfection into TV as he does into his radio programs which he, by his own admission, "edits, furnishes ideas for and co-writes." I would supervise every detail of my television show," he states comprehensively.

Benny himself is not an ardent TV looker. He has had a set in his home for about two years and the

(Please Turn to Page 39)

October 30, 1949

Page Thirty-three

Behind the Scenes

(Continued from Page 34)

desk. He had to send the crew out, order the lines, spend three hours trying to get the broadcast lines into the vacant lot at San Marino.

"And election night is always frantic," he sighs. Though everyone is prepared, the unforeseen always happens. During the last election, Christman was on the phone to New York, where the official on the other end of the line told him that the remotes from Albuquerque could be discontinued. He called Albuquerque and told the station that they could fold up and go home. Just as he hung up, the radio loudspeaker at his elbow announced, "This is New York, We take you now to *Albuquerque.*" He called the station back and got the newsmen at the mike in time to continue election returns from that city. "They were all puffing as if they'd run back up a flight of stairs." Throughout election night he would hear the network loudspeaker announce from New York, "We take you now to Hollywood," and with a couple of seconds' grace he'd get someone into a studio with copy.

Anything Can Happen

All networks have line failures from time to time and there's nothing much that can be done about it. There's always some industrious farmer between here and San Francisco bulldozing up cables and tearing the network off the air. When this happens, Christman must call the telephone company and get the lines re-routed. His record at this is three and a half minutes in ordering, buying and getting the lines working between here and San Francisco.

One of the night supervisor's biggest crises occurred the time that the Bergen-McCarthy show couldn't get through from Pomona, where the show was being done. Christman had three minutes' advance notice of the line failure. He found Louella Parsons' pianist, Joe Enos, just coming off the air and got him to a piano—but Joe had another broadcast in fifteen minutes. Christman switched to New York, where he'd ordered another stand-by pianist, and the time was filled without so much as a bump.

There's a little matter of a $10,000 rebate if the commercial is missed on a network show. One night on the Bergen-McCarthy show, a failure occurred on the special line that was to carry the commercial on a cut-in from New York. Christman rushed down to master control and, from his memory of the cues he'd seen in the script, cued the switch of the network to Chicago, where he'd called for a stand-by.

Details, Details

In between these big excitements there have been the minor ones... the lady who called him and raised the roof because NBC was playing "Slow Boat to China" at the time of the Nationalist defeat... the girl who fainted in the "Take It or Leave It" line... the noisy man who had just that morning decided to become a singer and somehow or other suddenly burst into the NBC corridor carolling in full voice... the star who decided to go to the movies while the rest of the cast stood around waiting to record his show.... The night supervisor tries to make them all happy—failing that, he points out the hard and fast rules that must be observed or else.

In spite of all this, Christman is calm, contented, his face is unlined and his shoulders unbowed. He regards his job happily. So do many other people. It's the best place in the organization to put into practice what you've learned about the network and to learn what's under any stone that you've left unturned. Trent Christman started learning network operation from the page staff up, with stops in the parking lot, maintenance and traffic and a tenure in the army. A graduate of the University of Minnesota, he came to NBC when the network employed only college graduates on its page staff. "We had two Ph.D.'s and a Rhodes scholar," he smiles reminiscently. In college, Christman was one of three editors of the school publications. The other two were Thomas Heggen, later author of "Mr. Roberts," and Max Shulman, humorist and author of "Barefoot Boy with Cheek." The three of them wrote a joint column. He came to Hollywood in 1942 after having worked on the Minneapolis Star Journal, and went right to work at NBC, where he made his way up to the crisis department.

In the matter of reactions—they're all delayed. Christman is calm throughout all excitement. "Then when it's over, I get excited—and sometimes mad!"

Year of Decision

(Continued from Page 35)

only thing he really likes is the baseball games. "I would like to see 'The Goldbergs,'" he continued, "and mysteries." He is convinced that as time goes on people will be much more selective about TV. "It is harder to sit still and look than it is to listen," is his argument. "You can listen and still be doing something else."

How does Benny think Fred Allen would look on TV?

Ah! That's an idea for Benny's first television-series show.

"You could *see* the bags," Benny says expectantly.

Is Mary afraid of TV?

She's not keen about anything in show business, states her husband with finality. Like radio, Mary will do TV because it will be important to help her husband.

"Hail the Champ!"

(Continued from Page 35)

and flirtatious blinking by the girls, while the shiny-faced boys blush to their toes in shock that such a thing should happen to them.

Adults on Show

Just as much fun is had by the adults, who appear on the average of once a month to compete with the younger set. One show featured the mothers and sons against the fathers and daughters, and while the mothers stood behind a backdrop of football players, catching greased cantaloupes, the fathers adorned themselves in hula skirts and pushed coconuts with their noses across the floor. Only a proud father, not wishing to be outwitted by some other child's equally proud father, would reveal knobby knees and risk splintering his proboscis in the hope of hearing his youngster chortle, "That's my pop!"

More than $500 worth of prizes each week is given to both contestants in the studio and watchers at home. All the participants are gifted with the sponsor's product, Powerhouse candy bars, and the *almost* "champs" receive prizes just as nice, and sometimes better, than what they wished for. Every boy or girl appearing on the stint is asked to tell what he would like to have if he becomes "champ." Surprisingly, the wishes are simple, and include bicycles, parakeets, footballs, skates, dance lessons, and meetings with the Hollywood stars.

Of course, there are a few innocents who fondly cherish the thought that if they become "champ," their most far-fetched dreams will come true. Like the wistful little chap with a gleam in his eye who sighed hopefully, "I want a swimming pool if I win!"

TOM MOORE is emcee of the new "Ladies Fair" show recently advertising on MBS-KHJ (heard 10:30 a.m.).

 **FAN CLUB**

15430 LOST VALLEY DRIVE
FORT WAYNE, IN 46845

THE JACK BENNY TIMES

Volume X, Number 5   INTERNATIONAL DISTRIBUTION   September-October 1990

WOW...WHAT MORE CAN I SAY?

☺☺☺ PRESIDENT'S MESSAGE ☺☺☺

Jell-o again...do you believe, do you believe? Yes, two consecutive issues of the <u>Times</u> can actually be ON TIME! Wait a minute, isn't that one of the signs of armageddon? Well, incredible as it may seem, I wanted to see this issue set an "on-time" precedent. Keep your fingers crossed folks, and I'll keep my nose to the grindstone!

First let me note that the International Jack Benny Fan Club has been expanding at a breakneck pace since the original in garnering other countries. We now have members in America (of course), Canada, England, Scotland, Egypt, Australia, Germany, Tunisia and Israel. Smile, folks! We've come a long way; and we've got a long, wonderful way to go...am glad to have you (yes YOU!) being a part of it all!

The Museum of Broadcasting has been setting up a Jack Benny retrospective for some time now; I have seen some of their written material, and it looks very good. Irving Fein has informed me that the dinner to commence the exhibit has been delayed from the end of January to around March or April. Hope to possibly be able to give you an "on the scene" report; am in the process of querying the museum for information, and will keep you posted on everything as soon as I know.

Los Angeles? Did someone say Los Angeles? YES! Must say I probably had the best five consecutive days of my life out there, and many upcoming issues will be reflecting the fruits of my research during the stay. Will spare you the minute details and just hit the high spots. Got some great shots of both of Jack's houses; or should I say house locations, as his last house has since been torn down. (Full story in later issue.) Loved the people on the tour buses going by who snapped MY picture and looked at me as if to say, "Are you somebody?" Yes, that IS Phil Harris and me on the cover! Nirvana! Equally as exciting was my meeting with George Balzer, and a continuation of our discussions about Jack and himself. I can't even begin to put into words my euphoria in meeting these gentlemen--just suffice it to say "It doesn't get any better than this!" Keep your eyes peeled for the transcriptions of these interviews in the future. Also did several other things, all in regards to Jack, that will show themselves in future issues. Oh, and had dinner at Lawry's the Prime Rib (Beverly Hills) and Chadney's (Burbank). If you're there some time, you MUST go to at least one of these restaurants. And ask for Miss Griem at Lawry's--she's the BEST!

Now for some greatly-deserved thank-yous. Thank you to: George Balzer and Phil Harris for making my trip one of the most memorable experiences of my life (also thanks to GB for the recommendation of the radio station and backing my car out; and to PH for the greatest glass of iced tea I have ever had); Mike and Melissa for their hospitality (food, etc.!) during my stay; Gerald for giving me the grand tour, all his time, and for being a generally fantastic human being; Billie for her time, help, and patience--and for also being a fantastic human being; everyone backstage for giving me a "hand in time of need," and especially Kevin for being so very kind and understanding (while I went completely nuts), keeping me company, and for the diet Coke (in lieu of a Bud...ha ha); Mrs. Goldman for being very nice, even when I accidentally got her out of bed; Irving Fein for being a superb person; Chris for being
© Copyright 1990, Laura Lee

wonderful, and recommending Chadney's; all those nameless, patient people who helped with my research; Miss Griem at Lawry's for the wonderful service and conversation; the people who snapped my photo at Jack's houses for giving me a good laugh; the fellow who delivered my lost luggage to the house; the lady sitting next to me on the returning plane for being a graduate of Jack Benny Junior High School (do you believe it?); to the weather for clearing up on Thursday (while being sunny and warm in Ft. Wayne until my return); and finally to a most important factor, my little sparkle blue Geo Metro for making it all possible.

OK...next order of business: Vice-Presidency. I have been asked by someone about running for Vice President of the IJBFC, and I am taking this opportunity to open the position for nominations. Feel free to nominate yourself or another member. Tasks are basically mainly gathering of information, research, and generally making whatever informational contribution to the club that is possible. If you have any questions, please feel free to write or call (as ever, see proverbial address at the end of the newsletter!). Please submit nominations before December 1st: a listing of nominees will be printed in the next issue.

Also note that we have received note in the British fan magazine Idols (thanks Paul for the copy!), and in Bob Burnham's Listening Guide Newsletter. Bob's newsletter is undoubtedly of interest to many, if not most of you, so if you are not receiving it yet, his address is: P.O. Box 2645, Livonia, Michigan 48151. Subscription rates are $12.00 for four issues, jam packed with information.

Oh, and...Peter Tatchell is "eager to get some correspondence going with American comedy buffs as...I don't have any regular contacts in the comedy line. I suppose I should drop a line to the Burns & Allen Fan Club [Ed.: Is there one? I had not heard of it, please let us know if there is one.]...feel free to give my name and address to any of your members who'd be interested in being part of a 'worldwide' network of humour fans who keep each other posted on what's happening on T.V., records, books, magazines and whatever else is being released." OK!...40 Bambra Road, Caulfield. Victoria Australia 3161. (03 211 3577 for you affluent people who would like to call!)

I think I've exhausted my space here...now on with the show!

JOAN BENNY'S BOOK!!!

Yeah! Sunday Nights at Seven by Jack and Joan Benny is scheduled for release on **NOVEMBER 7th** (a date which will live in infamy...). So pack your thermos and sleeping bag and camp outside the bookstore on the night of the 6th... Joan is going on a book tour across the country, and will be on numerous shows including The Tonight Show and Good Morning America. Keep your eyes open and your VCR's ready...and get those page-flipping fingers ready! Included with this issue is a copy of

a review that Joan sent me which will "fill you in" on all the details. JACK BENNY FANS UNITE AND REJOICE!

NEW MEMBERS

**** CHERYL WENNER **** FRANK POZZUOLI **** ROB CRAWFORD **** JOHN KRAMER **** MICHAEL LEANNAH **** LARA COFFER **** ROBERT STARRETT **** PAUL PINCH **** JOE KENNEDY **** MOHAMED EL LOUADI **** ROBERT L. GARLAND **** DONALD STRAIN **** BENTSY WILLIGER

***** BETTY GOLDMAN ***** SHELDON LEONARD

NEW ACQUISITIONS

The following acquisitions have been made by the IJBFC tape library (some are replacements with improved sound and/or speed quality):

```
6-18-33    2-11-34    2-18-34    5-18-34    8- 3-34    8-24-34
1-19-36   11-22-36    2- 7-37    4- 4-37    4-11-37    4-18-37
4-25-37    6- 6-37   11- 2-47    2-29-48    3-21-48    9-16-51
9-23-51   12- 9-51
```

and 5-29-56 <u>Biography in Sound</u> -- the career of Fred Allen

Infinite gratitude to donors supplying these shows. Thank you very much!!!

DIAMONDS IN CLUBS

First, would like to give note to the <u>Listening Guide Newsletter,</u> published by Bob Burnham, BRC Productions, P.O. Box 2645, Livonia, Michigan 48151. Have received the September 1990 issue of it, and it looks to be a wealth of information on OTR in general. It is a quarterly publication, rates are $12.00 for four issues.

The Abbott and Costello Fan Club is making breathless headway, growing at a rapid pace and organizing oodles of interesting meetings. This is a great club, folks--check it out! For information: P.O. Box 2084, Toluca Lake Station, North Hollywood, California 91602.

Jim MacKenzie is interested in starting a fan club for the famous animator Don Bluth. He is looking for potential members, and suggestions for activities for the club. If you or someone you know would be interested or has an idea, please write him at: 2642 Putnam Drive, Erie, Pennsylvania 16511-1272.

Also am certain that most of you already know about SPERDVAC, but if you do not, their <u>Radiogram</u> is also a wealth of information on OTR in general. For information: Barbara Watkins, P.O. Box 561, South Pasadena, California 91030.

Please mention the <u>Times</u> when writing--we appreciate it!

VIDEO TAPE LIBRARY

Well, I have received a few suggestions in response to my mention of the video tape library. There is one person in California who is willing to do some dubbing, and another person locally who has a beta and VHS recorder that could be used. Also another person suggested that if everyone chipped in about two or five dollars (depending on the number of "chippers"), then a VHS machine could be purchased EXCLUSIVELY for the use of the fan club library.

What do you all think? I will make note that due to a prior incident, I have a policy to never ship my originals in any manner (just too much risk involved in potential loss by carriers). Is there possibly someone who knows of (or has) a decent quality VHS machine that would/could be for sale at a reasonable price? Also, (and this does not commit you to anything) who would potentially be interesting in being a "chipper," if that option is judged most feasible? Please let me know.

DO YOU KNOW?

Three quick items for this column: Firstly, what is the name of the replacement for Mel Blanc? I thought it was his son, Noel, but I have been informed that it was someone by the name of Jeff. Also, it seems that somewhere out there is a screen test that Jack did for The Sunshine Boys. Anyone seen it? Finally, Alan Grossman has a little white plastic safe or "vault" that has Jack's picture on the front of it. Have you seen anything like it, or know if it is an authentic piece?

THE TALE PIECE

Another favorite Jack Benny anecdote:

As Edgar Bergen's guest on the New Edgar Bergen Show (11-27-55), Jack plays the owner of the Blue Skies Trailer Park in Palm Springs. Who else but Benny would think to install parking meters in the bathrooms?
--K. Weigel

Have a favorite Benny scene or anecdote? Even just want to share your memories of how you became an aficionado while sitting by the radio, the television, etc.? We want to hear from you! Tell us about it!!!

ETHER ONE

The Jack Benny Program is broadcast on:

WOR-TV, Channel 9 in New York City on Saturday nights at 10:30 p.m.

KNX (Radio) in Los Angeles on Saturdays at 9

KFRC Magic 61 (Radio) in San Francisco on Sundays at 6:30

♪♫♪♫♪♫♪♫♪♫♪♫♪♫♪♫♪♫♪♫♪♫♪♫♪♫♪♫♪♫♪♫♪♫♪♫

Please send all questions, comments, additions, corrections, etc. to:

Laura Lee, c/o International Jack Benny Fan Club Offices, 15430 Lost Valley Drive, Fort Wayne, Indiana 46845   (219) 637-2287

Please friends, send no bombs.

TRADE NEWS

EDITED BY GAYLE FELDMAN

Warner Evokes 'Sunday Nights at Seven' with Jack Benny

BY ROS SIEGEL

Can the life story of a nice guy who's no longer around to promote his memoirs become a bestseller? It can if the nice guy is Jack Benny and the coauthor is his daughter Joan—at least, that's what Warner Books believes. And the company believes in *Sunday Nights at Seven: The Jack Benny Story* ($19.95) strongly enough to risk a substantial six-figure advance and a 75,000-copy first printing for the November title.

Critics used to say the secret of Benny's success was timing. The story of *Sunday Nights at Seven* is about the kind of timing that can reach across generations to link the early days of radio and TV with this fall's publishing lineup.

Joan had been scribbling reminiscences about her father ever since he died in 1972. To help tickle her memory, she had a 400-page unfinished autobiography Jack had begun with a ghost writer in 1968. Some mystery surrounds the fate of this manuscript, which was never published. According to Joan, "The reason my father always gave was that my mother was upset by references to romances he had had before he was married."

But to the comedian's daughter, the problem wasn't too much sex—it was not enough. Who in the world would want to read a memoir with no scandal, no adversity and no gossip? She didn't think seriously about publication until three years ago, when the title suddenly popped into her head. "I'm not very creative," Joan insists, "but when I thought up 'Sunday Nights at Seven,' I knew I had to write a book to go with the title!"

She found a writer, Joan Pollack, to help her edit her father's manuscript and organize her own. Then she went looking for an agent.

Enter the father-son team of Arthur and Richard Pine, literary agents with a list of show biz clients that includes bestselling author George Burns. In a fitting example

Siegel is a New York–based writer and editor.

of old-boy networking, Arthur's longtime pal Irving Fein, now George Burns's theatrical agent—and formerly Benny's agent as well—suggested that Joan show her material to the Pines.

Pine senior, who quickly lined up Burns to do the introduction, says, "I asked myself who would go for this show biz story—and Warner seemed the logical choice." He called Mel Parker, editor-in-chief of Warner's paperback division, the next day.

"As soon as I heard about the project," Parker says, "it struck an immediate nostalgic chord. I remember my parents never missing *The Jack Benny Show*." Two days later, Mel had arranged a meeting with Warner publisher and president Nansey Neiman and Laurence Kirshbaum, to hear Joan's ideas for the book.

"We didn't show them anything on paper," Pine confides, "but when they saw and heard Joan, they were sold." That Benny shows were being rerun weekly on National Public Radio didn't hurt, either.

For Joan's part, she thought she was going to a meeting to get some advice on how to organize her material. But three days later, she was offered a substantial six-figure advance.

It was decided that Parker would edit the book, and for him, the major problem was how to merge Joan's reminiscences with Jack's autobiography. "We needed to strike a balance between her voice and his, and weave them together harmoniously to have a comment and gloss, a one/two comedy punch," says Parker—not to mention an all-important link between the past and the promotable present.

The appeal of the book is, however, ultimately a nostalgic one. It features a 32-page photo insert that not only shows a private Jack Benny playing his violin to his first grandchild, but a public Jack Benny whose guest stars included virtually every imporant figure of the era—from Marilyn Monroe to Harry Truman.

The book evokes a world when every window was open to catch a breeze on Sunday night and the whole street reverberated with *The Jack Benny Show*. The secure, happy life of a Hollywood family—the image of a little girl in pajamas sitting at the head of the stairs and peering down on a gala Hollywood soirée—is Warner's answer to the harsher descriptions of life in most other celebrity books. "At a time when so many stand-up comics are given to vulgarity, it's refreshing to remember Jack Benny, who had only to raise an eyebrow to get a laugh," says publicity director Ellen Herrick.

"Even though Jack can't sign books, both authors will sell books for us," says Herrick. "The day after the book was announced in *New York* magazine, I got calls from every important talk show in America." A 12-

Benny père and fille in an earlier collaboration.

city national tour is planned for Joan, who, despite her self-effacing manner, has so many friends in major cities that three book parties are planned in New York, Washington and L.A. Advance quotes have already been garnered from the likes of Gregory Peck, Alan King and Jack Parr, and the title is an alternate selection of the Literary Guild and Doubleday Book Clubs.

In January, New York's Museum of Broadcasting will dedicate a new building and celebrate its opening with a retrospective that focuses on *The Jack Benny Show*. How's that for good timing?

▲ SOME DAY SARA BERNER would like to have "a shop of her own", featuring her peasant-style originals and self-designed hats. Right now, she's too occupied being one of the most expert voice and character impersonators in the business. Sara, by the way, also plays Jack's uninhibited girl friend "Gladys Zybisco" on the show.

▲ BEA'S JUST had her hair cut into a short swirling halo and dyed a soft red, but she's still the same swell gal this picture shows. You also hear her as the violent "Mrs. Anderson" on "Day in the Life of Dennis Day" and as "Eve Goodwin", schoolmarm friend of "Gildy", in addition to other roles.

Benny's Switchboard Sweeties

Introducing the Two Very Adept Actresses Who Are Jack's "Number Plee-yuz" Problem

By Judy Maguire

(BUZZERS LOUD, AS IN A SWITCHBOARD)
Bea: Oh, Mabel.
Sara: What is it, Gertrude?
Bea: Your outside line is flashing.
Sara: You get it, will you?
Bea: Okay. (SOUND, CLICK OF PLUG). National Broadcasting Company. Oh, hello. What? Just a minute, I'll connect you. (SOUND, CLICK OF PLUG). Oh, Mabel, it's Mr. Benny.
Sara: I wonder what Spam-face wants now.
Bea: He wants me to connect him with the mimeograph department, because they haven't delivered his scripts yet.
Sara: Scripts? Well, how do you like that? And he palms himself off as an ad-lib comedian.
Bea: Yeah. He couldn't ad-lib a click if he had false teeth.
Sara: Ain't it the truth.
Bea: But I don't care if he can ad-lib or not, I think he's cute.
Sara: Why should you think he's cute? He's gone out with me more times than he has with you.
Bea: He has not.
Sara: He has too.
Bea: Oh Mabel, let's not argue. When we look like we do we should be happy we've got each other.

Brooklynesing this dialogue for the past three seasons as the sassy PBXers who make Jack Benny's life an open book are two of radio's most adroit character experts, Bea Benaderet, who's "Gertrude Gearshift," and Sara Berner, who's "Mabel Flapsaddle," started as a one-time-only comedy spot with Jack, have been on the show ever since.

Neither of them, incidentally, could operate a switchboard if she tried. NBC knows, because the girls *did* try, when they took over the station's Hollywood board for some publicity pictures. Bea was pregnant at the time. Photographers, regular operators and press agents had to work around her. In the confusion, cords flew, dialers yelped, ousted "help" tried to save what calls they could, Sara and Bea wailed "What'll we do *now?*" and one important coast-to-coast executive cooled his heels on a call for a fine ten minutes.

The place has never been the same since, declares NBC's head operator, Billie Clevenger, who is nonetheless the girls' most loyal fan. Coincidentally, another Gertrude (Smith) regularly works the Hollywood Vine and Sunset board right next to Billie.

Not Likes

But, while they're identically gum-popping, short-skirted and flip-commented on the program, Bea and Sara could hardly be paired as like types away from the studio.

"WELL, WHAT does old Spam-face want now?" says Sara "Mabel Flapsaddle" Berner, as Bea "Gertrude Gearshift" Benaderet takes another call from "Mr. Benny". The girls took over NBC's actual Hollywood switchboard for these pictures, disconnected half the stations and made one executive wait on a call for a full ten minutes.

Bea, who has just had her hair pouf-cut and dyed a soft feathery red (from its previous long page-boy black) is a swinging, adjusted soul who effects a "gosh, don't mind me" congeniality. She is the very happy wife of Jim Bannon, announcer and actor, and the mother of seven-year-old Jack and five-month-old Maggie. Professionally, she is: "Eve Goodwin" on the "Great Gildersleeve" show; "Mrs. Anderson," henpecker of Dink Trout, on the Dennis Day show; "Mrs. Carstairs" on "Fibber and Molly"; and "Gloria" on "Ozzie and Harriet", as well as one of Benny's switchboard sweeties. She's more interested in her family, she admits, than anything else.

Whereas, little, quiet, big-brown-eyed Sara Berner, by contrast, is absorbed in her career of mimicry. "Sara's a real ham," says Bea with affection. And gentle, soft-voiced Sara will indeed exert any effort to

(Please Turn to Page 52)

NOVEMBER 9, 1947

Benny's Switchboard Sweeties

(Continued from Page 7)

achieve an impersonation of character which has intrigued her.

"I've often wanted to be a telephone operator," she offers with enthusiasm, "so I could listen to all those wonderful people who call in!"

Sara spent four years in vaudeville with her "Impressions," and traveled the country during the war with them. She's "Little Jasper" on the "Puppetoons." She's the animated mouse who said "Lookit me, I'm dancin'." In "Anchors Aweigh." She was one of the two talking camels on "The Road to Morocco." And you ought to hear her get going on her take-offs of Edna Mae Oliver, Bette Davis, Mrs. Roosevelt, Una Merkel, Fannie Brice, Gracie Allen!

On the air, she plays both Ida and daughter Marilyn Cantor, a complete assortment of colored characters for 'Amos 'n' Andy", Jack Benny's girlfriend "Gladys Zybisco" (in addition to switchboarder "Mabel"), dramatics and dialects on call.

Sara, who went with the Benny troupe on its tour to Canada, knows a story of the trip that few have heard. On the way out of Corvallis, Oregon, the plane (a giant DC-3) hit a thunderhead, went up 2000 feet, down 2000 feet and finally the pilot turned the ship back.

When they landed again in Corvallis, the entire company piled shiveringly into the town's hotel. "And there in the lobby," relates Sara, "were a whole lot of people sitting around an old radio listening to the Jack Benny rebroadcast. You can imagine what happened when Jack himself walked in. Nothing in the place was too good for him!

"We all crowded into Jack's room then... the cast, WAC's and gen-erals from the nearby army camp and folks from all over the town... for a big party that lasted all night. Wonderful ad-libs! Phil said to Rochester, 'Boy, you look like a bottle of sour Milk.' and Roch said, 'Me? No mo' airplane rides fo' me, I'm goin' home by ox.' We blamed the plane trouble on Don... he'd just dropped off to sleep in the ship's tail.

"What a night! What a party!" enthuses the little veteran actress who loves every inch of her career. "It was just like being born again!"

RADIO LIFE

When you hear mention of Jack Benny, people always say "... What a swell showman."

"With Eddie Cantor, it's '... What a comedian that guy is!' But when my name comes up, it's always 'I wonder how old Jolson is?'

"Why don't they worry about those other two ... I bet they're a hundred and one years old if they're a day!"

Jack Benny FAN CLUB

15430 LOST VALLEY DRIVE
FORT WAYNE, IN 46845

THE JACK BENNY TIMES

Volume X, Number 6   INTERNATIONAL DISTRIBUTION   November-December 1990

A tightwad and a miser to his public, Benny is often forced to be extravagant in his personal life. And who could doubt his generosity after his recent party in a New York Automat—where each guest received $2 in nickels? Of course, Jack cut costs by providing the music himself (accompanied by violin virtuoso Kokomo).

45

☺☺☺ **PRESIDENT'S MESSAGE** ☺☺☺

MERRY CHRISTMAS!
HAPPY HANUKKAH!
HAPPY NEW YEAR!!!

Jell-o again folks...hope that this has been an enjoyable and prosperous holiday season for all of you. My sincerest thanks to all of you for making 1990 the best year ever for the International Jack Benny Fan Club. Now, to borrow an old phrase, ONWARD AND UPWARD!!!

Was Joan Benny's book under your tree or Menorah? If not, IT CERTAINLY SHOULD HAVE BEEN! Therefore if you (or someone you love) has not already purchased (or received) a copy, my suggestion is that you run (do not walk) to your nearest bookstore (enough parentheses in one sentence?). It is a DEFINITE MUST for any Jack Benny fan, and would make an excellent Valentine's Day gift!

As noted in the previous Times, we are currently having an election for Vice-President of the IJBFC. As I was putting together some packages of back issues, I noted that VP nominations had been requested at least twice in the past to no response...now FINALLY someone wants the job! Please refer to pages five through seven for full election details.

I am also very pleased to report that I had the great fortune and pleasure to talk with Tony Butala, an original member of the Lettermen. The group appeared on the Jack Benny show, and opened for Jack in Lake Tahoe--but I am jumping ahead of myself. I very much enjoyed this interview, and I know that you will too!

Another new feature is in store--we now have our very own comic strip, which will debut in the next issue. It portrays Jack and all his radio cast as children (a la Muppet Babies). As of this writing, it has no formal name. Therefore, I hereby christen a "Name the Strip" competition; contribute a name (or more than one, if you get creative) for the comic strip, and if selected, you will win an original copy of one of the strips. Go for it!!!

One other addition to our "Diamonds in Clubs" column; I have received a copy of the newsletter Bear Facts from the Cinnamon Bear Brigade. It is a very well-assembled and entertaining newsletter for fans of this show. For further information, contact: The Cinnamon Bear Brigade, 10419 NE Knott, Portland, Oregon, 97220. Please mention the IJBFC. Thank you.

Now on with the show!

♪ ♪ **A PERSONAL NOTE** ♪ ♪

Please indulge me a small bit of space here for a personal note. As several of you know, I will be graduating in May, and am actively seeking a job in the California area. My degrees will be: a Master's in Business-Administration, and a Bachelor's in Mathematics with minors in Telecommunications and Business. I am interested in a middle-management position in any of the following areas: computers, telecommunications, economics, finance, and/or mathematics. If you or someone you know might be able to help in this endeavor, please write or call me as soon as possible. Thank you very much.

© Copyright 1991, Laura Lee

♪ ♫ **$6.39 DUE** ♪ ♫
DON'T BE LATE!!!!

♪ ♫ JACK ABIZAID ♪ ♫ JAMES ADAM ♪ ♫ JOSEPH W. BAVETT, JR. ♪ ♫ BERNARD BECKERT ♪ ♫ HAL BOGART ♪ ♫ SCOTT BRICK ♪ ♫ JOHN BURNS ♪ ♫ JOHN W. CAIRNES ♪ ♫ PHIL EVANS ♪ ♫ CHARLES FAIR ♪ ♫ J. ED GALLOWAY ♪ ♫ ROBERT L. GARLAND ♪ ♫ THE HARDINGS ♪ ♫ DARRYL HENLEY ♪ ♫ RICHARD HILL ♪ ♫ THE HUCKS ♪ ♫ THE JONASES ♪ ♫ WILL JORDAN ♪ ♫ TOM KLEINSCHMIDT ♪ ♫ JOHN KRAMER ♪ ♫ MICHAEL LEANNAH ♪ ♫ KEITH LEE ♪ ♫ WALT MITCHELL ♪ ♫ JACK PALMER ♪ ♫ LORA PALMER ♪ ♫ PAUL PINCH ♪ ♫ FRANK POZZUOLI ♪ ♫ CLIVE ROBERTS ♪ ♫ DAVID M. ROGERS ♪ ♫ THE SADOWSKYS ♪ ♫ THOMAS SALOME ♪ ♫ L. SELSMAN-JONES & A. SELSMAN ♪ ♫ SCOTT SEVERSON ♪ ♫ MEL SIMONS ♪ ♫ GEORGE SKARZYNSKI ♪ ♫ W. ROBERT SMITH ♪ ♫ ROBERT STARRETT ♪ ♫ ANDRE STOJKA ♪ ♫ THE TAYLORS ♪ ♫ MARY LOU WALLACE ♪ ♫ SANDRA J. WEBER ♪ ♫ CHERYL WENNER ♪ ♫

♪ ♫ TONY BUTALA SINGS JACK'S PRAISES ♪ ♫

First a brief background of the Lettermen is in order. This group has been together for over 30 years; their first single, The Way You Look Tonight, debuted in 1961. The original group consisted of: Tony Butala, Bob Engemann, and Jim Pike. This trio performed on The Jack Benny Show of March 31, 1964, singing their hit Love Is a Many-Splendored Thing. Upon Jack's request that the group sing a second song, Dennis appears from the wings, angry that he never gets to sing two songs (sound familiar?). Jack quiets Dennis (for the moment) and the song starts...I will let Tony tell you the rest of that story! Then the skit of the second half centers around Jack playing a college Freshman, rooming with the Lettermen. (I love this show...have it on tape and watched it innumerable times!)

Jumping to today, the current group consists of: Tony Butala, Donovan Scott Tea, and Bob Poynton. They are still touring all over the world, and sound just as wonderful as ever! If you have a chance to see them, I guarantee you an excellent show. I would also like to mention the Lettermen Fan Club (of which I am a member); they have an excellent package of information about the group, as well as the Harmony newsletter to keep you up-to-date on the group's activities. Membership is $10.00 for the first year (less after that, but cannot find the exact figure); for more information, write to: The Lettermen Fan Club, 10010 Shoshone Avenue, Northridge, California 91325. Please mention the IJBFC and Theresa Yates when you write. Many thanks to all those in attendance that night who made me feel so welcome! Take it, Tony!

T: In 1964, [we had spent] a year...playing in Fresno at the Hacienda and...up at the Cave in Vancouver, British Columbia with George Burns and Dorothy Provine...His best friend, Jack Benny of course, came to see us...Jack was very, very surprised that in 1963 that there could be a vocal group that was having hit records on the charts that would still be relevant to his people. So not to be outdone by George Burns...Jack Benny said, 'Look, you guys should come to my show."...So he signed the Lettermen, and we worked on his television show, and we worked in Lake Tahoe at Harrah's club on Christmas of 1964, and December 31st through January 1965. [It was] one of the first times we worked the holiday, the main showroom, the Harrah's south showroom, and Jack gave us about 20 minutes of his show. We did a couple songs with him on the show, we did a shtick in the audience with him, and we played there for several weeks...It was one of the most enlightening times I ever had, to be around a genius, a magnificent performer who could really relate to his audience.

In those days, Jack had his television show...and he did a whole episode on "The Letterman" [the aforementioned skit]--I'm sure most people have seen it--where Jack has a long Beatle-type wig, and he joins the Lettermen as being one of our group. He shares a dormitory in the college...[Before the skit] we do a song, and he gives us another song, and Dennis Day is very jealous, so Dennis Day plots to get rid of the Lettermen. He drags one of us under the curtain [after hitting him with a sandbag], drags one of us behind the curtain, and he pulls me in the air.

L: ...Did you do that yourself, or was that a stuntman?

T: No, that was us! They actually flew me with wires...That's one of the most popular Jack Benny shows that they replay. Jack was so helpful to us then in going over our script and rehearsing our lines, and giving us hints about how to read the lines. We were three guys that were having hit records, but we were not actors as such. I had done some acting when I was a kid, but Jack was a real great help. The thing I remember about Jack Benny was that when my mother and dad came up to South Tahoe at Harrah's to spend Christmas with me, Jack Benny was completely thrilled and enthralled with that fact that my mother had 11 children...I slept in the same bed as my three brothers. Jack loved...and respected her for all the children and how young she looked. My mother...is 80 years old now, but she had a special thing with Jack that they joked about his age, and that was at a time when he started really believing that he should start telling people his real age. I think at the time he was about [70], and I really loved Jack for spending as much time and caring about my mother and father as he did. He was very much a humanitarian; and he really, with respect to me, just an act that was working for him...he went out of his way to be nice to my parents...He was a very sensitive and a very caring man. So he rates up there, number one.

I learned a lot about show business and about comedy and timing. To see Jack Benny on stage after a punch line, to be able to milk that punch line for a minute and a half by a look--first of all to the left of his audience, slowly turning his head toward the center, looking at people's eyes, passing the center, then slowly his eyes to stage right and looking all the way over, taking about a minute and a half, just milking the laugh of the joke before, where people were laughing at his expression and not necessarily at the punch line after a while. So you ought to have seen the Lettermen after we worked with Jack Benny; all three of us in our concerts were caught trying to do 'takes' like Jack Benny to make the audience laugh as long as he did, of course with no success, because there was only one Jack Benny! But we learned a lot about show business timing from Jack Benny. He kept up a good correspondence with us for years afterwards, and followed through.

We were very nervous about working in New York shortly after working with him, and he said, 'Boys, I'll come and introduce you at the Plaza Hotel in New York, if you're nervous about your first New York opening.' Lo and behold, a big television show came up and he couldn't come to New York to introduce us, so he did the next best thing. He made a tape for us to play...We used it that night, and it got thrown...in one of my back files. Then about four years ago, I discovered a dub of this tape, and I said, 'Oh my gosh, I think Jack would really love it if we used this tape to introduce...the oldies part of our show now.' The tape goes, 'Good evening ladies and gentlemen, this is Jack Benny. I'm sorry I can't be with you this evening, but I want to introduce a wonderful group of guys that I used on my television show and in Lake Tahoe.' Of course, Jack's up in Heaven now, but whenever I play that tape, I think that Jack would be proud that we still care enough about him to use his tape to say, 'Sorry I can't be with you tonight, ladies and gentlemen.' What he's saying is, I can't be physically with you, but I'm here in spirit. And he introduces the Lettermen, and we come out in our letter sweaters, and we recreate some of the hits of the early '60s, when we worked with Jack Benny. So he'll always have a fond spot in my heart, and I can only say the kindest and most wonderful things about this wonderful human being.

L: ...Since you've seen him work on both stage and television, what was the main difference in how he approached each one?

T: Well, it's so hard to answer that question--I will say this, though. There are so many television actors that are only one-dimensional. They can only perform to that little lens.

Whereas with Jack--we had live audiences, of course, which helped--but I think a lot of the vaudeville entertainers like Jack Benny and George Burns, they didn't perform for that little lens. They performed for the live audience **and** the television audience, knowing that that lens would be there that would magnify them and take them and their sincerity into people's homes...I think now, so many of the people that bomb on television do not make that transition. They work toward themselves in that lens, instead of realizing that lens is going to transport what they do to a live audience, into people's living rooms. So that's what I noticed--the lens was there, and he was aware that it was there, but [it wasn't the major focus], and I think that's a secret. The major focus was the ability to get a sincerity out, to expose it to that lens, but beyond that lens to the audience that was there. That's, I think, somewhat a trick that so many of the newer television artists don't master...They think they can put all their eggs in that focus of just that little lens, and I think somehow it gives them a one-dimensional visual aspect of that lens...If you perform beyond that lens, your soul to the people, that lens is...going to pick up that sincerity that is there behind that.

...Anything I can do to promote Jack Benny...and his feeling that he gives an audience, I feel very fortunate to be one of the younger entertainers that was able to be blessed by the presence of working with him, and I hope that I carry that through in my work. I think of him every performance that I make...If people can see our performance and get some sincerity, and I can say...that Jack Benny was one of the people who helped inspire me to do what I'm doing, I'm proud to say that.

[My sincere thanks again to Tony Butala and everyone who made this interview possible.]

>> A HAPPENING IN WAUKEGAN <<

News flash! This just in from the Waukegan Park District!

"[The Waukegan Park District is] nearing the fourth annual Benny Birthday Bash! at the Jack Benny Center for the Arts. On February 9 at 8:00 p.m. in Goodfellow Hall, we will produce a show reminiscent of the glorious vaudeville days in Waukegan. Jack Benny took part in these fine performances and appeared numerous times at the Majestic Theatre in downtown Waukegan [Ed. note: Plus the Barrison and Genessee Theatres.] We are very excited about the show and hope that you can attend this year.

Ticket prices are $25.00 per person and include the show and cake and champagne during the intermission. In addition, we will have hawkers selling small glass bottles of pop, popcorn, and candy [E.n.: How do you get the popcorn out of the little bottles?] The performers will include an eight-year-old Benny impersonator [E.n.: The son of our own David Spangler, no less], along with some of the most famous vaudeville skits ever (Willie and Al's "Nursey, nursey" sketch). The cast and crew are made up of our Friends of the Benny Center and talents from our theatre and opera companies. We certainly hope that you can attend. If you have any questions, please do not hesitate to contact me at 708-360-4741."

   ## ELECTION SELECTION

Here they are--the "campaign speeches" of the candidates for Vice President of the International Jack Benny Fan Club! However before we get to that, I should explain the actual voting procedure. The official ballot is printed on the back page of this newsletter. Please detach it (and your address label, for anonymous voting), mark your selection, and return the ballot to the IJBFC offices **NO LATER THAN FEBRUARY 14, 1991**. The winner will be announced in the January-February 1991 issue of the Times. Additionally, I believe in some states there are laws about campaigning within 100 yards of a voting place. Thus before you read any further, please detach the ballot. Then carry the remainder of this newsletter to a distance greater than your state's allotted "campaigning yardage," and proceed to read the candidate information, which is presented in alphabetical order.

Our first nominee is Rob Crawford:

I must say that our second nominee was quite a surprise to me. In any event, this person has been very active in the club since its very beginning, and has devoted extensive time to its activities through the years. Our second nominee is...Laura Lee. (Thank you George, for nominating me. I am very flattered. ☺)

Our third nominee is Rex Riffle:

"The past ten years have seen the International Jack Benny Fan Club grow into a well-established and respected old-time radio club. The time has come for a Vice President to be elected to assist and enhance the workings of the club, and I would like to offer my services in this position. My qualifications are as follows:

- I have an excellent knowledge of club management through my work as Publicity Director of the National Lum and Abner Society since its inception.

- I actually listened to Jack's shows on radio from circa 1952 through the Best of Benny of 1958.

- I started collecting his shows in 1975, and have continued amassing my collection over the past 15 years.

- I sat up until 4:00 in the morning just to see The Horn Blows at Midnight on the Late Show!

- I was lucky enough to get autographs from Mary and Dennis.

- Since I began listening to him at such a young age, I believe he had an effect on my personality!!!

I would like to put my knowledge and skills to work for you as your Vice President. Thank you."

****

There you have it, folks...the candidates for Vice President of the IJBFC. Remember, votes will be accepted NO LATER THAN FEBRUARY 14, 1991.

♪♪♪♪♪♪♪♪♪♪♪♪♪♪♪♪♪♪♪♪♪♪♪♪♪♪♪♪♪♪♪

Please send all questions, comments, additions, corrections, (and employment information!) to:

Laura Lee, c/o International Jack Benny Fan Club Offices, 15430 Lost Valley Drive, Fort Wayne, Indiana 46845   (219) 637-2287

Please friends, send no bombs.

OFFICIAL IJBFC VICE-PRESIDENTIAL BALLOT

Please mark an "X" on the line in front of the candidate of your choice.

_____ Rob Crawford

_____ Laura Lee

_____ Rex Riffle

_____ Write-in:_____

Jack Benny FAN CLUB

15430 LOST VALLEY DRIVE
FORT WAYNE, IN 46845

THE JACK BENNY TIMES

Volume XI, Number 1 — INTERNATIONAL DISTRIBUTION — January-February 1991

Collier's
FEBRUARY 19, 1954 • FIFTEEN CENTS

A Week Inside the WHITE HOUSE
By ROBERT LEWIS TAYLOR

Labor's New Demand: 52 PAYDAYS Guaranteed EACH YEAR

AFTER 39 YEARS— I'M TURNING 40
By JACK BENNY
(See Page 32)

☺ ☺ ☺ PRESIDENT'S MESSAGE ☺ ☺ ☺

Hello again, folks! I am pleased to announce that you are looking at the

39th ISSUE

of the <u>Jack Benny Times</u>. Additionally on January 1st, we celebrated our 11th anniversary. We are approaching 300 members spanning nine countries; quite a victory, to my way of thought! Our tape library is constantly growing, and several other facets of the club are changing and improving. This issue also announces our new Vice President. All these things are enormously encouraging, and a strong sign that your love for Jack Benny will maintain and nourish the International Jack Benny Fan Club for many, many years to come.

I would like to take this opportunity for a few words on the happenings since the last issue of the <u>Times</u>. Not to sound flip about it, but it seems we have had a war since the last time we talked. We do have some members in that part of the world (Israel included), and they are all safe and doing well. Our congratulations go out to them, and to all members with close friends and family who were involved in the Gulf conflict.

I would also like to take a moment for a special note on one of our honorary members, Bob Hope. He had kidded a lot recently about the fact that the soldiers say, "My father saw you during World War II," (or in Korea, Vietnam, etc.). This time Mr. Hope took his humor to "the world's biggest sand trap;" he said to the troops, "Are you ready?" and was answered with a tremendous cheer. It has been said ad infinitum, and yet it bears repeating; what Bob Hope has done for "our boys" over the years and millions of miles in immeasurable. The shows he has presented have surpassed the point of being pure entertainment, and have become a symbol of home, of family, of pride in the country...of the fact that our love and prayers go with them to the ends of the earth. Where there are American troops, there is Hope...laughter, and love.

One more note that member Will Jordan was featured in the recent Ed Sullivan tribute, and appears as the effervescent (ha ha ha) Mr. Sullivan in Oliver Stone's new movie, <u>The Doors</u>.

Yes, I have a tremendous pile of letters to answer. With my California job search, school, and all the usual and unusual items on the agenda, free time has not been a plentiful commodity. Please bear with me!

Now on with the show!

© Copyright 1991, Laura Lee

☺☺ NEW MEMBERS ☺☺

****DONALD STRAIN ****RICK ABRAMS ****MARGIE JONES ****JEFF ELLIOTT ****TOD IRZYK ****DON VISOVATTI ****JOEL S. ROTHMAN ****HOWARD D. LEIB ****J. KENT COSCARELLY ****MARY McINTYRE ****DEE CRAWFORD ****JOHN SMOTHERS ****STEVE DILLIE ****STEVE METZGER ****CLYDE BENGE ****DIANA WHITLEY

£ ¥ ₧ ƒ **$6.39 DUE** £ ¥ ₧ ƒ

DON'T BE LATE!!!!

♪ ♫ STEVE BRENT ♪ ♫ ALAN GROSSMAN ♪ ♫ THE LAKES ♪ ♫ GLENN LAXTON ♪ ♫ STEVEN M. LEWIS ♪ ♫ JAMES A. LINK ♪ ♫ FRANKLIN LOPSHIRE ♪ ♫ ROGER NELSON ♪ ♫ ROBERT OLSEN ♪ ♫ MICHAEL POINTON ♪ ♫ JOHN SCHLAMP ♪ ♫ JOYCE SHOOKS ♪ ♫ KEN WEIGEL ♪ ♫ CHARLIE WILLER ♪ ♫ DOUG WOOD ♪ ♫

➢→ ELECTION SELECTION ←⇐

May I have the envelope, please? (Drumroll) And the winner is... (dramatic pause)

 **REX RIFFLE**

I must say that I have never seen a closer race than this one; it was tied THREE-WAYS at least three times, and was won by just three votes. (That is a lot of threes!) In classic election style, the votes were cast into a genuine antique silk top hat before tallying. Our congratulations to both Rex and Rob for running a fine race. Received notes from some of you that were concerned that I was relinquishing my post of President; not to fear...if you will have me, I would like to remain in my capacity for as long as possible. Thank you for participating and making the first IJBFC Vice-Presidential election a success.

☺☺ OUR VERY OWN COMIC STRIP ☺☺

As mentioned in the previous issue, our very own comic strip is debuting in this issue. It is drawn by Rob Crawford; professional artist, standup comedian, and forklift truck operator. He also proudly notes that he was born on the day of Joan Benny's second appearance on The Jack Benny Show. As The Mouse That Jack Built portrayed the show's characters as mice, our strip will portray them as young children. Since the strip does not yet have a name, we would like to turn that task over to you. Submit your ideas to the address at the end of this newsletter (as always), and the chosen name will be awarded original artwork from selected strips. Good luck!

? ! ? ! DO YOU KNOW ? ! ? !

Firstly, Phil Evans has noted that between October 15th and 27th of 1927, Frankie Trumbauer was playing at a 14th Street theatre in New York. The orchestra was backing Jack Benny, of course. Phil would like to know the name of the theatre, and any further information about Jack's act at the time. One book mentions that part of the routine was to have Joe Venuti direct the band; and when Jack took the baton, "the result was disastrous." Personally, I believe that this bit was redone with Lawrence Welk on the 10-23-62 program. On this show, Jack claims that a conductor is not necessary for an orchestra. Jack takes the baton, and the orchestra playing is chaotic. Welk grabs the baton from him, and all musicians fall perfectly in step. When the baton is passed back to Jack, chaos returns. Can anyone confirm or deny this supposition?

Peter Tatchell is trying to put dates on three pre-1958 Jack Benny television shows that were circulated in the syndication package distributed to Australia. He supplies these synopses:

> "**THE HONEST FACE**: Sheldon Weeks is a piano tuner who has a face that is so honest that everyone trusts him. A jewel robbery of a quarter of a million dollars takes place, and the thieves put the jewels in Sheldon's instrument bag.
> **THE FACE IS FAMILIAR**: Tom Jones robs a bank for a gang, not knowing what he is doing. Because he has an 'average' face--so average no one can remember it--he does not suffer for the robbery, although the gang is caught.
> **THE FENTON TOUCH**: A respectable bookkeeper robs the company for whom he works of $50,000. The cashier tells him the books show a theft of $82,000 and threatens to go to the police."

I know that the second one was done on radio for the Suspense program of 1-18-54, but I have as yet been unable to find a record of these being done on Jack's television show.

Rex Riffle recently mentioned to me a low-budget science fiction short entitled Jet Benny, and was an actual take-off on Jack and Rochester (Heaven help us...). Does anyone know of any information on this...eh...unusual piece of work?

Finally, does anyone have a complete list of companies who are distributing Jack Benny videocassettes? We know that there are some movies on the market (To Be or Not to Be, thankfully being one of them), along with at least two television shows. Your help in all these matters is appreciated.

§§ JACK BENNY CLASSIFIED §§

§§ Paul Pinch has xeroxes of London Palladium programmes from three of Jack's appearances, which are available for trade. 75 Priory Avenue, Haverfordwest, Dyfed SA61 1SG, United Kingdom.

§§ Terrence Goggin is interested in obtaining a videotape copy of Love Thy Neighbor. 213-286-9825.

§§ J. Kent Coscarelly is seeking a copy of Tamahine by Selma Nicklaus, published in Britain in 1957. 2173 Willester Avenue, San Jose, California 95124.

§ §   Need a book? (Kent take note!) Crabtree's Collection is a fabulous resource; has found many rare volumes for me over the years. Penny Crabtree, c/o Crabtree's Collection, 310 Baptist Road, Box 330, Canterbury, New Hampshire 03224.

§ §   The following people are early additions to the tape trading list:

** David A. Howell, 1300 Kennedy Boulevard, #419, Cuyahoga Falls, Ohio 44221

** Tom Kleinschmidt, 5815 Tree Moss Lane, North Ridgeville, Ohio 44039

** Jack Palmer, 145 North 21st Street, Battle Creek, Michigan 49015

** John Smothers, 22 Townsend Drive, Freehold, New Jersey 07728

** Peter Tatchell, 40 Bambra Road, Caulfield, Victoria 3161, Australia

♪ ♫ JUST SOME GENERAL NOTES AND SUCH ♪ ♫

The software on which The Jack Benny Times is produced has been upgraded from WordPerfect 5.0 to WordPerfect 5.1. While we are on the topic of computers, do any of you have access to Internet or Bitnet computer nodes? (Bitnet is a computer network linking many educational institutions; Internet has a much broader spectrum, including military bases, etc.) Selected members with such access have elected to receive their issues in ASCII files via these networks. If you have this capability and are interested, let me know.

As far as a preview of coming attractions, the Sam Perrin interview is not yet completed! Yes, the next issue should contain its continuation. Would also like to whet your appetite with two phenomenal interviews with Phil Harris and George Balzer, which will be appearing in future issues. Further, (as time permits) I am pursuing several other interviews (since you all have told me that you are simply in love with new interviews...who can blame you?) for your reading pleasure.

Now for my own anxiety time: in looking toward May, my graduation, and a job-hunting trip to California, there are a few things that I should mention. I fully anticipate maintaining the Times through this period, perhaps (and I enforce that PERHAPS) even sending out the May-June issue early to alleviate any unforseen problems. I DO anticipate suspending service of the tape library for a period of at least two to three months, beginning in May. However, this service will be reinstituted when my situation and location are more well-defined. I will be perfectly honest; I am scared out of my flipping mind about my future, but am maintaining a positive attitude. My future location will be determined mainly by my ability to secure gainful employment. During this time, please continue to send mail to the address below.

♪♫♪♫♪♫♪♫♪♫♪♫♪♫♪♫♪♫♪♫♪♫♪♫♪♫♪♫♪♫♪♫♪

Please send all questions, comments, additions, corrections, (and employment information!) to:

Laura Lee, c/o International Jack Benny Fan Club Offices, 15430 Lost Valley Drive, Fort Wayne, Indiana 46845   (219) 637-2287

Please friends, send no bombs.

After 39 Years—

The old man with the scythe has finally gained ground on the

The bloom of youth still appears on the Benny cheeks. You just have to look a bit harder

THE day started like any other in Beverly Hills. The sun forced its way through the early morning smog, the birds in the trees began to cough and I tumbled out of bed, happy, carefree and ready for the next 24 hours—like any healthy young animal.

Early rising is a ritual with me. Unlike my nocturnal brethren in show business, I am matutinal by nature. (I have always been matutinal, but never knew how to say it until I made an appearance on the Omnibus television program with Alistair Cooke. He slipped me the word, as he put it, "as a lagniappe." I don't know what lagniappe means, but the next time I see him I intend to ask.)

Anyway, the morning to which I refer began normally enough. I flung open the bedroom windows and started my daily dozen. I had just gotten around to the knee-bending exercises when I heard the stairs creaking and I knew that Rochester was on his way up with orange juice and coffee. Then I remembered that this was Rochester's day off. Suddenly I realized it wasn't the stairs that were creaking. It was my knees.

The shock straightened me up. I tried the knee-bending exercise again to make sure I had heard right. There was the same creaking—only this time louder, like somebody scraping a fiddle string. I winced. I can't stand bad violin playing.

I've always expected that sooner or later I'd start showing signs of wear. But I never expected the signs to be audible. I stood there, listening, and my eyes settled on the wall calendar, as they frequently do: it was a gift from Marilyn Monroe. After a moment or two, I glanced down at the date. It was February 1, 1954! In less than two weeks, on February 14th, I, Jack Benny, would be forty!

Forty! I shuddered, and my eyes fogged. The clock on the dresser seemed to be ticking faster, in a deliberate effort to hasten the fateful date. Cold chills and hot flashes coursed intermittently through my body. In a sort of hazy stupor, I could visualize myself sitting on a park bench with Barney Baruch, feeding the pigeons.

As reason slowly returned, I realized that Father Time had been waving his scythe under my nose, and I had been too comfortably ensconced in the sage and durable age of thirty-nine to heed the closeness of the blade. Trifling occurrences that I had dismissed as unimportant came back now to plague me with their full significance.

Lately, I had noticed that the Martinis were getting stronger, the hills on the golf course steeper, flirtations scarcer. Perhaps I had been cutting too fast a pace for a man on the brink of forty. I would have to change my habits. No more carousing with the boys. From now on, Charlie Coburn, Guy Kibbee and Lionel Barrymore would have to fun around without me.

In the following days, I underwent a transformation. I brooded and fretted, found fault with everything. I changed from a bright, lovable young man to a bitter, churlish, middle-aged curmudgeon. Rochester was on the verge of quitting. Polly, my parrot, wouldn't talk to me. I insulted the people on my radio and television shows. I even began to hate myself—and I was the last person in the world I thought I'd ever hate.

Finally I decided I would have to adjust. After all, it isn't a crime to be forty. A pity, maybe, but not a crime. I got a grip on myself and went to see my doctor. That is, I didn't exactly go to see him. I invited him over to my house for dinner. It was friendlier than going to his office ... and much less expensive.

After a modest meal, I led the conversation around to the state of my health and my impending birthday. The doctor was reluctant to talk business at first, but a couple of quick ponies of brandy loosened his tongue.

"When most men reach forty," the doctor said, "they find themselves up against a psychological block. Forty is considered the gateway to middle age and nobody wants to make the trip."

I refilled his glass and he continued his dissertation: "A man seems to feel, and with some reason, that while he's in his thirties he's within shooting distance of his youth, but when he hits forty he's all shot."

He helped himself to some more cognac.

"That all depends on the health of the individual," he went on. "Now, I'm forty-eight and

The first sign of advancing years: Jack met Marilyn Monroe—she looked the other way

I'm far from shot. Why, I can outdrink two twenty-four-year-olds put together."

I hastily put away the cognac bottle.

I had drawn some cheer from the doctor's observations. But I still was not satisfied. I yawned in his face a couple of times so he could get a look at my tongue. I saw his quick professional glance, and his lack of comment was reassuring.

I took the little wooden hammer out of the nut bowl and casually put it down on the table within easy reach of his hand. Then I crossed my legs and waited. Sure enough, he took the bait. He picked up the hammer and tapped me on the knee. I hadn't realized my reflexes were so fast. If he hadn't pulled his head back just in time, I would have punted his teeth into the kitchen.

The doctor remarked that he hadn't seen such knee action since Nijinsky. If I took care of myself, he said, I could live to be a hundred and forty.

Keeping the doctor's visit on a social basis, I said, "Doc, if you had a patient like me, what kind of diet would you put him on?"

He told me everything I wanted to know and it didn't cost me a quarter (including the price of the cognac). However, the diet he prescribed was disquieting. I was limited to expensive steaks and chops, lean cuts of meat, fowl and a few green vegetables. Bread and gravy, potatoes and rice, the old standbys that regularly graced my table, were taboo. Under my tutelage, Rochester had become proficient at preparing some wonderfully economical dishes ... braised beef hearts, fried pork livers and country gravy, breaded fishcakes and the hundred different kinds of hash that help the housewife stay within her budget. I was loath to discontinue this fare, especially since my freezer was full of beef hearts and fishcakes. Besides, Rochester was now so expert at preparing this type of food it would be a pity to make him stop.

Rochester Offers an Ideal Solution

After turning the problem over in my mind, I finally found a way out of the dilemma. Rochester was not on a diet. There was no reason why he couldn't go on eating beef hearts and fishcakes, even though I was stuck with steaks and chops.

As I walked the doctor to the door, I felt reassured. Still, I had been unable to think of a way for him to take my basal metabolism. I began toying with the idea of inviting him to dinner again. I could make the invitation for two and ask him to bring his machine with him.

As we shook hands, I held the grip, and fed the doctor one more leading question.

"So you think I'm in good shape, eh, Doc?"

"Yes," he said, struggling vainly to get his hand loose, "but I think you ought to drop by the office for a checkup in a week or so."

"Another checkup?" I asked, taken off guard. "But you just gave me one."

"Well, you can't be too safe," he grunted, tugging at his hand. "Besides, a man of your age can change overnight."

All my old fears overwhelmed me again. In fact, I was so staggered that my grip turned to mush, and the doctor, released suddenly, went flying out the door.

The doctor's pessimistic remark left me frus-

Collier's for February 19, 1954

I'm Turning 40

By JACK BENNY

young fellow with the fiddle—but it was some race while it lasted. They're both winded

trated and disappointed. But I was able to find consolation in the fact that even though the body was beginning to sag a little as birthday number forty crept closer, mentally my faculties were never sharper. I still retained all my old cunning and guile. Besides, I decided, even though I might change by tomorrow, I was still in good shape tonight, so the money expended on food and drink for the doctor had not been entirely wasted.

When the Plumber Comes to Dinner

Feeling a little better, I checked my supply of cognac and was pleased to find there were still a few pints left. Not that I drink myself, but I like to keep some in the house for my guests. Next week, I'm having my plumber over for dinner. There's an annoying leak in the kitchen drainpipe, and I'm sure that after Herman imbibes a few samples of the grape, he'll be under that sink like an old firehorse. I'm counting on quite a saving, because the plumber's fee is usually higher than the doctor's.

The next morning I could find no perceptible change in my health, in spite of the doctor's dour warning. Nevertheless, I bathed and dressed carefully to avoid taxing my strength, and, wary of my protesting knees, I had Rochester help me with my socks and my shoelaces. Then, after a cautious breakfast of orange juice and hot vitamin-fortified milk, I set out on my program of readjustment.

First I dropped in to see my old friend and colleague, Eddie Cantor. Eddie had long since endured the experience I was now undergoing, and I hoped to acquire a few tips on how a man should dress, behave and adapt his philosophy when he reaches forty. Eddie proved to be a disappointment. He beat around the bush and seemed reluctant to discuss the subject.

Finally, I put it to him point-blank. "Eddie," I said, "did you feel that your whole psychological structure changed when you became forty?"

Cantor answered that he wouldn't know; he never had been forty and he never intended to be.

You see, Eddie went from thirty-nine to sixty overnight, and the only one who ever suspected it was Ida.

After lunch, I left Cantor's house, still groping for a panacea to restore my confidence and bolster my shattered morale. As I walked down Sunset Boulevard, I felt that everyone was staring at me. I could almost hear people saying to themselves, "Look at him. He must be forty if he's a day."

I decided a few holes of golf might help my frayed nerves. I was going to take a taxi out to my club, but it was such a pleasant day I chose to walk. It was only seven miles and I knew a short cut, most of it paved. The only bad stretch was a half mile through a beanfield, but I knew the terrain like the back of my hand.

I started out briskly enough, but after a few blocks the pace began to tell. My strides were slower and my breathing was faster. I thought a cup

For Benny, the voice of Time was soprano. It said, "I'm awfully sorry, Jack, but I have a date for that night. Unless you'd like to go along as chaperon?" Note stunned expression

FAN CLUB

15430 LOST VALLEY DRIVE
FORT WAYNE, IN 46845

THE JACK BENNY TIMES

Volume XI, Number 2   INTERNATIONAL DISTRIBUTION   March-April 1991

Scene from "Hollywood Daffy"

☺ ☺ ☺ PRESIDENT'S MESSAGE ☺ ☺ ☺

Jell-o again folks! Well, so much for the on-time policy. However, I believe that I have a very fair excuse. As just about all of you know, my graduation is approaching on May 13th (how lucky can one get?). I will be receiving my Master's degree in Business-Administration with a concentration in Economics and Finance. I find it rather appropriate for a Jack Benny fan to be majoring in such subjects.

One other note of importance, since it seems to have been overlooked in the previous issue.

THE TAPE LIBRARY IS TEMPORARILY CLOSED.

In other words, for the moment I am not accepting orders. If you send me one, I will send it back. Why? Because if I hang on to your tapes, they will probably have to be sent out to California anyhow. Also, I do not want to lose any tapes. Moreover, I am certain that you do not want your tapes consumed in the great void of magnetic dormancy while I job-hunt. I foresee August* as a reasonable reopening date for the library, as by that time I hope to have a job and a place to live (I hope I hope I hope). Until that time, please hold all orders. Thank you very much, and get ready to deluge me in August; I will be prepared.

Now on with the show!

☺ OUR VERY OWN COMIC STRIP'S NAME ☺

In the last issue of the <u>Times</u>, our own comic strip made its grand debut. As you recall, it features Jack and the gang as children. We turned it over to you to supply the name. These names were then perused by the strip's artist, Rob Crawford, and a winner selected. THE WINNER IS (drumroll):

THE LUCKY TYKES PROGRAM

submitted by Frank Pozzuoli of the Bronx, New York. Congratulations, Frank! You are the proud winner of an original drawing of the strip, certainly soon to be a collectors' item and exhibited in galleries around the globe. (Gee, I do not even have one of those!) Congratulations again, and thanks to all our contributors!

© Copyright 1991, Laura Lee

*~~mid-September~~ It <u>was</u> reasonable, but I can't get my tapes here yet!

? ! ? DO YOU KNOW ? ! ?

Jack Benny Does a Bing Crosby;

Bing Crosby Starts Something! It happened when Bing did a bit part in "My Favorite Blonde" with Bob Hope. He wasn't billed with the cast, and movie audiences got a bang out of the stunt he and Bob pulled, because Bob's "it can't be" reactions exactly paralleled their own. Now Jack Benny pulls the same stunt on the set of "Casablanca" with Ingrid Bergman and Humphrey Bogart in a cafe scene. If movie-goers have sharp eyes, they will see Jack scurrying around among the waiters at the small tables that form the background of the scene . . .

At the left is a clipping on a matter that has been haunting me for some time now. Jack is somewhere in Casablanca, but unfortunately I have only been privy to rather fuzzy tape copies of copies. Ergo, the picture has not been clear enough for me to truly discern individuals who may or may not be Jack. Does anyone know exactly WHERE Jack appears in the movie? If you are able to supply a precise time (e.g., 32 minutes into the film) it would be very helpful. However, any exacting description of the scene and Jack's location would be of great value. Get those VCRs up and running!

§ § JACK BENNY CLASSIFIEDS § §

§ § **WANTED:** Liberty article, "Produced by Jack Benny," March 1949. Contact: J. Kent Coscarelly, (408) 377-0733.

§ § **WANTED:** Ethel Merman memorabilia. Offer Jack Benny items in trade. For instance, "Merman was on the Johnny Carson show, mid-1970's, and brought a framed letter from Jack. Johnny reads the letter and shows extended close-ups of Jack's handwriting. [The videotape] is quite clear, and the letter is studied in its entirety." He also has a copy of The Mouse that Jack Built, transferred directly from the 16mm print (I wish I had some Merman items to trade for THAT!!!) Contact: Skip Koenig, 1298 Wickapecko Drive, Ocean, New Jersey 07712.

§ § The Autograph Quarterly and Buyers' Guide is an impressive volume filled to the brim with information and advertisements for autograph collectors and enthusiasts. Items range from Napoleon to George Gershwin to Eric Clapton. Truly a must-see for collectors. Autograph Quarterly, P.O. Box 55328, Stockton, California 95205.

§ § Personalities on Parade is a limited edition LP containing rare recorded performances of all your favorites, including: Jack (soundtrack from Bright Moments), Jolson, Crosby, Ethel Merman (Skip, take note), and many others. *The only known recording of Harpo Marx's voice is also included.* There are four volumes, and only 750 copies of each volume will be pressed and individually numbered. The cost is $50.00 for all four volumes, or $12.95 per volume purchased separately. Contact: John Newton, P.O. Box 471, Claymont, Delaware 19703.

See also Watt's article.

♪ ♪ THE TALE PIECE ♪ ♪

The following Benny moment is brought to us by our cartoonist, Rob Crawford:

"One of my favorite excerpts from the Benny program comes from a 3-44 broadcast from the Hollywood Canteen:

Jack: Gosh, I wonder if the lemonade is ready? Oh Rochester!...Rochester!! Hmmm...he never hears me....Phil, give me a pair of dice, will ya?... Thanks.
(Sound of dice rolling in someone's hands and being thrown)
(Sound of footsteps running)
Roch: Who's doin' it?!...For how much? And what's the point?!
Jack: Rochester!! Rochester...he went right down on his face! Rochester...where were you when I rattled those dice?
Roch: In Pomona!
Jack: Way out in Pomona?
Roch: Yes Boss...I would have been here sooner, but I came here on my knees!
Jack: Well get up off your knees...people will think you're Al Jolson!
Roch: Al Jolson? After it rains I'm still Rochester, but who's he?!
Jack: Well, get up! You're supposed to be in the kitchen mixing some punch!
Roch: Well Boss, as long as I'm here, I wanna help entertain the boys...I rehearsed a song.
Jack: Well...that's a nice gesture Rochester--but you can't sing!
Roch: Who can't sing? You just don't appreciate my soft, tender voice.
Jack: Soft, tender voice?
Roch: Yeah! In my part of town, they call me "the sentimental fellow with the mellow bellow."
Jack: Oh sure, sure!
Roch: Really Boss! I used to sing with the Hall-Johnson Choir.
Jack: What happened?
Roch: Johnson threw me out in the hall!!

♪♪♪♪♪♪♪♪♪♪♪♪♪♪♪♪♪♪♪♪♪♪♪♪♪♪♪♪

Please send all questions, comments, additions, corrections, and job information to:
Laura Lee, c/o International Jack Benny Fan Club Offices, 15430 Lost Valley Drive, Fort Wayne, Indiana 46845
(219) 637-2287

Please friends, send no bombs.

And Likewise— JACK BENNY

By Howard Wilcox

If You're Looking for the Secret of Jack Benny's Hold upon His Public, Hippodrome Along with Him and Get His Mastery of Satire

Jack shows Nancy Carroll and innumerable other attractive femmes in his latest motion picture Transatlantic Merry-Go-Round that Casanova has been outclassed

From lingerie buyer to air fame has been Mary Livingstone's jump since she became Mrs. Jack Benny

Picture a fellow at the top of his profession with sponsors begging for his services, whose slogan is "Situation wanted"—and you have Jack Benny.

It's not a job Jack wants. His crying need really is for situations—scenes about which he can build those comedy circumstances which have made him the most beloved of all the jesters of the air.

Puns are not in his line. An occasional play on words necessarily finds its way into his scripts, but the premise upon which this polished performer has built his outstanding popularity is that of the clown of the old Greek hippodrome, the buffoon whose heart bleeds while he smiles and gibes to amuse King Public.

And how that regal audience smiles with him!

Under-dog—that's the Jack Benny of the air. In his program somebody forever is getting ribbed. And that somebody is inevitably Benny himself.

Mary Livingstone, his wife, plagues him; the orchestra leader deserts him in his hour of need; the announcer turns the tables on him, and seemingly everyone on the program conspires to defeat him. But Jack jests bravely on. Sympathy is his by virtue of every human and humane trait, and in that bond of commiseration lies the adoration of a nation.

Of course, it's all make-believe, but in Jack's capable hands it is all so real, so natural in its portrayal, that listeners subconsciously find themselves lined up as supporters in his misery. This is the essence of good comedy. Almost anyone with a flair for snappy presentation can take the comprehensive English language and twist it into the ribald jest or the merry mot, but their mouthings, save to a moronic few, have none of the quality of endurance.

Back of the Benny motif are sweetness and charm, the principles upon which personality and its attendant success are built.

Perhaps it is because Jack many times has needed public sympathy in his personal life, that he knows so well the value of soliciting it for the character which he portrays on the radio.

The Benny of today who names his own weekly salary—and who has been playing tag for two years with a needed vacation but can't run fast enough to escape the would-be sponsors who hem him in—is a far different figure from the disappointed artist who saw eclipse in the decadence of the vaudeville theater, and consequently faced the future with uncertainty.

But in the interim he encountered the kind of experience which mellows evaluations and which, in his case, made him turn from the edged sort of wit to the more subtle field of satire. In short, he had faced situations. Nothing more natural than that he should turn to them as the background for his later comedy efforts. He had learned that to be on the wrong end of a joke and take it gracefully and courageously won him more attention than a shopworn quip which was worth little.

Benny looked about him when radio was presented as an outlet, and quickly determined that a certain group of theatrical stars were trading almost 100 per cent on their prestige from the stage. He knew his safety lay in his material rather than in his name. It had to be different and it had to be instantaneous in its appeal. Radio is the short-order restaurant of entertainment. Listeners will not sit around and wait for a "guy to get good." So his flair for satire was invoked.

An instance of Jack's experience was his first encounter with Goodman Ace. This scintillating quipster was then a columnist on a Kansas City paper.

Benny, not long out of the Navy, and still just a fiddler who gagged as he played, was at a Kansas City vaudeville house, and in his hunt for paragraphic material Ace saw the show. His adverse criticism of Jack wasn't even cleverly subtle.

Following his natural inclination, Jack looked up the columnist. He placed himself in the position of a chap needing a helping hand, and won Ace's sympathy. He sought suggestions and he got them—good ones, too—suggestions that have helped him on his way to success. A friendship was established that still endures, and many a gay quip in Benny's radio acts today is the fruit of Ace's facile ingenuity.

Another sympathetic and guiding influence in Jack's life has been Mary Livingstone, the Pacific coast girl who deserted a lingerie buyer's remunerative job to cast her lot with the tall funny man. Between them they do a deal of bantering; but her complete consideration for him, whatever his trials, has been just another window through which to admit the sunshine of sympathetic tolerance.

Thus the marvel of Jack Benny's success is dissipated. It rests securely on the Waukegan, Illinois, boy's hard-won knowledge of the world's love for the clown, on the current of concord that flows from the contented to the oppressed—and on Jack's mastery of satire.

Jack Benny is on the air Sundays at 7 p. m. EST or 6 p. m. CST. The network is NBC-WJZ. The makers of Jello are the sponsors.

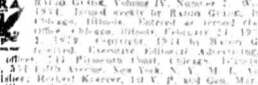

Radio Guide
December 8, 1934

MORE RECORDS BY JACK BENNY
Written Especially For THE JACK BENNY TIMES
Your Host: Walt Mitchell

Greetings to Club members worldwide from a collector of old phonograph records. As such, it has been my regret that Jack Benny didn't make more records than he did. With a career on radio spanning more than two decades, he proved himself to have been one of the century's great masters of spoken comedy. So the lack of an extensive recording career on his part is certainly a mystery to me. However, I am pleased to report to all of you that I have a few more records featuring Jack's voice than those already spotlighted by Laura, and here they are.

The first issue I'd like to describe is the oldest Benny record and also the newest! That paradox is explained by my saying that the lp containing the performance in question was released as a limited edition record in 1988, but was recorded by Jack sixty years earlier! It is the oldest known example of the recorded sound of Jack's voice and it was performed circa January of 1928. It bears the rather generic title, "A Few Bright Moments." The master number cited in the liner notes as being on the original disc was one of a series which was totally unfamiliar to me. Moreover, the performance didn't sound to me as though it had been recorded at 78 rpm, which was obviously the case with most of the other tracks by the other stars heard on this lp. A check with John Newton, the owner of the rare originals and compiler of the lp, confirmed what I suspected. "A Few Bright Moments" was not made for release as a record. Rather, it was a primitive method of recording the sound for an early talkie film short on a disc rather than on the film itself! The film short apparently is missing and may even be long gone forever, but at least part of the performance still lives in the grooves of that lone 16-inch 33 1/3 rpm sound track disc. The commercial release is part of the album called "Personalities On Parade," which is also the name of the label. This is Volume One in a series of four, of which only 750 copies of each volume were produced.

In 1956 Jack made a Capitol lp for children. On this record, he greets the children at the beginning, then proceeds to tell Mary the story of what happened to him while he was learning to play the violin as a child. This record was a fantasy story produced and written by Alan Livingston. For the virtuoso violin performances heard throughout the lp, the great Isaac Stern was borrowed from Columbia Records to "ghost" the soli for Jack. Although Mr. Stern was indeed subbing in Jack's place, unlike most "ghost" performances, he did not do it anonymously. Quite to the contrary! The front cover of the album shows what appears to me to be an oil painting of Jack and Isaac standing side by side in matching tuxedos, their violins poised to begin playing. This is despite the fact that Isaac does not speak nor performs as himself on the record. Mary gets no credit on the record label or cover for her dialogue speeches with Jack. However, my dear friend the late Mel Blanc provides two voices (including a straight performance as a <u>gentle</u> Professor LeBlanc!) and gets "Voice characterization credit both on the label and the back cover! The album was designated as one record in Capitol's "Music Appreciation Series," and was released on catalog number T3241. The title was "Jack Benny plays The Bee ably assisted by Isaac Stern." Part of the title ("The Bee") was an error, so the story's title was changed to a more accurate "Jack Benny Fiddles With The Classics" when the lp was reissued in 1978. The latter pressing was issued by commission of Wonderland Records, and Capitol put it out on its own Special Marketing label with catalog number L-8108. This time, the cover showed a cute cartoon of Jack as a little boy.

(MORE RECORDS BY JACK BENNY,   )

The radio reruns of Jack's program were sponsored by The Home Insurance Company during the 1957-58 season. As a sideline, my late father was an independent insurance agent representing several national companies in our area, including The Home Insurance Company. This firm hearalded its sponsorship of the show in a surprising, unique way. They sent out a postcard to each of their agents. On the postcard was a black-and-white photo of Jack and Rochester in a gag pose in the Maxwell. Laminated onto the picture was a small 78 rpm record pressed on see-through plastic--a sheet as thin as cellophane! Since the record was not sold in stores, it has no catalog number. (An inner-margin master number--PM 3196-2F--does appear on some copies, but not all!) Printed on the front of the card next to the photo is the following announcement: "A PERSONAL MESSAGE FROM THE JACK BENNY GANG FOR HOME AGENTS ONLY!" The underlined words are shown that way on the card. The back of the postcard reads, "Play this card on any standard 78 rpm phonograph--it will give you an idea of how we can work together to get good business for you! THE JACK BENNY SHOW sponsored by THE HOME INSURANCE COMPANY on your local CBS Radio station for you!" The record is so small that it cannot be played on automatic changers, even those old enough to be equipped with 78 rpm speed. But when played on a manually operated machine, this is what is heard:

   "Oh, Rochester!...Rochester, what's this message about Mr. Zanuck
    calling?"
   "Oh yes, Mister Benny. He phoned this afternoon from 20th Century-Fox
    Studios."
   "Whaddidie want? Whaddidie want? What? What? What?...What?"
   "You owe 'im a dime! The Coke machine is out of order!"
   (Audience laughter.)
   "Heh, heh! Well, I hope that sounds familiar. This is Don Wilson,
    speaking on behalf of Jack Benny Mary Livingstone, Rochester, Dennis
    Day and all the Gang, to tell you how very happy we all are to be
    working for you and The Home Insurance Company starting September 29th
    on the CBS Radio Network. Every week I'll be speaking on behalf of
    the Home agent in every community, and will be reaching millions of
    prospects with your message. So be sure to be tuned in on Sunday
    beginning September 29th at Jack's traditional time."

There are probably other copies of this record kicking around among collectors of old postcards, but so far I have seen only two copies.

Finally, I have an advertising record made on a record-cutting machine, which chisels the record groove into a metal-base acetate disc. The Gotham advertising agency produced this 10-inch 33 1/3 rpm record, with data for this particular disc typewritten on a paste-on label. Since each record was made this way by hand, there's no telling how many or how few were manufactured. Considering the facts, however, there can't have been thousands of them. All they contain are five 30-second radio commercials (all on one side, with nothing on the back) for Bradlee's Department Store. All five commercials feature Jack as a customer in the store, with a small supporting cast, store-noise sound effect in the background, and Jack's hilarious penny-pinching dealings in the store.

That's all of the additional Jack Benny records that I know of. If anyone knows of others that are not in Laura's discography nor mentioned here, please drop me a line with full details on what you have. My address is Box 201, Oriskany, New York 13424 USA.

  FAN CLUB

```
3561 Somerset Avenue
Castro Valley, California 94546
```

THE JACK BENNY TIMES

Volume XI, Number 3 INTERNATIONAL DISTRIBUTION May-June 1991

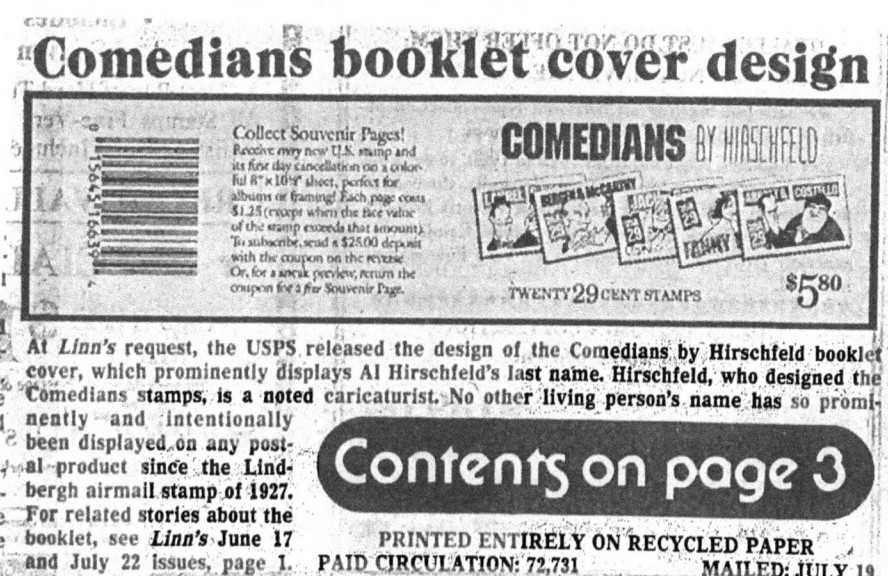

FINALLY!

☺ ☺ ☺ PRESIDENT'S MESSAGE ☺ ☺ ☺

Jell-o again, folks! Unimaginable changes have occurred over the past two months. Above all, I am happy to announce that I am wildly, madly, desperately, and deeply in love. The object of my affection is a city called San Francisco. I had visited here in September of 1980 at which time it was quite rainy, foggy, and cold. However, I now have traversed the area under much better climatological conditions. What a wonderful place! So many things to see and do, or it is equally enjoyable to merely wander about with no specific intent or goal other than having a good time. One cannot do this among the Indiana cornfields. Accidentally discovered an absolutely ethereal (Jell-o is, of course, not ethereal, it's a dessert) pleasure which I will pass along here. Sit out on the dock next to Pier 39 (a natural location, to be certain) during the day after the fog rolls out and before it rolls in again, and eat fresh clam chowder by dipping pieces of sourdough in the bowl. Who needs a spoon?

As far as actual drive out here goes, it was blissfully uneventful. On the first, second, and fourth days my locales were setting record or near-record highs, and the third day brought near-record lows. Plus, my car has no air conditioning. There were several tornadoes just north and east of me when I stayed in Cheyenne, and vicious winds blew across the salt flats in Utah. Yes, I took 69 north, and then 80 all the way. House- and cat-sat for different friends who were on vacation. Am temporarily working in Palo Alto, and still seeking more permanent employment in the general vicinity. This brings me to an important piece of information--my new address and VERY OWN PHONE NUMBER (miracles still happen!):

NEW ADDRESS:
3561 Somerset Avenue
Castro Valley, California 94546
(415) 886-3321

Please make a note of it. Also note that after September 1st, the area code of the phone changes to 510. I am still receiving the mail that is sent to Ft. Wayne, but there is a considerable delay. Ergo, please send any packages/letters/mail (but no bombs) to the above address. Thank you. I hope that all of you who are awaiting a response to your letters will take the above as an explanation for the delay. I have toted all my backlogged correspondence with me, and have every intention of answering as soon as I become settled at my address.

The tape library is still closed until ~~August.~~ further notice. As of this writing, it is in the process of being shipped to me in sections.

© Copyright 1991, Laura Lee

My apologies for taking all this space with my own affairs, but I hope that it at least serves to keep you abreast of the move of the IJBFC offices to the west coast. West coast...my, my...that **does** sound nice! Now on with the show!

♥ ☺ ♥ JACK BLOOM PASADENA CHAPTER ♥ ☺ ♥

The time has come again for the induction of members to the Jack Bloom Pasadena Chapter. This is an honorary society for non-honorary members who have been active for four or more years. Jack Bloom (see May-June 1990 issue for the complete story) was a fabulous human being who dedicated incalculable time and effort to the IJBFC and the perpetuation of Jack Benny. A complete list of JBPC members follows, with asterisks next to new "entrants."

JACK ABIZAID	TOM MASTEL
JACK BLOOM	BILL OLIVER
BRUCE BAKER	ROBERT OLSEN
HAL BOGART **	JOHN SCHLAMP
PHIL EVANS	JOYCE SHOOKS
MARILYN FILLENWARTH **	BENJAMIN SPANGLER **
LE ROY FILLENWARTH **	BONNIE SPANGLER **
ALAN GROSSMAN	DAVID SPANGLER
JAY HICKERSON	STEVE SZEJNA
TIM HOLLIS	BARBARA WATKINS
SAREE KAMINSKY	KEN WEIGEL
LAURA LEE	DOUG WOOD
GEORGE LILLIE	

!!!!! YOU DO KNOW !!!!!

Three questions were posed in a past "Do You Know?" column, and all were answered within a few weeks. Fantastic! First of all, Peter Tatchell had asked about three television shows featuring Jack. The titles of these were: The Face is Familiar, The Fenton Touch, and The Honest Face. Tom Kleinschmidt informs me that all the shows he mentions were originally broadcast on G.E. Theatre. Tom has a copy of The Face is Familiar, and would like to know if anyone has video copies of these shows. Contact him at: 5815 Tree Moss Lane, North Ridgeville, Ohio 44039 (nice zip code!).

The next question on Jack's screen test for The Sunshine Boys. Walt Mitchell writes: "My recollection of having seen it is somewhat vague, but I do recall that it was shown on one of the talk shows, introduced by someone who was on the program to promote the film just as the final product was going into the theatres. I believe the program in question was The Mike Douglas Show. The scene for which Jack tested was the one in which the former partners are brought together at Jack's (later George's) character's home to talk about doing their act on a TV variety show. The dialogue here conveys the fact that the vaudevillians still don't get along well with each other. The things I distinctly remember about this brief clip are the living room setting and one of Matthau's lines. In an exasperated tone of voice, Matthau says at one point, "It wasn't the Belasco Theatre; it was the Morosco Theatre!" That's all I remember about the scene, except that it lasted (the clip as aired, that is) only a minute; perhaps 90 seconds."

Finally, Frank Pozzuoli supplies this information regarding the distribution of Jack on video tape: "The best distributor of Jack's TV shows and guest appearances is Shokus Video...P.O. Box 8434, Van Nuys, California 91409. Their catalogue of many different 50's an 60's TV shows is $3. They have 5 tapes each containing 4 episodes of Jack's show. A few other shows with Jack (his own series and guest appearances or specials) are scattered on 'variety' tapes. They also have an episode of The Dennis Day Show and Dennis guest starring in an episode of Betty White's Date with the Angels. Shokus is a great source and you can even see their name on certain TV specials, as they helped to supply the old TV clips.

"As for movies, It's in the Bag is distributed by Republic Pictures Home Video. Also Transatlantic Merry-Go-Round is available from MCA Distributing Corp." To Be or Not to Be is also available, we believe from CBS/Fox Video.

Loads of kudos and gratitude to Tom, Walt and Frank for their help!!

AND EVEN MORE WITH SAM PERRIN

L: What do you think about today's comedy and comedians?

S: I don't understand it...I just don't understand it. I don't like to mention names.

L: Is there any particular one you like? Steven Wright, Robin Williams...?

S: Well, you cannot pick an isolated case when you say 'comedy today'...Robin Williams could be great. I think he could make me laugh, but bigger names than Robin Williams can't make me laugh...A lot of the things I don't understand, so I figure it must be me.

L: I am the same way with some comedians, that perhaps **I** am missing the point. Is there anyone you feel who has the talent or the capacity?

S: As a comedian? Well unfortunately, I don't know whether I would vote for a comedian. Even Milton Berle I would say is a **personality**. Bob Hope is a personality; incidentally, the most modest man you ever met in your life. So was Jack. They don't know they're such big stars. He was absolutely wonderful. I just don't watch that much...I used to. There is no comedian--personality or comedian--who everybody likes...There is a man I like, who is not supposed to be a comedian. He's doing a show now called Dear John [Judd Hirsch], and most of the shows are good...But he himself is not a comedian, and he underplays beautifully. I like him...I don't like a show where the people know they're funny.

L: That was probably the element to Gracie Allen's comedy, that she 'believed' it.

S: She was very nice. She was sincere and gentle. [EN: Tape jumped here...alas!! Now switch topic to Jack and the writers.] There were five of us, four writers and Jack. Now when Jack sat in the room with us, he was not the star. He was one of us...he was one of five. With the five of these talents, who has to come up with a **great** joke? The secretary, Jeanette!

L: I've heard a lot about Jeanette. Is she still around?

S: Yes. Jack had just come back from England, and Danny Kaye was over there. [Kaye] was invited every place. [Jack] said, "Danny Kaye comes and they make such a fuss over him at Buckingham Palace. It doesn't matter for me...Although I almost made it. I was invited to dinner at number 9 Downing Street!" That was Jeanette!

L: I think it was George [Balzer] who said that there were almost six of you: the four writers, Jack, and Jeanette; and Jack and Jeanette were the editors of the show. [EN: Complete digression] How long ago did Tack [John Tackaberry] die?

S: It seems like a long time ago...I loved this guy, because he did everything that I didn't do. He drank, he was a real Texan!...My wife also is from Texas. Tack would make steak dinners. He would call me and say, "We're making some steak. Come on down!"...I lived in an apartment a little bigger than this, and there was a girl who lived in this complex. She said, "I'd like to meet him [Tack]." I said, "I'll introduce you to him." He had called me to come on down...So this one day I said, "Tack, can I bring a girl down with me?" He said, "Sure!" So we came down. I didn't go home with her. She stayed there, I think one or two days later they were married--they fell so in love!...She works now for a music publisher...

[Still a little more to go!]

♪♩♪♩♪♩♪♩♪♩♪♩♪♩♪♩♪♩♪♩♪♩♪♩♪♩♪♩♪♩♪♩♪♩

Please send all questions, comments, corrections, additions, and job information to:

Laura Lee, c/o International Jack Benny Fan Club Offices, 3561 Somerset Avenue, Castro Valley, California 94546   (415) 886-3321

Please friends, send no bombs.

Promotional potential of stamps appears to influence USPS approach to new issues

By Gary Griffith

The new United States "Comedians by Hirschfeld" booklet will break new ground in several ways, as the promotional potential of some stamps now appears to dominate the U.S. Postal Service's approach to new issues.

As Linn's reported in its June 17 issue (page 1), the name of a stamp artist will be used on a postal product for the first time. The name of Broadway caricaturist Albert Hirschfeld will prominently appear on the booklet cover.

No other living person has been intentionally honored in such a prominent way on a postal product since 1927, when the Post Office Department issued the Lindbergh commemorative stamp. Several souvenir sheets bear names of postmasters general.

The Postal Service has released the design of the stamps, but is still withholding the design of the covers, which were printed by the Bureau of Engraving and Printing more than a month ago.

In another marketing move, the Postal Service is reporting that "the stamp issuance will launch a joint promotional campaign by the Postal Service and MCA/Universal Home Video."

MCA/Universal is releasing two new Abbott and Costello home videos. The booklet stamps depict the team as one of five subjects on the se-tenant pane.

The videos will be priced at $14.95 and will be sold at a profit as part of the private firm's product line. No part of the profits will go to the Postal Service.

According to a Postal Service news release, Robert Blattner, president of MCA/Universal Home Video, was to accompany Postmaster General Anthony Frank at unveiling ceremonies in Las Vegas, Nev., during a convention of video software dealers.

Asked why the Postal Service was promoting a private commercial venture, spokesman Dickey Rustin told Linn's, "There is nothing to stop us from doing anything that is mutually beneficial."

MCA/Universal will, according to the Postal Service, promote the stamps with a "special insert" included with the videos.

The Postal Service will also be using the stamps and Hirschfeld's name to sell what it calls "a limited edition Abbott and Costello art print" for $14.95.

According to the Postal Service, the poster will be "signed" by Hirschfeld "in the plate," which means that the signature will be mass produced, and that the artist will not approve the final product.

The 11- by 14-inch print is also described as including "the highly-collectible official first day of issue postmark and a certificate of authenticity."

Art dealers who use such language in describing so-called "limited edition art prints" are often accused of deception.

Actual art prints by Hirschfeld start at $450, according to the New York gallery that handles them.

Known for the caricatures of New York theater figures that he has drawn for more than 60 years, Albert Hirschfeld is still active at age 88. He continues to draw for the New York Times on a weekly basis, and he also underlakes commercial work for other publications and advertising agencies.

The rule against secret marks in stamp artwork or engraving has been waived for Hirschfeld, to allow him to continue his practice of including his daughter's name, "Nina," somewhere in his

(Please turn to page 21)

A booklet pane of ten stamps showing the five different designs of the U.S. Comedians by Hirschfeld stamps.

Christmas stamps to be without denominations

By Gary Griffith

Another rate change, this one to 30¢ for a first-class letter, now seems likely, and the United States Postal Service is taking steps to implement it before the end of the year.

Linn's has learned, and the Postal Service has confirmed, that this year's Christmas stamps will be printed without denominations.

At present, the Postal Service has ordered approximately 2 billion Christmas stamps.

McDowell told Linn's that no non-denominated make-up rate stamp is contemplated.

The 1¢ Kestrel stamp issued last month and printed by the inexpensive offset lithography process is expected to serve that purpose.

"If the rate goes to 30¢, we know what the makeup rate will be," McDowell said.

About 2 billion non-denominated make-up rate stamps were ordered for the Feb. 3 rate change. Current production of the Kestrel stamp is estimated at about now wait for a response from the PRC.

There is no mandated time in which the PRC must respond, and it may agree or disagree with the Postal Service that new rates are warranted.

However, the board of governors can raise the rates on its own, regardless of the PRC's response, by voting unanimously to do so.

The board was unanimous in its July 2 rejection of the 29¢ rate case, and it appears to have the votes it needs to

District of Columbia Bicentennial

used on overprints of a set, the color used for a particular stamp is noted in the description line of that stamp.

Se-tenants — including pairs and blocks, will be listed in the format most commonly collected. If the stamps are collected as a unit, the major number will be assigned to the multiple and the minor numbers to the individual increments. When the items are usually collected as singles, then each individual stamp is given a major number and the entire se-tenant item is given a minor number of the last item in sequence.

The manner in which an item is listed generally depends on the stamp's usage in the country of issue. Where stamps are used widely for postal purposes, even if se-tenant issues will be collected as a unit, each stamp will be given a major number, such as the stamps of the United States, Canada, Germany, and Great Britain.

For further information about the 1992 Scott catalog, write to Scott Publishing, Box 828, Sidney, OH 45365.

Comedians by Hirschfeld data

(Continued on page 1) drawings, often several times.

"We felt that 'NINA' has become such a distinctive element in Al Hirschfeld's art that our stamp designs would not be true Hirschfelds without them," Postmaster General Frank has explained in a prepared statement.

While current law prohibits the honoring of a living person on a stamp, the Postal Service appears to be coming close with "Comedians by Hirschfeld," as the stamps will be officially known.

Hirschfeld's signature will be included in the "art prints" the Postal Service will be selling, and his name will be much more prominent on the booklet covers than any of the names of the subjects on the stamps.

In fact, the comedians who are the subject of the stamps have so far gotten less mention by the Postal Service than Hirschfeld has.

The five designs of the stamps depict Bud Abbott and Lou Costello, Jack Benny, Edgar Bergen and his ventriloquist's dummy Charlie McCarthy, Stan Laurel and Oliver Hardy, and Fanny Brice.

Linn's hasn't counted the number of "Ninas" in the stamp drawings, but it has counted the number of "Hirschfelds" in the Postal Service's two press releases on the issue. He is currently leading Fanny Brice 11 to 2.

Originally planned for release in September, the issue date is now expected to be moved forward to August to allow the booklets a longer period of sale.

However, no first-day or production details have been released by the Postal Service. Linn's will report them as they become available.

Scouts at jamboree

Five United States members of the Scouts on Stamps Society International will leave for Korea Aug. 1 to help publicize stamp collecting.

They will attend the international scouting jamboree scheduled for Aug. 8-16 in Soruk Park, Korea.

Laurence Clay, Carl Schauer, Warren Wheeler, Fred Bruhne and A. Camp Hopkins will operate an SOSSI booth at the jamboree. Other SOSSI members helping at the booth will be from Japan, Korea, Hong Kong and, possibly, the Philippines.

SOSSI members attending the jamboree in other scouting capacities may also participate in the booth activities.

The men will set up a display of World Jamboree stamps. Scouts visiting the booth will be given free postcards and the SOSSI emblem will be applied to their passports.

On sale at the booth will be SOSSI patches, pins and cacheted covers.

Look for Nina in the Mail

Fans of famed caricaturist Al Hirschfeld, 86, who is widely known for hiding his daughter's name, "NINA," in his drawings, now have an opportunity to look for the name in a recent issuance of commemorative stamps. The Hirschfeld drawings are included in the new series of 29-cent stamps featuring Bud Abbott and Lou Costello, Jack Benny, Edgar Bergen and Charlie McCarthy and Stan Laurel and Oliver Hardy. The stamps will not include the artist's signature with its clue for the number of "NINAs" in the drawing, but Postmaster General Anthony Frank said, "We felt that 'NINA' has become such a distinctive element in Al Hirschfeld's art that our stamp designs would not be true Hirschfelds without them."

Al Hirschfeld puts his stamp on the mail.

GRENADA COMMEMOR[ATES] THE "COMING EX[PLORATION] OF MARS"

On June 21, 199[1] Grenada, an East Carib[-]bean country, commemo[r-]ated the coming explora[-]tion of Mars by issuin[g] four miniature sheetlets ta[in]ing nine stamps and t[he corre-]sponding souvenir sheet[. Man has] long been fascinated wi[th the] fourth planet in our solar [system.] Like the Earth, it takes o[ver two] months for Mars to ma[ke a com-]plete revolution of the Su[n. The clo-]sest planet to Earth. The [corre-]sponding souvenir sheet [is mini-]sarhelyi and depict variou[s famous] astronomers, Kepler, Gali[leo...]

This is the second phila[telic inci-]dent African nation, Sierr[a Leone,] lets of nine stamps and o[ne sheet,] despite its very high face [value, the] four miniature sheetlets [total of] 117 East Caribbean dolla[rs. We feel] this issue and expect den[and to sell] promptly. We must, howev[er, limit per cus-]tomer. A small quantity of [...]

Incidentally, a second s[ouvenir ex-]ploration of Mars was rel[eased and] also immediately sold out.

Whether you are a coll[ector who] want to partake in this [issue on] Mars, we encourage you t[o...]

SPECIAL OFFERING:

Mint Unit pe[r...]
Complete first day [(of issue] covers) $75.46

Sierra Leone: Th[e issue of] four miniature shee[ts (nine to a] sheet). Mint Unit p[er...]
Complete first day [(of issue] covers) $209.95

Sierra Leone: T[he souvenir] sheet II released [...]
Mint Per 1: $8.[...]

Exploration [of Mars]

MARLEN Stam[ps]

We offer a comprehensive ne[...]
☐ Sets ☐ FDC'[s]
☐ Plate Blocks ☐ Error[s]

3561 Somerset Avenue
Castro Valley, California 94546

THE JACK BENNY TIMES

Volume XI, Number 4   INTERNATIONAL DISTRIBUTION   July-August 1991

.00 PAGES OF EXCLUSIVE PICTURE STORIES, ENLARGED TELEVISION SECTION

RADIO ALBUM MAGAZINE

WINTER
25c

DELL

MURDERERS ROW
Special photo section on crime shows

☺ ☺ ☺ PRESIDENT'S MESSAGE ☺ ☺ ☺

Jell-o again folks...excuses come first, as always. I was working for Quintiles Pacific (an experimental pharmaceutical contractor) in a temporary position until I could find a permanent job. A software company in Oakland made me an offer shortly after the Labor Day weekend, and I accepted. After a couple weeks, Quintiles decided they wanted me back (and I was somewhat disillusioned by the atmosphere of the software company anyhow). After a couple weeks of negotiations, I returned to Quintiles. I now manage their shipping and receiving department, as well as project-specific inventory. I am in love with my job and the company, and am happy as a bug in a rug. Furthermore (and having more direct impact on the IJBFC), I had sent off the previous Times to be printed quite some time ago. After a significant period, the envelope returned to me. Attached was a note informing me that the store had been destroyed in the earthquake and that my printer was out of business. Then I had to shop around for another printer, which I obviously have found. OK...enough excuses.

A note from Mary Lou Wallace brought a couple of interesting items. The first, for those of you who never heard, is that Noel Blanc (son of Mel) returned home March 15th (yes, it's a little outdated) after his helicopter crash. He said that he would be completely recovered within six months. Ergo, we all hope that all is back to normal for him now.

Secondly, some of you may recall a movie released earlier this year (or late last year) entitled Awakenings, starring Robert DeNiro and Robin Williams. It seems that the concert master on its score was...take a guess...Stewart Canin! Yes, the boy who played The Bee on Fred Allen's show and "started" the feud. Interesting, n'est-ce pas?

Now on with the show!

☺ * ☻ NEW MEMBERS ☻ * ☺

**** BOB SWELLIE **** RUSSELL MYERS **** STUART JAY WEISS **** DAVID BONDEHAGEN **** RUSS HOFFMAN **** RON LA MARRE **** ANDREW STEINBERG **** GUS STORM **** EDWARD McGUIGAN **** SHIRLEY FITZPATRICK **** TONY DI FABIO **** FRANK GREGORY **** NEIL J. BASKIN **** STUART YEDWAB **** RIC ROSS **** BOB NATHAN ****CHARLES NIREN **** ERIC S. BRAVO **** JOHN R. JUVINALL **** ALVIN W. POST **** LILLIAN SPENCER

***** EDDIE CARROLL ***** JACKIE MASON

© Copyright 1991, Laura Lee

$ $ $ 6.39 DUE $ $ $

♪ ♪ J. KENT COSCARELLY ♪ ♪ JEFF ELLIOTT ♪ ♪ WAYNE ENNIS ♪ ♪ LARRY GASSMAN ♪ ♪ DAVID HOWELL ♪ ♪ TOD IRZYK ♪ ♪ MARGIE JONES ♪ ♪ BERNIE KELKER ♪ ♪ HOWARD D. LEIB ♪ ♪ PATRICIA LINK ♪ ♪ JOEL S. ROTHMAN ♪ ♪ DON VISOVATTI ♪ ♪

♦ ♥ TAPE TRADING LIST ♣ ♠

Ellen Barker, P.O. Box 1402, Reseda, California 91335

Hal Bogart, 2029 Aldersgate Drive, Lyndhurst, Ohio 44124

Yosef Braude, 25 Longhorn Road, Providence, Rhode Island 02906

Rob Cohen, 6635 Helm Avenue, Reynoldsburg, Ohio 43068

The Everills, 1558 Knox Drive, New Haven, Indiana 46774

Andrew Haskell, 160 West 39th Avenue, Vancouver, British Columbia V5Y 2P2, Canada

David A. Howell, 1300 Kennedy Boulevard, #419, Cuyahoga Falls, Ohio 44221

Tom Kleinschmidt, 5815 Tree Moss Lane, North Ridgeville, Ohio 44039

Laura Lee, 3561 Somerset Avenue, Castro Valley, California 94546

John Malone, Rural Route #2, Wee-Ma-Tuk, Cuba, Illinois 61427

Bill Oliver, 516 Third Street NE, Massillon, Ohio 44646

Jack Palmer, 145 North 21st Street, Battle Creek, Michigan 49015

Lewis and Sedalia Pearson, 240 Ridge Drive, Marion, Iowa 52302

Michael Pointon, 11 Kings Court, Kings Road, London SW19 8QP, England

Keith Scott, 4 Bellbird Crescent, Forestville 2087, N.S.W. Australia

Joyce Shooks, P.O. Box 307, Sparta, Michigan 49345

Steve and Kim Smith, 1945 Coit NW, Grand Rapids, Michigan 49505

John Smothers, 22 Townsend Drive, Freehold, New Jersey 07728

Steve Szejna, 3334 South 15th Street, Milwaukee, Wisconsin 53215

Peter Tatchell, 40 Bambra Road, Caulfield, Victoria 3161, Australia

James E. Treacy, Jr., 900 Hargrove Road,, Apt. 234, Tuscaloosa, Alabama 35401

Want to be listed here? Lemme know!

!! !! JACK BENNY CLASSIFIEDS !! !!

§ § Ric Ross is in search of the Jack Benny Programs from December 17, 1944, and February 22, 1948, both with Frank Sinatra as a guest. Ric had a brief time with Sinatra at an airport--FAS saying that Jack was the greatest comedian he ever knew. Can't miss good taste when you see it! He has all other appearances of Sinatra on Jack's program. 325 East Hillcrest Drive, #205, Thousand Oaks, California 91360.

§ § Peter Tatchell has published the first issue of Laugh: The Comedy Magazine. It includes an article on Jack's television work, as well as write-ups on Monty Python, The Young Ones, and other comedians. It is Peter's hope to catalyst a worldwide network of comedy aficionados and traders; something to which I know many of us would be able to contribute. Check out Laugh for $5 (or £2 U.K.) to: Peter Tatchell, 40 Bambra Road, Caulfield, Victoria 3161, Australia.

§ § Member Randy Skretvedt and Jordan Young have released The Nostalgia Entertainment Sourcebook: The Complete Resource Guide to Classic Movies, Vintage Music, Old Time Radio and Theatre. The volume provides listings of over 1,100 sources of such information, from clubs to dealers to you-name-it! (Including the IJBFC, thank you!) Excellent reference. Paperback is $9.95, limited edition hardcover is $24.95. Check your local bookstore, or contact Moonstone Press, P.O. Box 142, Beverly Hills, California 90213; 1-800-677-1927.

§ § Wavelengths is the quarterly magazine of RCR (Revival of Creative Radio). It focuses on OTR shows, stations, and the actual radios themselves. $12 annually. Check it out! RCR, P.O. Box 1585, Haverhill, Massachusetts 01831-2285.

ETHER ONE

Hooray, hooray...Jack's shows are being broadcast on The Nostalgia Channel, Thursdays at 8:30 p.m. eastern time, 9:30 p.m. pacific time. (Thanks to Rex Riffle and Neal Berezin for this information.)

Frank Pozzuoli brings us the next four tidbits. An episode of Alfred Hitchcock Presents... with Dennis Day is being broadcast on Nickelodeon (Nick at Nite). Dennis has the starring role in "Cheap is Cheap." Dennis plays a man who is so cheap that he makes Jack look like the world's greatest philanthropist! Next, an episode of F Troop with Phil Harris as a guest is also on Nickelodeon. The title is "Where Were You at the Last Massacre?", and is a color episode from the second to last season.

Thirdly, the American Movie Classics (AMC) is showing a This is Your Life of Phil Harris, with Jack, Alice, the kids, and Frank Remley making appearances. Lastly, Salute to the States on AMC has an episode on Illinois. Two minutes of the program are concerned with the Jack Benny Junior High School and the Jack Benny Center for the Arts. All four of these will appear in the normal rotation, so keep your eyes open!

♪♪♪♪♪♪♪♪♪♪♪♪♪♪♪♪♪♪♪♪♪♪♪♪♪♪♪♪♪♪♪♪

Please send all questions, comments, corrections and additions to:

Laura Lee, c/o International Jack Benny Fan Club Offices, 3561 Somerset Avenue, Castro Valley, California 94546   (510) 886-3321

Please friends, send no bombs.

Through the Tears with Jack Benny—

Mr. Showbusiness Himself

Wanting a family, Jack and Mary found "their girl," when they adopted Joan.

His father saw Jack rise to fame; his mother died early—confident he'd win.

By PAULINE SWANSON

EVERYBODY loves a rumor. And a guaranteed gasp-provoker going the rounds in Hollywood at the moment is that Jack Benny—Jack Benny!—will quit radio for good to devote all his time to television.

It's a monstrous notion. Jack Benny, after all, is radio, on the top for at least eighteen of the twenty years he has been hello-ing everybody within earshot on Sunday nights—some 25,000,000 everybodies, at latest count.

Two thousand of his show business pals crowded into the New York Friars Club last November, on the occasion of his twentieth anniversary on the airways, to call him the greatest—Mr. Show Business himself. You readers of RADIO-TELEVISION MIRROR have been voicing this sentiment in your own way, year after year voting him your Favorite Radio Comedian. Why, Jack Benny even has an Act of Congress to guarantee that the 7 P.M. Sunday night hour on the air is his forevermore.

Jack Benny quit radio? It's a nasty rumor, and it shocks everybody—everybody, that is, who doesn't know Jack Benny.

His close friends aren't (Continued on page 97)

The Jack Benny Program is heard Sundays, 7 P.M. EST, on CBS; sponsored by American Tobacco Co. for Lucky Strike.

Benny spends plenty of time, talent—and money!—to entertain "those wonderful guys" in uniform.

Jack Benny—Mr. Showbusiness Himself

(Continued from page 61)

...ked. Most of them have known Jack for almost all of the 43 years he has been in show business (he's been entertaining people, you know, for four years more than the 39 he grudgingly admits to—*Who's Who* says he's 58). Friends have seen him do some crazy things. Crazy like a fox. Like quitting vaudeville, when nobody could top his earnings or his audiences, to take a flyer in the new "talkies"—then as immature and brassy a medium as a lot of people think television is today. Like quitting films in turn, when he had an iron-clad, gold-lined contract for something approximating life, to go back to the stage because he couldn't stand being cut off from direct contact with the audience, with the people out there in front.

And, of course, everybody knows by now the legend of Jack's third big walkout—when he left the stage where he commanded a weekly salary in four figures and the biggest, brightest lights on the marquee, to "go into radio."

Legend by now, too, his first broadcast back in 1932—a guest shot, for free, with Commentator Ed Sullivan. Jack walked up to the terrifying mike, his jitters concealed by dint of heroic effort, and said, "Hello, folks. This is Jack Benny talking.... There will now be a brief pause while you all say 'Who cares?'"

Twenty-five million of you cared, it turned out ... Jack Benny floated, with apparent ease, to the top of the heap again. Radio was his. His mother, had she lived to see it, would have been pleased. It was she who had dinned into her young son's head the maxim he has lived by: "It is not enough, Benny, to be good enough. It has to be as good as you can make it."

The last words she said to him, as he sat beside her deathbed, were: "You'll keep on studying."

A new medium, new techniques, a whole field of younger, fresh competitors ... of course he would have to accept the challenge, and never stop "studying" until he had licked it—not just when it was good enough, but when it was as good as he could make it.

Mrs. Kubelsky would have understood. So, for the record, does the other woman who has molded Jack Benny's life ... his wife for twenty-five years, Mary Livingston.

It was for Mary, really, that Jack in the early thirties took his first flyer in films. They lived a normal life for a while. They had a house—rented, but it stayed in one place—and they actually went to bed at night for a change, and got up in the morning! Mary was in seventh heaven, until she began to feel that Jack was not.

"You'd better go and see Mr. Mayer," she said, "and tell him 'thanks so much but I quit.'"

He did.

Mary's place in the radio show came about even more accidentally than her bit in the vaudeville act. An actress failed to show up for a broadcast, and Mary was on.

That was twenty years ago, and Mary has been a fixture on the show ever since. It could have been twenty minutes ago to Mary's stomach. She has never gotten over her stage fright, her show-time jitters—original source of her now famous giggle.

Mary would have begged off radio years ago if Jack—and their audiences—had permitted it. Now, especially, that their daughter Joan is a Stanford freshman, all pal and no problem, Mary would like to be free to enjoy their new comradeship.

Mary could see Jack go into television—and without her—without a pang. And the rumors that he might don't shock her one bit.

And, let it be said without further ado, they don't shock Jack.

They couldn't, inasmuch as he started them!

From the day he made his first TV appearance—those first shows, incidentally, may have delighted the audience, but they didn't satisfy Jack; they weren't "as good as he could make it"—Jack has hammered at everybody who would listen to him that he is fascinated with television.

"It's like going back to the theatre ... you know you make contact ... the audience is *there*," he says.

It's the old, intimate show business again, and Jack Benny feels thirty-nine again, experiencing it. But there are a few problems. A sponsor, a contract ... to say nothing of his high-powered and high-priced staff. Some of them have been with him for eighteen years. And TV doesn't pay their kind of prices.

It wouldn't surprise anybody who really knows Benny if Jack made the leap, anyway, and shelled out the money himself to keep his co-workers in the style to which they have grown accustomed.

People who buy the picture of Jack Benny—which he has created himself, of course—of the nickel-pinching skinflint, who exacts a lawn-mowing as well as a solo for Dennis Day's weekly twenty-five dollars, would simply never believe that Jack Benny is unmindful of the importance of the dollar. They would never believe he could exchange radio's lush profits for television's comparative peanuts cheerfully once he was convinced that, in the new medium, he could entertain more people more effectively. But it's true.

Some of his greatest shows he has done for considerably less than nothing—in Iran, for instance, and Egypt, and Sicily, Italy, New Guinea, Australia, the Marianas, the Marshalls, the Gilberts, the Solomons and Kwajalein, where he took his troupe during World War II. Ask any G.I. if Jack Benny was funny under front-line pressure? And even they, probably, wouldn't believe the actual fact that Jack spent $100,000 of his own money in telephone line charges in order to be able to get the show to them.

But he did; entertainment is *giving*.

Last summer, he took a troupe to Korea—when many a younger, hardier man was begging off—traveled 30,000 miles in everything from a jeep to a helicopter, slept—no more than four hours a night—in a dirt-floored tent, and gave.

He came home, a friend says, "Looking like hell ... broken physically and mentally."

But he caught up on his sleep, told the world that it was the greatest experience of his life and he would go again at the drop of a hat.

He talked of nothing but "those wonderful guys" slugging it up and down Korean mountains.

And *their* wonderful jokes.

Their jokes—just as on the air it's always Rochester, or Phil Harris, or Mary, or Dennis Day who grabs off the big laugh, while the boss brings down the house with "We ... ll."

A great entertainer, Jack Benny.

A giver.

And once he decides, if he does, that he can give you more on television than on radio—which has called him the Greatest and made him rich—you'll be seeing him regularly in your living rooms.

HOLLYWOOD IS YOURS!

All the color, extravagance and romance ... all the splendor and fascinating allure of Hollywood ... all this is yours when you open the pages of

Photoplay Annual 1952

the most exciting book of the year! Over 200 Photographs! Over 2000 Facts!

- FULL-COLOR PORTRAITS
  Exclusively photographed in gorgeous four-color you'll find pictures of Farley Granger, Doris Day, Tony Curtis, Ava Gardner, Mitzi Gaynor, Ann Blyth, Alan Ladd, Steve Cochran, Elizabeth Taylor, Debbie Reynolds, Dale Robertson, Gordon MacRae.

- THE GREATEST SCREEN MOMENTS IN 1951
- 31-PAGE ENCYCLOPEDIA OF ALL THE STARS
- STARS OF THE FUTURE
- PHOTOPLAY'S COLLECTOR'S ALBUM

Don't Miss This Gorgeous Book Of Hollywood In Review

Photoplay Annual 1952

50c at all newsstands today! Get Your Copy Early!

3561 Somerset Avenue
Castro Valley, California 94546

The Jack Benny Times

Volume XI, Number 5 — INTERNATIONAL DISTRIBUTION — September-October 1991

Jack Benny

A Special One-Man Tribute

Starring
Eddie Carroll
As Benny

☺ ☺ ☺ PRESIDENT'S MESSAGE ☺ ☺ ☺

Jell-o again folks...would like to start right off by thanking Murray Frymer of the San Jose Mercury News for his time and the lovely article that resulted. It was a fantastic two-page spread in the November 3rd (Sunday) Arts and Books section, with good pictures of both Jack and myself (separately, of course!). Definitely one of the best (if not **the** best) article ever done on the club. The response to it has been tremendous; the "New Members" column in the next issue will be quite sizable! Welcome to all new people, and I hope that the club will serve you well in your pursuit of Jack Benny shows, memorabilia, and information. Thanks a million, Murray!

Since the season to be jolly is rapidly approaching, would like to remind you all that a very economical gift to give to your favorite co-Jack Benny fan is a membership in the International Jack Benny Fan Club. Economical? Hey...membership is **free**! Also as you know, a year of The Jack Benny Times is a mere $6.39 as an added option. Send all requests and inquiries to the ever-present address at the end of this newsletter.

Now on with the show!

!! !! WE INTERRUPT THIS INTERVIEW TO BRING YOU... !! !!

Another interview! Remember a few issues back I had asked for information about an individual who was doing a one-man show of Jack Benny? Well, the man I was seeking is Eddie Carroll, who wrote me about two weeks after that publication. Chris Costello, daughter of Lou Costello and a mutual friend, had passed my name and address along to him. Eddie and I spoke via phone on October 24th, and talked about his career, the Jack Benny performances, and his future plans. Enjoy, folks!

E: Just to give you a little background on me, I have been a professional actor for about thirty years. I was born in Alberta, Canada, and Robert Goulet and I went to high school together; we were in a theatre group called the Orion Musical Theatre--we did two revues and a light opera production a year. I played a lead in Oklahoma, Finian's Rainbow, and Brigadoon--all the current musicals of the day. I then went to Toronto to go to school, Robert Goulet went to the Canadian Academy of Music, and I studied radio and television production along with theatre arts. I then worked in radio, television and theatre and won a scholarship to come to Los Angeles. I worked at NBC as a page, which was wonderful. It was very exciting to come to L.A. and suddenly be thrust right in the middle of the television industry...That was 1957. At that time they still had a draft going for the Army, and here I was a Canadian citizen down here, but since I had applied for an immigration visa to work here, I got drafted. So I went in the Army for two years, and while I was in the service I worked in Armed Forces Radio, and then was transferred to the motion picture section of the Army--I wrote and directed two training films. I also produced a big jazz show and did a lot of entertaining for the troops. Then in the last year in the service, I was a master of ceremonies for a very elite singing corps, the Sixth Army Soldiers' Chorus. We travelled all over various camps and

© Copyright 1991, Laura Lee

places to entertain, plus we did an awful lot of public relations entertaining at civic groups--we performed with the San Francisco Symphony, and a bunch of other things. So actually, even though I had to be in the Army for two years, it turned out to be great fun!

When I got out of the service, I started to begin my acting career in earnest...then started doing a lot of commercials. I did probably over 250 television commercials over the years.

L: Any particularly memorable ones?

E: It's hard to say--I've done so many of them over the years. I mean, you name the product, I've done everything. Every possible car commercial you can think of, food products, beer, soft drinks...almost everything. It was very lucrative...There was one year that I had 17 national commercials running at the same time, and those were wonderful because the residuals just pour in. Also I did a lot of guesting, the situation comedies...everything from All In the Family, Maude, a lot of segments of Alice, Fantasy Island...the list goes on and on and on. I've probably done over 50 or 60 television shows. Then for a season, I was a co-star on the Don Knotts Variety Hour...and that was great fun. Big guest stars coming on every single week, so it was really enjoyable.

L: How long did that show run?

E: It ran for a full season. That was terrific...In 1963, my wife [Carolyn] and I got married. We had met doing a show, after I got out of the service and doing a lot of television work and so forth...there was a show put together by a producer who did a lot of work in Las Vegas. He put together a very lavish revue called A la Carte from Las Vegas. We toured through the midwest. That's where I met my wife; she was a singer and a dancer. She had started professionally at the age of sixteen on the radio, and then went to Hollywood Professional School. At that time, the Hollywood Professional School was formed because there were so many kids in show business that were working on series every day and in films that still had to get their high school education. So Hollywood Professional School was formed for them to go to school half-days, and still get all the basics that they needed in order to graduate...A lot of the big stars of the day, when they were teenagers had gone to Hollywood Professional School. Then when Carolyn was seventeen and eighteen, she travelled in an extensive tour with Marlene Deitrich, and she worked in Las Vegas, Reno, Tahoe with Dan Dailey and Donald O'Connor, Milton Berle, and a lot of big stars. So when we got married, she decided to quit show business because she felt that marriage in itself a difficult situation if you are separated all the time. She said, "I don't want to be somewhere out of town, or you're out of town, or whatever. It's not a good thing."...Then about three years after we were married, our daughter came along. Then a few years later, our son. Once our kids got to the point of grade school and beginning to grow, she went back to school and got her degree and is now a psychologist. So it was a very big change from show business to this field for her, but she's excellent at it...

But anyway, as the years went by, I was doing very well in my career. Before th series M*A*S*H started, Jamie Farr, who played Klinger on M*A*S*H, he and I had known each other before either one of us was married. In fact, both of us were in the service at the same time, but we did not know each other; he was stationed in Europe, and I was stationed here. When I got out of the service, when I was working as an actor I was still going to drama school...and I met Jamie there. So Jamie Farr and I became very dear friends. When I was dating Carolyn, he was dating his [future] wife Joy at the time, and we'd double date together. I was at his wedding...and he was at mine. Then a number of years later when my children were still quite young, I was always busy in many other things, too. I was doing a lot of voice-over work, animation voices and so forth. I did the voice of Jiminy Cricket for Walt Disney, and I've been doing that for 18 years...There's an awful lot of work in that, because [Jiminy Cricket] does a lot of educational work, stuff for schools, industrial, and so forth.

L: Were you the official heir to the throne after Cliff Edwards...?

E: Yes...Cliff Edwards did it until just about 18 years ago when he passed away. Disney had a massive call to find somebody who could not only do the character, but do it exactly the same way he did it, so the character was always perennial...I auditioned for it, and months went by until they finally made the decision. Then one day my agent called up and said that there would be a lot of work in Disney, that they were going to take the I'm No Fool series and the educational things...They're going to wipe the track, and have you retrack everything. So I did all of that stuff, and everything since then...In addition to all of that...the University of Cambridge in Boston had negotiated a deal with the educational division of the Japanese government to create a training package for children of the ages three, four, and five to learn how to speak English...It's very difficult to get children to concentrate or to get their attention on something unless you make it entertaining. Of course the Disney characters are known all over the world. So when I got to Boston, we had to do a series of many cassettes plus wordbooks that went along with it. We started with words, and then went to sentences, and then paragraphs, and then songs and so forth; but the problem we ran into was that at the very beginning, these children only understand Japanese! So Jiminy Cricket had to explain to them in the beginning in Japanese what they were about to learn, and express to them what this was in Japanese. So the first cassette was enormously difficult. In addition to that, we had to bring in a Japanese linguist from Columbia college in New York to make sure I pronounced the words properly in Japanese. If I had screwed up their language, I would lose credibility if they're going to giggle over the way I talk with dialect or slang or whatever, then they certainly wouldn't pay attention to the terms of the English. So that was a very, very interesting project. Then later on we did another project for the Lowrey organ company, which was losing tremendous sales because with rock and roll, kids were into guitars and everything else, and the organ was just a stuffy old instrument. So to make it more appealing and to let kids know that it was not that difficult an instrument, the Lowrey organ company put together a package when you bought an organ, you got this huge package, and in it were many cassettes where Jiminy Cricket actually taught a child how to play the organ, right from one note all the way through chords, songs, and all the rest of it. So I spent almost a week in Milwaukee going through that, so there's been a myriad of things...going on that's always been interesting...

So at this time, Jamie and I were very dear friends and we would talk a lot about the industry...and he and I would occasionally have ideas. So one day he called me and said, "I have an idea for a show, a sitcom, but I'm having problems developing it. Can you get together with me?" So we put that thing together...took it to an entertainment attorney who had worked for ABC for a while and had gone into business for himself. He presented it to the network, and from that point on, Jamie and I started doing an awful lot of developing. Evenutally, we got a developer deal with Screen Gems, a division of Columbia, and over a period of time, we created and developed several game shows, a couple of sitcoms, a pilot for CBS called Our House, and then created and sold a show to MGM called Man to Man, which was a sports talk show with a special approach...So it's been a myriad of education that I've gotten from this industry--not only as an actor, but producing, writing, developing, all of the areas of it. Then of course, when M*A*S*H came along, Jamie got so busy with the series that he wasn't able to devote any more time to us working together. It was just as well, though, because M*A*S*H was wonderful for him...

So about eight years ago, my wife and I were watching the Johnny Carson show, and George Burns was on, and as usual, somewhere along the line they got into a conversation about Jack Benny. We both know that very special relationship that Burns and Benny had, but also Johnny Carson just *idolized* Benny. He even admitted many times that he styled his approach and his timing after Benny's comedy, and in fact, Jack Benny gave Johnny Carson his first big break...On occasion, stars who had a series-- during the hiatus period in the summer, their production company would produce summer replacement shows. He gave Johnny Carson the opportunity to do a comedy-type show.

L: Carson's Cellar?

E: Yes, I think so...Then after the [Tonight] show was over, Carolyn and I were talking about it, and I said, "Jack Benny was not just a comedian, he was not only legendary-- most people are called legends after they're gone--but he was a true legend...while he was still alive...He was also an American institution. There are people who wouldn't leave the house on Sunday night unless they had heard Jack Benny's radio show, and even on television...then he did specials, and everything else. He was on the air for 33 years...from radio to television. I don't think there's going to ever be a performer who will have that kind of run on continuous broadcasting." At that time, they hadn't done a special or a tribute to him, nothing. It's like nobody cares...I said, "Somebody should do something about this. I think I'll noodle some ideas in my mind, maybe to write a special or to write a play." I wasn't sure yet what, but something should be done for him, not thinking really in terms of *my* being involved with it, only from the standpoint of maybe writing and producing it. So interestingly enough, when the time is right, something is meant to happen, all the pieces just seem to fit. I had been working on a film as an actor, and it was a very tense day. It was taking so much time, and they were doing take after take after take, and either the camera wasn't in the right place or the lighting was off or an actor blew his line or whatever. So after about take 45, it was going smoothly, we were almost finished, and somebody dropped something backstage. I saw the director start to really get hot, and I learned a long time ago that when you see a lot of tension, it's best to try to relieve it with laughter rather than waiting for the anger to come. So just out of a reflex action, I said [a la Jack Benny] "Oh for goodness sake, Rochester! I told you when I'm working to just sit down and not touch anything! Gosh, he spoils everything for me!" and just started carrying on as Benny. Of course it got the laugh, everyone was giggling, and the director came over to me and said, "You do that very well." I said, "Well, it was kind of fun." He said, "Well, what's interesting Eddie is that you not only sound like him, but you start to *look* like him!" I said, "That's interesting, because nobody, in all my years in show business, nobody ever said I even resembled Benny." So he said..."There's a guy in New York who is going to be doing Jack Benny as a one-man show. He's a producer, and he already has the play written, a one-man show done. He's casting people for it. In the next week or two, if I were you, I'd fly out there." I said, "I don't want to go out to New York. My family's here," so I never thought about it. About a week and a half later, I get a call from a guy I'd never met before, and he introduces himself on the phone. He says, "You don't know me, but I'm a friend of a man by the name of Ted Snowden who is producing Jack Benny as a one-man theatrical show. I heard from my director friend that you do Jack Benny very well." I said, "Well, I'm not a mimic or an impressionist, I'm an actor. I just had fun with the character." He said, "Well, look. He's coming out here to L.A., so if he's coming out here, would you like to meet him and audition?" I said, "Well, if he's going to be here, sure."

So I got all dressed up, I went to a place in North Hollywood called Eddie Brandt's Saturday Matinee, and the guy's a film buff. If you want *anything* picturewise, or any film, or any lobby card or movie poster from any film from the beginning of time, he has it. So I went in to see him, and I said, "Give me everything you have on Jack Benny." So he gave me a stack about a mile high! I found wonderful pictures--an early tintype of Benny when he was a teenager, a couple of shots of the entire radio gang when his hair was prematurely almost white, just various stages--shots of him at a party, shots of him with George Burns, all kinds of stuff. What was interesting was clotheswise, he was a very snappy dresser. A very handsome dresser, and he liked wearing dark suits and so forth; but one of his favorite outfits was a blue blazer and grey slacks. And I noticed that in the later years, he started wearing horn-rimmed glasses. So I didn't want to put makeup on or anything, so using my facial muscles and kind of widening the grin and the mouth formation and the eyes, I found that if I put on horn-rimmed glasses, it emphasized the large eyes that he had. And when I combed my hair straight back and flat down, my hairline is identical to his! So I put this all together, worked on the character--the walk, the stance, the look, the attitude, and I got to the audition...He had rented an office just for a week here in town, and there were about four or five other actors that were seeing him, so I waited until they had all gone in first, waited down at the end of the hall. By the time he was ready for me, he had opened up the door to the office. The hall was very dark, and the light was spilling out from behind him into the darkened hallway. He was tring to peer through the darkness to see where the last actor was, and from way down at the end of the hall in the darkness, I said [in Jack's tone],

"Oh Ted! Hang on a second. Now listen, I heard," saying this as I'm walking towards him, "that you're going to be doing a play about my life, and I decided that I'd better come down and check it out because nobody's going to do me except me!" By this time I'd walked into the light...and he freaked, did a double-back, had his hands around his heart like Redd Foxx used to do, and said, "I'm going! I'm going!" So anyway I walked in and he sat down and turned to his associate and said, "I don't think he has to do anything, he already did it!" So we talked for a while, and I picked up the script and he said, "Read a few lines for me." I started to read a few lines, and he said, "You know what? You don't have to do any more. Listen, I have to go back to New York because Frank Gorshen is coming in from Australia, and he's going to read for me, and another guy who's done impressions for Ed Sullivan for years...

L: Will Jordan.

E: Will Jordan, who's done Benny and is going to read for me. So I've got all these people, and I've already committed to seeing them...Let me go back to New York, and I'll let you know in the next week to ten days or two weeks, or whatever. Within a week to ten days I should know. But I must tell you, I am very impressed. Up to now, either somebody sounds like Benny and does a very credible vocal impression, but they don't look anywhere near him. I'm getting people 6'2, 300 pounds...I don't care if the person doesn't really look exactly like him, but as long as an illusion can be created, that's the best I could hope for. You have *everything* right there! But I can't make a decision yet until I see everybody." ...So as I was leaving, I stopped and turned to him and as an actor, I've never said this to any producer, director, or anybody of authority, but I said, "I don't really care how many people you see or interview. It doesn't matter, because I'm going to do this show. It is not ego, it is not brag--it's just a fact. I know it in my gut, here in the pit of my stomach, I know I'm going to do this. I don't know how else to tell you that. I just know for a fact that I'm going to do this show." So he kind of gave me a strange look, and he was a nervous kind of a guy anyway, and he gave me almost a Cary Grant-like double take...Within a couple of days, Carolyn and I and our children had planned to go to Hawaii on vacation, so we went and had a wonderful time. Carolyn turned to me after a couple of days and said, "Aren't you kind of like a little nervous or antsy to know what's going on?"...I said, "No, I know I'm going to do the show."

♪ ♪

Stay tuned for more with Eddie Carroll!

♪ ♪

Please send all questions, comments, corrections and additions to:
Laura Lee, c/o International Jack Benny Fan Club Offices, 3561 Somerset Avenue, Castro Valley, California 94546　　　　　　　　　　　(510) 886-3321

Please friends, send no bombs.

 FAN CLUB

3561 Somerset Avenue
Castro Valley, California 94546

THE JACK BENNY TIMES

Volume XI, Number 6   **INTERNATIONAL DISTRIBUTION**   November-December 1991

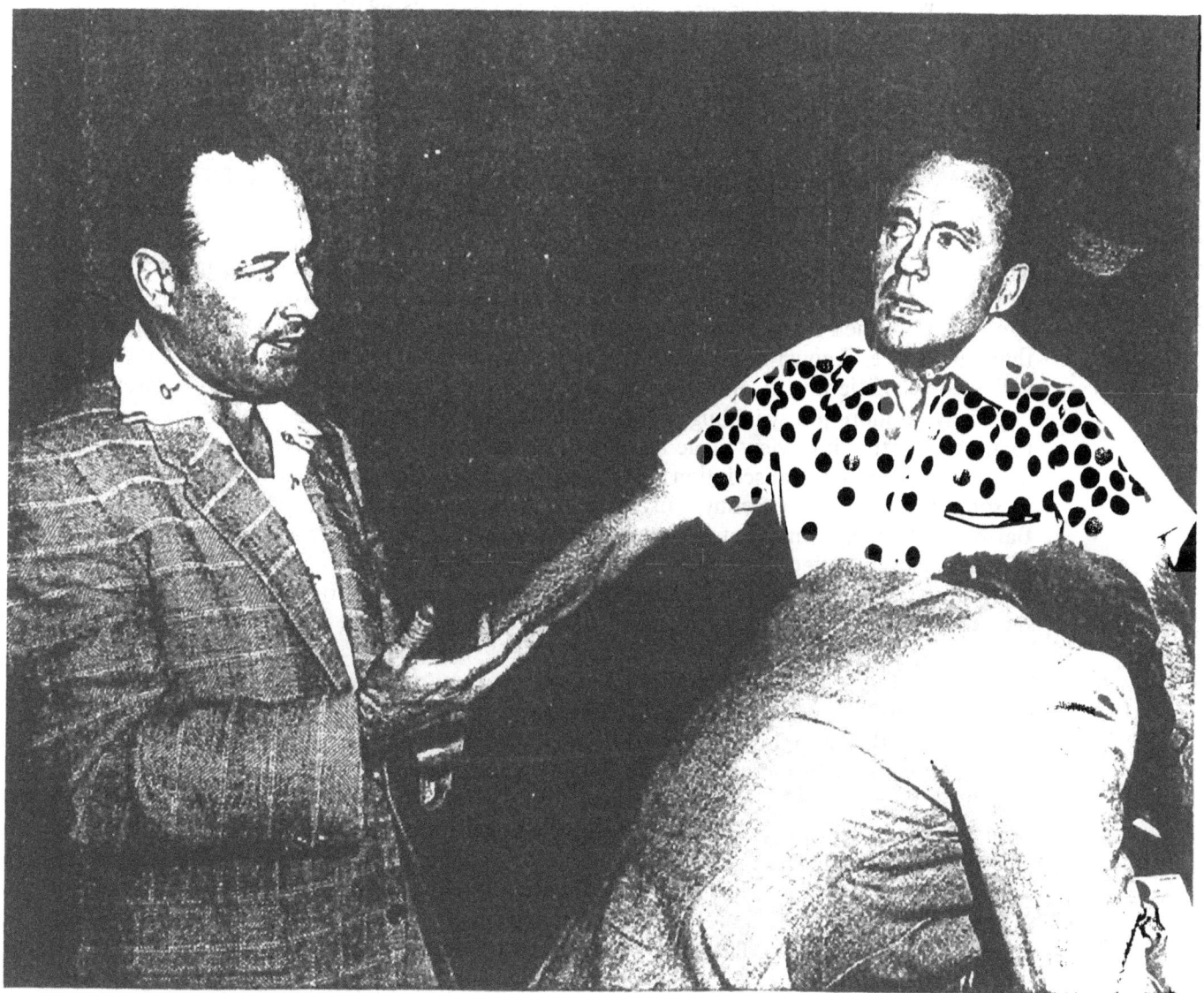

George Balzer and Jack during rehearsal for the television episode "How Jack Met Mary"

☺ ☺ ☺ PRESIDENT'S MESSAGE ☺ ☺ ☺

Jell-o again folks! Well, the family certainly has grown by leaps and bounds since we last talked! Welcome to all the new members, and greetings again to all continuing friends. First things first. On January 1st, we celebrated our:

12th ANNIVERSARY

Three cheers; a snifter of Sabra (good stuff!); and, as always, a hearty **THANK YOU** to <u>you</u>, the members, who make it all possible. Just wait until we get to our 39th anniversary!!!

Thought it would be a very opportune time to give a quick once-over on the general workings of the club. Hope this will be informative and helpful to all. <u>The Jack Benny Times</u> is published in six issues per year. I will openly admit (as evidenced by this issue) that I have been known to be tardy at times in its distribution, however I hope that things will settle sufficiently to alleviate this problem (i.e., no more final exams, theses, and hopefully no more job switching). There are two basic types of issues, between which I try to alternate: the "interview" issue and the "column" issue. The interview issue is one which is taken mostly by a transcription of an interview I have conducted with someone related in some way with Jack Benny. In the past, these have included: Dennis Day, George Balzer, and Irving Fein. Future interviews include Phil Harris, among others. This issue will most closely reflect this type, as the interview with Eddie Carroll is continued. (Just a quick update for those of you wondering: Eddie portrayed Jack Benny in a one-man stage show.)

The "column" issue contains a potpourri of information, trivia, want lists, and the like. We have a tape trading list for those individuals interested in trading or buying Jack's shows in any media; this is published annually, with additions as required. Other frequently-published columns include: "Do You Know?", "Jack Benny Classified", "Ether One", and "The Tale Piece." "Do You Know?" contains questions from members on any facet of Jack Benny or his associates; responses are published, appropriately enough, in "You *Do* Know!" "Jack Benny Classified" is fairly self-explanatory. This is an open forum for specific material requests from members. This is usually contained to either requests for Benny material, or swaps of Benny memorabilia for non-Jack-related items. "Ether One" is a listing of stations--television or radio--airing Jack's shows; such information is generally supplied by members (ergo, if you know of one, let *me* know!). Finally "The Tale Piece" is a column for favorite stories about Jack, reminiscences of family life revolving around the program, anecdotes about meeting Jack or his colleagues, or (probably most frequently) brief transcriptions of favorite scenes from television or radio shows.

Copyright 1992, Laura Lee

Back issues are available for 50 cents apiece. In total, there are 43 back issues (not including this one). I am currently stocked out on several of them, but hope to replenish the supply in the very near future.

The log, 39 Forever, has gone into its fourth printing. It is available for $15.00. Hope that I may be able to sit down with it in the coming months and do some revisions on it for a second edition. This volume has been used by many organizations as a reference for other works (e.g., Jack Benny: the Radio and Television Work by the Museum of Broadcasting).

Now the tape library. Even after going home over Christmas, I did not have quite enough room to bring all of it back with me. Moreover, my main Christmas gift was a lovely new dubbing machine for the club. Both the rest of the library and the machine are boxed and by the door, awaiting shipment to me. I have been told that this will be done in the next week (but I have been hearing that for a very long time). When I obtain these items, the library will be officially reopened. The ordering process is as follows: a listing of the library contents is available for $1.00 and a SASE. Make out your pick list, along with an appropriate number of alternate shows (just in case). Send this list to me, along with enough blank tape to hold your wants and a service charge of $1.00 per hour for the first five hours, and 50 cents for each additional hour. The maximum order is ten hours. I will dub your desired shows onto the blank tape and return them to you via USPO. **Please hold your orders until I get the rest of the tape library.** This problem has been one of the main banes of my existence since last July, so please bear with me. Hopefully it will be resolved in the near future (I hope I hope I hope).

One other thought:

LET'S GET TOGETHER!

With so many new members in the Bay (and surrounding) area, I thought it would be a lovely arrangement if those of us within a reasonable (you decide what is reasonable!) distance could get together somewhere for dinner on February 15th. Was going to suggest February 14th since it is Jack's birthday, but figured that a Saturday would enable people from a little further distance that would desire to join us to trek in to the area. Further, you would not have to come straight from the end of a tiring work week to dinner. So how about it, gang? Have not settled on a location as yet, since I do not know how many people are interested; probably somewhere in San Jose, since many of the new members reside in or near that city. Please give me a call at: 510-886-3321 to let me know if you would like to participate. If you get Jack on the answering service, you obviously got the right place! Based on the response, I will select somewhere suitable and notify you by phone. Am really looking forward to this, so let's make it BIG!

Now on with the show!

_____   If this box is checked, $6.39 is due for another year.

♪ ♪ HOW TO PUT ON A ONE-MAN JACK BENNY SHOW ♪ ♪

E: We got home, and...I went to get the mail...and there was a letter from the New York Production office that [Ted Snowden] was working out of...It looked like a form letter, you know the kind. Even though it's personally typed, it looks like something from which a lot of copies were made. It said, 'Dear Eddie: We thank you so much for auditioning for the Jack Benny show...you're very talented, we enjoyed meeting you...however at this time, we have decided to go in a different direction. We thank you anyway, and maybe in the future we will get together on another project.' Now as I'm reading this, even though what they're saying to me is 'You didn't get it,' I know that I don't believe it. Something is terribly wrong here. As I'm reading this letter outside the house, my daughter comes through the front door and says, 'Dad, Ted Snowden is on the line from New York.' So I get on the phone and Ted says, 'Hey how ya doing? How was Hawaii?' I said, 'Terrific.' He said, 'I'm glad you're home because I need to talk to you...' and I interrupted him and said, 'Well gosh, I appreciate you calling me, but what's interesting is that I just got a letter in my hand that says 'Thank you very much, but you didn't get it." Well, he started to scream a profanity, 'I don't believe it! &*&(% it! I *told* that woman in the office that *these* people [should get the letter], but tell Eddie Carroll that I have to call him. Forget it, throw it away! You weren't supposed to get that letter!' I said, 'I knew it.'

L: Talk about timing!

E: So he said, 'Look, I'm coming out in another week. It's down to one person and you. Because it's been a while since I've seen you, I'm not sure if you were really that good, or if the impression you gave was so startling. I've got to be sure before I make my mind up... So I'm coming out to L.A., and I'm going to give a guy another reading here in town...and we'll sit down and go through it, and then I'll know for sure one way or the other.' Well, I already knew that it was etched in rock, but he just didn't want to make a commitment yet. So he and I had a good laugh over the rejection letter that shouldn't have happened. So he came out to L.A., we had a meeting, started talking, and he said, 'Why don't you get up and read some of this for me?' I read about three pages, and he said, 'Oh h--l, let's just roll up our sleeves and go to work!' So from that point on, we worked very, very hard...This had to be 1983. We spent months rehearsing it, working on timing and nuances and so forth. In the two weeks of previews we had before we had our official opening to test the material and see if it was working, I found that there were vast passages that were very historical and very entertaining from the standpoint of information about Jack's life, growing up, going through stages and so forth, but there were moments throughout where it needed bigger laughs in there. If someone recreates Harry Truman, for example, or does some historical character with some serious bent, he can take time and get very dramatic. But someone coming from a comedy background, even if they tell you about something that's sad, to get off it you go to a joke. It just needed 'punching.' The writer kept insisting that I punch the lines that are there harder, and I tried to explain to him after doing comedy for so many years, that if there's joke that gets a chuckle, no matter what you do with it, that's all it's ever going to get is a chuckle because of the construction of the joke. You can't time it or stomp on it or force it or push it...if it's going to get a three on a laugh meter, that's all it's ever going to get. He kept insisting only because he was resisting doing any more writing; he had literally written himself out. He was giving me notes, the director was giving me notes, and I said, 'Look, guys. Don't give me notes any more. I will try everything you ask me to do, but if it doesn't work then you have to start [working on it].' After four nights of this, I finally said, 'I've done everything you want me to. If you listen to the audience, the audience will tell you where it needs work."...Three days [the writer] was gone, and I thought, 'He's going to come back with blockbuster stuff!' He came back...and I said, 'Well?' He said, 'I'm working on a line.'

L: *A* line?

E: *A* line. Not that he even had a line...I said, 'If it's going to take three days to come up with one line, we're in very deep trouble.' In the interim during the preview days, almost every writer that worked for Benny came to see the show. Al Gordon, Sam [Perrin], George [Balzer], Milt Josefsberg, and so forth. They came backstage and were very, very encouraging...So I finally said to the producer, 'Look, we need help here. Even the best playwrights in the world--even Neil Simon--after a zillion smash hits on Broadway and film, still takes it out of town and goes through massive rewrites again because comedy needs an audience to tell you where the comedy plays...Who better to write for Benny than the guys who **wrote** for Benny?' So...the way the writers worked, Sam and George were a team, Milt Josefsberg and John Tackaberry were a team; and if they worked on a show, one team would take the first half, and the other would take the second half. Then of the two, they had it broken down that Sam would work on the construction of the joke, and George was the joke master--he was the one-liner, the puncher. So I said, 'That's the guy we need.' We talked to George and said, 'How would you like to write for Benny again?' He said, 'I'd love it! Who gets a second chance in life? That's wonderful.'...We would get together early in the morning in an office in Santa Monica, and we would work for three, four, five hours, and find sections of the show that needed work, started adding material, and that night I would plug it in. It was a bear, because we were taking stuff out of the second act and putting it in the first act, pulling stuff out of there and putting it in the second act. Now when you've got almost an hour and forty-five minutes worth of material in your head and you don't have another actor on stage cuing you, and you're so far forward that even if someone has a book backstage you can't hear them to throw you a line if you get lost, you've got all this information in your head and you've rehearsed it for months. Now when you're out there in front of the audience and you're approaching a section, you're reminding yourself 'Don't do that now--that comes later in the second act,' and you have to put the new piece in. It's like a little guy running around inside your head like a traffic cop! I had seasoned, well-known performers and actors who came backstage and said, 'How do you...go out there every night by yourself and face down an audience with no one else on stage in front of you? I wouldn't have that courage in a million years!' But I loved it. I felt so privileged to be able to be the one to carry on the tradition and bring this man's special wonderment and his special talent back again. So to me it was a joy...

The playwright had a great deal of trouble adding new material, but with George's stuff in it, it did help a lot...So the show ran and did very well, but then when we got down to a point where Dick Clark wanted to produce it as a special, we talked about bringing in writers so that we could now adapt it to an hour or hour and a half...the playwright went nuts. He became totally self-sabotaging...it was his baby and he didn't want anybody else touching it. Even though the jokes that were added and the way the show was rearranged, it's like arranging a song with a full symphony orchestra, having the tympani come in just at the right time, and then you bring in the strings, and then the French horns, and then suddenly the music begins to stir and move you emotionally, it starts to pay off. Well, [the playwright] was furious...'Your material is in there,' I said. 'We've added elements. We've rearranged things.'...He said, 'My deal is that if it goes to television, no other writers are involved.' I said, 'You can't do that! You'll get single play credit--Teleplay by:, and then there will be an additional card after that with 'Additional material by:." He just wouldn't have it. Then at the end of the year when the play had to be reoptioned again, the playwright brought in his attorneys, and they got into such a negotiation...that the producer almost had an epileptic fit over it. So as a result of it, I put together my own version of Benny, without plagiarizing material. Then for the next number of years, I performed all over the country with a show called Legends in Concert, played Las Vegas, the Nugget in Reno, Caesar's Palace in Atlantic City and Miami and Boston and Toronto, and then did a very special version of Legends on Broadway with people who did Al Jolson and Judy Garland. Then intermittently between that, I did another version of Benny's presentation for various companies for their conventions all over the country. I then did a series of commercials--radio spots--for Zenith, and those were great fun because we got Frank Nelson [Yeeeeeessssss?]. We did the commercials, and with sound effects we made them sound just like they were lifted out of the Benny radio show. You hear the door open and close, you hear people mumbling about, and so forth, and Benny's, 'Excuse me...Oh mister, mister!' 'Yeeeesss?' 'I'm looking for a television set, I'm thinking of buying a new one.' 'Oh, is the one you bought during the Civil War broken?' 'Now cut that out!' We had a laugh track and all the rest of it--it was great, great fun. Then I did a series of television and radio commercials for the cable company in Miami, to promote their new fall season on television. Then I did another commercial for the Warner cable company in Chicago...The commercial I did there used two Bennys. The whole thing was that they hired three actors, and they wanted to do one of those things where a guy is talking to himself. They were so silly, because it didn't occur to them to frame your shot, you divide it in three, shoot it once with a guy on one side of the frame, then you do a center piece, and so forth. Then in your editing, you put it all together. What they did was got three actors, and when they put them all together, they had three people who may, by themselves, give an illusion of Benny, but all together looked like three totally different characters! It was bizarre! One guy was 6'1, and the other guy was smaller than me! To make us all the same size, they put huge blocks of wood under our feet, and we had to walk in and make an entrance! The whole commercial was like a Saturday Night Live sketch. A *bad* Saturday Night Live sketch! I didn't want to say anything, but I finally said, 'Guys, don't you just want to use one actor, and frame your shot?' They looked at each other like, 'Why didn't we think of that before?' They had flown me in from L.A., another guy from New York, and they went through so much.

So in the interim, after this period of time that I had done the show on Broadway, a producer by the name of Donald Saxon and his partner Bob Bloom...started saying to me, 'You know, you really should do your own show.' I said, 'Well, I had done it before.' They said, 'Well, you should do it again. Only on rare occasions is there an actor that is perfect for the role. Anthony Quinn was Zorba. There was no question about it, even though there never was a real Zorba. The public, especially the younger people today, really need to know what Jack Benny was all about. You should do it again.' So I said, 'Well, if you're interested, let's try to work something out.' As time went by, we kept in touch with each other. They were trying to get hold of a writer entrepreneur in New York to help with the material, and he was in Israel or London or someplace, and as usual, time went by and time went by. I met a producer out here by the name of Chuck Carson, and he was after me to do it as well. So he and I put together a portfolio, a prospectus for investors, and then Don Saxon came out from New York because they were doing Milton Berle's life story as a musical comedy. While they were out organizing everything with Milton Berle, we had a meeting with them...so together the two of them are going to put this whole thing together. We now have a writer in place who is excellent. He is in his late 50's-early 60's and knows Benny from radio and television...is excited and enthusiastic about it and has wonderful ideas. Now we're looking forward to getting this on, and we hope that if all the pieces come together and the financing starting to come in so we can get the writer started, our hope is some time late spring-early summer we can open with the show in Waukegan at the Jack Benny Center, with the tremendous cooperation of the people who are in charge of the Jack Benny Foundation for the Creative Arts. Then our plan from there is that if we have just a limited run there, maybe three weeks, and then either--if time warrants--to go to Milwaukee or, depending on how well the show is received, to move it into Chicago...Then from there our plan is to take it to London, and then bring it into New York. Then if it does well there, it can go on an extended city tour across the country. Also by that time,... we've already had meetings about presenting it to HBO, Showtime, or one of the large cable companies as a television special.

Please send all comments, questions, additions, and corrections to:

Laura Lee
c/o International Jack Benny Fan Club Offices
3561 Somerset Avenue
Castro Valley, California 94546   (510) 886-3321

Please friends, send no bombs.

FAN CLUB

3561 Somerset Avenue
Castro Valley, California 94546

THE JACK BENNY TIMES

Volume XII, Number 1 — INTERNATIONAL DISTRIBUTION — January-February 1992

☺ ☺ ☺ PRESIDENT'S MESSAGE ☺ ☺ ☺

Jell-o again, folks! Guess what? I have moved again. The new address is:

322 Palmetto Avenue, #154
Pacifica, California 94044
(415) 355-3723

Am right by the Pacific Ocean--have the window open now to get the sea breezes. Am very happy, very busy, and enjoying life to the fullest. Please send all correspondence, etc. to the above address. Enough about me.

As you will notice, we have an incredible list of new members. Warmest of welcomes to all of you, and hope that you will find your membership in the International Jack Benny Fan Club to be most profitable and amusing. If there is anything that you would like to see in the newsletter or services that you would like to recommend for the club to provide, please let me know. In the move and everything, I must ask if all of you received your membership certificates. If you ordered <u>39 Forever</u>, a tape library listing, or anything other than a basic membership, did I send it? I am quite certain that I caught everyone, but I just want to double-check.

Remember about our tape trading list, members new and old; this list is for anyone interested in buying or trading tapes of Jack's shows, appearances, or anything else audio or video related to Jack. If you are not on it now and would like to be, please drop me a note.

A quick anecdote before I close this section. I have a copy of Jack's Texaco "I'll try a gallon" ad hanging in my office at work. Upon seeing it, a young co-worker asked who it was. I replied that it was Jack Benny. "No, it's not," she said confidently. "Yes it is," I said. "No, it's not," she repeated. "O.K., why is it not Jack?" I questioned. "Because he's not black!" she said proudly. Apparently she had him confused with Ben E. King, because she made a comment about Jack's jazz singing (a talent of which I...ahem...was unaware). Perhaps she was thinking of Al Jolson? ☺

Now on with the show!

© Copyright 1992, Laura Lee

♪ ♫ TAPE LIBRARY ♫ ♪

Can you believe it...

THE TAPE LIBRARY IS NOW OPEN.

I finally got all the tapes out here, and a working tape dubbing machine set up to fill your orders. For the new folks out there, here is how it works. Make your selections from the listing of the tape library (available for $1.00 and a SASE if you do not already have one). Please be certain to select some alternates, in addition to your "priority" list. Send this list, accompanied by an appropriate number of CASSETTE tapes and an appropriate service charge amount (see below) to the ever-present address at the end of this newsletter. I then dub off your requests and return the tapes to you. The service charge is $1.00 per hour for the first five hours, and 50 cents for each hour thereafter. The maximum order is ten hours. Questions? Drop me a note. Happy ordering!

☺ ☺ ☺ NEW MEMBERS ☺ ☺ ☺

****BOB SWELLIE ****RUSSELL MYERS ****STUART JAY WEISS
****DAVID BONDEHAGEN ****RUSS HOFFMAN ****RON LA MARRE
****ANDREW STEINBERG ****GUS STORM ****EDWARD McGUIGAN
****SHIRLEY FITZPATRICK ****TONY DI FABIO ****FRANK GREGORY
****NEIL J. BASKIN ****STUART YEDWAB ****RIC ROSS ****BOB NATHAN
****CHARLES NIREN ****ERIC S. BRAVO ****JOHN R. JUVINALL
****ALVIN W. POST ****LILLIAN SPENCER ****NEAL BEREZIN
****ELIZABETH ANDERSON ****LARRY BURCH ****HOWARD R. CLEMENTS
****GERALD OSTER ****VIRGINIA B. WOODDELL ****C. A. CARAMELLA
****GORDON HUTTON ****BEVERLY HUTTON ****DALE W. SPROCK
****LARRY ELLIOTT ****DAVID B. WARD ****MARY LOU FAIRBANKS
****DEBORAH OVENS ****TOM OVENS ****JULIA ROGERS ****PAUL ROGERS
****EMMA R. ELJAS ****YVES ELJAS ****ROSE ELJAS ****MIRIAM ELJAS
****ROBERT O. WHITESELL ****JOE M. VALENTINE ****JOAN STARK
****ROBERT J. CARUSO ****CHARLES LILYGREN ****ALLAN MARX
****BILL TWILLIE ****KAREN ACKERMAN ****GAIL MOORE
****CHARLES BURTON ****A. J. ROBERTS ****MARY ANN ROBERTS
****BONNIE BAUSKE ****RICHARD RUBENSTEIN ****BARBARA THUNELL
****TOM WINSTON ****ERIC SUNDIUS ****JOAN NASS ****W. L. LOWREY
****HELEN SONGER ****DENNIS BURK ****BILL HOUSOS ****DAVID ADLER
****KENNETH KLEIN ****JOSEPH STEIDL ****GARY TALLMAN ****AL SHACK
****RICHARD WOLFSIE ****DONALD CRANE ****GERALD RUARK

_____ If this box is checked, $6.39 is due for another year.

****ELTON T. RIDLEY ****SAM RABER ****ELIZABETH TEICHER ****LORETTA ZERBY ****SCOTT SMITH ****GERTRUDE BARDOLPH ****MRS. MARTIN KAPLAN ****RICHARD GOLDFARB ****GORDON HUTTON ****LOUIS PHILLIPS ****JOSEPH PHILLIPS ****CHARLES MOORE ****AL CATE ****KAREN SIMONIAN ****JIM PROBASCO ****DENNIS BENEDICT ****JIMMIE HICKS ****RICHARD LARSON ****PATRICK CAREY ****KIM CUNNINGHAM ****MEL HOLT ****TROY A. KAIB ****WAYNE SCHULMAN ****LISA MELCOMBE ****EMERSON WILLIAMS, JR. ****CHRIS REALE ****JAMES R. STEWART ****THEODORE RIDLEY ****RICHARD NATHAN ****DAVID Z. JOSEPH ****TERRY HEATH ****MORRIE K. BLUMBERG ****MARIA ROSA PIERAMICO ****RONALD EBERHARD ****DIANE BERKOWITZ ****MYRNA CHARET ****LEV MAILER ****CINDY CHESSER ****A. C. ETTINGER ****DAVID ETTINGER ****RAY DRUIAN ****CHRIS TURNER ****ROBERT NYSTROM ****ALICE RAMSEY ****MARTIN BRAUN ****PALMA CABILES ****TOMMY HOUSOS ****JIM SEITZINGER ****DAN SCHRYVER ****M. T. FISHER ****STEPHEN H. WOODS ****MICHAEL AVEDISSIAN

Honorary Members: *****EDDIE CARROLL *****JACKIE MASON

WOW!

THE FIRST-EVER IJBFC GET-TOGETHER

The world premiere gathering of International Jack Benny Fan Club members was held on February 15th, 1992, at the White Lotus restaurant in San Jose. Attending were a total of twelve people (pretty good for the first time ever!) ranging in age from teens to seventies. As I looked around the table, I noticed that every basic "type" of Jack Benny fan was there: those that had known him firsthand through radio, the slightly younger crowd that knew him through television, those that had acquired the taste through a hobby or friends, and those introduced to him by their parents. Members were greeted with a large poster made by Rob Crawford wishing Jack a happy birthday, and a fantastic portrait of Jack playing the violin. A very hearty thanks to Emma Eljas, who was very instrumental in assisting with making plans and contacting members. She even wrote the following menu:

Jack: Hi everybody. This is Jack Benny speaking, and I'm so glad you got together for my birthday. But it was really yesterday the 14th, ya know.

Mary: Jaack, don't be rude. You know it's been raining cats and dogs so that's not very nice of you.

Jack: You're right, Mary. I'm sorry folks.

Don: You know Jack, Tu who is the chef here gave us a few possible dinners that might work well together.

Jack: Well, that's very nice of her. Did she throw in dessert for free?

Don: No, Jack.

Jack: Hmmmm. How about my birthday cake?

Don: They didn't have 39 candles, and it would pose a fire hazard.

(Menus then listed)

Mary: I hope they don't give us a collective bill--we'll be here all night figuring it out.

Jack: You mean the sponsor didn't pick up the tab?

Don: Nope.

Jack: Well folks, have a good time ANYWAY.

It was definitely a very lovely evening of talk about Jack Benny (needless to say), comedy, and other various topics of collective interest. I am so pleased to have finally met some people who have been members of the club for years, and those who have been members for not so many years! Everyone agreed that we must do this again in the near future, at the very least on an annual basis, and I heartily concur. Toward the end of the dinner, the chef came to the table, leaned over to Emma and whispered, "Which one of you is Jack Benny?"

♪ ♫ JACK BENNY CLASSIFIED ♫ ♪

§ Alan Grossman asked me if there was any chance of publishing a photo of Mary's sister, Babe Blum. Good question...I would if I knew where to find one. Does anyone possess a photo of her, or has seen one? If so, please let me know at the address at the end of this letter.

§ Richard Nathan is looking for the Christmas program where Jack buys Don shoelaces. I know that there are several people out there who have been looking for this show; has anyone found it? 347 1/2 North Ogden Drive, Los Angeles, California 90036.

§ Wayne Schulman is looking for the Jack Benny television shows on which Ann Margret appeared (4-2-61, 4-30-63), a copy of <u>A Love Letter to Jack Benny</u> (which

I wouldn't mind having myself), and any photos of Jack with Ann Margret. 18619 Collins Street, #F15, Tarzana, California 91356.

§   Michael Avedissian is interested in purchasing 8x10 glossies of Jack Benny. 31 Morris Drive, New Hyde Park, New York 11040.

☼ ☼ THE TALE PIECE ☼ ☼

This story comes to us from Sam Raber:

"In 1944 and 1945 I became actively involved in two big dinner meetings--one at the Beverly Hills Hotel and one at the Beverly Hilton Hotel...We obtained a handful of sponsors through my friendship with Oscar Hammerstein and then mailed to a large list of notables asking them to become sponsors for the 1945 dinner, at which Norman Cousins, then editor of the Saturday Review and Carlos Romulo, then Philippine Ambassador to the U.N. were my speakers. I was volunteer Executive Director of the dinner. A response came back accepting to be listed as a sponsor from Jack Benny, including an unsolicited, <u>unsigned</u> check for $50.00.

The phone number of his manager was on the check, so I called Jack's manager. He laughed and gave me Mr. Benny's unlisted phone number. I phoned Mr. Benny and he invited me to come over to his Beverly Hills home. When I arrived, a maid opened the door and directed me upstairs. Mr. Benny had just come out of the shower, was dressed in a rich-looking purple robe with a towel around his neck. He greeted me cordially and we sat in his bedroom and had a nice chat. I showed him the unsigned check, he belly-laughed just as one would hear him on stage, and signed the check."

If you have an anecdote like this one, a favorite story about Jack (not necessarily involving yourself), or a favorite scene from one of his shows, we would love to have it in "The Tale Piece."

OTHER CLUBS, ORGANIZATIONS, AND PUBLICATIONS

I have received quite a bit of mail from other groups regarding their Jack Benny items and related services. Worth a look for finding material!

Radio Spirits, Inc. Their catalog states that their radio shows are digitally remastered and enhanced; an idea which I have been advocating for a long time. Have not heard any of their recordings yet, but they do have a large supply of Benny material. P.O. Box 2141, Schiller Park, Illinois 60176.

Modern Radio Drama: Collecting, Creating, Restoring, Enjoying A magazine worth a look for all general radio fans. Like their notation that "The pictures are better on radio." c/o J. Steven Coleman, P.O. Box 12631, Berkeley, California 94701.

AntiqueNet This is a 24-hour computer bulletin board concerned with antique dealers, restoration services, periodicals, flea markets, and clubs (like ours) specializing in particular fields. Call 1-414-375-0756, and set your modem to full duplex, 8 bits, no parity, 1 stop bit, 2400 bps. 6920 Kingswood, Cedarburg, Wisconsin 53012.

My Book Heaven Looking for an out-of-print book (perhaps a Benny biography) or a rare edition? Try here. Rick Boyles/Laurie Aldrich, P.O. Box 2715, Alameda, California 94501, (510) 521-1683.

♪♪♪♪♪♪♪♪♪♪♪♪♪♪♪♪♪♪♪♪♪♪♪♪♪♪♪♪♪♪♪♪

Please send all questions, comments, additions and corrections to:

Laura Lee, c/o International Jack Benny Fan Club Offices
322 Palmetto Avenue, #154, Pacifica, California 94044   (415) 355-3723

Please friends, send no bombs.

NEWSWEEK, MARCH 31, 1947

The Lifetime Guarantee: Out of the fact that the Bennys live next door to the Ronald Colmans in fashionable Beverly Hills, Calif., Benny got one of his funniest situations: the socially correct and veddy British Colmans entertaining the social climbing, inelegant Benny. Last year the comedian brought the names of three small Southern California towns into the show. Now the mere mention of Anaheim, Azusa, and Cucamonga brings a laugh. Jack started a national nuisance when he got involved with a character named Kitzel who sold him a hot dog with "peekel een the meedle and the mustard on top."

This year's major contribution to the nation's giggles is Benny's quartet. He hired them first for laughs and secondly to help hurdle that necessary evil, the middle commercial. The quartet, professionally known as the Sportsmen but around the Benny show as "Mmmmmm," take the middle plug for Lucky Strike cigarettes and sing or chant it in ridiculous and clever verse. The commercial is written by Benny himself, with the help of Mahlon Merrick, the show's musical director.

For comedy reasons, Benny accepts the quartet only as a major nuisance and recently "fired" them to get a laugh-provoking situation. Last week the situation had been built up to a temporary substitute—and extraordinary—quartet consisting of Dennis Day, Dick Haymes, Andy Russell, and Bing Crosby. In the million-dollar clambake that followed baritone Bing stumbled on a high note and nearly broke up the show by ad-libbing loudly "Who the hell picked this key, Dennis Day?"

Only a Crosby could get away with profanity on a Benny show. Throughout his radio career, Benny has avoided any off-color, muddy humor. His care to keep his show clean is even greater than his reliability in coming up with comedy 35 Sundays a year.

For as long as Benny cares to stay in radio, listeners can be sure they may tune him in on the 7 p.m., EST spot Sundays. In 1941, when it looked as if Benny might move to another network, NBC made the unprecedented move of giving him a lifetime option on what is one of radio's most valuable half hours. So long as he has a sponsor satisfactory to NBC, Benny can use that half-hour as he sees fit. Two weeks ago he was assured of NBC's satisfaction for three more years when the American Tobacco Co., Benny's fifth and current sponsor, renewed his contract through 1950. The terms: $25,-000 a week for the packaged program which Benny owns, plus $250,000 a year to advertise and publicize the show. Benny will earn it.

International Jack Benny
Fan Club
322 Palmetto Ave. #154
Pacifica, CA 94044

The Jack Benny Times

Volume XII, Number 2 — INTERNATIONAL DISTRIBUTION — March-April 1992

☺ ☺ ☺ PRESIDENT'S MESSAGE ☺ ☺ ☺

Jell-o again, folks! I would like to officially announce the formation of our

UNITED KINGDOM BRANCH!

Paul Pinch of Dyfed, U.K. had suggested this idea to me some time back, and had some excellent ideas. On January 1st of this year, the U.K. branch was born. Paul is setting up both an audio (and potentially video) library, and has published the first U.K.-specific newsletter which accompanies copies of the <u>Jack Benny Times</u> that is supplied to all members. The membership list is already starting to blossom:

William Hardwick
Michael Mills
Mike Waring
John Poole
Dan Peat
Paul Ruddock
John McGregor
Alison Grimmer
J. D. Bain

in addition to Paul himself. My heartiest congratulations and sincerest thanks to all of Paul's help and energy, and best wishes for continued success! For further information or the terminally curious, Paul's address is: 75 Priory Avenue, Haverfordwest, Dyfed SA61 1SG, United Kingdom.

Many of you already know about the Jack Benny biographical special: **Jack Benny: Comedy In Bloom**. Am in contact with the producer, and will bring you all the behind-the-scenes information that I possibly can. Look for it on Home Box Office on a television set near you. More details to follow.

Since Don always gave you a Jell-o recipe near the end of the Jell-o shows, it is only fair that we supply you with one here. However, this is one recipe that Don would NEVER have given you! Be forewarned that this has a very powerful, yet seemingly unassuming result; consume it sparingly!

© Copyright 1992, Laura Lee

Poison Jell-o

2 cups water
1 large box or 1 small boxes Jell-o
2 packets Knox unflavored gelatin
1 cup corresponding schnapps
1 cup corresponding liquor

Boil 2 cups water in saucepan. Add Jell-o and Knox; return to boil, stirring constantly with wire whisk. Immediately reduce heat to medium, and cook until Knox is fully dissolved, stirring frequently with whisk. Remove from heat and add schnapps and liquor; pour into pan. Chill until set. Cut into blocks.

Recommended combinations: Peach Jell-o, peach schnapps, vodka
Mixed fruit Jell-o, tropical schnapps, rum
Tropical punch Jell-o, tropical schnapps, rum
Small lemon and small lime Jell-o, margarita schnapps, tequila (sprinkle with salt)

I have passed this recipe on to several friends, all of whom had excellent results. If you have any more combinations, please let me know. Enjoy!

Now on with the show!

? ! ? DID YOU KNOW ? ! ?

Jimmie Hicks set me straight on a topic that apparently has caused some confusion in the past. The Jack Benny show with guest star Claudette Colbert, listed in 39 Forever as being aired on April 5, 1951, actually was aired on April 1, 1951. He enclosed two clippings from The New York Times which confirm this date, and a New York air time of 7:30 P.M.

Tom Winston supplied this tidbit:

"Did you ever see the show with Clint Walker as the guest (E.N.: 10/15/63)? That's the one where Jack wants to audition for the part of Clint's brother in a new movie. Somebody else has the first audition, so Benny waits. It is one heck of a fight scene. Benny does nothing but react. Now...did you know that was a remake? The first show was with Gary Cooper (E.N.: 9/21/58)...When Cooper died, the show could not be rerun, so it was redone."

Thanks Jimmie and Tom--appreciate the information!

_____ If this box is checked, $6.39 is due for another year.

? ! ? DO YOU KNOW ? ! ?

There has been quite a push lately to find copies of the <u>Shower of Stars</u> appearances of Jack. Is it possible that anyone has access to these, or that they might have any leads on them? It certainly would be a blessing for early Jack Benny video memorabilia to be able to unearth any existing copies of these. If you have any information whatsoever on these items, please contact me (at the address at the end of this newsletter, of course); the Museum of Television and Radio, 1 East 53rd Street, New York, New York 10022; and/or Harry D. Arends, c/o 12th Street Productions, 338 North Palm Drive, Beverly Hills, California 90210.

Chuck Harris would like to know if there were ever any games or toys that were produced in conjunction with <u>The Jack Benny Program</u>. The first thing that came to mind was not actually a toy, but merely a radio premium: <u>Jack and Mary's Jell-o Recipe Book</u>. For those of you who have not had the pleasure of seeing it, it is a 24-page booklet containing various Jell-o recipes, suggestions, and tips along with color cartoons of Jack and Mary throughout. Often Jack is playing straight to bad puns from Mary: e.g., Jack: "Honest, Mary, I can't imagine why Jell-o is like a man with his chair pulled out from under him." Mary: "Because it <u>sets faster</u>!" (There will be a slight pause while everyone says, "Oy vey!") Oh yes...the copyright is 1937.

Still, that is not a toy per se. However, about ten years back, there was a Dennis Day bear produced. It was dressed in an Irish outfit, and had a recording inside of Dennis singing and telling a little story about the bear. Dennis himself was involved in the production of these (beyond simply lending his name and making the recording), but then the production rights were sold to Korea. According to Dennis, the quality deteriorated at this point, and he discontinued his association with the project.

That is about as close as I could come to a toy with the show. Do any of you know anything which I have overlooked? If so, please contact me and/or Chuck Harris, c/o Visual Arts Group, 323 South Orange Drive, Los Angeles, California 90036.

♪ ♪ THE TALE PIECE ♪ ♪

Richard Nathan sends this story:

"I saw Jack Benny once in person. That was when Groucho Marx did his show at the Los Angeles Music Center. This was the same show Groucho did at Carnegie Hall (E.N.: entitled <u>An Evening with Groucho</u>), except that he had a stroke in between the time he did the New York show and the time he did the Los Angeles show, and he wasn't in very good shape for the show I saw. Anyway, I went with a friend of mine, and after the show we rushed to the stage door to see if we could get another look at Groucho. My friend was in such a hurry, he nearly ran into Jack Benny and George Burns. When we got to the door, someone from the theatre announced that Groucho had left immediately after the show. My friend was very disappointed, and I said to him, 'Well, at least we got to see Benny and Burns.' His eyes got huge and he shouted 'WHERE????' I told him he'd almost run into them. So we stood around for a few moments listening to Benny and Burns. They were also disappointed that Groucho had left so early, and they didn't have the consolation of almost running into themselves."

☼ ☼ ETHER ONE ☼ ☼

The Jack Benny Program is being broadcast on:

WAMU-FM, 88.5 FM, Washington, D.C. Sunday nights at 7:00 P.M. (of course). It is followed by The Phil Harris-Alice Faye Show at 7:30 P.M.

KCMO, Kansas City, Missouri. A full hour of shows on Sunday mornings at 8:00 A.M.

KNX, 1070 AM, Los Angeles, California. Saturday nights at 9:00 P.M. (But you knew that.)

Thanks to Roger White and Bernard Beckert for this information.

OTHER ORGANIZATIONS AND PUBLICATIONS

Laval Archives, 1009 Autumn Woods Lane, #106, Virginia Beach, Virginia 23454. Send $2.00 for their catalog of old radio, including Jack Benny shows.

Illinois Old Radio Shows Society, Nancy Warner, 10 South 540 County Line Road, Hinsdale, Illinois 60521. Has a new service called "The Source," a computerized database of information on OTR clubs, organizations, and programs.

Wavelengths, RCR, P.O. Box 1585, Haverhill, Massachusetts 01831. Their annual expanded edition of their publication includes an article on the Maxwell.

Collector's Information Clearinghouse, P.O. Box 2049, Frederick, Maryland 21702-1049. CIC is now offering their Antiques and Collectibles Resource Directory for dealers, clubs, and all other facets of antiques. 8 1/2 x 11, 352 pages. Softcover, $19.95; hardcover, $27.95. Add $4.00 for postage and handling, MD residents add 5% sales tax.

Kurt R. Krueger Autographs, 160 North Washington Street, P.O. Box 275, Iola, Wisconsin 54945-0275. Has ongoing mail and phone auctions, as well as a fixed price list.

♪♪♪♪♪♪♪♪♪♪♪♪♪♪♪♪♪♪♪♪♪♪♪♪♪♪♪♪♪♪♪♪♪♪
Please send all questions, comments, additions or corrections to:

Laura Lee, c/o International Jack Benny Fan Club Offices
322 Palmetto Avenue, #154, Pacifica, California 94044   (415) 355-3723

Please friends, send no bombs.

"ROCHESTER": Eddie Anderson

The actor who became a household name through his portrayal of Jack Benny's valet was born on September 18, 1905, in Oakland, California. His parents, Big Ed and Ella Mae, worked as aerialists in circuses and on the vaudeville circuits. When Eddie was twelve years old his voice left him completely after a day of hawking newspapers on a San Francisco street corner. When it returned it had the scratchy quality that years later would bring him success on radio.

In the twenties, Eddie worked in vaudeville as one of the "Three Black Aces," along with his brother Cornelius, and toured with the California Collegians, a band that included an unknown Fred MacMurray. Eddie also worked at the Cotton Club for two and a half years, six nights a week.

After working around Los Angeles in nightclubs, he debuted in movies in *What Price Hollywood* (1932), which was the original version of *A Star Is Born*. He was in *Three Men on a Horse* (1936) with Frank McHugh (living in Cos Cob, Connecticut), *Green Pastures* (1936), playing the character Noah, *Melody for Two* (1937), with Sally Blane,[3] *Gold Diggers in Paris* (1938), with Rosemary Lane (now a real estate dealer in Pacific Palisades, California), and as Uncle Peter in *Gone With the Wind* (1939).

His first appearance (after he auditioned for Benny) as Rochester Van Jones, a Pullman porter on Benny's Sunday night radio program, was on Easter Sunday, 1937. Benny liked Eddie's distinctive voice and felt he would register with radio audiences. Soon Anderson had a running part as Benny's valet and the Van Jones was dropped. One of his duties was to look after Carmichael, the polar bear Benny kept in the basement to guard his vault. From time to time Rochester would make references to the gas man Carmichael was supposed to have devoured. The character continued to appear almost every week right into the 1950s and was featured on many of Benny's TV shows as well. His popularity at one point brought two thousand letters a week; this was NBC's figure, and while no one disputed the count, little was said about some of the audience's disapproval of the characterization. Many listeners were particularly offended by Eddie addressing Benny as Boss.

If Anderson ever objected to the stereotype casting, on the air and in films, it was done very quietly; certainly nothing came of it because he continued to play the chauffeur, factory worker, or janitor. By 1940 he was so identified with the radio character, he was even billed as Rochester on film credits, and not only in the Jack Benny vehicles *Buck Benny Rides Again* (1940) and *The Meanest Man in the World* (1943), with Priscilla Lane (Mrs. Joseph A. Howard of Derry, New Hampshire). Some of Rochester's other pictures are *Cabin in the Sky* (1943), *Brewster's Millions* (1945), *The Sailor Takes a Wife* (1945), and *The Show-Off* (1947). He was also often part of the stage presentation at New York's famous Roxy Theatre, as well as at the Apollo Theatre in Harlem.

The fifties brought change. In 1952 his son Willie was given a suspended sentence for possession of marijuana, in 1954 his wife, Mamie, died of cancer, and two years later son Willie, who had become an outstanding athlete in school and for a while was a professional football player with the Chicago Bears, was sentenced to five years in prison for the sale and possession of marijuana. And Rochester figured less and less in the Benny shows. During rehearsals for a Benny TV show in 1958, Eddie suffered a heart attack from which he has never completely recovered. The recent difficulty he has had with his sight and speech have further curtailed professional engagements. But as the new image of the black man emerged, Eddie had further submerged. His appearance in *It's a Mad, Mad, Mad, Mad World* (1963) was his first since 1947, and his last.

Three Anderson children, by his second wife, whom he married in 1956, live with the couple in the largest house on a dead-end street in a fashionable black neighborhood in Los Angeles. Almost daily during racing season Eddie can be found at the track, and he is often accompanied by his old friend Jack Benny. Eddie is delighted to oblige fans with autographs, signing them "Rochester."

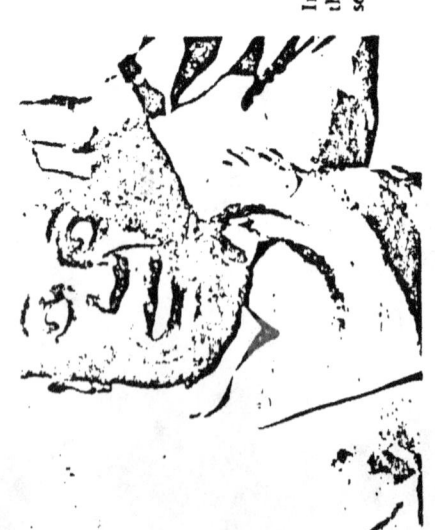

In *Topper Returns* (1941), where the script required Eddie to kiss a seal.

With Edmond Anderson on the grounds of their Los Angeles home. *Chris Albertson*

Source unknown

JACK BENNY 3-30-47

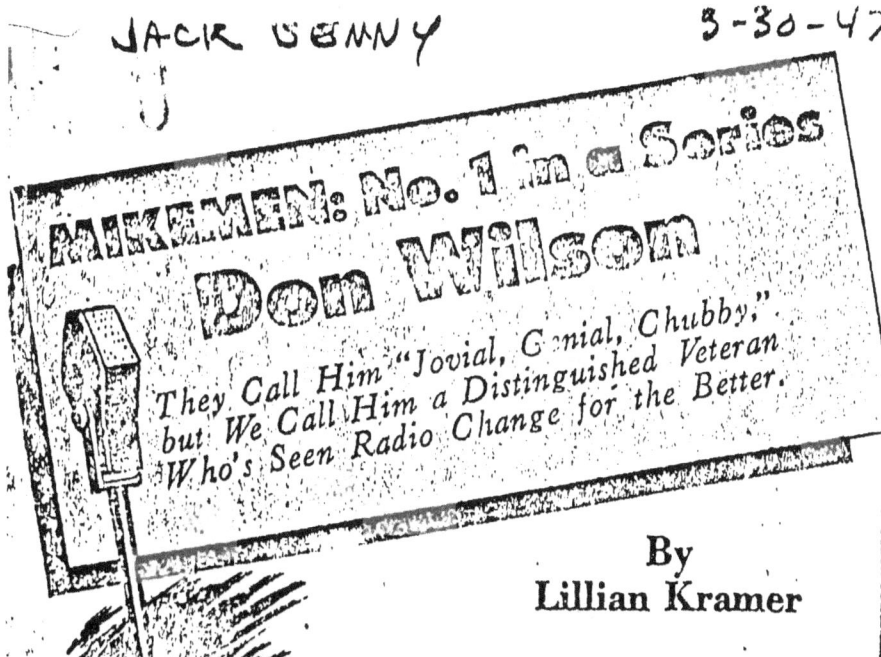

MIKEMEN: No. 1 in a Series
Don Wilson

They Call Him "Jovial, Genial, Chubby," but We Call Him a Distinguished Veteran Who's Seen Radio Change for the Better.

By Lillian Kramer

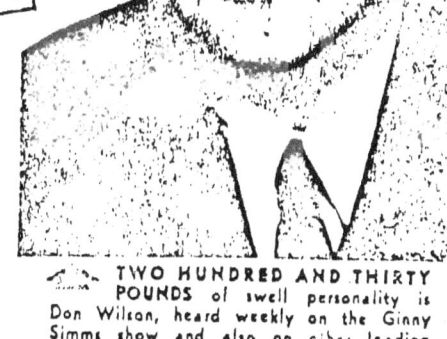

TWO HUNDRED AND THIRTY POUNDS of swell personality is Don Wilson, heard weekly on the Ginny Simms show and also on other leading airers. He's still going strong after twenty-four years in radio.

DON WILSON, rotund winner of Radio Life's 1946-47 Distinguished Achievement Award for the Most Enjoyable Commercial, has been "at it" for twenty-four years now, and that's a long time.

Don has seen radio change from a fad to a giant industry. When he started dabbling in radio back in 1924 they weren't as fussy about production, sound and timing as they are now.

"Before commercial radio, it didn't make much difference if we ran over a minute or two," Don recalls.

"As a matter of fact, if we didn't have anything to put on the air—or if someone failed to show up for a broadcast—the station just signed off for a while."

A bit more informal than things are today!

Don confesses there wasn't much money then in radio, "but it was a lot of fun and we learned as we went along".

Most people got into early radio because they were musically inclined, either instrumentally or vocally, since most radio programs consisted solely of music. Don started out as a singer over a Denver transmitter. It was several years before he took up sportscasting and then announcing.

Our chubby voice of experience says that announcers, along with technique, have changed for the better since those early days.

"Announcers today have finer diction and a much greater command of the language.

"They must have more than a good voice and a knowledge of pronunciation, however. They have to be able to project a 'selling' voice over the microphone and to have an acceptable radio personality at the same time", he points out.

According to Don, the radio microphone is the daddy of the lie detector.

"The mike is the greatest detector of insincerity, and by the same token it reflects honesty and sincerity in an announcer's voice", he claims.

His Advice

Every week Don receives countless letters from would-be announcers seeking advice on how to succeed in radio. He answers them all:

"Be yourself. Don't try to mimic someone else. Your own personality is your greatest asset.

"Have an honest enthusiasm about the product you're selling and your voice will register successfully."

He certainly knows whereof he speaks. The Radio Life citation is latest in a ten-year-long string of firsts in popularity polls which have picked him as favorite announcer.

Don has been with Jack Benny for thirteen years. Besides his Sunday stints for Benny, the Wilson verve also adds lift to Ginny Simms' Friday night airers, the Victor Borge-Benny Goodman show, and Kenny Baker's five-times-weekly early morning broadcasts.

Most of his fans write about his infectious laugh. Those background chuckles are not prop laughs. Don doesn't laugh at a joke because there's a paycheck in the shadows. He really enjoys a funny line and it's second nature for him to boom out with the hearty ho-hos.

After all those references to Don as a "Hemo Boy," comparisons to Mt. Wilson, and what not, the popular conception is a Don Wilson weighing in the neighborhood of 400 pounds, more or less.

Actually, Don weighs a trim 230—not bad for his six feet, two.

Ginny's warm-up shows make a lot over Don's avoirdupois. A make-believe storm at sea calls for a line like "Make Wilson stay in the middle of the ship—it's listing!"

Pounds don't worry Don, and he claims he diets only when he's asleep. His favorite midnight snack is a bowl of graham crackers and milk.

Wilson is married to Marusia Rudunska, a refugee Polish countess and a very talented dress designer. A couple of weeks ago Marusia had her new spring opening in Beverly Hills. Hollywood stars and Beverly Hills society were well represented.

Ginny was one of the hostesses at the opening, which was emceed, as you might guess, by Don Wilson. Marusia modeled her creations herself and caused quite a flurry.

Don is very proud of Marusia's success. He likes to talk about her workshop in downtown Los Angeles, about the clever things she does with fabrics, and about the gowns she whips up for Esther Williams and other stars.

"They call her the Valentina of Beverly Hills", he says gleefully.

The Wilsons have just moved into a new apartment in Beverly Hills and are now in the happy throes of decorating. They used to live on a ranch in the Valley, but their busy careers made town living more to be desired.

Besides his multitudinous radio assignments, Don finds time to be President of Acro-Speed, Incorporated, an automotive tune-up equipment plant located in Pasadena—and to be radio's number one gin-rummy addict.

International Jack Benny
Fan Club
322 Palmetto Ave. #154
Pacifica, CA 94044

ADDRESS CORRECTION REQUESTED

Volume XII, Number 3 **INTERNATIONAL DISTRIBUTION** May-June 1992

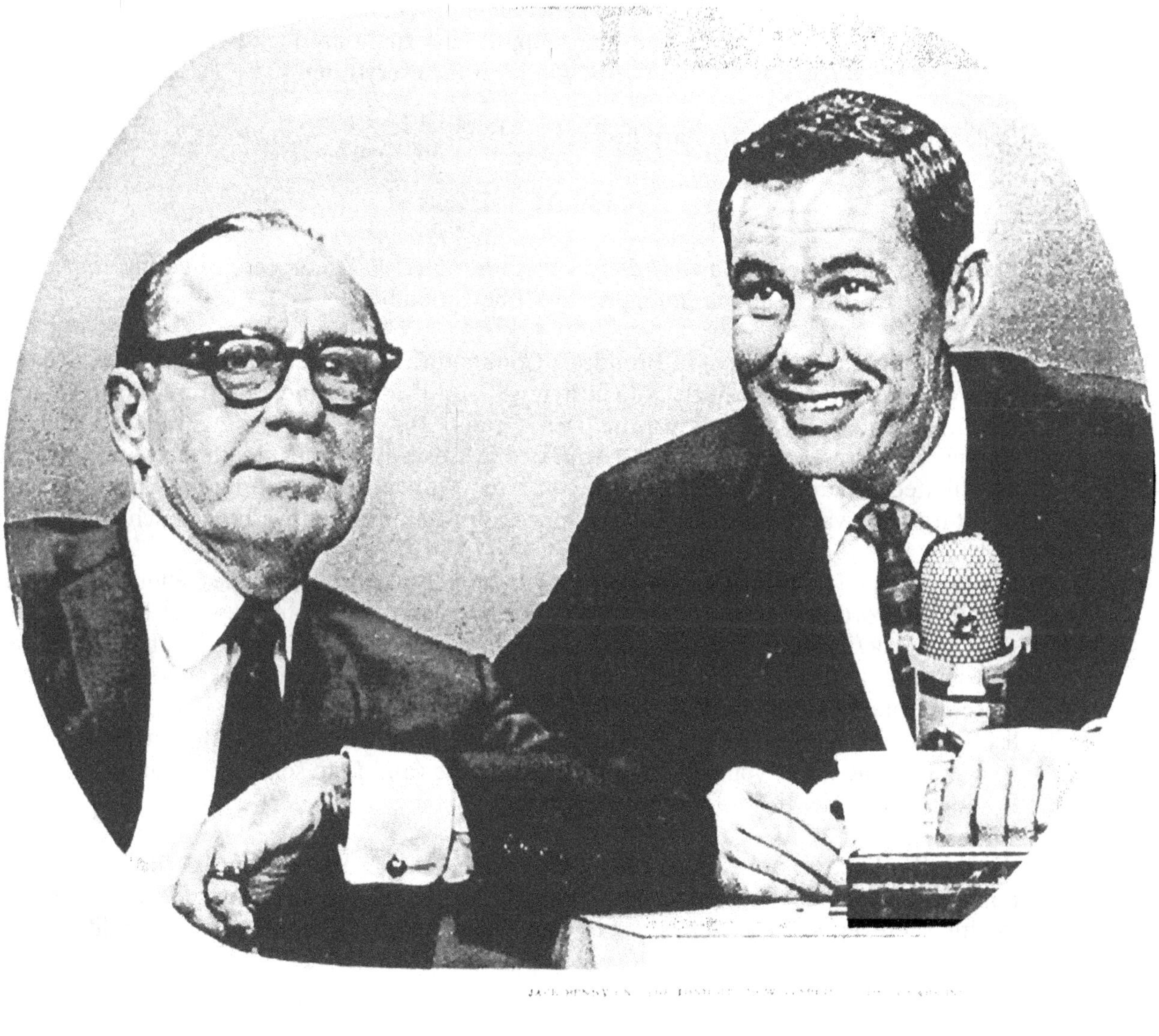

☺ ☺ ☺ PRESIDENT'S MESSAGE ☺ ☺ ☺

Jell-o again, folks! Hope that you all have been enjoying your summer thus far; things have been wonderfully busy as usual for me, and all is quite well here in Pacifica. Figured that since Johnny Carson completed his last show in May, it would be an appropriate time to reprint the photo from the March-April 1988 <u>Times</u>. Was fortunate enough to run down to Los Angeles for a day to see the last public show (w/Robin Williams and Bette Midler); it was a definite delight, and emotions appeared to be high on both sides of the cameras. I would like to take this opportunity to publicly thank Frederick de Cordova (Jack's director and <u>Tonight</u> show Executive Producer) and Billie Freebairn-Smith for all the help they have given me over the years. Without their help, the International Jack Benny Fan Club would not be nearly what it is today. Thank you both for **everything**.

Speaking of milestones, we have just reached

400 MEMBERS!

Our 400th member is Dawn Adler, daughter of Rich Adler (conveniently, our 399th member). Welcome to you both, and to all new members!

Must note that the Museum of Broadcast Communications in Chicago and Chuck Schaden have opened an exhibit entitled "**Jack Benny's Vault**" at their new location in the Chicago Cultural Center. It features various Benny radio and television shows, as well as other "Benny broadcast memorabilia." Know that several of our members have already contributed generously to this exhibit; rah rah! Am currently waiting for Chuck Schaden to return from vacation; will give you more information when we both touch base.

On the subject of the tape library, there have been several inquiries about the "Other Related Recordings" section. The listing does not currently note the exact length of each show/excerpt/interview/etc., so it makes ordering from the list difficult (i.e., how much tape do you send?). Ergo, I am going to sit down and compile a list of exact time lengths for all these offerings and publish it in the <u>Times</u>. In the meantime, if you wish to order from this list, just send me your **pick list only**. I will then note the time lengths on your list and return it to you. Thus you will know how much tape (and $) to send with your order. Sorry for any inconvenience this may have caused.

Would also like to note that on May 20th, member Doug Wood went into the Army. He renewed his membership before his departure, so the <u>Times</u> will continue to wing its way to him wherever he goes. Good luck to you, Doug, and to all our members on military duty.

Now on with the show!

© Copyright 1992, Laura Lee

♥ ☺ ♥ JACK BLOOM PASADENA CHAPTER ♥ ☺ ♥

It is the May-June issue again, and time to run down our annual Jack Bloom Pasadena Chapter list. For those of you just tuning in, Jack Bloom was a very dedicated member of the IJBFC. He did extensive research on Jack, as well as making very large donations to our archives and tape library. Jack's contributions to our log, <u>39 Forever</u>, were invaluable. Additionally, Jack and I kept a running correspondence for a great deal of time, discussing Jack Benny and all other related topics. His passing in June of 1990 was a great loss for all IJBFC members; his humor and kindness will never be forgotten, and we are all indebted to him for his great generosity. (For the full story, see the May-June 1990 <u>Times</u>.)
I still miss you, Jack.

The Jack Bloom Pasadena Chapter is an honorary society for IJBFC members who have been active for four or more years. Below is the full JBPC membership, with members added this year indicated by 3 asterisks.

JACK ABIZAID	TOM MASTEL
JACK BLOOM	BILL OLIVER
BRUCE BAKER	ROBERT OLSEN
HAL BOGART	JOHN SCHLAMP
FRANCIS W. DALY ***	JOYCE SHOOKS
PHIL EVANS	BENJAMIN SPANGLER
LE ROY FILLENWARTH	BONNIE SPANGLER
MARILYN FILLENWARTH	DAVID SPANGLER
ALAN GROSSMAN	STEVE SZEJNA
JAY HICKERSON	EVA TINTORRI ***
TIM HOLLIS	MARION TINTORRI ***
SAREE KAMINSKY	BARBARA WATKINS
LAURA LEE	KEN WEIGEL
GEORGE LILLIE	DOUG WOOD
JAMES A. LINK ***	

JACK BENNY GALA

My thanks to Lisa Melcombe for sending me information on the dedication of the Jack Benny statue at the Television Academy Hall of Fame Plaza. Alas due to my work schedule I was unable to attend. However, Lisa was in attendance that evening (I am envious!) and gave me the whole low-down.

In a place where it never rains, it almost rained on July 8th. However, knowing that Jack has connections in high places (I mean, God was his best friend for almost 60 years!) the clouds held their peace. A statue of Jack standing in the traditional three-fingers-on-the-cheek pose and holding his violin and bow was officially unveiled. (Looks **very** good in the pictures!) Joan Benny and Irving Fein were in attendance, and told a few anecdotes about

_____ If this box is checked, $6.39 is due for another year.

Jack. One that was mentioned was the incident detailing Jack's request that Abby Lane (hope that is right...cannot find the actual written account) be given 100% billing in his show. (100% billing meant that her name was just as large as his on the marquee.) A Jack look-alike also did a comedy routine during the proceedings (could it have been Eddie Carroll or Will Jordan?). The special Jack Benny: Comedy in Bloom was then screened at the Academy Plaza Theatre; it is scheduled to debut on HBO later this year (more information on that ASAP). Clips of many JB appearances are included, such as interviews with Steve Allen, Dinah Shore, and Merv Griffin. (I would wager that some Carson clips should be there as well.) Interviews with many of Jack's associates are also interspersed.

As for the guests, we have already noted Joan Benny and Irving Fein, and Gisele MacKenzie was also in attendance. Various non-Benny people were also there, such as Doris Roberts (character actress, also featured in Remington Steele), and Al Haig (have I spelled that properly?...of Fame). Thanks again Lisa for all your help.

DO YOU KNOW?

Just a short one this time, and something that I should already know. Jay Wild wants to know if Jack Benny has a star on the Hollywood Walk of Fame. I believe I recall that Ed McMahon's star was placed between W.C. Fields and Jack Benny, but I just am not certain. Can anyone clue us in on this matter?

§ § § JACK BENNY CLASSIFIEDS § § §

§ Tony and A.J. Boyce of Doncaster, England are interested in securing some of Jack's television shows. Please note that England has a different television system than America, so USA tapes need to be converted. A script for such shows would also be a welcome addition, as they are hearing-impaired. They are also interested in any information on Eddie "Rochester" Anderson. 49 Whitton Close, West Bessacarr, Doncaster DN4 7RB, England.

§ Lisa File is offering copies of Jack Benny's will for $11.00 plus $2.00 for shipping and handling. I have received a copy of it from her, and found it to be an interesting addition to the collection. She also has copies of many other wills and legal documents; just looking over the listing is interesting! 9291 Golden Leaf Way, Indianapolis, Indiana 46260.

§ James Fisher is compiling a bio-bibliography of the great Al Jolson (those four words are, of course, inseparable). I have discovered over the years that being a fan of Jack Benny and of Al Jolson seem to frequently go hand-in-hand. If any of you would be able to supply Jolson-related information (not necessarily relating to Jack Benny), please contact him. c/o Theatre Department, Wabash College, Crawfordsville, Indiana 47933.

§   Vice President Rex Riffle has amassed a very large collection of Jack Benny stamps with various postmarks from around America. He also collects postmarks with non-Jack stamps. 1 Kepner Street, Buckhannon, West Virginia 26201.

☼ ☼ ETHER ONE ☼ ☼

This information comes from Frank Pozzuoli:

"At the beginning of April, Nickelodeon's Nick-At-Nite started showing <u>The Lucy Show</u>. Jack made two appearances on that series [E.N.: Plus at least one on <u>Here's Lucy</u>]*. The first one was around the start of the third season. It's called "Lucy and the Plumber" and has both Jack and Bob Hope. Jack also appears in the sixth and final season [October 16, 1967]...Also in the final season, there was one episode with Dennis Day and another one with Phil Harris. So check out that last season!"   *9-28-84*

The other <u>Lucy Show</u> appearance was the one in which Lucy is trying to persuade Jack to put his money in the bank for which Lucy works. Jack states that the bank must be able to prove that it has a better security system than his vault. Lucy then shows Jack the system constructed for him, ending in the most expensive television sight gag at that time. Just FYI, the <u>Here's Lucy</u> show featured Lucy being sent to help Jack write his life story. As Jack dictates, certain scenes in Jack's life are played out with Lucy being all the women in his life. In my opinion, both shows are absolutely delightful.

OTHER CLUBS, PERIODICALS, ETC.

<u>BRC Productions</u> marches on...member Bob Burnham continues to sell a wide variety of radio shows on cassette, including a large number of Benny shows. BRC listings are available through an on-line service 24 hours a day: dial Gateway On-line, (313) 291-5571. Select the letter O from the main menu, then BRC Productions. BRC Productions, P.O. Box 2645, Livonia, Michigan 48151.

<u>Flashback</u> is a newsletter concerned with old television. Their May issue includes articles on Lawrence Welk, Johnny Carson, Robert Reed, <u>The Untouchables</u>, and Art Linkletter. <u>Flashback</u>, 16 Robin Hood Lane, Jackson, Tennessee 38305.

<u>Hi-De-Ho Collectibles</u> offer a wide variety of memorabilia through their sales catalogs. These include memorabilia on movies, television, cartoons, westerns, and many other items of interest and nostalgia. Hi-De-Ho Collectibles, P.O. Box 2841, Gaithersburg, Maryland 20886-2841, (301) 926-4438.

♪♪♪♪♪♪♪♪♪♪♪♪♪♪♪♪♪♪♪♪♪♪♪♪♪♪♪♪♪♪♪♪♪

Please send all questions, comments, corrections and additions to:

Laura Lee, c/o International Jack Benny Fan Club Offices, 322 Palmetto Avenue, #154, Pacifica, California, 94044   (415) 355-3723

Please friends, send no bombs.

*Actually, he was on four 12 <u>Here's Lucy</u>s. More later.

Yes Please!

Dennis Day Got His Job Because He Said, "Yes, Please, Mr. Benny"

By SUZANNE WARNER

OH, DENNIS! Jack Benny was calling one of the many applicants for the singing spot left vacant on his NBC show by Kenny Baker.

"Yes, please," returned Dennis Day McNulty.

Jack Benny slapped the desk. "That's it," he whooped. "A character who would be deferential and perhaps show up with his mother." A new avenue of gags appeared before Benny.

But it didn't come just by accident that Dennis was at that rehearsal. Mary Livingstone was his discoverer. She had heard him sing on a talent show and had requested that he make a recording.

This he had done, and Mary had asked that the audition record be forwarded to Jack Benny.

When it came time to hold an audition, Dennis' voice was one of those picked out of the hundreds and hundreds of recordings that were sent in.

So here he was, a young Irish lad, fresh out of college, being picked for the singing role on a transcontinental show. He might not have gotten the job if his parents hadn't always insisted that his manners be of the best. As Dennis says, "All six of us minded, but pronto. We had to or it would have made too much work for mother."

So when Dennis looked up when Benny called and said, "Yes, please," that was just what he was used to saying at home.

The character you now hear on the radio as naive Dennis Day is quite like the real Dennis Day McNulty—only enlarged upon.

Even being in Hollywood and feted by everyone hasn't changed him a bit. He still follows his rule of being in bed by 11, and rising by nine. He has never smoked. He remembers too clearly the time he was in the lot with the neighborhood kids smoking a dried stalk of golden rod, when his sister saw him and told his mother. Mother Mary said, "Faith and I'll be tellin' your father when he comes home." And she did. Father didn't do much talking except to say he'd have no son of his smoking, Dennis was whisked away to the bedroom, and came into rather close contact with the razor strap. He hasn't smoked from that day to this.

Now that he is grown up he supports his mother and father and three brothers, two of whom are ensigns in the naval reserve.

Dennis says the greatest handicap he has had to overcome is shyness.

It has always bothered him. When as a child he sang "Ave Maria" in Latin at a church festival, he forgot the words. After the first strain, he began to blush, stopped singing and said, "That's all, folks" and ran off the stage. He still is afraid of forgetting words.

To Radio Life's way of thinking, he has one of the finest singing voices on the air. Each succeeding week it seems to get better—if that is possible. Also as we tear pages off the calendar, Dennis becomes a better and better comedian. It is our prophecy that in the near future he will have a show of his own, and appear as singing emcee.

Paul Whiteman also backs up this opinion. He says of Dennis, "He has a fine legitimate voice. God gave him good equipment and he is making the best of it. Also, he is very funny. I think he delivers lines the best of any singer. His timing is perfect." And that is from Paul Whiteman, the music director of the Blue, a rival network.

When Dennis sings over the air, he sings to his dream girl . . . the girl he's never met, but hopes to. She's five foot, three inches—light brown hair, blue eyes . . . and maybe has a bit of Irish in her.

Dennis was asked, when he came to NBC, to fill out the routine questions. Here are some of them which give an insight into the real Dennis and show his clever sense of humor.

Q. Did you participate in the world war?
A. Yes. I was a member of the 149th diaper division.
Q. What is your pet aversion?
A. Eccentric women's wear.

(Please turn to Page 32)

"I'LL TAKE CHARGE OF THIS SITUATION," says Dennis' radio mother (Verna Felton). "But mom, I'm the singer," cries Dennis. "No matter, no matter . . . you go and sit down, I'll talk for a while," commands mother, "Yes, please," condescends Dennis.

Nicky Left Us
(Continued from Page 37)

fight, but I can produce food.' So she has. And that's how the pigs come into her life."

Besides the pigs—so prolific that now the families of her original four sows and a boar all but crowd her off the place—she has four beautiful soft-eyed "bossies"—and does a thoroughly capable job as a milkmaid. She also raises white-faced Hereford cattle for the beef market and will greatly enlarge her herd on the newly-acquired acreage at Fontana.

"Churns her own butter, too,—just enough for her morning toast and daily cooking duties," Nicky bragged. Miss Rich admits that butter-making still is too strenuous to be a full-time chore.

"Everywhere about the ranch, and in the radio and screen star's charming Early American type residence, especially, we saw ample evidence of how she has made a fascinating game of solving today's perplexing conservation and rationing problems.

"You may think I'm prejudiced, but really, I think she is the most ingenious woman in the world," Nicky whispered at the first moment his favorite human turned out of earshot. "Why, do you know, nearly all the wood in this house was salvaged from some former construction? But, stained, polished and rejuvenated, who'd know it now?"

Lengths of telephone poles went into a new bedroom's foundation. The wooden floors are unfinished and hand-painted. For heat, an old-fashioned and very picturesque Franklin stove. Bits of wood and pine cones from the ranch grounds crackle cheerily in it on snappy Fall and Winter days. And then it becomes Nicky's special pet among the household furnishings, because it provides such pleasant warmth for his not-infrequent naps.

Hand-crocheted rugs of heavy white cotton and lengths of the same material upholster quaint Colonial chairs and foot-stools. The simple, attractive furniture throughout the residence has been fashioned from second-hand pieces, rejuvenated with just a little paint, a bit of varnish and lots of ingenuity.

"The government has asked women to do more and more of their own dressmaking, it seems," said our canine informant. "So, she's turned one corner of her boudoir into a 'Fashion Center.' And there she pores over style catalogs and patterns in her spare moments—when she has any.

Instead of buying new garments for the coming season, Miss Rich has made over scads of her last season's dresses, apropos of the latest fashion ideas—and they're so smart!"

Did you know—(we didn't until Nicky told us)—a "lady farmer" looking for clothes-creating inspiration is aided and abetted by the manufacturers of chicken feed,—no less! It seems the feed is sold in sacks made of ready-to-sew cotton, printed in gay patterns of plaids, stripes, polka dots and floral designs. Nicky nearly tore the house down, trying to show us all the clever sports dresses, aprons, tablecloths and curtains his versatile "Ma'am Boss" has fashioned from the sacks.

"I don't know how she does it," breathed Nicky, adoring her with his eyes. "All this is just leisure-time work, you know, for most of my boss lady's time on the ranch is spent supervising the big job of raising foodstuffs to help feed a nation at war.

"She seems to be one of those people that just have the knack of making things grow. I don't know how she— Well, of course, I've never planted anything but bones, but not even one of the thousands I've put into the dirt have ever sprouted into a T-bone steak, or even the dinkiest lamb chop!"

Yes, Please!
(Continued from Page 38)

Q. What is your idea of nothing to do?
A. Sitting in a hotel lobby, waiting for someone who's late.

Q. What instrument did you first learn to play?
A. I didn't.

Q. What things annoy you most?
Q. Other singers rehearsing, and I'll bet it's mutual.

Q. What was the first job by which you earned money?
A. Peddling papers on a Bronx route. Earned $12.00 a week.

Q. What did you do with the money?
A. Gave it to my mother.

Q. Do you keep pets. What kind?
A. Yes. Mutts. I don't want 'em if they're pedigreed.

Q. What was the funniest incident you ever experienced in the studios?
A. Finished song and went out of studio for drink of water. Maestro Ray Block confused cues, and went into introduction of my next song instead of a band number. I reached mike on cue, but with a mouthful of water. My first note had to be run through a wringer.

Q. Clothes. What is the extent of your wardrobe?
A. From hat to shoes.

Q. What is your fondest memory?
A. Having to forsake law school.

Q. Why did you go to New York. How?
A. You'll have to ask my parents that. I came via the birth route.

Q. Name your pet aversions.
A. Spinach, peroxide blondes, road hogs, loud ties and sox.

Q. What is your favorite radio program?
A. Fred Allen.

Q. What do you wish to do when you retire?
A. Be a gentleman farmer, with large country estate and equally large family. (If I marry).

Q. What is your favorite anecdote?
A. The one about the two Irishmen.

Q. What do you do with your savings?
A. What savings?

Q. Have you ever saved a life?
A. Yes. Saved a woman from drowning. She was middle-aged, though.

Q. What is your earliest recollection?
A. Hating fried mush and tossing it on the floor when mother turned her back.

Q. Do you think that radio marriages are happier than the usual run of stage or musical or screen tie-ups?
A. I'd be quoting propaganda if I answered that one.

Q. What sort of women do you prefer—blonde, brunette, short, tall, or are you married and already committed?
A. I like 'em all, as long as they are pretty.

Q. Have you any accomplishments that aren't well known?
A. I can bake a cake. I can wiggle my ears, too.

Q. Is there some interesting item of information not covered by the above questions?
A. Could there possibly be?

★ ★

FREE COFFEE A LA JARVIS

Al Jarvis, originator of the famous "Make Believe Ballroom", has a new wrinkle in contest prizes coming up. During the week of May 17-22, he plans to give away more than 400 pounds of Breakfast Club Coffee to lucky listeners to this show.

It's a six-day contest called "Breakfast Club's Guessing College of Entertainment." Each day 50 lucky contestants will receive a pound of coffee, free. Topping these fifty daily prizes, Al will give away a **whole year's supply** of Breakfast Club Coffee to the two participants who come out best in each day's contest—a total of twelve grand prizes of a year's supply of coffee.

Next to getting a letter that a rich uncle has left you a fortune, this is about the best windfall that could come one's way, these days. All that is required to listen to Al's Make-Believe Ballroom and "guess" by mail. As a tip, though, it is suggested that listeners have a pound of Breakfast Club on the shelf. That may make a difference between winning only one pound of coffee or a whole year's supply.

★ ★

Entire radio, theater and film career of Chester Lauck and Norris Goff for 12 years has consisted of portraying Lum and Abner.

Hey NLAS members!

Tape trading list in next issue... let me know if you want to be on it!

 FAN CLUB

322 Palmetto Ave. #154
Pacifica, CA 94044

ADDRESS CORRECTION REQUESTED

THE JACK BENNY TIMES

Volume XII, Number 4   **INTERNATIONAL DISTRIBUTION**   July-August 199

Jack and Mary are really happy in the company of Babe Marks (seen just at left), but her resemblance to sister Mary certainly causes complications. But the crowning blow came when baby Joan (below and on the opposite page) cast her vote in the "Mary mix-up"!

☺ ☺ ☺ PRESIDENT'S MESSAGE ☺ ☺ ☺

Jell-o again, folks! All is well here in California, and I hope that things are the same in your neck of the woods. Well, it is time to warm up those VCRs for the long-awaited special Jack Benny: Comedy in Bloom on HBO. The big day is

OCTOBER 5TH

so keep your eyes open and your television listings handy.

Speaking of the special, in the last issue we gave you a synopsis of the Jack Benny gala in Los Angeles. This featured a screening of Comedy in Bloom, and the official unveiling of the Jack Benny statue at the Television Academy Hall of Fame Plaza. I received a letter informing me that the gifted sculptor of the statue is Ernest Shelton of Shelton Sculpture Studios. (Thanks, Lyn, for the info!) If you are in that area, it is certainly a worthwhile endeavor to see this fantastic statue. Will try to get a reproducible photograph of it at some time in the future.

Would you believe that Grenada is issuing a Jack Benny stamp? Bill Oliver sent me an AP article about Grenada's stamps for U.S.O. stars, which is reprinted at the end of this newsletter. Not bad! As Bill said, Jack is practically turning up as many places as Elvis!

Regarding the afterthought last time about Jack being on four Here's Lucys, here is a list of all exact titles and dates, as taken from a list supplied to me by Tom Kleinschmidt:

"Lucy Visits Jack Benny"	September 30, 1968 CBS
"Lucy and Jack Benny's Biography"	November 23, 1970 CBS
"Lucy the Crusader"	February 8, 1971 CBS
"Lucy and the Celebrities"	November 15, 1971 CBS

Additionally, Jack was on two The Lucy Shows:

"Lucy and the Plumber" (w/Bob Hope)	September 28, 1964 CBS
"Lucy Gets Jack Benny's Account"	October 16, 1967 CBS

Another item from this list since a question had arisen in previous Times over the exact dates/origin of the following three shows. They are all G.E. Theater:

"The Face is Familiar"	November 21, 1954 CBS
"The Honest Man"	February 19, 1956 CBS
"The Fenton Touch"	March 3, 1957 CBS

_____ If this box is checked, $6.39 is due for another year

© Copyright, 1992, Laura Lee

In response to Alan Grossman's plea to see a photograph of Babe Blum, we have one on our cover, supplied to us by Barbara Thunell. Have also seen later pictures of her, and it looks as though she could practically pass for Mary's twin.

Now I had intended for this issue to start the transcription of the Phil Harris interview. I went looking for the tapes of it, and discovered that they are sitting in my fireproof safe (vault?) in Fort Wayne. Ah! I am so upset with myself. Alas...will try to obtain them to start the transcription in the next issue. Know many of you have been waiting for it eagerly!

Now on with the show!

* * TAPE TRADING LIST * *

Ellen Barker, P.O. Box 1402, Reseda, California 91335

Hal Bogart, 2029 Aldersgate Drive, Lyndhurst, Ohio 44124

Yosef Braude, 25 Longhorn Road, Providence, Rhode Island 02906

Rob Cohen, 6635 Helm Avenue, Reynoldsburg, Ohio 43068

Rob Crawford, 2818 Altos Avenue #B, Sacramento, California 95815

The Everills, 1558 Knox Drive, New Haven, Indiana 46774

Andrew Haskell, 160 West 39th Avenue, Vancouver, British Columbia V5Y 2P2, Canada

Dick Hill, 1802 Bateman, Hastings, Nebraska 68901

David A. Howell, 1300 Kennedy Boulevard #419, Cuyahoga Falls, Ohio 44221

Tom Kleinschmidt, 26101 Country Club Boulevard #706, North Olmstead, Ohio 44070

Steve Lake, 7780 North Pinesview Drive, Scottsdale, Arizona 85258

John Malone, Rural Route #2, Wee-Ma-Tuk, Cuba, Illinois 61427

Bill Oliver, 516 Third Street NE, Massillon, Ohio 44646

Jack Palmer, 145 North 21st Street, Battle Creek, Michigan 49015

Lewis and Sedalia Pearson, 240 Ridge Drive, Marion, Iowa 52302

Michael Pointon, 11 Kings Court, Kings Road, London SW19 8QP, England

Frank Pozzuoli, 2830 Waterbury Avenue, Bronx, New York 10461

Keith Scott, 4 Bellbird Crescent, Forestville 2087, N.S.W. Australia

Joyce Shooks, 2026 Lafayette NE, Grand Rapids, Michigan 49505

Steve and Kim Smith, 1945 Coit NW, Grand Rapids, Michigan 49505

John Smothers, 22 Townsend Drive, Freehold, New Jersey 07728 (Open reel preferred)

Steve Szejna, 7806 West Waterford Avenue #1, Greenfield, Wisconsin 53220-2275

Peter Tatchell, 40 Bambra Road, Caulfield, Victoria 3161 Australia

James E. Treacy, Jr., 900 Hargrove Road, Apartment 234, Tuscaloosa, Alabama 35401

If you want to be added to this listing, just drop me a line!

YOU >DO< KNOW!

In response to Jay Wild's question about Jack's star on the Walk of Fame, Tommy Housos supplies us with the answer from the Hollywood Walk of Fame Book. Jack's star is located at 6650 Hollywood. It is bordered on one side by the stars of Red Skelton and Norm Crosby, and on the other by Smilin' Ed McConnell (featured on radio's The Buster Brown Gang) and Bessie Barriscale (Vaudeville actress, also in silent Wooden Shoes, 1917). Now we know. Thanks, Tommy!

§ § § JACK BENNY CLASSIFIEDS § § §

§   Frank Pozzuoli reports that Shokus Video is offering Shower of Stars from November 1, 1956, with guests Nanette Fabray and Johnnie Ray. Also on the same tape is Stars in the Eye from November 15, 1952, with Jack, Burns and Allen, Lucille Ball, Desi Arnaz, and the Amos and Andy cast. All told, the tape is two hours, $24.95 plus $3.65 for postage and handling. Ask for it by number...tape #473, TV Variety XXVI.

§   From Jimmie Hicks: "I am doing a study of the career of actress Claudette Colbert and for this work I am compiling a list of all her appearances on film, stage, radio, and television. I know that she was a friend of Jack Benny and his wife and that she made, at least, three professional appearances with him. One was on his radio show (February 6, 1949) and one was on his television program (April 1, 1951). She apparently made, at least, one more appearance with him on the Gulf Screen Guild Theatre (October 20, 1940) but I have no information on the contents of this program. I would appreciate any information I could obtain on her appearances both with Jack Benny and otherwise. I am especially interested in finding out about any appearances she may have made in short films." 5657 Lexinton Avenue, Hollywood, California 90038.

§ Rob Cohen would like to trade for Jack's radio shows or videos of Jack's specials, movies, documentaries, etc. 763 Oaksedge Drive, Gahanna, Ohio 43230.

§ George Lillie, 4021 Flicker Lane, Cedar Rapids, Iowa 52402. George is selling his collection of media-related magazines. Listings give Title years (quantity):

The American 28	(1)	Radio Guide 34-38	(59)
Modern Screen 48, 56, 57	(3)	Radio Land 34	(1)
Motion Picture 49, 56, 59	(3)	Radio Stars 34	(1)
Photoplay 47-49, 58	(6)	Sat. Eve. Post 74	(1)
Radio Album 49	(1)	TV Life 58	(1)
Radio/TV Mirror 48-49	(3)	TV/Radio Mirror 61-62	(4)

♪♪♪♪♪♪♪♪♪♪♪♪♪♪♪♪♪♪♪♪♪♪♪♪♪♪♪♪♪♪♪♪

Please send all questions, comments, corrections and additions to:

Laura Lee, c/o International Jack Benny Fan Club Offices, 322 Palmetto Avenue, #154, Pacifica, California, 94044   (415) 355-3723

Please friends, send no bombs.

SUNDAY AUGUST 2, 1992

Grenada issues stamp series honoring USO's 50th birthday

By SYD KRONISH
For AP Special Features

The USO (United Service Organizations) has been entertaining American service men and women during war and peace for more than 50 years.

To honor the magnificent efforts of those who performed for our service people, the Caribbean island nation of Grenada (and its dependency Grenada-Grenadines) have released a series of 16 stamps and four souvenir sheets.

The new stamps belatedly salute the golden anniversary of the USO, since the organization actually began operation in 1941. However, these new adhesives are part of an ongoing philatelic tribute to the 50th anniversary of World War II events. Grenada is a former British colony.

Famous USO performers are seen on the Grenada and Grenada-Grenadines stamps. Included is a famous dummy, Charlie McCarthy, and an English music hall artist (Gracie Fields), who lifted the British spirits during the "blitz" with her songs.

The Grenada stamps also feature such stars as Jack Benny, Jinx Falkenburg, Frances Langford, Joe E. Brown, Phil Silvers, Danny Kaye and Frank Sinatra.

Shown in the first of two Grenada souvenir sheets is Bob Hope. The second sheet depicts Chinese-American movie actress Anna May Wong.

Included among those featured in the Grenada-Grenadines stamps are James Cagney, Ann Sheridan, Jerry Colonna, Spike Jones, the Andrews Sisters, Dinah Shore and Bing Crosby. Illustrated in the first souvenir sheet is Marlene Dietrich. The second sheet portrays Fred Astaire.

Collectors interested in acquiring the new stamps from Grenada and the Grenada-Grenadines can contact the Inter-Governmental Philatelic Corp., 460 West 46th St., New York City, NY 10001. The cost of the stamps is $10. The souvenir sheets are $10. A special price for the stamps and

JACK BENNY: He's Been 39 for 28 Years

While men half his age moan that TV is too exhausting to do more than six programs a year, Benny, at 67, this year doubled his load to a show a week. Two things keep him going: his unmitigated-ham personality and his "think-young" philosophy.

by LARRY WOLTERS

JACK BENNY was sitting with friends in a hotel suite. He stepped to the phone and ordered coffee sent up.

"Please, make it so hot that you can't carry it," he told room service. Hanging up the phone, he said with a chuckle, "To be honest about it, that line is stolen from George Burns."

"That reminds me of a story," put in a friend of Benny. "There was this kid—three or four years old—who seemed normal in every way except that he couldn't (or wouldn't) talk. His parents were worried about it. They took him to doctors, they took him to speech experts—they tried everything but the boy wouldn't say a word.

"Finally, one morning when they served him his cocoa, he tasted it and yelped, 'It's too hot!' His parents burst into tears of joy, kissed him, and asked, 'Why haven't you ever spoken before, dear?' 'Well,' he said, 'there wasn't anything to complain about before.'"

Benny laughed and said that he could use that joke. However, another comedian present said he would get it out on the air ahead of Benny. Jack was philosophical about it. Never one to complain, he certainly wasn't going to kick over the loss of one joke.

Despite all that has been printed about Benny as a worrier, he never frets, stews, or grumbles. He's as relaxed as Perry Como, Bing Crosby, and Dean Martin, divided by three.

Jack Benny is the only guy in the world who has been 39 years old for 28 years. More than that, he expects to go right on being 39. And he actually looks and says that he feels more like that age than the 67 he is.

On radio in 1954, Benny got a perennial 39th-birthday kiss from his wife, Mary Livingstone.

MARCH 1961

This is a nice article — I'm going to publish it over the next few issues due to length.
—LL

"To stay young in heart, think as young people do. Look forward, never backward. Work, instead of worrying."

At least 12 different cars have subbed for Jack's famed Maxwell, a figment of writers' imaginations.

What Ponce de Leon searched for fruitlessly—perpetual youth—Benny had handed to him by his writers, although he didn't realize it at the time.

"That 'I'm only 39 gag' my writers came up with," Benny insisted, "was just about the best thing that ever happened to me. The cliché, 'you're only as old as you feel,' happens to be true. I feel young and so far as I can find out I'm healthy.

"Of course, I don't kid myself into believing I'm young," the elder statesman of comedy admitted. "I just look in the mirror. That snaps me back to reality.

"To stay young-looking and keep healthy you have to give some thought to it and work at it. I play golf almost every day—but I don't overdo it. I used to play 18 or more holes but now I take nine. I get a lot of sun and keep tanned. I work with my violin an hour or two every day. It gives me pleasure and satisfaction—although that isn't true for those who are around me.

"And I watch my food intake. This is important and it's not likely that you can keep your weight where it belongs without counting calories. You can't be a fat slob with three chins and look young, or even acceptable. So I watch out about starches, sugar, and fats. I use sugar substitutes. I always drink skim milk. I hated it at first, but now I can't stand whole milk anymore. And I've stopped smoking cigarettes.

"But I am convinced that more important than diet and exercise is your mental attitude," said the most durable comedian of the century. "You've got to keep young in heart. You've got to think as young people do. It means you've got to look forward, never backward. Work, instead of worrying, is one of the chief reasons I feel good."

Not so long ago Benny and Ginger Rogers were to rehearse an athletic dance routine. Benny moaned with a rueful grin that he was too weak to get into an overcoat alone. A few minutes later he disproved this when he lifted Ginger off the floor and whirled her through the air.

"I did that?" Jack asked. "George Burns will never believe this—for that matter even I don't believe it." In another show he did a 10-minute skit in which he played football in the living room. He jumped over chairs and couches and rolled about the floor with the agility of a kitten.

Another time he did a fencing scene in the Tower of London which actually had touches of the swashbuckling of Douglas Fairbanks, Jr. and the late Errol Flynn. This, as anyone who has ever fenced knows, means countless hours of hard work. It is a Benny rule that anything he can do himself he will never relegate to a stunt man.

TODAY'S HEALTH

WE'VE BEEN SEARCHING ALL OVER AMERICA FOR ONE MISSING SUPER-MILLIONAIRE!

Ed McMahon

If you return the grand-prize winning entry, we'll say...

INTERNATIONAL JACK BE IS THE UNDISPUTED TEN MILLION DOLLAR WINNER WE'VE BEEN SEARCHING FOR ALL OVER AMERICA!

THE SUPER-MILLIONAIRE SEARCH HAS COME TO 322 PALMETTO AVE. 154 PACIFICA CALIFORNIA

BEAT THIS DATE

CAR-RT SORT **CR29
INTERNATIONAL JACK BE   AEJ
FAN CLUB
322 PALMETTO AVE. 154
PACIFICA, CA 94044

WILL YOU COME FORWARD AS THE MISSING TEN MILLION DOLLAR WINNER?

Hmmm...

International Jack Benny
Fan Club
322 Palmetto Ave. #154
Pacifica, CA 94044

To:

The Jack Benny Times

Volume XII, Number 5   **INTERNATIONAL DISTRIBUTION**   September-October 1992

☺ ☺ ☺ PRESIDENT'S MESSAGE ☺ ☺ ☺

Jell-o again, folks! This issue begins the long-awaited interview with Phil Harris; I am certain that you will find that it was worth the wait. I also am including the first installment of a piece by our Vice President, Rex Riffle. Through this article, you will get to know more about Rex's background and the beginnings of his interest in Jack Benny. I personally always enjoy stories such as this because they reflect both the cultural diversity of Jack's fans, and point out different aspects of his appeal. In other words, the characteristic that may have sparked interest in one person may have gone almost unnoticed by another.

Hope you enjoy it all. Now on with the show!

REX RIFFLE: UP CLOSE AND PERSONAL

"Some of us are blessed, or cursed, with a great capacity for memory. I, for one, can remember times before I could walk. For some reason certain things and certain people made an impression on me that I have strongly remembered to this very day. Jack Benny was one of those people.

"I was an only child, born to a couple whose post-WW2 romance did not last long. I was born in 1947--my father was gone by 1949. My mother had already been employed since 1942 in a glass factory in Clarksburg, West Virginia. She continued to work there until she retired in 1975. We lived with her parents, my primary caretakers. They had a farm about two miles south of the little village of Johnstown, WV. I was an only child, out farm was isolated, and in my early years, contact with other children was very limited. My mother spent long hours at her factory job, and when she did get home, she was very tired and hardly in the mood for doing much with me. My grandparents had a working farm to run, there were cows to be milked, chickens to be fed, hogs to be slopped, clothes to wash, etc. There was work seven days a week on a farm.

"As a result, I was left mainly to my own devices. I developed a first-rate imagination. I learned early to read, and devoured comic books, children's books, and anything else I could get my hands on. Things changed when I was given my own RADIO!

"There *were* radios in the house--I can remember my Grandmother listening to soap operas in the afternoon while she did work around the house. I vividly remember <u>Our Gal Sunday</u>, <u>The Romance of Helen Trent</u>, etc., along with commercials for "Pink Ice", which I believe was a type of cosmetic.

_____ If this box is checked, $6.39 is due for another year.

© Copyright 1992, Laura Lee

"BUT--my great uncle Roscoe sold us a huge floor-model console radio. My great memory just cannot recall the brand name of that radio, but I remember just about everything else about it. I believe that we got it about 1953. Yes, a lot had left radio by that time, but Jack Benny was still on the air!

"I soon learned to turn the massive dial to 100 and got station WMMN, Fairmont, WV. It was a CBS station, and on Sunday nights when my grandparents' friends would come up to visit and play cards, they would go into the dining room and leave me in the living room with that great radio all to myself. I can remember that the evening started off with Gene Autry's Melody Ranch program. (Gene is another one of my all-time favorites.) Then, I believe, came Suspense, with "tales well-calculated to keep you in...*SUSPENSE!*" Some of those shows scared me so badly that I would move the couch out from the wall and get behind it to listen. But then it came on like a breath of fresh air--Don Wilson's booming voice, after the few bars of "Love in Bloom"...THE JACK BENNY PROGRAM!

"Even to a young boy from the hills of West Virginia, Jack Benny on the radio was a person who was very easy to get to know. I soon learned all about him, and all of the other characters on the program. They all became very real to me in a very short time. Some of the routines were priceless--I can remember almost getting hysterical when Jack was at the local public library and meets Don and the Sportsmen. He's already had a run-in with the librarian about the noise, and tells the Sportsmen to whisper, causing them to break into a very loud version of the song Whispering. The resulting pandemonium was hilarious. I remember laughing so hard that my mother came in to see what was wrong with me.

"I guess I never realized that Jack went off radio in 1955. His shows were repeated up to 1958, and I really don't remember when it was that I last listened, because around that time my mother cashed in some savings bonds--and bought us a television.

TUNE IN NEXT TIME FOR MORE FROM REX!

THE ONE YOU HAVE ALL BEEN WAITING FOR: PHIL HARRIS

On August 15, 1990, I had accidentally passed the address where I was to see Phil Harris. As I was doubling back, a familiar figure, deeply tanned and clad in a purple-and-white print top and black shorts, appeared from a house and waved at me. I sat there stunned for a moment, just looking at him. I had been waiting for this moment for *years*. He motioned for me to park at the side of the house, which I recovered my senses enough to do. Phil greeted me as warmly as an old friend, and I immediately felt comfortable and welcome. As I sat in a huge rocking chair (feeling almost a bit like Lily Tomlin's "Edith Ann"), I regarded the walls, covered almost to capacity with photos, mementos, a gold record, and other memorabilia. Yes, there were several bottles of wine and spirits scattered around, but many appeared to be more for decoration than consumption. One of the first things that Phil said to me was (this is from memory, not tape), "You know, I don't drink nearly as much as they said I did on the show! If I drank that much, I couldn't stand up." I queried that he wasn't a complete teetotaler, though. "No," he replied, "but that was one of the keys to the show to take the person's characteristics and just make them 'larger than life', exaggerate them."

The interview did not have a formal beginning, in fact, I would not even call it an interview per se. It was more just spending a couple hours talking about this and that. As always, I will transcribe my tape verbatim; just know that this is a more casual, free-flowing chat, which is probably all to the good! The tape starts with Phil talking about his practice of saving the show scripts, which were later donated:

PH: Well, you were supposed to throw the script up on the desk. For some reason or another, don't ask me why, it isn't my habit, but I'd stick mine in my pocket. And I gave them sixteen years, all leather bound, of 39 shows in each year. Sixteen years, and I gave them to the Bing Crosby Library quite a few years ago.

L: Where is that?

PH: Gonzaga University. It's in Spokane, and they have a beautiful library for Bing in there. Then for seven years that Alice and I had our program, I have those and also have the acetates you know, we eventually put them on tape because there was no tape then, and I have those in our library that we have in my hometown of Linton, Indiana. So I'm very proud of that, because...if they were left, if Jack kept all the scripts, I imagine that he did...

L: Yes, he donated them to UCLA in 1968...

PH: Have you talked to Irving Fein?

L: ...Yes, I've talked with him several times...I was hoping to get together with him when I came out here, but he was having an operation on his eye [E.N.: The operation went very well, and Irving is...well...fine!]...

PH: Well, he's about the only one alive now...He's with George Burns now...George is a very nice fellow...Now what are you collecting this material for?...

L: I'll transcribe the interview in our newsletter, and the tapes will go into the tape library.

PH: You have a library, too?

L: Yes, it's exclusively audio tapes, but we're trying to branch out into video...Oh before I forget, George Balzer has been trying to reach you. I was at his house yesterday.

PH: ...Well, I'm here everyday. Of course I've been in the hospital, I had a little problem, but I'm all right now. But I think, you know, when I first met Jack Benny was in 1933. I was staying at the Essex House, and he was staying there. And I had my own program then, too, I was on for Cutex nail polish, I was with J. Walter Thompson. In fact, I was on it for something like 78 weeks, and he was kind of in between shows because it had been when he was on for [Canada Dry], and they didn't like the idea of his format, which was kidding the product. [E.N.: This bears breaking for a moment to refresh your memories as to the commercial that sparked the ire of Canada Dry, and produced one of the very first funny commercials: "While walking through the desert, I came across a caravan of explorers who had been lost in the Sahara for six weeks. Their water supply had been exhausted a long time ago, and they were all dying of thirst. Quickly, I rushed to them and gave each one a bottle of Canada Dry, *and not one of them said it was a BAD drink!*"] And then I think he went from there to Chevrolet, and then [after a brief time with General Tire]...naturally he went to Jell-o. And what happened was that I was on a circuit at that time, and my contract ran out with J. Walter Thompson, so I was playing like the national hotel chain, which, at that time, was run by a man by the name of Ralph Pitts. In other words, he had the New Yorker in New York, the Netherland Plaza in Cincinnati, the Adolphus in Dallas, the Roosevelt in New Orleans, and then the Hollywood in Galveston, and right back around. I'm in New Orleans, and I get a call from George Burns, and George Burns wanted to know if I had a program. I said "No, my program, I just finished with it." And he said, "How would you like to go on with me?" I said, "Well, I'm under contract, but I'll see if I can get away." So I managed to get away, but in the meantime, by the time I brought my band and got out here, Music Corporation, for some reason or other, had kind of messed around some kind of way and they'd given it to Wayne King. So I found myself back on the coast without a job. Mary and Jack and I had become very good friends, in fact I was there when they adopted Joanie, their little baby...I was invited to the Trocadero, which was one of our top spots at that time, by Jack and Mary and during the conversation, he said to me..."What program have you got this year?" I said, "I don't have one." He said, "Well, you're with me." That's the way it happened....[E.N.: Phil's first appearance on Jack's show was October 4, 1936.]....When we were in New York, Mary happened to [hear a record] of Dennis, so I went over to the Bronx, or wherever it was, and I had dinner with the McNulty's, and that's when Dennis came with us [E.N.: Dennis' debut was on October 8, 1939]. Now as far as Eddie Anderson [goes], Eddie Anderson was working in a place called Sebastian's Cotton Club, and a very good friend of mine because we musicians all used to hang out there because they had a great band there called Les Heidt [sp?]. That's where Armstrong, Louie, and all the top black people used to come to play. So naturally, we musicians hung out there. Well, Rochester had an act with a guy, if I remember correctly, it was a comedy act, something like Anderson and Bloomfield, or something of that order. But anyway, Jack was looking for this black comedian, you know, that was supposed to have been a porter on the Chief. But I told Rochester, because we had two or three people try out, and naturally they were well-educated, they were all pronouncing their "ing"s and "*cahn't*"s and "*shan't*"s and I told Eddie, I said, "Look, that's not what Mr. Benny wants. Mr. Benny wants a real good Southern black man that talks that way." So Rochester tried out and he got the job, and...he and I were very close, and I think that I was the first one, I'm *sure* that we were the first ones that got him into a white hotel, and that was in St. Louis, Missouri, and...we took him in with us, and the week after that we heard that Marian

Anderson, the big opera star, came in and tried to get in the hotel and they wouldn't let her. She had to sleep in the Pullman or something, and she blew the whistle on Rochester. She said that Rochester got in, and you don't let me in...but that's how tough it was for those people that far back. And I can remember when I first took Eddie, Rochester, into a top restaurant. I was in Seattle in a place called Ripley's or something, because in those days, I mean, it was kind of tough. They went mostly to Chinese restaurants in those days. So all those things, but I think one of the most amazing things that happened, it'll never happen again, is that on Sunday, if you didn't stop the picture in the movie house and put on Jack Benny, they wouldn't have anybody. Or Amos 'n' Andy. Just those two. And I think one of the most interesting events that ever happened was when he left [General Foods] and went to Lucky Strike. Now in those days, when you went to a cigarette program, it was a market death because all cigarette programs were using whoever was hot, even bands or anybody that was hot, they'd use them for 13 weeks, and then maybe 26 weeks, you know. So at that time, we were broadcasting from Sunset and Vine--that's before Burbank--and Jack and I were very close because, like I said, he didn't find me, I had a job before and we became very close. And he came in one morning and I met him in the parking lot, and he says, "We're leaving Jell-o." Well, now, that's like leaving your mother, you know...because it was like Pablum, you know Pablum had never advertised. I wrote a letter one time asking about Pablum, and you'd never heard Pablum advertised on the air--they don't have to. Well, Jell-o's a household word, you know what I mean...So he said, "We're leaving Jell-o." I said, "Jack, please, please...where are you going?" He said, "We're going on for Lucky Strike." I said, "Oh my God! How can this happen? How can you possibly?" He looked at me and said, "We have to." I said, "What do you mean we have to?" He said, "They can't make Jell-o fast enough now!" Can you imagine?

L: It also was during the war. [E.N.: General Foods moved Jack off Jell-o in 1942 due to a combination of sugar rationing and high demand for Jell-o. The following October, Jack started for Grape Nuts, also under the General Foods banner. Jack did his last show for General Foods on June 4, 1944, and moved to the American Tobacco Company (Lucky Strike) on October 1, 1944. In his biography of Jack, Irving Fein attributed the impetus of this change to Jack himself, seeing that five different sponsors had made him offers of more money (as Phil indicates below). The ATC was chosen because their President, George Washington Hill, had "agreed to hire the Steve Hannagan publicity office to publicize the program", and that "Jack felt [they] would be instrumental in bringing his show back to the number one spot again in the Hooper ratings." OK...enough of my aside.]

PH: He said, "I have no chance of ever getting any more money." You know what I mean?...However, that's another smart move, or was a great move of Jack Benny, you know. We were all exclusive. We couldn't work anywhere else without his permission. Like I say, he was very, exactly the opposite of what he played, his character, because he was very generous, and the fact of the matter, when somebody he knew would pass away, it would take him two or three days to get over it. I never will forget, *many* times we had a place across the street on Vine where we used to go to get a sandwich or something, you know...before the Derby, you know. And he'd come over...Myrt Blum's the manager [E.N.:

Mary's sister Babe's second husband, and became Jack's business manager in 1936], and he'd come over and he'd say to me, "Go to Myrt and tell him to give you a little raise." You know, maybe every six months or so, because I had all three- or four-year contracts. And I never had a home before, you know, I'd always been on the road, you know, in a bus. I put sixteen years in a bus. So I said, "What for? I'm very happy, Jack. All I'm saying is, 'Hello Mary! Here comes Rochester!' That's all I got to say, and you're paying me pretty good." He said, "Well, go ahead. Go ahead and tell him I said give you some more." And he said, "By the way, have you got a quarter? I want to get a couple of cigars." He never carried any money, you know what I mean. At that time, he smoked, I think it was White Owls or something, and then when Burns started using his cigar, Benny quit smoking. See, he used to use it as a prop, you know what I mean? And the minute that Burns started, he stopped. He just didn't use it any more. I don't know why...

L: He still smoked, though, didn't he?

PH: No, he stopped smoking entirely. Oh yeah. He quit smoking for years before he even went into television, I mean, but he used to carry them, you know, when he talked, like Burns did. I guess he thought that there was some kind of similarity, because they were like brothers anyway. But he was something else, you know. He liked me. I used to go in the writing room...of course, you know, all the credit goes to Morrow and Beloin [E.N.: Bill Morrow and Ed Beloin worked with Jack from 1936 to 1943.]. You see, they did the bear [Carmichael], they did the guy in the safe, you know, down in the basement [E.N.: I assume this means the gas man who was eaten by Carmichael, as the vault did not debut until 1945.], they did the cheap bit, they did the Rochester bit, everybody else played off of that. Beloin and Josefsberg and Tackaberry and those guys. The only guy that he used to bring in right at the first when Morrow and Beloin were the only writers, he used to bring in Boasberg [E.N.: Al Boasberg had supplied Jack with some jokes for vaudeville starting in 1926, and had written many one-liners for Jack during his very early radio days when his character was more of an emcee. Boasberg went on to also write for the Marx Brothers.], and Boasberg would sit with his raincoat on...and he used to bring him in on Sunday, and all he would do is sit there and listen to us run through the program, and then he'd punch it up, two or three gags, that's all.

More with Phil Harris coming up soon!

♪♩♪♩♪♩♪♩♪♩♪♩♪♩♪♩♪♩♪♩♪♩♪♩♪♩♪♩♪♩♪♩♪♩♪♩

Please send all questions, comments, additions or corrections to:

Laura Lee, c/o International Jack Benny Fan Club Offices
322 Palmetto Avenue, #154, Pacifica, California 94044   (415) 355-3723

Please friends, send no bombs.

 FAN CLUB

International Jack Benny
Fan Club
322 Palmetto Ave. #154
Pacifica, CA 94044

THE JACK BENNY TIMES

Volume XII, Number 6   **INTERNATIONAL DISTRIBUTION**   November-December 1992

How about some holiday J-J+B:
Jessell, Jolson, and Benny!

☺ ☺ ☺ PRESIDENT'S MESSAGE ☺ ☺ ☺

Jell-o again, folks! Hope that you all had a good holiday season. Had some interesting things happen since the last time we talked: spent Thanksgiving weekend in Monterey/Carmel (and petted a RAY at the aquarium! Neat!), spent the holiday back in the way-backs in Indiana (and had a smashingly good time, amazingly enough), became engaged on New Year's Eve (in San Francisco...not Indiana), and contracted chicken pox (blech!). These things are not related to each other in any way...I hope! Those of you that know me fairly well are now marvelling that the eternal bachelorette has become engaged (and those who aren't marvelling are probably deservedly laughing). Will just give you the basics so as not to take up too much space here: his name is Danny Leff, we both work at Quintiles (where, obviously, we met), his parents are both moderate Jack Benny fans (and he's learning quickly, but likes Rochester best of all), and we have not set a date (but it will be a while due to the financial demands a wedding makes). Want more info? Let me know. Nuff said. The only good thing about chicken pox (which I am in the depths of now) is that it allows me to stay home and get the Times done.

I find this next thing so much fun that I just have to share it with you. Member Margie Jones (nee McKee) was paging over a recent issue of the Times, when she noticed that she had something in common with two other members: Bob Garland and Alvin Post. All three of them are from the Hoover High School class of 1949 from Glendale, California! Guess that shows that they had taste as well as class...

A new entry to our tape trading list:

Stephanie Bonifant, 1807 West 14th Street, Ashtabula, Ohio 44004

Stephanie moved recently, so if you sent her a letter at the Georgia address and not received a response, please write her again.

Now on with the show!

REX RIFFLE: THE TELEVISION YEARS AND BEYOND

(E.N.: In our last episode, it was 1958 and Rex's mother had just bought a television...)

"Yes, I know that Jack had already moved to TV, but, to me, it just wasn't the same. Even though I had seen pictures of Jack and the entire cast, when I saw them on television they

_____ If this box is checked, $6.39 is due for another year

© Copyright 1992, Laura Lee

just didn't look like they should. Something was missing. I believe that it was my imagination of the show. However, I did watch occasionally, but I just didn't have the eagerness for it like the radio show. Plus, I had to move on to other things.

"I graduated high school in 1965. The farm was now gone, lost to coal developers who destroyed the house, fields, and the entire landscape in their frantic rush to get at that dirty black rock. Neither of my wonderful grandparents lasted long after that. I went to the military, and it took until 1972 for me to enter college and get a degree to teach social studies in the public schools of West Virginia.

"I was first married in 1973, my oldest daughter, Molly, was born in 1975. It was about that time that television, to me, was becoming less and less entertaining. Molly loved to visit her grandmother who has always lived in Johnstown, and who has subscribed to the Good Old Days magazine for over 20 years. I happened to pick up one of those magazines and saw an ad in the back for cassette tapes of old-time radio shows. It came as a shock to me that the old shows had been saved. I had figured that once they were broadcast they just went out into outer space, lost forever. I was very pleasantly surprised to find that most had been recorded.

"I wrote to the dealer. I asked him if he had any of The Jack Benny Program.

"The rest is radio history. I have been collecting Jack's shows ever since. My son Paul arrived in 1981, and then another marriage (a much better one) brought another daughter, Emily, in 1988. All three of my kids can tell you about Jack Benny. From infancy each of them have heard Jack's voice, Mary's voice, Phil's voice, Dennis' voice, Rochester's voice, and his truly, Don's voice.

"Jack has always been part of my life, even to the point that I didn't even realize it. I think I picked up some of his character's traits! I once risked life and limb on a dark, busy street, dodging traffic to pick up a smashed roll of pennies that someone had dropped. I sat up until 3:00 A.M. on a Sunday morning just to see The Horn Blows at Midnight. Yes, I stayed awake through the entire thing. I was really surprised at the plot. All those years I thought it would be about automobiles. Seriously. I made a big hit at a party once by saying, "I don't know where Mom is, but I got pop on ice." The folks there thought it was really funny. (Thank you, Phil Harris.)

"I really do believe that Jack would be greatly pleased to know that, though he's been gone for over 18 years, he is still bringing laughter and joy to those of us who are intelligent enough to appreciate it.

"I think it would be a good idea for more of you folks to write to the Times and share your enjoyment of Jack and the gang with the rest of us. I would really like to know if and how many of you were lucky enough to see Jack in person. Or if you have met any of the cast. Also, what are your favorite stories, situations, routines, etc. Plus, do you have shows to trade, any information that you might need, etc., etc., etc.?! Please feel free to write to me, and I will see to it that Laura puts it in the next available Times...or I'll send her a bomb.

"Write to: Rex Riffle, 1 Kepner, Buckhannon, West Virginia 26201-2117. Good night, folks!

YOU *DO* KNOW!

Frank Pozzuoli, always a marvelous repository of information, alerted me to the fact that Who Was That Lady? was being broadcast late on a Saturday night on TNT. Jack's cameo role goes thusly: Dean Martin is a writer for CBS, and he is walking through the studios with friend Tony Curtis.

C:	That's President Eisenhower!	Man:	Hey Mr. Cosgrove!
M:	(To "Eisenhower") Hi Sam!	Jack:	Yes?
"Sam" waves at Martin		Man:	Go make up those two extras in Studio B.
C:	Sam?!?!		
They walk a bit further		Jack:	Yes, sir.
C:	He looks like Jack Benny.	C:	Jack Benny, huh?
M:	It *is* Jack Benny.	Martin shrugs	
Man approaches Jack			

The scene occurs early in the movie, so if it is on late and you do not want to see the whole film, you need not lose an inordinate amount of sleep. Overall, I would say that if you like a somewhat more muted version of the Martin/Lewis pictures, you will enjoy it.

Frank also sent an invaluable excerpt from Quinlan's Illustrated Registry of Film Stars. This listing of films in which Jack appeared (star and cameo) lists many that I had not heard of before. Will give you the run-down here of those not listed in 39 Forever (* indicates a short--3 reels or fewer):

Strictly Modern (1930)
The Rounder (1930)*
A Broadway Romeo (1931)*
Cab Waiting (1931)*
Manhattan Merry-Go-Round (a.k.a. Manhattan Music Box) (1937)
Show Business at War (1943)*
Screen Snapshots No. 109 (1943)*
Without Reservations (1946)
Screen Snapshots No. 166 (1948)*

Radio Broadcasting Today (1948)*
The Lucky Stiff (1949)
A Rainy Day in Hollywood (1949)*
Memorial to Al Jolson (narrator only) (1952)*
Hollywood's Pair of Jacks (1953)*
Susan Slept Here (1954)
The Seven Little Foys (1955)
Fabulous Hollywood (1958)*
Who Was That Lady? (1959)

Have just seen the Memorial to Al Jolson--it's good, and definitely a plus for the many of you who, like myself, have a soft spot in their heart for Jolie's way with a song. Any more information on these--particularly the early ones and shorts--would be appreciated.

And here's a question from Frank: on Stars in the Eye (11/15/52), a special commemorating the opening of CBS' Television City, there is a skit with Jack, Rochester, and the Maxwell, complete with Mel doing the sounds. Was this the first time the Maxwell appeared on television? Please let me (LL) know if you know!

§ § § JACK BENNY CLASSIFIEDS § § §

§ Barbara Thunell would like to know if anyone has assembled any scrapbooks of Jack Benny photos/clippings/etc. over the years. 8472 Delco Avenue, Canoga Park, California 91306

§ Dennis Duffy is looking for original or reproduced stills (any size) of the stars and cast of the Jack Benny show or any other old radio shows. 634 Lost Pine Way, Absecon, New Jersey 08201, (609) 652-0105

§ Dick Hill is searching for the 1-1-49 Gene Autry's Melody Ranch on which Jack was a guest star. 1802 Bateman, Hastings, Nebraska 68901

→ OTHER CLUBS ↔ PERIODICALS ↔ ETC. ←

File this in the "Well, it's about time" section. A group calling themselves "The Vitaphone Project" has organized to "locate and file in our database ALL existing sound-on-disc recordings of early sound films." The basic purpose is to locate and pair up the film and sound portions of as many early talkies/soundies as possible. (Gee, speaking of those films that we were just mentioning...) They are putting out a quarterly newsletter called the Vitaphone News, including copies of old Vitaphone ads and updates on their work. For more information, write to: Ron Hutchinson, 5 Meade Court, Piscataway, New Jersey 08854. There are no official subscription prices as yet, but a donation of $5.00 is appreciated. Check it out--they are doing (and finding) some great things!

If you reside in the Chicagoland area (thank you, channel 9) or are planning to visit it, be certain to stop at the Museum of Broadcast Communications. You've heard all about it, and some even helped with the construction of the Jack Benny vault exhibit. Member John Juvinall rates it highly. Plus, they have a positive quote from The Grand Rapids Press (my hometown newspaper) on the back of their brochure, so I *know* it's got to be good! Hours are Monday through Saturday 10:00 A.M. to 4:30 P.M., and Sunday Noon to 5:00 P.M. (just enough time to get home to catch Jack at 7). It is located in the Chicago Cultural Center near the intersection of Michigan Avenue (another good sign!) and Washington Street. Admission is free, so fans dedicated to truly epitomizing Jack's character don't have an excuse. For more information, call (312) 629-6000.

The Illinois Old Radio Shows Society (ILORSS) is offering their computer databank of OTR sources called, aptly, "The Source". As they put it, "We have computer files of clubs, libraries, dealers and private collections. We can tell you who has the shows you want to find." We have told you about this before, but they are having a little trouble getting the system off the ground due to lack of publicity. This looks like a very valuable resource, folks! Try 'em out...I probably should have them do a search for all the shows the library is missing (hmm...mental note). Pass the word around. For more information about services and costs, send a SASE to: The Source, 10 S 540 County Line Road, Hinsdale, Illinois 60521.

In Monterey I found a small shop dedicated mainly to OTR, but has branched out a little into the almost-obligatory Marilyn Monroe/James Dean/Elvis merchandise (not obligatory by **my** standards, just the public's, it seems). Sorry, just one commercially-produced JB cassette there, that's all. If you are in the area, check it out: Phillips Museum Shop, Fisherman's Wharf, Monterey, California, (408) 373-5911. And if you go there, go over a few steps and eat at Abalonetti's. They have the best clam chowder I ever ate!

Received a flyer on a video called <u>In Times Past: Radio Days</u>, featuring "segments from 75 original broadcasts, over 200 archival photographs, and classic film clips." Runs 71 minutes, but their flyer says "segmented into four parts for easy viewing." Egad...has the nation's attention span *really* become that abbreviated? And whatever happened to the "pause button"?... Oh well, I'm not trying to criticize the tape--I have not seen it. However, if any of you order it, please let me know how it is and how much JB material they include. Cost is $29.95 plus $3.50 shipping. Call 1-800-426-3812 and have your MasterCard or Visa ready!

♪♪♪♪♪♪♪♪♪♪♪♪♪♪♪♪♪♪♪♪♪♪♪♪♪♪♪♪♪♪♪♪

Please send all questions, comments, additions or corrections to:

Laura Lee, c/o International Jack Benny Fan Club Offices
322 Palmetto Avenue, #154, Pacifica, California 94044   (415) 355-3723

Please friends, send no bombs.   (You too, Rex! ☺)

Michigan Jell-O capital

By ELAINE VIETS

I can't say the earth shook when I heard the news, but it might have wobbled a little.

Grand Rapids, Mich., is the Jell-O capital of America. The city has earned its place as the jewel in Jell-O's crown.

"Grand Rapids consumed 82% more Jell-O than the average marketing area," said Cliff Sessions, spokesman for General Foods, the Jell-O makers. "People there ate 25.5 servings per household, as opposed to 13.5 servings per U.S. household."

What molds Grand Rapids into a city of mighty Jell-O consumers?

"Traditional family values are strong there," Sessions said. "They sit down to meals prepared with care. Jell-O takes time to make. You can't nuke it in the microwave and serve it 30 seconds later."

Maybe. But I have my own theory. Grand Rapids also has more churches than any other place in America. And Jell-O is the official food of the church supper. It is the modern manna, made for any occasion. Jell-O with celery is a salad. Jell-O with pineapple is a dessert. Jell-O with whipped cream and strawberries is for special occasions.

The mayor of Grand Rapids, Gerald Helmholdt, took the news with cautious pride.

"It's got to be because we have such happy, jolly people here," he said. "We like to see that Jell-O shake and jiggle on the plate."

Somehow, I can't see the 600,000-plus people of Grand Rapids sitting around watching their Jell-O wobble. But His Honor would not speculate further.

"I've got to be careful," he confided. "A few years ago, some survey said Grand Rapids was the largest buyer of rat poison. A reporter called me for a comment. I said those weren't rats, they were chipmunks. I said that tongue-in-cheek, but the neighborhoods got after me."

Jell-O wasn't always identified with homey ho-hum "family values."

In the early 1900s, glamorous actresses such as Ethel Barrymore revealed their Jell-O recipes. Young Jack Benny pushed it on his radio show in the '30s. He started his show with a cheery "Jell-O, everybody!"

Maxfield Parrish and Norman Rockwell illustrated Jell-O ads.

Rose O'Neill, the artist who invented the Kewpie doll, also did a Jell-O girl. Her ads were not saccharine-free. A 1921 ad shows a group of sweet, beribboned children being served red Jell-O for a birthday party.

"Dorothy is 5 years old today," the ad begins. "As usual on such occasions, Mama has made up a big Cherry Jell-O dessert and while Nan brings it in and serves it, cousin Betty and Peg congratulate each other on their good fortune."

I'll spare you the passage about "Bobbie's gleeful face."

But Jell-O was not an instant success. The first stirrings of interest in gelatin desserts were in 1845. In that historic year, Peter Cooper invented the prototype of Jell-O.

He called the stuff a "transparent, concentrated substance containing all the ingredients fitting it for table use in portable form, and requiring only the addition of hot water to dissolve it."

In 1895, Pearl B. Wait, who made corn plasters and cough medicine, adapted Cooper's gelatin dessert. His wife, Mary Davis Wait, gave it a snappy new name, Jell-O. In 1897, the first Jell-O was on the shelf.

It stayed there. The public was not bowled over. Even the official Jell-O history admits the new product "... didn't set any sales records. A few years later it was sold for $450 to a neighbor, Orator Francis Woodward."

Jell-O flopped for Woodward, too. In fact, he couldn't even sell the formula for $35.

Then, everything jelled. Woodward started an expensive advertising campaign. It had "... women with wavy curls and fashionable buns" (put your eyebrows down; buns were a hair style at the turn of the century) "... dressed in white aprons and proclaiming 'America's Most Famous Dessert.'"

Actresses and opera singers gave their favorite recipes in lavishly illustrated booklets. Suave gentleman salesmen turned up at summer picnics, church socials and country fairs and gave away Jell-O.

By 1906, the ads were true. Jell-O was America's Most Famous Dessert, with sales just under $1 million.

I've always believed that Jell-O enjoyment was sex-linked. Men liked it better than women. Anyway, the men in my family did. My brothers always asked for Jell-O for their birthday dinners. And they could have had anything they wanted, even steak and ice cream.

But spokesman Cliff Sessions said gender has nothing to do with Jell-O.

"Jell-O enjoyment is not sex-linked," he said. "Males and females are not always equal, but when it comes to Jell-O, they are."

 FAN CLUB

International Jack Benny
Fan Club
322 Palmetto Ave. #154
Pacifica, CA 94044

THE JACK BENNY TIMES

Volume XIII, Number 1   **INTERNATIONAL DISTRIBUTION**   January-February 1992

☺ ☺ ☺ PRESIDENT'S MESSAGE ☺ ☺ ☺

Jell-o again, folks! Well, the only comment I will make here is an apology for a misspelling in the September-October issue. Phil Harris mentioned the name of Les Hite, and I spelled it "Les Heidt" (as in Horace Heidt). To be perfectly honest, when I was transcribing the tape and came to that name, I stopped the tape and chewed on my finger for a while. Know that I have 78s of both Horace Heidt and Les Hite, but I just could not recall the correct spelling of Les' last name. Further, pretty much my entire record collection is still in Indiana (and will be for the foreseeable future), and I could not access it for the spelling.

I am always obsessive/compulsive about the accuracy in this newsletter (as far as the documents at hand can help me), and I am glad to know that such accuracy is appreciated (as evidenced by the barrage of letters I got correcting the spelling of Les Hite's name). Sorry! So now I'll save any other comments for a later time so that you can have just that much more of the Phil Harris interview. Now on with the show!

MORE WITH...YOU KNOW WHO!

(We rejoin our conversation where Phil was relating about Jack working with his writers.)

P: This man [Jack], as I started to say a few moments ago...they had office hours. They'd go to work when he was there. It's not like it is now. Two writers took this piece home, and two writers took that piece home. They all sat around a desk, and they worked like office hours. They'd work till maybe 1:00, then they'd go and they could go to the health club and take a rub or a steam and have lunch and come back and work till five. Jack would sit right at the head of the table while all this was being written, and I've heard gags for me that would break the building down, and Jack says, "No, that spends too much time." In other words, he protected his characters, but he had to find something to magnify. There had to be something he overdid...if I drank that much, I couldn't lift 20 pounds. It was just so exaggerated. The thing that put Dennis on right away was at the first rehearsal, Jack said to him, "Dennis!" and he [Dennis] said "Yes please!" And that was it. But he had to find something to magnify...Like I say, he paid you so well that you didn't have to worry about a thing. Like I said before, I'm repeating myself because we were all under contract to him, but he was very lenient. In other words, if we wanted to go on another show as a guest, all we had to do was ask him...Fact of the matter is, to show you what kind of man [he was]...why didn't I go to CBS? What actually happened was when they made that move, when Edgar Bergen and Jack and Amos 'n Andy and all of them made the move to CBS, which in fact was only one block down the street from NBC, I was supposed to go with them, but I was still supposed to follow Jack Benny. So something came up--who knows--you know, I mean all of a sudden "No" they were going to let Amos 'n Andy follow him. So it just hit me wrong--you know what I mean? I mean because we would go so well, and everything was working, and I knew that it had to be a piece of conniving because you know
© Copyright 1993, Laura Lee

know when you follow Jack Benny you already had a ready-made audience. You didn't have to worry about the Nielsens, you know. You had it. So it was, you know, I mean it was too tough to give up. So in other words, and then I manipulated--or I got--a ten-year contract with NBC because I was the only thing left on Sunday night! Everybody else left! And now they were in a terrible fix had I gone, they had nothing whatsoever. But I had a legitimate reason that to show you what kind of guy Jack was, he used to put me on the first 15 minutes on his show, and I'd run through the alley then and warm my audience up, because I was going on in my 4:30 time [7:30 Eastern time]. So that's what kind of guy he was. Nobody else would have done that, because here I am doing a family show with two children and Alice, and on his show I'm loaded! You know, playing pool and chasing women!

L: I do remember hearing some shows where you are talking on the phone to your daughter, though. How was the transition made from the "loaded and shooting pool" to more of a family man?

P: Well, people...they know it isn't true. You know, they know it's just to make a joke. And then we had Frankie on our program, and it worked. And the only reason that I just had had enough and I didn't want to go into television, I didn't want to dress up in funny clothes and you know, I mean, as far as I was concerned [if I had done] Ozzie and Harriet and Desi and Lucy had done, I could have made a fortune I guess. But I don't know, I just...I was making a few pictures at the time and Alice didn't want to work. She wanted to raise her children. Of course we didn't use our girls [on the shows], those were two little actresses that we had on the program. But it all worked out, and it worked out beautifully. It was **the** most memorable [time] and the epitome of my life was the time I spent with Jack Benny. There's only one.

L: You were on the television show just a couple of times...

P: I went on the anniversary show.

L: That's right; you did "That's What I Like About the South" and Jack brought out a map. [I'm fairly certain that this was done on Jack Benny's Twentieth Anniversary.]

P: Yeah, and the other time on his anniversary, he says, "What do you think of my anniversary?" I said, "I'd spend more on a rabbit hunt than you did on your anniversary!" He didn't know I was going to say that. He used to let me [ad lib] once in a while...I was pretty cozy about it because...I was born in show business and I've been around it all my life. My mother and father were in the circuses...But he used to let me ad lib a little bit, you know, I mean that I never abused it. When the time came and I had a pretty good [line]...that I figure it's gonna play, you know. Course that's hard to do. That's one thing you can never do, and I learned it with Jack Benny--you can never tell whether a gag is going to play or not. If anybody tells you it is, because I can't tell you, I'd have a roomful of nuts! Especially seeing we were getting our audiences from off of the street, and it got so bad that we didn't know what to do because the same people were there every week.

They've got nowhere else to go, and they knew more about us than **we** did! And we tried to mix it up--we even got to the point where we were taking tickets to the colleges and everything because these same people, every Sunday, they're **there**!...And they might as well have reserved seats!...They could make the Maxwell motor themselves!

L: Give Mel a run for his money!

P: That's right! It was tough, but we couldn't do anything about it. We loved them, they were terrific fans. I mean, they knew what a gag was going to be before we got to it. But it was fun. It was great. Those were the great days.

L: I should know this, but I don't. How did the "That's What I Like About the South" start?

P: Well, I tell you, it started in Cincinnati. I never used to call a set. In other words, I'd call one tune, and while we were playing it, the people would come by and I'd say, "What do you want to hear? You got a tune you want to hear?" So in the meantime, when the tune had stopped, while we were looking for that [requested] tune, I'd see people standing on one foot, one leg, and you know, kinda awkward and they didn't know what to make of it. They'd dance together just the first time and all. So I started what we call a little eight-bar turnaround, just a little vamp, you know what I mean? [E.N.: For the uninitiated, a "vamp" is generally a very short piece of music that can be repeated as many times as needed before going into the actual musical piece. If you look at sheet music of many vaudeville songs, you will see a couple bars marked "vamp" just at the end of the introduction, but before the verse.] And truthfully, we started making up lyrics in the band, and they were risqué, you know. We were doing it just ourselves, you know what I mean? So finally, these people started gathering all around. They wanted to hear this. So I said to myself, "Well, if they want to hear it, we'll do something about it." So me coming from the South [E.N.: Southern Indiana, to be exact. But if you've lived there, you'd agree it's pretty much the South.], the first thing I thought about was food. But that's why I never had it published because I don't remember who, but I put in three or four verses, maybe five, maybe the drummer did one about cornbread or something, and somebody else...so actually it was kind of a [mix of authors], and in that way, see, when we'd stop a tune, we'd start this vamp. And then I'd get a tune and play it in the same tempo, and that would keep the music from stopping, and keep the people from feeling uncomfortable. But I wouldn't keep it too long--I'd keep it equivalent maybe to four tunes, and then when I'd play my one-nighters, I would never stop the music, because in the towns and all where I was going, they had to be 175 miles apart. And people drove that far just to go to a dance. But if you stop, then they wanted to get familiar with you, you know, and I mean this and that's pretty rough, Texas and all, panhandle and all down in where I was. So I would keep five men, I'd start with my full band and then after they'd played a while I'd put on the dixieland group. Take five out of it. Then I always had a bar set up in the back, my guys never overdid it [E.N.: Sorry to be smashing so many of your long-standing impressions here!], they could have Coke or they could have a drink if they wanted to, smoke a cigarette, and then when we came back with the full band again, then I'd take the five that didn't do it, and I'd put on a waltz set. So consequently I had music on all the time, cause in those days we had to go from like nine to one. Then you get in the bus, and drive till you got to the next town because you couldn't stop and eat, because there was only one restaurant. So if you'd eat in a town where you'd [played], you'd never get finished. So it looked like the Safeway [grocery store] when you'd walk on the bus. Everyone had their special kind of food up on the bus. But it was fun. I'd like to do it again.

L: How many from the band are still around?

P: ...Only one that might be is, and I doubt it, is the bass player. You know it's kind of...I don't like to talk about that, you know. I don't mind, but you know it's kind of frightening that I'm the only one left...

[E.N.: I had mentioned before the interview started that George Balzer wanted to get in touch with Phil, since they had not been in touch for quite some time--I had talked with George the day before. I gave Phil his phone number, and I was rather surprised that Phil immediately picked up the phone and called him. Well, no time like the present!]

P: Mr. Balzer?...Well, when they find a safe place to bury my liver, I'm gonna call you!...I'm fine, and I'm sitting here with Laura Lee and she say's you've been trying to get hold of me...Well, I'll tell you, I just got back. I went fishing in Alaska, and I went from there to the Bohemian Grove, and I was feeling kind of lousy, and I go to the infirmary and the guy gives me the wrong medication, so I just spent five days here in intensive care. He almost knocked my roof in, but I'm all right. They gave me a thing called [], way, way too much, and I was terribly...Oh yeah, so...Oh, he's got to be just about 60!...I'l be darned...What ever happened to Tackaberry?...Is that right?...[E.N.: John Tackaberry passed away in the 60s or so; cannot find an exact date at the moment. Help!]...Listen, let me ask you again, what happened to the kid, what was the name of the kid who was in Russian and was friends with Jack and me and was in a couple of shows in New York...He was like Nelson, or like Sheldon Leonard, or like Elliott...only he was...no,no not a writer. An actor...You know him well. He was studying Chinese some time, and sometimes Russian...[E.N.: Anyone have any ideas on this? I'm stumped.] You knew this guy well. Everybody liked him. He was real tall and skinny and he looked Russian...no, he lived out here. He was part of the staff. He worked a whole lot with you...No, not the Jewish guy...He used to do like if you were doing Russian or something like that...I can't think. How about Perrin, is he gone? Are you the only one left? [E.N.: Happily, Sam Perrin is still around!]...
♪♪♪♪♪♪♪♪♪♪♪♪♪♪♪♪♪♪♪♪♪♪♪♪♪♪♪♪♪♪♪♪♪♪
Stay tuned for more with Phil!
Please send all questions, comments, corrections and additions to:
Laura Lee   c/o International Jack Benny Fan Club Offices
100 Pasito Terrace, #108, Sunnyvale, California 94086   (408) 730-JACK

Please friends, send no bombs; I'm not affiliated with any educational institution.

Harris

Vi 18152 My Syncopated Melody Man/Paradise Blues
Vi 18343 Some Sweet Day/They Go Wild, Simply Wild Over Me
Vi 18398 When I Hear That Jazz Band Play
Vi 18482 There's a Lump of Sugar Down in Dixie
Vi 18509 After You've Gone
Vi 18535 A Good Man Is Hard to Find/For Johnny and Me
Br 2309 I'm Just Wild About Harry/Cradle Melody
Br 2345 Hot Lips/Aggravatin' Papa
Br 2361 Mississippi Choo Choo/Who Cares?
Br 2370 Rose of the Rio Grande/I Gave You Up Just Before You Threw Me Down
Br 2443 Who's Sorry Now?/Waitin' for the Evenin' Mail
Br 2458 Dirty Hands, Dirty Face/Somebody Else Walked Right In
Br 2552 St. Louis Gal/I Don't Want You to Cry Over Me
Br 2610 How Come You Do Me Like You Do?/It Had to Be You
Br 4663 Nobody's Using It Now/Funny, Dear, What Love Can Do
Br 4806 You Do Something to Me/Wasn't It Nice?
Br 4812 I Remember You from Somewhere/Nobody Cares If I'm Blue
Br 4873 Little White Lies/If I Could Be with You
Br 6016 Blue Again/He's My Secret Passion

778. HARRIS, PHIL   d vo B
Born January 16, 1904, Linton, Ind.

Famous bandleader, later personality in radio, movies and TV. Excellent showman, performed well on rhythm and novelty tunes in raspy, half-talking manner. Grew up in Nashville, played drums locally with Francis Craig. With Henry Halstead in mid-20s; toured with bands in U.S. and abroad. Co-leader with Carol Lofner of band on west coast early 30s. Formed hotel-style band to play Cocoanut Grove in Los Angeles. A sensation with showmanship and novelty vocals. Made 1933 movie short SO THIS IS HARRIS; later in year in movie MELODY CRUISE. On own 1934 radio show Let's Listen to Harris. Later did radio series from New York. In mid-30s had good band; could swing, featured vocalist Leah Ray. Played hotels, theatres. *Rose Room* theme. Joined Jack Benny radio show late 1936, became big name. Band played each show and Phil had important comic role as wise-guy hard-drinking musician stereotype. With show until 1946, filled in on Kay Kyser show 1944-5. 1947-54 co-starred with wife Alice Faye on long-running radio show. Harris associated with novelty songs *That's What I Like About the South*, 1950 hit *The Thing*. A natural for TV, often on in 50s and 60s. TV specials by himself and co-starring with wife. In later 60s and 70s concentrated on country and western songs, handled them well. Still active in early 70s. During career in numerous movies as single or leading band.

MOVIES
1933—MELODY CRUISE
1937—TURN OFF THE MOON
1939—MAN ABOUT TOWN
1940—BUCK BENNY RIDES AGAIN; DREAMING OUT LOUD
1945—I LOVE A BANDLEADER
1950—WABASH AVENUE (best role)
1951—STARLIFT; THE WILD BLUE YONDER
1954—THE HIGH AND THE MIGHTY
1956—ANYTHING GOES; GOODBYE LADY
1963—THE WHEELER DEALERS
1964—THE PATSY
1967—THE COOL ONES
1969—KING GUN

RECORDS
HENRY HALSTEAD
Vi 19511 Bull Frog Serenade
Vi 19514 Panama
LOFNER-HARRIS ORCHESTRA
Vi 22830 I'm Sorry Dear/I Got the Ritz
Vi 22831 Was It Wrong?/River, Stay 'Way from My Door
Vi 22832 Big "C" March/Hail to California March
PHIL HARRIS
Vi 22855 Constantly/When It's Sleepy Time Down South
Co 2761-D What Have We Got to

Lose?/You've Got Me Crying Again
Co 2766-D Was My Face Red?/How's About It?
De 564 I'd Rather Listen to Your Eyes/I'd Love to Take Orders from You
De 565 Now You've Got Me Doin' It/As Long as the World Goes 'Round and Around
Vo 3419 You Can Tell She Comes from Dixie/Where the Lazy River Goes By
Vo 3430 Nobody/Jelly Bean
Vo 3447 Goodnight My Love/Swing High, Swing Low
Vo 3488 Too Marvelous for Words/Sentimental and Melancholy
Vo 3533 Jammin'/That's Southern Hospitality
OK 3583 That's What I Like About the South/Constantly
OK 6325 Nobody/Woodman, Spare That Tree
Vs 8197 Careless/Faithful Forever
Vs 8272 Buds Won't Bud/What's the Matter with Dixie?
Vi 20-2089 That's What I Like About the South/If You're Ever Down in Texas, Look Me Up
Vi 20-2143 The Preacher and the Bear/Where Does It Get You in the End?
Vi 20-2401 Fun and Fancy Free
Vi 20-2614 One More Time/Old Time Religion
Vi 20-2684 Minnie the Mermaid/Pappy's Little Jug
Vi 20-3968 The Thing/Goofus
Vi 20-4070 Southern Fried Boogie/Oh, What a Face
Vi 20-4342 Where the Blues Were Born in New Orleans/Rugged but Right

PHIL HARRIS-BELL SISTERS
Vi 20-4993 Hi-Diddle-Diddle

LPs

PHIL HARRIS
Cam CAL-456 That's What I Like About the South (Vi RIs)
Vi LPM-1985 The South Shall Rise Again
Vi(10")LPM-3203 You're Blasé

779. HARRISON, JIMMY   tb vo
Born October 17, 1900, Louisville, Ky.
Died July 23, 1931, New York, N.Y.

Probably best early jazz trombonist. Career cut short by death at 30. Although influenced by New Orleans trumpet stars King Oliver and Louis Armstrong, veered from New Orleans tailgate style. Sure attack and execution, warm tone; still developing at death. Influenced trombonists. Grew up in Detroit, played jobs there, moved to Toledo. As teenager toured with minstrel show as trombonist-singer. Played 1919-21 with Charlie Johnson, Sam Wooding, Hank Duncan, James P. Johnson and others. To New York 1922, worked with Fess Williams, June Clark, also with Clark in mid-20s. In mid-20s with Billy Fowler, Elmer Snowden, Duke Ellington. Most important period with Fletcher Henderson 1927-30 (except for 1928 interval with Charlie Johnson). In 1930 serious stomach operation. Tried comeback with Henderson late 1930-1 but remained in ill health. With Chick Webb awhile in mid-1931, collapsed on job, died a few weeks later.

RECORDS

CHARLIE JOHNSON
Vi 21712 The Boy in the Boat/Walk That Thing

FLETCHER HENDERSON
Co 1059-D I'm Coming Virginia/Whiteman Stomp
Co 1543-D King Porter Stomp
Co 1913-D Wang Wang Blues/Blazin'
Co 2329-D Somebody Loves Me/Chinatown, My Chinatown
Co 14392-D Easy Money/Come On, Baby
Vo 1092 Fidgety Feet
Br 4119 Hop Off
Vi 20944 Variety Stomp

CHICK WEBB
Vo 1607 Soft and Sweet/Heebie Jeebies

CHOCOLATE DANDIES
Co 2543-D Bugle Call Rag/Dee Blues
Co 35679 Goodbye Blues/Cloudy Skies
Co 36009 Got Another Sweetie Now

FAN CLUB

International Jack Benny
Fan Club
322 Palmetto Ave. #154
Pacifica, CA 94044

THE JACK BENNY TIMES

Volume XIII, Number 2 — INTERNATIONAL DISTRIBUTION — March-April 1992

With Ginger Rogers, November 3, 1957

☺ ☺ ☺ PRESIDENT'S MESSAGE ☺ ☺ ☺

Jell-o again, folks! Again I'll reserve my commentary for the next issue, so we can get back to a man who needs no introduction to this crowd. Now on with the show!

MORE OF WHAT YOU'VE ALL BEEN WAITING FOR...

(E.N.: When last we saw our hero, he was on the phone with George Balzer. Also for the terminally curious, "E.N." means "Editor's Note".)

P: ...That was too bad too about Dennis, you know...Just happened all of a sudden, didn't it?...I was telling this young lady about Boasberg, you know, about how he used to come in at maybe the last reading and sit down with the raincoat on, and put maybe in a couple of gags you know...Well, yeah, but then he had two writers before you guys, friends of his from vaudeville. What were their names? [E.N.: I assume he means Hugh Wedlock and Howard Snyder, who at times worked in conjunction with Bill Morrow and Ed Beloin. Wedlock and Snyder were preceded briefly by Sam Perrin and Arthur Phillips, who wrote for three weeks following the dismissal of Jack's first writer, Harry Conn. Ed Beloin was recommended by Fred Allen, and Bill Morrow came from Chicago. Wedlock and Snyder were previously columnists, and Sam Perrin and Arthur Phillips were loaned to Jack by Phil Baker. Harry Conn was recommended by George Burns. Sam had written a few lines for Jack in vaudeville, and my memory says that Harry Conn had written some for Jack on stage also. Most of this info comes from Irving Fein's book. OK...enough of me.]....Yeah, he was one of the first writers. And then they had two guys that came around once in a while, I think, when you guys were there...That's it! Wedlock and Snyder [E.N.: Ah. Well, I'll leave my comment in for your information.]...And then they had that young little kid. What was his name? A little short guy--he worked with you guys. Goodman or something?...Al Gordon! Wasn't he a kind of a little short guy?...Yeah...That's right...I never will forget when we picked that guy up in New York, and coming out on the train he was asking me all the questions and all this and "What kind of a girl is Mary?" and "What kind of a guy is Jack?" and he said he couldn't write with anybody. You remember?...Cy Howard! Right! I don't think he wrote a thing, did he?...Twenty minutes or something...[E.N.: Cy Howard was hired for the season beginning in the fall of 1943. Three other writers began with him: George Balzer, Milt Josefsberg, and John Tackaberry. Sam Perrin joined a couple weeks later. Cy had met Jack in Chicago, and Jack hired him. Cy Howard left the show after thirteen weeks, and went on to write <u>My Friend Irma</u>, <u>Life With Luigi</u>, and Martin and Lewis' <u>That's My Boy</u>. He also directed <u>Lovers and Other Strangers</u>. All this info is taken from Milt's book, page 124.]...Hey listen, do you ever get down this way?...I'll tell you what you do. You've got my number, haven't you? And now I just got yours. So here's what's gonna happen. I had it, but I don't know what. But here's what's gonna happen. The next time maybe that they have one of those things at [], maybe we get together...Maybe I can get my guy, you know Audrey's friend...From <u>Green Acres</u>....One of my best pals...Pat Buttram....All right, it's sure nice talking to you...Well I'm glad I got you. Now I won't let you get away. I'll check in once in a while...All right, partner. Right. [Hangs up.] Nice guy!

L: [During the call I had been looking at the pictures and mementos which leave very little of the wall uncovered. Several times, my eyes had set upon a gold record hanging up near the ceiling.] I must ask, which record went gold?

P: Oh, I had...four, I think. I think that one is "The Thing". [E.N.: If you don't know about the song "The Thing", run--do not walk--to your nearest rare/used record store and look for it. It's great.]...We just needed something to put on the other side, and it was an old English sailing song that...we dressed up the lyrics....The things I'm proud of, they're in my library, are the albums, the big things are from like <u>Jungle Book</u> and <u>The Aristocats</u> and <u>Robin Hood</u> [E.N.: Disney movies]. I just finished one that will be out in November called <u>Rock-a-Doodle</u>, and it's gonna be pretty good.

L: Animated Disney?

P: Animated, yeah. But they're fun to do because they can make you clever. Make you dance and do everything...So you live in from Fort Wayne? [E.N.: I did at the time.]...Yeah, I played Fort Wayne 14 years....[E.N.: I mention a friend of his in Fort Wayne, for whom he leaves a phone message.]

L: You were mentioning about the song "The Thing".

P: Oh yeah, then we just changed the lyrics, but everybody says "What was it about?" But nobody knows what it was about.

L: It was about a percussion section!

P: Yeah, that's it. We just stomped our feet. Everybody stomped their feet. Then "That's What I Like About the South" and "Poker Club" and "The Preacher and the Bear". We start talking about people, my God, Gene Autry's got a roomful of them. I think he got more gold records than anybody living. Course in those days, you know, there were very few. One tune. I can remember when a tune would stay popular for a year. The same way if you'll notice with a picture. It will be on top for one week, and then the next thing you know it'll be fourth, fifth, and then out of the first ten. Got new cream coming on all the time....The girl that had my fan club for years and years, passed away last year, from Allentown, Pennsylvania...I met her in the Earl Theatre in Pittsburgh. She was in Allentown, Pennsylvania. Nice lady...She gave me all the stuff for the library that she had collected. Scrapbooks, you know...Alice's biggest fan club is in England...She has a couple of them. They get together in London and show one of her pictures...[E.N.: Phil asks if I am going to college at Indiana University. I am.]...See, I'm right near there. I'm in Litton, and Litton is halfway between Terre Haute and Bloomington. Southern Indiana, down around Vincennes...It's right near the Tennessee border, you know...

L: Actually, one of the Maxwells is in that vicinity. By the way, would you have any idea how many Maxwells there were?

P: I think about two or three. [E.N.: Think that three is right, as the first one was purchased to be donated to the scrap drive for World War II, and I have seen publicity photos of Jack in two different Maxwells. A member once told me that one was a 1916 Maxwell, and the other was about a 1924 Maxwell, but I am not positive of this info.] It was the sound, you see, Mel Blanc. Mel Blanc together with our sound department, two or three other guys. He was doing all the belching, I mean. So I actually don't know...When we'd go someplace, they get one. But I'll tell you, when Mark Sanders made the picture--with all due respect to Mark because he was a great genius, he did all the Fred Astaire/Ginger

Rogers pictures later--but when he showed the bear, I mean, Carmichael, when he showed the Maxwell and the [vault] down where they kept the money, we never got the laughs that we got [on radio] because, see, people had a different [vision]. That's one good thing about radio, you know, you can draw your own pictures....Does he have anything at all in the library in Waukegan?

L: There's the Jack Benny Junior High School, but just about the only major thing that's related to him is the Genessee Theatre, where you did a number of broadcasts when you were in Waukegan. [There is also a display in the Waukegan Historical Society, and the Waukegan Public Library has some selected holdings.] Also Am Echad [the synagogue co-founded by Jack's father, Meyer]...

P: Where they planted the tree that died. [E.N.: Regarding the tree that was planted in Jack's honor that died, Fred Allen said, "How can a tree live in Waukegan when the sap is in Hollywood?"]

L: ...What are your recollections of Fred Allen?

P: Oh, I like him. Oh, and that feud was one of the greatest things that ever happened. Course they used to do that, you know, when the ratings would get low or something. Bernie had a feud, too. Ben Bernie had a feud with somebody [E.N.: Walter Winchell]. But the feud with Allen and, of course they were very close friends. But they were all vaudevillians, they were all vaudevillians, you know, like Burns and Allen....

L: [The phone rings again, this time with someone inviting him to a golf tournament. He notes that he does many of those.] About how many golf tournaments do you do per year?

P: I do too many. I'm cutting down. I do a lot of them.

L: Just want to spend more time here at home?

P: No, just too much to do.

L: [Phil hands me a glass of iced tea] There's no vodka in here, is there?

P: No, you want some in there?

L: No, no...I'm always curious if people have favorite episodes of the Benny shows.

P: One show? Oh, no--we did 39 a year. I can never know, because that's what's most amazing about it. I could hardly pick a bad one. We didn't have any bad ones. You know what you call "bad", I can't ever remember when we came off of there on a Sunday saying, "Hey, wait a minute. We didn't get too many laughs." I can't remember that, because the show was so well-written. We were so fortunate, I'm telling you, Beloin and Morrow, regardless of what anybody tells you, they never improved on their basis...The whole foundation was their idea. Rochester, Kenny Baker, all of those people--with all due respect--they were all good writers, but they didn't create it...And Beloin, they tell me, this is just heresay, but back in Massachusetts he was a typewriter salesman. With all that talent. And this [where the interview took place] was Morrow's house. This is who I bought it from. Course he was a bachelor, and it was nothing like this...it was many years ago, and nobody lived up here. This was just a little hideaway in the desert, and fact of the matter is that room you came through there was a breezeway, and it had one bedroom because he was single. I planted all this stuff [E.N.: There was a lot of beautiful vegetation around the place]...but this is where he used to come to from L.A. to relax.

L: [Tape ran out, so there is a jump here] Exactly how did the Fitch Bandwagon start?

P: That started by using a different band every week. That's way before me...I just went on with my band like everybody else, and they liked it. And that's when Jack gave me permission to do that, too.

L: So basically now you're working in the golf tournaments and with Disney...

P: That's it. I do quite a few benefits...I do as far as nightclubs are concerned or any of that kind of work no more. I spent 25 years in Vegas, and I was very proud of the fact that I only worked for one man, Moe Dalens [sp?], most of the time, and I worked only in two places, and they were both owned by the same people: the Desert Inn and the Frontier.

L: Also, I know I saw you once on a hunting show with Bing Crosby.

P: Oh, I made a lot of American Sportsman.

L: One other thing, a friend of mine said that he thought he had seen a movie from the thirties where there was a fellow who was trying to impersonate you to impress a girl, and you were playing the impersonator.

P: Oh yeah, well that was a Gold picture that was made years ago at RKO, where [in the movie] I owned...an escort service, and so I saw this girl and I liked her. It was a cheap picture. And so I posed as somebody that I'd sent, but I went myself. Very cheap.

Phil had another appointment and I had taken up plenty of his time, so here we ended. You can make up your own jokes about the interview focused so much on Jack ending with the words "Very cheap."

♪♪♪♪♪♪♪♪♪♪♪♪♪♪♪♪♪♪♪♪♪♪♪♪♪♪♪♪♪♪♪♪♪♪
Please send all questions, comments, corrections, and additions to:

Laura Lee   c/o International Jack Benny Fan Club Offices
100 Pasito Terrace, #108, Sunnyvale, California 94086   (408) 730-5225

Please friends, send no bombs.

FROM RICHARD LAMPARSKI'S SERIES "WHATEVER HAPPENED TO...." VOLUME 8

Phil Harris and Alice Faye were one of America's most popular married couples when they had their own network radio program for eight years.

Phil Harris

The musician-comedian was born on June 24, 1904, in Linton, Indiana. He says his real first name is "Wonga," meaning "swift messenger" in Cherokee.

Harris's mother was a clothes buyer. His father played clarinet, professionally. Phil was raised mostly by his grandparents, who allowed him to take a job when he was eleven years old playing drums and creating sound effects as an accompaniment to silent movies. When he was sixteen he joined his father, who was working with a band in Nashville.

Phil's first job of note was with Henry Halstead's band, which had a youthful Lew Ayres playing banjo.

By the late twenties Harris had acquired a widespread reputation among professionals as a drummer and was beginning to develop a following as a jazz singer.

In 1928, shortly after he became co-leader of the Lofner-Harris band, the group was the first to play the Rendezvous Ballroom in Balboa. The following year they were such a hit at the St. Francis in San Francisco that the hotel held them over for or three years.

Their next engagement was at the Coconut Grove. By this time it was called the Phil Harris Orchestra. They caught on immediately with the movie crowd who frequented the Los Angeles nitery. Harris's asides to his musicians had a lot to do with their success. They were audible to the dancers and, on some nights, to those listening to their radios. It was on those programs that the Phil Harris radio personality, which later became such an important ingredient of *The Jack Benny Show*, emerged and developed.

His greeting "Hiya, Jackson!" soon became known throughout the country. Thanks to Benny's writers he became the personification of the jazz talking, hard-drinking musician with little education and a huge ego. He often referred to his own "wavy hair and baby blue eyes."

When Harris growled, "Oh, you dwwwwwg!," listeners knew that he was gazing at himself in the mirror. Probably the biggest laugh Jack Benny ever got on the air was when Phil's name was mentioned during a meal, prompting Benny to exclaim, "*Please, not while we're eating!*"

Phil Harris and Alice Faye first met in New York City in 1933. At the time she was the vocalist with Rudy Vallee's orchestra. Both barely remembered that encounter when they were brought together again years later by Jack Oakie.

When Alice and Phil married in 1941 after a brief courtship, even some of their close friends were stunned, even though negative predictions were rampant. She was the reigning queen of Twentieth Century-Fox, where her public image had been carefully shaped. Her studio and many of her fans were very disappointed that she had become the wife of a man who was thought of as a carousing lush.

The pair who at first seemed so poorly matched have proved their critics to be mistaken. Not only has the marriage lasted, but Phil and Alice starred as themselves for eight years on their own radio program. Her warmth and down-to-earth attitude complimented his brashness perfectly. Their attraction to each other was obvious and understandable even to those who had heretofore found Harris only flashy and coarse.

Phil Harris has been in more than two dozen movies, beginning with *So This Is Harris*, a three-reeler that won the Oscar as the Best Short Subject-Comedy of 1932-33. He made many guest appearances on television over the years, but now prefers to live quietly in Palm Springs.

The Harris-Faye home is on the green at the Thunderbird Country Club. His office is a few miles away at the Ironwood Country Club and also faces the golf course. Phil, though still interested in the game, now limits his playing to Scrabble.

His close friend as well as hunting-fishing-business partner and drinking companion was

Richard Lamparski

In March 1984, three months away from his eightieth birthday, Phil Harris said, "I've never endorsed any brand of booze. Wouldn't want to slight the others. They're all just great!"

Bing Crosby. The Crosby sons, with the exception of Gary, stay with him whenever they are in the desert. Of Gary Crosby's controversial book about his upbringing, *Going My Own Way*, Phil says, "I couldn't finish it. Maybe it's all true. Bing was very hard on those boys, but he meant well and he took care of all of them financially."

Harris never became the jazz singer many thought he could have been, although his records of "That's What I Like About the South" and "The Thing" were both big hits.

He says he has no regrets about his career, although before Robert Preston accepted the role in *The Music Man*, Phil turned it down as being "too corny to work." It was Phil Harris who suggested Forrest Tucker when he rejected the national company, as well.

Dennis Day

Dennis Day was associated with Jack Benny from 1940, when he was first hired, until the comedian's death in 1974.

The singer-comedian was born Owen Patrick McNulty on May 21, 1917, in New York City. His father was an engineer for the city. The McNulty family home was in the Bronx.

He had been in his high school glee club, but when Dennis graduated from Manhattan College his intention was to go to law school. Hoping to earn some tuition money by singing, he made a recording of "I Never Knew Heaven Could Speak." He sent copies of the record around to various radio producers. Someone played it for Mary Livingston, who insisted the tenor be considered for her husband's radio program, *The Jack Benny Show*.

By 1940 Benny was well established as the Sunday evening listening habit for much of the nation. Tenor Kenny Baker (now a Christian Science practitioner in Solvang, California) had made a name for himself as the show's vocalist, but objected to the scripts, which had him playing a likable but scatterbrained character. He gave his notice.

An audition was set and Dennis Day was one of the many singers who were called. He did not know he was being heard as a possible replacement or that the job would require comedy. When his name was called he responded with, "Yes, please!"—a phrase that was to become a familiar one to millions of radio listeners. Jack and his wife felt the moment they heard it that Dennis had the perfect attitude for the part he was to play, a good-natured schnook.

"Jack and Mary sized me up quite accurately," Day explains. "The writers did the rest. Now, I wasn't as green as they made me out to be but, frankly, I was naive."

Usually in his exchanges with Benny it was Day who got the laughs. Today when he is told by former listeners of their vivid recollections of his contributions to that show Dennis is greatly flattered but says, "What people are astounded to learn is that my part on all the programs was never once more than a page and a half of script."

Dennis Day's career was managed skillfully so as to allow him to strike out on his own as a regular on other shows and to star in two of his own without leaving the Benny cast.

A Day in the Life of Dennis Day was a successful situation comedy on NBC radio for five years beginning in 1946. From 1952 to 1954 *The Dennis Day Show* was seen on TV.

His on-the-air relationship with Jack Benny was never more cleverly exploited than when the late Verna Felton would guest as Dennis's mother. Her character was that of a pushy old lady who bested Benny in every exchange.

Dennis married in 1948 and is the father of six sons and four daughters. He has eight grandchildren. His brother, an obstetrician, is the husband of Ann Blyth (living in Toluca Lake, California).

He has narrated movies for Walt Disney and worked as a single in nightclubs. Several times Dennis has toured the country as the star of *Brigadoon*. He is still active as a lecturer, which gives him an opportunity to expound on one of his favorite subjects—the defense of ethnic humor.

After taking his professional name legally in 1944 he returned to court to have the order reversed three years later. His family had strongly objected.

Dennis Day is almost as well known for being Roman Catholic as he is for being Irish. He is an outspoken opponent of anything he considers "blue." In 1962 he canceled a $5,000 booking in Seattle when he learned that he was expected to work on stage with strippers. He holds the titles of Knight of Malta and Knight of the Holy Sepulchre, both high honors in his faith.

Dennis brought up his family in a large Cape Cod house in Mandeville Canyon. For several years he was honorary mayor of that wealthy area in West Los Angeles. In 1983, when most of their children had moved away, the Days put their property on the market for $2,750,000 and planned to move to Santa Barbara. They have since decided to remain where they are, but have sold The Old House, the antique shop they owned and operated for years in Santa Monica.

When queried about Jack Benny's well-publicized stinginess Dennis answers, "To me, he was generous in every way and really happy about my success. God rest the immortal soul of my dear friend."

Dennis Day's home in the Mandeville Canyon area of West Los Angeles is furnished with fine antiques.

Donna Schoeller

International Jack Benny
Fan Club
100 Pasito Terrace, #108
Sunnyvale, CA 94086

THE JACK BENNY TIMES

Volume XIII, Number 3   **INTERNATIONAL DISTRIBUTION**   May-June 1992

☺ ☺ ☺ PRESIDENT'S MESSAGE ☺ ☺ ☺

Jell-o again, folks! Whew...the last of three issues. I owe you all my sincerest apologies; there are many reasons the newsletter has not been written for a while. Here are the major ones: I moved in March (see end of newsletter for new address), have been searching for a new job (found one, and have been settling in for the past month), am studying for conversion, had the computer in the shop for about a month (it went down the night I sat down to work on the newsletters back in May), am planning my wedding, and went to New York, New Jersey, and Indiana. As one member put it, I always have at least one foot in the fast lane. You long-timers know this already, but it bears repeating: although the fan club may not be the first priority in my life, it is never forgotten (and I am constantly making myself guilty for not spending more time with it). Just as these newsletters indicate, the <u>Times</u> may be late, but it always is published. Thanks to all of you for having a great deal of patience and understanding--thank you, thank you, THANK YOU!

Now having delayed so long, I have a great stockpile of stuff to put in this issue. I think we will all be surprised that it is so chock full of information. Speaking of things that bear repeating, I have had a lot of questions on the procedures for the tape library. OK...here's the scoop. Make your selections from the listing of the tape library (available for $1.00 and a SASE if you do not already have one). Please be certain to select some alternates, in addition to your "priority" list. Send this list, accompanied by an appropriate number of CASSETTE tapes and an appropriate service charge amount (see below) to the ever-present address at the end of this newsletter. I then dub off your requests and return the tapes to you. The service charge is $1.00 per hour for the first five hours, and 50 cents for each hour thereafter. The maximum order is ten hours. Questions? Drop me a note. Happy ordering! Also, I have been somewhat more diligent about my attention to the tape library than I have been to the newsletter!

Also, last January or so I finally got my back issues restocked. Now there is only one problem: the list of back issues that people ordered was inadvertently discarded by my family in Indiana. Therefore, I have no record of **who** has gotten **what**. Ergo, here is a plea to all people who have ordered back issues to please let me know which issues you ordered but did not receive. I can tell **how many** you ordered, but I cannot tell **which issues you received**. Please let me know.

Now on with the show!

LET'S GET TOGETHER PART 2

The last gathering of Jack Benny Fan Club members was so successful that WE SHOULD DO THAT AGAIN! I was not able to do such a thing this year, owing to the impending move, etc. Now you have plenty of notice. I am thinking of a gathering on February 12

© Copyright 1992, Laura Lee

and/or 13 (Saturday and Sunday), incorporating radio shows, television shows, and/or movies if possible. What happens depends largely on how many people are interested in attending. (Obviously, if five people want to attend it will be much different than if fifty people want to attend.) So please let me know if you would be interested in attending such a function. Oh yes...this event would take place somewhere in the Bay Area (between and inclusive of San Francisco and San Jose). Again, let me know ASAP if such an event would be of interest to you.

♥ ☺ ♥ JACK BLOOM PASADENA CHAPTER ♥ ☺ ♥

It is the May-June issue again, and time to run down our annual Jack Bloom Pasadena Chapter list. For those of you just tuning in, Jack Bloom was a very dedicated member of the IJBFC. He did extensive research on Jack, as well as making very large donations to our archives and tape library. Jack's contributions to our log, 39 Forever, were invaluable. Additionally, Jack and I kept a running correspondence for a great deal of time, discussing Jack Benny and all other related topics. His passing in June of 1990 was a great loss for all IJBFC members; his humor and kindness will never be forgotten, and we are all indebted to him for his great generosity. (For the full story, see the May-June 1990 Times.)
I still miss you, Jack.

The Jack Bloom Pasadena Chapter is an honorary society for IJBFC members who have been active for four or more years. Below is the full JBPC membership, with members added this year indicated by 3 asterisks.

JACK ABIZAID	TOM MASTEL
JACK BLOOM	BILL OLIVER
BRUCE BAKER	ROBERT OLSEN
HAL BOGART	EMILY RIFFLE ***
FRANCIS W. DALY	PEGGY RIFFLE ***
WAYNE ENNIS ***	REX RIFFLE
PHIL EVANS	JOHN SCHLAMP
LE ROY FILLENWARTH	JOYCE SHOOKS
MARILYN FILLENWARTH	BENJAMIN SPANGLER
ALAN GROSSMAN	BONNIE SPANGLER
JAY HICKERSON	DAVID SPANGLER
TIM HOLLIS	STEVE SZEJNA
SAREE KAMINSKY	EVA TINTORRI
LAURA LEE	MARION TINTORRI
GEORGE LILLIE	BARBARA WATKINS
JAMES A. LINK	KEN WEIGEL
PATRICIA LINK ***	DOUG WOOD

_____ If this box is checked, $6.39 is due for another year.

! ! ! YOU DO KNOW ! ! !

Well, let's start off with the Jack Benny-related sightings of our own Vice President, Rex Riffle:

1. Jack has been on the Disney Channel on the Classic Comedians, he was included in the TV comedians
2. Jack was briefly on the Discovery Channel's <u>The Way We Were</u>, about the war years. Jack was shown sitting on a table in a mail room reading "I Can't Stand Jack Benny Because" letters. He says, "Here's a letter from Fred Allen. It says 'I can't stand Jack Benny because he can't stand me any more than I can't stand him!'"
3. Jack's picture was in <u>U.S. News and World Report</u> connected with an article on how CBS had lured David Letterman away from NBC, like Jack had been lured many years ago.
4. Phil Harris was on a rerun of <u>Ben Casey</u> on the Nostalgia Channel, playing a wino (of all things)
5. Alice Faye was interviewed on AMC (American Movie Classics). They showed some very early pictures of Phil, but never mentioned his association with Jack.
6. The Disney Channel (again) had "An Evening with George Burns", where George was interviewed by members of the audience (sounds like Jackie Mason's "Interview with an Audience" series), and he sang some of his great songs. He also told great stories about Jack and the tricks he played on him.
7. Jack and Rochester were shown on a health insurance commercial (briefly), along with a lot of other classic folks.
8. AMC also had a special: "Stars and Stripes: Hollywood and WWII", which featured a section on Jack.
9. (You probably know this) The sports teams of Jack Benny Junior High School in Waukegan are called the "39ers".

Additionally, Walt Mitchell had the following to say after the publication of the first installment of the Phil Harris interview:

"Did you see 'This is Your Life--The Classics' (on AMC) when they reaired Phil's life--one anecdote after another? I was spellbound! And Phil himself is such a fun guy!...You know (or could have guessed) that both Phil and Alice made 78 rpm records back in the 1930s, and Phil had a more extensive career in this field. Each of them had hits, but did you know that they once recorded a duet together? This was for RCA Victor in 1951, and the song was called 'The Letter.' Phil made his first records in 1931, and Alice made her record debut singing with Rudy Vallee's orchestra in 1933--incredible, isn't it?"

Warren Debenham has been providing me with invaluable information on Jack's availability on disc--LP or otherwise. One LP to look out for at your local used record shop is "Every Night at Eight: The Classic Movie Musicals of Jimmy McHugh", Box Office Production JJA 19825, two-record set, released circa 1985. Side 2, cut 9 is "Say It (Over and Over Again)" from Buck Benny Rides Again, sung by Lillian Cornell, Virginia Dale, and Ellen Drew. Cut 10 of the same side is "My Kind of Country", a comedy narration by Jack Benny, with Dennis Day and chorus in tow. Also look for in CDs "Superstars of Comedy", a four CD set including:

- "Radio's Favorite Comedy Teams" Great American Audio Corporation #49010, 1992 Includes the vault, "Your money or your life", and a violin lesson from Professor LeBlanc

- "Radio's Favorite Bloopers" Great American Audio Corporation #49012, 1992 Includes the vault and a violin lesson (different cuts from #49010)

Thanks, folks...keep that information coming!

§ § § JACK BENNY CLASSIFIEDS § § §

§§§ Greg Seltzer has a "mint condition copy of Jack Benny: The Radio and Television Work, which was put out by the Museum of Radio and Television in New York...It's a big 8½ x 11 paperback with approximately 270 pages. Lots of photos of the radio show being performed. Also the TV shows being performed. It has sample scripts from both, details of particular shows, and articles about Jack. The pictures of the cast at the microphone doing the show are worth the whole book. The cover price on it is $24.50 and it's in excellent shape." Greg will let this copy go for $30; grab it quick--it's a steal! 39 Martin Cook Road, Richmond, New Hampshire 03470

§§§ John Moran is seeking three Jack Benny Christmas shopping shows: 12/8/46 Jack buys Don shoelaces [Does **ANYONE** have this show? I've had at least six people ask for it specifically. Please let me know if you have any leads on it.], 12/18/49 Mary buys Jack a pencil sharpener, and 12/2/51 Jack buys cufflinks for Don. 6351 Beck Road, Canton, Michigan 48187

§§§ I was able to pick up two copies of Irving Fein's Jack Benny: An Intimate Biography in New York. The books themselves are in near mint condition. Both books have the dust jackets, which have some minor tears and wear along the edges, but nothing affecting the writing or picture. For all of you who have been asking me all these years "Where do I find JB bios?", here is a chance. Will let them go for $25 per copy, plus $3.00 postage. 100 Pasito Terrace #108, Sunnyvale, California 94086

§§§ Emma Eljas is eager to get more videos of Jack Benny. Help her out! 1266 Willo Mar Drive, San Jose, California 95118

§§§ Melvin Steinmetz has the following items for sale:
Look Magazine May 9, 1950; Jack and Rochester on the cover. $20
"The Sweetheart Waltz", sheet music with Jack's picture $10

"Mary Rose", sheet music with Dennis Day's picture $8
"But I Loved You", sheet music with Phil Harris' picture $8
"Down Among the Sugar Cane", sheet music with Phil $8
"I'll Never Make You Cry Again", sheet music with Phil $8
"The Thing", sheet music with Phil $8
"Twenty-Four Hours In Georgia", sheet music with Phil $8

§§§ And speaking of Jack Benny on video, <u>Hollywood Revue of 1929</u> is available on laserdisc as part of the "Dawn of Sound" series. According to the <u>Intra-Tent Journal</u>, "Portions of the film were shot in primitive Technicolor, and these color sequences have been restored for the new edition." Sounds sharp! Check it out.

§§§ Moviecraft Home Video has also released some JB items on video. One tape features the 4/6/58 show with guest star Ronnie Burns (George/Gracie's son), complete with Lucky Strike commercials (this show is paired with Ernie Kovacs' "Take a Good Look" from 1957) Order Number MC-93, $19.95.

Also offered are two shows with some commercials intact. One is 1/24/60, and features Jack trying to get new TV talent. The other is 5/23/54, with guest star Bob Hope and a cameo by Martin and Lewis; the sketch is called "The Road to Nairobi". Order number MC-82, $19.95. Moviecraft, Inc., P.O. Box 438, Orland Park, Illinois 60462

§§§ And MORE of Jack on video! Actually, this too is the 4/6/58 show, but by itself for $19.95. Order number 1780. Video Yesteryear, Box C, Sandy Hook, Connecticut 06482, or fax your order to 1-203-797-0819

§§§ Sheldon Mulman will pay $200 U.S. plus postage for a copy in fine condition of <u>The Great American Comedy Scene</u> by William Cahn with Rhoda Cahn, Monarch Press (Division of Simon and Schuster), 1978. 4500 Bourret Avenue, Apt. 205, Montreal, Quebec Canada H35 1X2

♪ ♪ THE TALE PIECE ♪ ♪

Gregg Oppenheimer, son of the famous comedy writer Jess Oppenheimer, recently joined the club. He is currently working on his father's uncompleted memoirs, which include the following reminiscence about Jack:

"Jack was the master of controlling the audience. He'd say a line, and then lay his hand against his cheek, open his eyes wide, and look out at the audience, slowly changing his point of view, like a comic lighthouse. And as long as he looked, they laughed.

"There was a fellow named Al Boasberg who was one of the greatest 'wild' joke men in the country, and he used to work for Benny just on Saturday afternoon. The cast would come in and read the script and then they would re-write all afternoon after they heard how it sounded. And Boasberg always came up with three or four just tremendous jokes. Well, Boasberg died and then somebody recommended me to Benny. I was at Young & Rubicam, which had the Jello account, and I had just finished writing for the Packard Hour with Fred Astaire during the 1936-1937 season. Jack put me on at about one-hundredth of the salary that Al Boasberg had. So I wrote for Jack for six months and then I got a job as head writer on the Screen Guild Show. Well, Jack Benny is as easy to write for as anyone, but this job was especially easy for me because of the way we worked and the fact that the Benny character was so well-defined, as were the characters and attitudes of all of the supporting players. It was just a case of sitting around the table and thinking of things and saying them as they came out of your mouth. There was no construction--no having to work out a premise or an idea or a basis for anything. It was just whatever you could think of that was funny. That was certainly the easiest show I ever wrote for."

♥ ♦ ♣ ♠ DIAMONDS IN CLUBS ♠ ♣ ♦ ♥

- For you Laurel and Hardy fans, write to the Sons of the Desert. They are an enormous club devoted to L&H, with a quarterly newsletter entitled Intra-Tent Journal, which more resembles a newspaper. Tons of articles and photos, and some in COLOR! Very impressive; well worth a second and third look (at least!) Scott MacGillivray, P.O. Box 501, Ipswich, Massachusetts 01938

- How about Marx Brothers fans? Check out The Freedonia Gazette. Tons and tons and TONS of tsatskes to order, from sweatshirts to cloisonne pins to statues to napkins to climbing toys and MORE! Be forewarned that Paul and I have similar philosophies when it comes to doing newsletters--that's its better to be late and have quality than rush and be shoddy. But isn't that better anyway? Paul G. Wesolowski, Darien 28, New Hope, Pennsylvania 18938

- And for the myriads of Al Jolson fans out there, look for the legendary International Al Jolson Society, which started in 1949. Their Jolson Journal comes out twice a year, and is a veritable book every time. I have heard many plausible explanations for why there is so much crossover between Jack Benny and Al Jolson fans; I know that I'm one, too! Just write "Nyahhhh" on a piece of paper and send it to John H. Treasure, 235 Arundel Road, Pasadena, Maryland 21122, and tell him Jack Benny sent you.

♪♪♪♪♪♪♪♪♪♪♪♪♪♪♪♪♪♪♪♪♪♪♪♪♪♪♪♪♪♪♪♪♪♪

Please send all questions, comments, corrections, and additions to:

Laura Lee   c/o International Jack Benny Fan Club Offices
100 Pasito Terrace #108, Sunnyvale, California 94086   (408) 730-JACK

Please friends, send no bombs.

Actors on Actors
JACK BENNY

By George Riddle

Jack Benny and George Riddle backstage at the Empire Room of the Palmer House, Chicago 1967.

"Do you really know Jack Benny?" said the lady at the front desk of the theatrical hotel.

"Well, you know, we're both in show business..." My voice trailed off as I waltzed toward the elevator, clutching a phone message. The message said simply, "Mr. Riddle please call Jack Benny."...there was the phone number of The Palmer House and a room number.

It was March of 1967 in Chicago, and I was one of those fortunate creatures...a working actor! We had been informed by the producers that we were completely sold out for our limited two week run, and were settling down for an almost relaxing fortnight in the Windy City.

Mr. Jack Benny was appearing at the Empire Room of the famous Palmer House, and I had written him a note on my hotel stationery, asking if I could come back after his midnight show to meet him. I didn't really expect to hear from him, but I figured that perhaps he might leave my name with someone guarding his dressing room, and I would be allowed entrance. That was all I really hoped for.

The elevator delivered me to my floor and I was at my door fumbling with the key...once inside the room, I picked up the phone...the operator answered. (You see, theatrical hotels like this one, have the kind of switchboard that does not allow you to dial an outside number yourself.) Trying to keep my heart from leaping out of my throat, I give the lady the number ...but before she clicks off, I hear her say, "He's going to call Jack Benny, you wanna listen?" I hang up. I must not be found out! If either of those old ladies found out I really didn't know him, it would destroy my stay in Chicago. I couldn't risk it. I put my coat back on...down in the elevator... briskly through the lobby and out on the street. **This is ridiculous!** Jack Benny wants me to call him, and I'm afraid to call him from my room!

March in Chicago is cold! Into a phone booth...dime in the slot... number dialed.... "Thank you for calling the Palmer House."...I give the room number, it rings. (Damn. I have left my cigarettes back in the hotel room.) Another ring...a man's voice answers, "Hello?"

"May I speak to Mr. Benny please?"

"This is Mr. Benny."

"I wrote you a note. My name is George Riddle."

"That was very nice of you. What are you doing in Chicago?"

I've got Jack Benny on the phone, and he wants to know what I'm doing in Chicago...I am freezing to death in a phone booth and he's probably just been handed the telephone by Rochester...(All my illusions must remain intact.)... and there he is sitting in an overstuffed chair, wearing a velvet smoking jacket.

"Well," say I. "I'm here with the National Company of the **Fantasticks** playing at the Studebaker Theatre.

"Oh, you're an actor?"

"Yes."

"Ya know, Mary and I saw that show in New York about four years ago...around Christmas. We loved it."

My heart stopped. I was playing the **Fantasticks** in New York when he saw it...I tried to be casual. "I was in the show in New York when you saw it." I had a feeling I said it twice.

"What role did you play?"

"Well, I was playing Hucklebee, the Boy's father in the original New York production...but now I'm

GEORGE RIDDLE

"A strong production of 'Desire Under The Elms' is this seasons tribute by the Provincetown Playhouse to Eugene O'Neill. George Riddle's Ephraim, the father, is the center of the evening. Hard as rock, bitter as salt, deep as the sky he would own, both majestic and pathetic, this character is the quintessential O'Neill. Riddle does him justice. O'Neill is the greatest playwright America has yet produced. Riddle is the one actor in this production who is in touch with that depth of spirit. His scenes are the strongest in the show."

Contact: George Riddle 260-8793

playing the Old Actor."

"You were the father in New York?"

"Yes."

"Are you tall and thin with a handlebar moustache?"

"Yes."

"You're a very funny young man."

I can't believe any of this is happening. I'm in a phone booth, in Chicago, freezing my buns off, listening to Jack Benny tell me that he thinks I'm funny!

Walking back to my hotel, my mind is racing... I've invited him to see a matinee this coming Saturday afternoon... and I've got to get to Albert Poland, the co-producer, and ask him for two tickets. Oh, my God! If we're sold out, how am I going to get him tickets? That's what I get for playing "Big Shot!"

I run into Wayne Martins, another actor in our company, who also happens to be a photographer.

"Wayne, you'll never guess who I just spoke to..."

"Who?"

"Jack Benny! I just spoke to Jack Benny! He's coming to the matinee on Saturday, and I'm going to meet him after his midnight performance. You want to come? Besides, I want you to be there to take a picture of me with him in his dressing room."

The rest of the week passed uneventfully. The necessary tickets were obtained for Mr. Benny and his manager. Wayne agreed to come along and be my personal photographer. And Don Babcock, the director, who was also acting... (What is that "old saw" about the doctor who treats himself, has a fool for a patient...) was also planning to attend the midnight show. Don and I had been friends for years, and often talked to each other in "Jack Benny type voices." We were all very excited about seeing him in person.

The day and hour had arrived. We had just finished our own evening performance, and found ourselves sitting in Chicago's very elegant Empire Room, awaiting the magic hour.

There was so much excitment at the theatre about the whole thing, that both David Cryer and Albert Poland, co-producers of our show, had decided to treat the entire cast to a night out on the town, and so the whole evening wasn't even costing us anything! It occurred to me later, that Jack Benny's reputation for thrift had rubbed off on me... and that only added to the thrill.

Everything was right. Wayne was on my left with his camera. Babcock was on my right talking to me like Jack Benny. We were ready.

The show opened with an Italian tenor, Frankie Fanelli, He did twenty minutes. He was good. I felt sorry for him because the room was packed, and not one person was there to hear him sing! He finished his set, and the MC announced, "The Empire Room of the Palmer House is proud to present Jack Benny." The band played several bars of **Love In Bloom**, and the spot light awaited his entrance. No Jack Benny.

Again the MC made the announcement. "The Empire Room is proud to present Mr. Jack Benny." Still no Jack Benny.

A third time the MC comes forward, "Presenting: Mr. Jack Benny!"

That famous face appears, "I **heard** you!"

That was all it took. The entire audience mostly over 39, jumped to their feet. The whistles. The screams. Cheers. They stamped their feet. They applauded! I've never heard an ovation like it in my life. He entered through the audience, swinging his arms and walking that silly walk he was so famous for. He had arrived.

An hour and forty minutes later, after three encores, it was over. I was drained. Exhausted. I had been entertained by the master.

Wayne and I weaved our way through the sea of people on the dance floor toward his dressing room. I checked to see if Wayne still has the camera. He did. I had left nothing to chance. I had personally bought the film the day before, and finally we were waiting outside in the hall. His dressing room door was open, and the man and woman talking to him had their backs to us. Mr. Benny looked up, saw us standing there... "George?" he asked.

I nodded. He had remembered my name.

"I'm glad you enjoyed the show, but a friend of mine is waiting to

"GEORGE RIDDLE plays Henry, the motheaten old actor with a BLEND of SHAKESPEARE and MARK TWAIN, and who said there were no great comic actors anymore."
(Contact: 260-8793)

see me..." I looked around, there was just Wayne and I, both sporting large handlebar moustache and blue blazers (looking like a modern version of the Smith Bros.) He must have been referring to me! He just told those people that I was his friend! Wayne was fiddling with his camera... I tried to look casual.

"Wayne, that camera better work or I'll break both your legs!" I whispered through clenched teeth ... and suddenly I was talking to Jack Benny. I noticed little things, like the fact that he had freckles on the back of his hands... he was shorter than I. He was such a giant out there on stage, it just never occurred to me that I was taller.

Wayne tells me that we talked for ten or fifteen minutes... and he wants to know what we talked about. He had some trouble with the camera, and only got two shots.

I can't remember! I had been so awe-struck that my memory of the actual conversation was nil... I think he did most of the talking ...asking me questions about myself. What the hell was Jack Benny doing interviewing me? It was a night I'll never forget... I know it happened, because I've two pictures of me standing and talking to him in his dressing room.

In two years I'll be 39... maybe I'll be thirty-nine for a while. I've always loved Jack Benny.

International Jack Benny
Fan Club
100 Pasito Terrace, #108
Sunnyvale, CA 94086

THE JACK BENNY TIMES

Volume XIII, Numbers 4-6   **INTERNATIONAL DISTRIBUTION**   July-December 1993

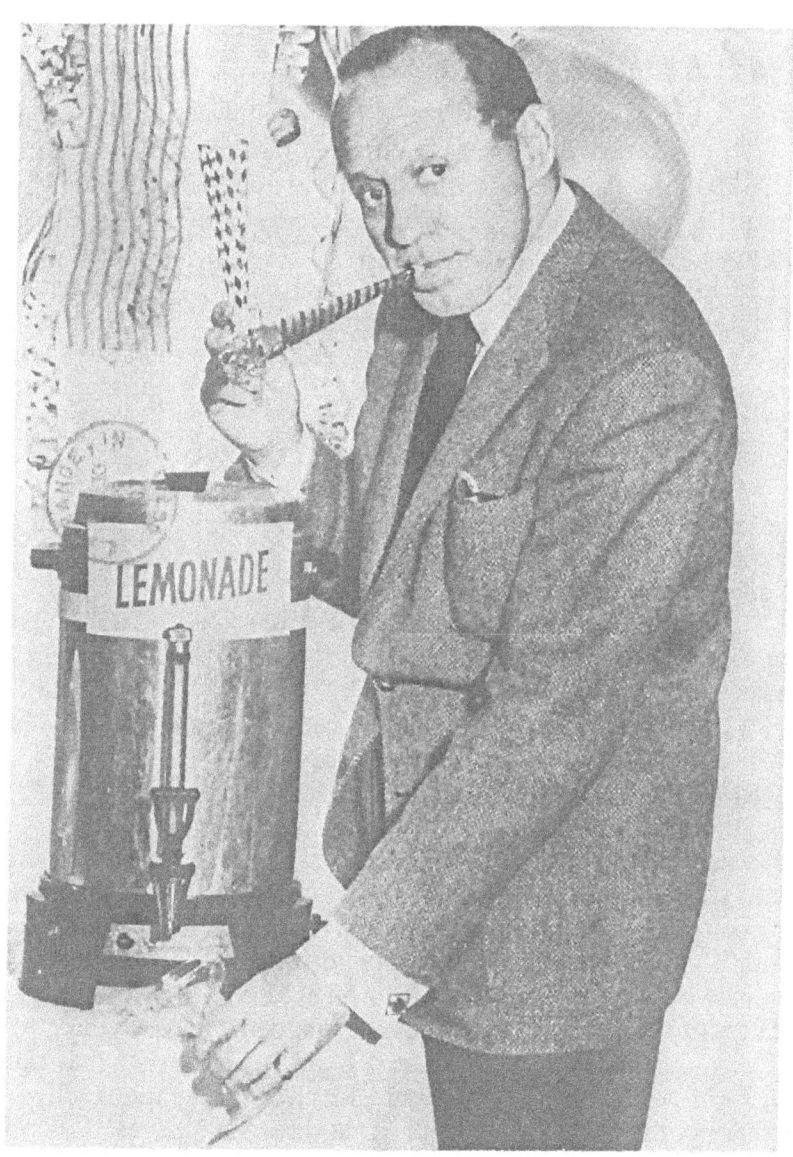

Happy 100th, Jack! - your fans

☺ ☺ ☺ PRESIDENT'S MESSAGE ☺ ☺ ☺

Jell-o again, folks! In the interest of time, I am combining the last three issues of 1993 into this one mega-issue to commemorate

JACK BENNY'S 62ND 39TH BIRTHDAY!!!

Also known as his 100th birthday... OK...for all the purists out there (of which I, admittedly, am one) it is 47th 39th birthday, as the "first" time he turned 39 was on the February 15, 1948 program. Jack thinks that everyone has forgotten his birthday, when they all were planning a surprise party for him. Mary orders a cake with 39 candles on it in the shape of a question mark. The previous year (2-16-47), Don brings a cake with 38 Lucky Strikes on it. Ergo, Jack was actually 54 when he turned 39. (Side comment: this answers a question for all you Letterman fans, since honorary member Tony Butala has been claiming for a while that he is "as old as Jack Benny was when he turned 39.") Am hoping to get these postmarked on the 14th; will jump up and down on my printer to rush the order.

Now for a little personal information: contrary to popular opinion, I AM NOT YET MARRIED. Thank you for all your good wishes--they are greatly appreciated. The wedding is in May, and is going to be, against the average, a comparatively small affair with family and close friends. Eat your hearts out--I was running around San Francisco earlier this evening doing errands for it--cruising across the Bay Bridge (always beautiful), around Van Ness and up and down Haight, and finally just outside of Golden Gate Park with my window down enjoying the lovely evening. Which brings me to comment that I hope that all members are well in light of the difficult situations all over the country: namely, the bitter wintery weather across a large part of the country, and all our members down in Los Angeles with the earthquake. Vice President Rex Riffle reported an air temperature of -44°F...BRRRRR!

And for the excuses of why no one has heard from me in so long--I'll try to be brief. The "new job" that I started in June was running me 12 to 14 hours a day, and then laid me off in October (long story). I still have not secured a permanent job, but a month and a half after the layoff, began working in a temporary position in Walnut Creek. Check it out on a map...I commute over 100 miles a day, and it takes about 2 hours one way by mass transit. My weeks are a write-off, and my weekends are jammed with everything I didn't do during the week. Every time I go to write letters, I am so exhausted that nothing would be coherent. So I will do the best I can; please, as always, be patient. My sincerest thanks. Also I know that I put the wrong date on the first three 1993 issues. I did not use the same covers, I just forgot to change the year on the template.

Enough of this, let's get to the real stuff. Just this evening I received a message that there is something happening in Waukegan in conjunction with Jack's birthday, but I don't have any

© Copyright 1994, Laura Lee

information on it. Would hold the newsletter, but then it wouldn't get out on the 14th. So we'll fill you in on it next time.

Now on with the show!

→→ LET'S GET TOGETHER, PART 2 ←←

Originally intended for this to happen the weekend of Jack's birthday, but that's obviously out of the question now. **How about February 27th at 4:00 P.M.?** I choose this date/time for several reasons: it is still in the same month as Jack's birthday, it is a Sunday and therefore compatible with different religious and business obligations, and 4 P.M. would have been when Jack and the gang did the show for the east coast, since 4 here is 7 there. I would give more notice for anyone electing to come in from out of town, but I think that this is going to be just a small, informal gathering anyway. **Please call me at: (408) 730-JACK** *as soon as possible* **if you would like to attend.** Then based on the number of attendees, I will select an exact place and notify all interested parties.

HAPPY BIRTHDAY, JACK!

In commemoration of Jack's 100th birthday, here is a brief summary of Jack's parentage and birth circumstances. This information is taken from the four major biographies on Jack (in author alphabetical order): Sunday Nights at Seven by Jack and Joan Benny; Jack Benny by Mary Benny, Hilliard Marks, and Marcia Borie; Jack Benny: An Intimate Biography by Irving Fein; and The Jack Benny Show by Milt Josefsberg.

Jack's paternal grandfather ran a tavern in a shetl (in either Russia or Lithuania, near the Polish border), and saved money for nearly ten years so that his son, Meyer Kubelsky, born in 1869, could travel to America to escape the unceasing problems Jews in that area were experiencing. However for whatever reason, the government denied Meyer the right to leave the country; thus he was smuggled out of the country at the bottom of a shipment of bottles, similar to the many Jews that escaped at the bottom of a load of hay (which Al Jolson and his family did). Travelling to Hamburg and then boarding a ship to America, after several weeks Meyer entered the country through Ellis Island.

His father had supplied the names of friends in Chicago, where Meyer journeyed to settle. After working twelve-hour days in a sweatshop and learning to read and write English at night, he eventually saved enough money to purchase a horse, wagon, and an assortment of household goods to peddle throughout the towns from Chicago, Illinois to Kenosha, Wisconsin. Keeping the laws of kashruth (kosher) was a challenge while on the road (and still is), and Waukegan was always a welcome stop because of the five Jewish families there. He stayed with Solomon Schwartz, the local tailor, who sought to enlarge the community in order to have a minyon, ten

_____   If this box is checked, $6.39 is due for another year

observant adult male Jews, which is required for the practice of many religious rituals. Schwartz eventually did convince Meyer to settle there.

Following in the footsteps of his father, Meyer purchased a saloon and billiard parlor on the corner of Genessee and Washington streets in 1892. Schwartz then referred him to a schadchen (matchmaker) in Chicago. This led to a meeting with the Sachs family in the Humboldt Park section of Chicago, their daughter Emma, born in 1870, being the eligible candidate. During the three-month courtship, Meyer's profession nearly caused disaster. He explained that he ran a restaurant that served alcohol, in order to soften his occupation and not destroy his chances of a marriage blessing from Emma's family. Early in 1893, Meyer and Emma were married, and settled in a two-room apartment on either Glendon Street or Sheridan Road. Emma's parents had no money for a dowry, but did supply them with one item--an upright piano.

Approximately a year later, on February 13, 1894, Meyer and Emma journeyed to Chicago for the birth of their first child. On February 14, 1894 in Mercy Hospital, Emma gave birth to a son, Benjamin. There are several reasons given for why this was done: Chicago was simply where the hospital was, Emma wanted to be near her family, and/or she "believed it was an honor to be born in a big city."

I have no data whatsoever to back me up on this next piece of information, but I imagine that the Kubelskys stayed in Chicago for at least a couple of weeks subsequent to Benjamin's birth. The reason for this is that there was no synagogue, or even minyon, and almost certainly no mohel (circumciser) in Waukegan. Jewish law mandates that every male child must be circumcised on the eighth day of life, ergo they probably performed the bris in Chicago. Per Irving, Jack joked about this in his Las Vegas act, saying "I was born in Waukegan a long, long, *long* time ago. As a matter of fact, our Rabbi was an Indian...he used a tomahawk...I was eight days old...what did I know?" On a similar topic, ten families had settled in Waukegan by Jack's first birthday. Am Echod ("God is one"), Waukegan's first synagogue, was founded in 1901. It is currently located at 1500 Sunset Avenue, presided over by Rabbi Furtzig, and Meyer's name is on a plaque in the entryway as one of the founders. Jack Benny Junior High School is behind it.

Jack's "aptitude" for music was first discovered when he began "one-fingering" the melodies played by his mother on the piano, for which she had taken lessons as a girl. It has been said (by Jack included) that the violin was a popular instrument for Jewish children to study at that time (as borne out by the high number of famous Jewish violinists) because of its portability during progroms. Although there were no pogroms in America, Meyer presented Benjamin with a half-size violin which cost either a whopping $50 or $100 for his sixth birthday. He studied twice a week with Professor Harlow, who charged 50 cents per lesson. Also in that year (1900), a daughter, Florence, was born on September 12. Benjamin later went to Professor Lindsay, who charged $1 per lesson. After two years, he began to take weekly lessons from Dr. Hugo Kortschalk at the Chicago Musical College. Jack would practice at the front parlor window of 224 South Genessee Street between four and six P.M., looking out at Lake Michigan (perhaps looking more than practicing). Emma might realize her dream of having a son who was a concert violinist.

At some point during this time--by my estimation, around 1901 or 1902, a drunk was shooting pool at Meyer's saloon and demanded a free drink. Upon Meyer's refusal, the drunk gave him a blow to the head with his pool cue. Emma, who had never liked the saloon, finally insisted that Meyer go into another business. He concurred, and after an unsuccessful try at a dry goods store, he opened a haberdashery which was across from their aforementioned Genessee apartment (which, consequently, was located on the second floor over a butcher shop).

For Benjamin's graduation from grammar school, Meyer purchased an imitation Amati violin for $75. He then began performing more in public, charging $1.50 per engagement. Upon entry into ninth grade at Central High School, he secured a position in the pit orchestra of the Barrison Theatre (which is now, alas, gone). Benjamin never cared much for practicing the violin or school. I have always liked the story related in Marcia Borie's book by a Central classmate: "It was obvious he didn't like to study...He thought of some pretty funny ways to avoid settling down. One day, he hid a piece of Limburger cheese behind the radiator. It was in November, I'll never forget...It was cold and raining. The classroom windows were shut and the heat was going full blast. Gradually, this awful smell filled the room. Our teacher told us to stand out in the hall, then she went to get the janitor. It only took a few minutes before the two of them discovered cheese melted all over the back of the heater. We were all instructed to come back after school and serve detention. But Jack 'confessed' he had been responsible..." After failing every class in ninth grade, Jack was thrown out of school. A study of bookkeeping in Waukegan Business College quickly gave the same results.

I have also enjoyed Jack's own story of working in his father's haberdashery. A man comes in and hands Jack a dollar, informing him that "It's on my account." When Meyer returns, he asks "What did you sell, Benny?" Jack responds, "Nothing--some man just came in and handed me a dollar on his account." "So--what was his name?" queries Meyer. "Do you have to know their names?" asks Jack. Dennis Day could have had a run for his money...

Getting you to Jack's work in the Barrison Theatre brings us up to the point at which many stories start, so this is where I will end. I will note that Emma's father died early in 1915, at which time she had surgery to remove a lump in her breast. Several months later, a double mastectomy was performed with a local anesthetic (not general due to Emma's diabetes). She eventually passed away in November of 1917 at the age of forty-seven. Meyer lived much longer, staying in the haberdashery business until retirement. He passed away from a heart condition on October 14, 1946 in Chicago.

(Please let me know if you particularly like this sort of article. I hesitate to write things like this since all the information is in the books, and I'm largely sitting here with them all open and taking as many facts from them as seems reasonable. There are always little things that are in one volume and not another, and I'm trying to present as complete a picture as possible without going overboard. Hope it's informative without being redundant.)

TAPE TRADING LIST

Ellen Barker, P.O. Box 1402, Reseda, California 91335

Hal Bogart, 2029 Aldersgate Drive, Lyndhurst, Ohio 44124

Stephanie Bonifant, 1807 West 14th Street, Ashtabula, Ohio 44004

Yosef Braude, 25 Longhorn Road, Providence, Rhode Island 02906

Rob Cohen, 6635 Helm Avenue, Reynoldsburg, Ohio 43068

Rob Crawford, 2818 Altos Avenue #B, Sacramento, California 95815

The Everills, 1558 Knox Drive, New Haven, Indiana 46774

Andrew Haskell, 160 West 39th Avenue, Vancouver, British Columbia V5Y 2P2, Canada

Dick Hill, 1802 Bateman, Hastings, Nebraska 68901

David A. Howell, 1300 Kennedy Boulevard #419, Cuyahoga Falls, Ohio 44221

Tom Kleinschmidt, 26101 Country Club Boulevard #706, North Olmstead, Ohio 44070

Steve Lake, 7780 North Pinesview Drive, Scottsdale, Arizona 85258

John Malone, Rural Route #2, Wee-Ma-Tuk, Cuba, Illinois 61427

Bill Oliver, 516 Third Street NE, Massillon, Ohio 44646

Jack Palmer, 145 North 21st Street, Battle Creek, Michigan 49015

Lewis and Sedalia Pearson, 240 Ridge Drive, Marion, Iowa 52302

Michael Pointon, 11 Kings Court, Kings Road, London SW19 8QP, England

Frank Pozzuoli, 2830 Waterbury Avenue, Bronx, New York 10461

Keith Scott, 4 Bellbird Crescent, Forestville 2087, N.S.W. Australia

Joyce Shooks, 2026 Lafayette NE, Grand Rapids, Michigan 49505

Steve and Kim Smith, 1945 Coit NW, Grand Rapids, Michigan 49505

John Smothers, 22 Townsend Drive, Freehold, New Jersey 07728 (Open reel preferred)

Steve Szejna, 7806 West Waterford Avenue #1, Greenfield, Wisconsin 53220-2275

Peter Tatchell, 40 Bambra Road, Caulfield, Victoria 3161 Australia

James E. Treacy, Jr., 900 Hargrove Road, Apartment 234, Tuscaloosa, Alabama 35401

If you want to be added to this listing, just drop me a line!

♪ ♪ THE TALE PIECE ♪ ♪

From Margie Jones:

"...I just thought of a great experience I had in the 70's sometime. Don Wilson and Dennis Day were making a personal appearance at an opening of a Home Savings in Santa Ana. I had some sheet music--song: "Say It (Over and Over Again)" from the movie Buck Benny Rides Again. I took it with me when I went to see them and they [both] signed it for me. They were so gracious. Don Wilson did not look well at all, but he was very sweet--so was dear Dennis."

From Barbara Thunell:

"I worked at CBS Radio (later television) from 1951 to 1960. During that time I had a chance to see many stars, but my favorite was Jack Benny. I would go up to the sponsors' booth, try to be unnoticed, and watch the rehearsals. Since they didn't know I was there, the cast was quit candid. Jack was usually nice, but on occasion he did make a sharp retort, though not nearly as many as Mary did. I remember Jack going to the vending machine and getting a candy bar and offering to share it with anyone. He also brought (diabetic) cookies, and offered to share them. Probably my greatest thrill was talking to Jack on the phone. I was working for awhile as receptionist at the rehearsal studios when Jack called. He asked if his TV director, Ralph Levy, was there. I said he wasn't in, but would he like me to give him his phone number. At first Jack said no, but then said, "You'd better give it to me." I did, and we said goodbye, and hung up, but I will remember that conversation always.

"In television I would also watch the rehearsals, but it was not as intimate as radio and they didn't have a sponsors' booth for me to hide in. The last TV show I saw in person was in January of 1974 with George Burns, Red Foxx and others. I sensed that Jack was afraid of getting old. He came out in the audience between takes and one lady said that she was 80. Jack said, "I'm almost there. Death can't be too bad, can it? Were you so unhappy before you were born?" Jack looked tired, and this was the last TV special he did before his death 11 months later.

"When Jack appeared in Las Vegas or in the Los Angeles area, I would get to his show whenever possible. He did a theatre in the round, which was a new thing for him. He did a hospital routine that was very funny, but certainly nothing he could have used on radio or TV! He always had poise and grace, and was one of the greatest showmen ever!"

♥ ♦ ♣ ♠ DIAMONDS IN CLUBS, ETC. ♠ ♣ ♦ ♥

BRC Productions, P.O. Box 2645, Livonia, Michigan 48151, (313) 721-6070 fax New additions to listing; more Jack Benny shows on audio and video. Write for a listing

Adventures in Cassettes, 5353 Nathan Lane North, Plymouth, Minnesota 55442-1978 Video and audio (more of the latter) tapes; write for catalog. One caveat: they list two tapes from "The Best of Television: Comedy Series" (Jack Benny and Burns and Allen) which my father tried ordering from a television ad. After several orders and a great deal of detective work on the phone with the Better Business Bureau, he was finally able to obtain them. So beware of television ads for these tapes. **To my knowledge, there is no connection between the television marketing of these tapes and Adventures in Cassettes.** Just wanted you to know that you can get 'em here instead.

Norma's Jeans, 4400 East West Hwy, #514, Bethesda, Maryland 20814-4505, (301) 652-4644, (301) 907-0216 fax No Jack, but lots of clothes/stuff belonging to stars, costumes from movies, etc. The catalog is REALLY NEAT to look through. Laura-Bob says check it out.

♪ ♪
Please send all questions, comments, corrections, and additions to:

Laura Lee   c/o International Jack Benny Fan Club Offices
100 Pasito Terrace #108, Sunnyvale, California 94086   (408) 730-JACK

Please friends, send no bombs.

His trick of making himself the butt of jokes, the amiable boob, makes every man in the audience 10 feet tall.

The dean of comedy aims for family entertainment, has some hard words for sick and smutty humor, TV violence.

No doubt of it, Benny at 67 has more energy, vitality, and bounce than performers half his age. While men much younger moan that television is too exhausting to do more than a half dozen shows a year, Benny has been doing his TV shows twice a month for 10 years. This season he is doubling his load. He'll be on every Sunday night for 32 weeks. Half a dozen of these shows were filmed last summer so he'll have a chance to follow his other interests, too, during the year.

He does many benefits, several TV specials, and solo appearances with major symphony orchestras. He's done 16 orchestra dates so far and expects to tackle several more in the future. One of these was done for the Kansas City Orchestra at the invitation of Harry S. Truman. This one got the orchestra out of debt. Truman conducted the "Stars and Stripes Forever" while Benny played. (Later the former President appeared on Benny's show.)

"These concerts started as a sort of joke with me," said Benny. "But now they are a source of great satisfaction. It's hard to say just how much they've taken in. We raised a million dollars in Bonds for Israel. The profits from the present concerts we're doing run from $25,000 to $60,000 each. All the proceeds currently are going to the musicians' benefit fund."

Last April, Benny traveled to the Orient, making appearances in Tokyo and Hong Kong. He may return to the Far East to shoot one or two TV shows there.

Benny never thinks of cutting back.

"Actually my work seems to grow easier as I grow older," the dean of comedians confided. "Last season was the easiest and I expect this one to go even smoother. I'm not an ulcer man; I don't suffer all day and far into the night.

"I insist on good programs because I can't stand lousy ones. In fact, I can't stand anything second rate. And I really like to work. I told Bob Hope that once and he said, 'You know, Jack, there's just one reason you go on working. It's because you're a bigger ham than I am.' So I admitted it. I like show business. I work because I enjoy it. Nobody has more fun than I do."

A man who says he had his greatest day when he was 66 can't have too much wrong with him.

"I got the biggest kick in my life," he recalled, "when Waukegan, Illinois, my home town, named a new junior high school for me and I turned the first spadeful of earth for it. This is just the nicest thing that can happen to a comedian.

"The other two junior high schools are named for Daniel Webster and Thomas Jefferson," Benny added.

"I don't kid myself into believing I'm young. But if you give some thought to it, you can stay young-looking."

"I can build a half-hour show around one joke," says Jack. Usually he's the straight man, giving punch lines to others in the cast—like Don Wilson.

"I guess the three of us are about the same age."

This is one of the ad libs that supports Benny's reputation for being funny without his writers. On the trip to Waukegan he visited an old home where Lincoln supposedly slept.

"Lincoln was my favorite president," Benny declaimed. "Any man who will walk barefoot in the snow to return a library book to save three cents is my kind of a guy."

Once when Fred Allen had him over a barrel in the radio heyday, Benny retorted, "You couldn't say things like that to me if I had my writers with me."

But he's had plenty of good writers with him, several for a dozen years. Besides building him up as the eternal 39, they also developed his reputation as a cheapskate and the world's champion miser with such jokes as these:

"Why in the world do you give Jack Benny only one glove?" one clerk asked another, and got the reply: "That's all he needs; he never takes his right hand out of his change pocket."

Then there was the time a holdup man poked a pistol against him and gave the ultimatum: "Your money or your life."

Benny remained completely silent while audience tension mounted. When the suspense reached a climax the gunman prodded him again. "I'm thinking it over," said Jack, hitting the laugh jackpot.

Actually, this tightwad character pressed upon him by his writers has cost him plenty of money, even though it has given him many of his best laughs. He is a notorious overtipper. Even for short hauls, taxi drivers collect dollar tips.

"I don't want cabbies going home and telling their wives that Benny is really stingy," he explains.

Jack has been a perpetual gift giver and charity contributor. Eddie Cantor told of the time he invited Benny to dinner. During the course of the meal, Cantor discussed a Bonds for Israel campaign.

"I could see Jack was interested," Cantor recalled, "but he floored me when he wrote a check for $25,000. The only reference Benny ever made to this incident came some time later when he told a mutual friend: 'Don't ever eat at Cantor's house. He serves the most expensive meals in town.'"

Another Benny myth is his lack of violin skill. At the turn of the century, Waukegan knew him as a child prodigy with the violin. (Often called a native of Waukegan, Benny only in recent years has explained that he was born in Chicago. "My mother had gone into Chicago for a day of shopping," he said. "She never made it home and I was born in a Chicago hospital. But since she carried me around for nine months in Waukegan, I don't think it's

A fine violinist who's done many concerts, Benny (here clowning with George Gobel) never reveals this on TV.

Always the fumbling, fouled-up fall guy, he plays the role of Chandu the magician on show with Dennis Day.

dishonest to claim that I'm a native of that town.")

Jack's father, Meyer Kubelsky, operated a small haberdashery. He had ambitions that his son, Benny Kubelsky, might become a good violin player. On Benny's sixth birthday, his father bought him a violin and put him to taking lessons and practicing.

"I would rather have played baseball, and I had no idea how much the violin meant to my father. The trouble was that I was lazy and I didn't practice enough to become a good violinist."

Nevertheless, Benny did well enough that at 16 he was playing in the pit orchestra at a local Waukegan theater. (He had been playing as a professional violinist since he was 13.)

"It was a short step up out of the orchestra," Jack says. "Soon I had a vaudeville act of my own. I started with a lady pianist named Cora Salisbury. I didn't tell jokes but managed to draw laughs by sawing away on the violin, with the little finger of the bow hand extended while my eyes followed its movement in mock curiosity."

Subsequently Jack joined another pianist, Lyman Woods, and they toured the country. They even made the Palladium in London at the outbreak of World War I. Benny decided to join the navy and that broke up the act.

At Great Lakes Naval Training Center, a few miles from Waukegan, Benny Kubelsky was put into a revue to aid recruiting. He played the fiddle between the acts without much applause, but one evening he paused to make a few wisecracks. That did it. The audience roared and Benny, the comic, was born.

"The sound intoxicated me—that laughter ended my days as a musician and I never put the violin back where it belonged except as a gag," Benny said.

For years he had been billed as Benny K. Benny. But after the war to avoid confusion with another fiddling comic, Ben Bernie, he changed his name to Jack Benny. He worked with great success in the two-a-day vaudeville and went on to further acclaim in Shubert and Earl Carroll shows on Broadway.

While playing in a musical, *Great Temptations*, in Los Angeles, he met Sadye Marks, a department store clerk. They were married the following year and she became famous as Mary Livingstone, his radio partner, who only recently retired from show business.

"We were married in Waukegan in the home of a friend," Benny recalled. "Six or seven people were there and the cost was nil. We were married in the afternoon and I had to grab a train almost at once for Chicago, where I was appearing in a show that night."

When Joan, their adopted daughter, was married, the Bennys threw a reception that reputedly cost $25,000.

Jack's first appearance on radio came on March 29, 1932, as a guest on Ed Sullivan's interview program. The first words *(Continued on page 63)*

Try to keep this a relaxed party. Let the guests take over and enjoy themselves, *by themselves.* Keep in mind that 11's need space, flexibility, active sport, plenty of chance to talk and to be alone.

And remember: "Although 11-year-olds are not always easy to manage at home," according to the Gesell authorities, "the right kind of party usually allows them to rise to their vigorous, enthusiastic, and boisterous best." END

(*Next month* TODAY'S HEALTH *will report the Gesell Institute's research on children's parties for ages 12 through 15.*)

FOR FURTHER READING
The Gesell Institute Party Book *by Frances L. Ilg, M.D.; Louise Bates Ames, Ph.D.; Evelyn W. Goodenough, Ph.D., and Irene B. Andresen, M.A.* (Harper, $2.95)

JACK BENNY
(*Continued from page 29*)

Benny spoke were: "Hello, folks, this is Jack Benny. There will be a slight pause for everyone to say, 'Who cares?'"

As everyone knows, there were people who cared. Jack Benny and the American people have been carrying on their love affair for almost 30 years.

A short time after the Sullivan appearance, while he was starring in Earl Carroll's *Vanities,* Benny got a call to an audition—and an offer. He consulted Mary about what to do. She thought it might be well for him to try the new medium. This meant giving up a $1350-a-week job for a third of that—a fact that Benny has had no cause to regret.

Benny feels he hit the radio jackpot through a series of happy accidents. He made fame and fortune in radio and TV by playing the perpetual fall guy.

"This wasn't planned," Benny recalled. "I played that sort of a guy in vaudeville. People got to know me as a fellow who was always the victim of his own jokes."

Thus in radio his writers made him targets of the jibes of others. The people laughed and demanded more and more. He typified the timorous, ineffectual fall guy; his auto was a museum piece, he always had trouble getting girls to go out with him, he wore a toupee.

He always played second fiddle. As Hedda Hooper once said: "His trick of making himself the butt of jokes, the amiable boob, makes every man in the audience 10 feet tall and has every woman thinking that her particular small-salaried guy has far more on the ball than Jack."

His "feud" with Fred Allen grew out of his early playing of "The Bee," butt of countless jokes during his earlier radio years. But if it had been planned, Jack often recalled, it would have lasted no more than three weeks.

Jack's feud with Allen got under way when Fred did a takeoff of the old Major Bowes Original Amateur hour. A moppet played the tune and Allen commented:

"Only eight and already you can play 'The Bee.' Why Jack Benny ought to be ashamed of himself."

The next Sunday night Benny retorted on the air that he would produce four persons who would attest that he played "The Bee" when he was six. The feud was on and flourished for many months and irregularly thereafter.

A decade or so ago, the entertainment and radio editors proclaimed Jack Benny the greatest broadcasting personality of all time. (Franklin D. Roosevelt ran second.)

"For my first sponsored radio appearances," Benny recalled, "I was paid $350; for my first television show, $10,000. The only similarity between those appearances was the amount of money the government let me keep."

This was a typical Benny crack. Even in a situation which others would have regarded as exceedingly fortunate, Benny made himself once more a fall guy.

The Benny glow was reflected from many of the performers he took into his group. Besides Mrs. Benny, they have included through all the intervening years Eddie Anderson (Rochester), his valet; Phil Harris, Bob Crosby, and several other band leaders; Kenny Baker, Dennis Day, and Frank Parker, three of his singers; Andy Devine, the gravel-throated comedian, and Mel Blanc, his man of a thousand voices. Among the roles Blanc created were Professor LeBlanc, Benny's violin teacher; Bugs Bunny, and Woody the Woodpecker. There were also Gisele MacKenzie and Sammy Davis, Jr., whom Benny helped on the way up.

The history of comedy goes back to the Greek philosophers and perhaps far beyond their time. No satisfactory definition to cover all aspects of humor has ever been devised. Plato, however, said a mouthful when he pronounced: "The pleasure of the ludicrous originates in the sight of another's misfortune." Thus, Plato might have found Benny funny. Jack Benny is ridiculous because he's a liar, he's a miser, a conceited ham, and insists he's 39 when everyone knows he's well into his 60's.

Steve Allen in *The Funny Men* said: "A fascinating thing about

---

The only way to keep your health is to eat what you don't want, drink what you don't like, and do what you'd rather not. —Mark Twain

---

Jack's humor is that he makes himself consistently inferior (hence, you superior)."

Allen also called Jack "a sort of straight man for the whole world; he rarely amuses actively, only passively. His is the 'true' sense of humor . . . One will search many pages of his scripts before finding Jack taking the punch line of a joke himself . . . The jokes are on him and the funny things are done to him."

Benny's sense of timing and spontaneity of delivery have often been cited by critics, fellow comics, and the public as unmatched.

Although a battery of top writers and directors whip together the raw material, Jack does the final editing, rewriting, unifying, and polishing. A London critic once wrote of Benny: "He is wonderfully refreshing. His mastery of timing and the relaxed approach to the cameras are a welcome contrast to the restless, high-pressure technique used by some of our comedians to assail the camera and exhaust the viewers."

Another critic said: "Quiet and unflurried, he throws off a very fancy and polished light."

Benny is modest about his formula:

"We don't press," he explained. "We just try not to have a bad show. By the time some comedians do one show, I could have done a whole season. I can take one joke and build a half hour's show around it."

Then he gave an example: Recovering from an illness at the time, Benny was in pajamas and robe in his hotel room. While awaiting for cast members to arrive for rehearsal, he introduced a trim brunette in white, standing in the background, to the press: "This is my nurse, Miss Donovan. I knocked on her door this morning to find out what she wanted for breakfast. She told me: orange juice, scrambled eggs, and coffee. I called her when it was ready."

He paused a minute, raised his eyebrows, and snorted: "She's supposed to be taking care of *me*."

His audience roared. Don Wilson, his longtime announcer-comic said: "That is a routine for next year. We can use that: Jack waiting on the nurse!"

Benny is one of the great comedians who is not bound by long-term contracts. He signs up for only one year at a time.

"I don't want to be stuck longer than that," he explained, "because I never know what I'll want to do the following year. I want to keep on doing violin concerts with symphony orchestras."

Since he doesn't get paid for these, it is truly a labor of love.

"I'd never do my concert violin act on television," he said, "for that would spoil it when I traveled to the various big cities, since all the concerts are similar.

"To get through the numbers at all," he chuckled, "I've got to practice like mad to play lousy."

Benny is thinking in terms of doing summer stock, perhaps this year.

"I'd like such a play as *Make a Million*, which Sam Levene did on Broadway. Sam and I don't think alike and our delivery is different, yet almost all of his comedies would be good for me without changing a word.

"I'd like to do a Broadway play but I wouldn't want to stay in it too long. If a special vehicle were written for me they'd want me to stick with it."

For a long time, Benny has worried about good taste on television. A few years ago he warned that we were inviting censorship if TV wasn't cleaned up.

"We're getting by with murder, too much murder," he said. "We have too much horror and the showing of the techniques of crime. Risqué jokes should be banned ... Ed Wynn in his heyday was the funniest man I ever saw on the stage. And yet he never had one off-color word or gesture in his material.

"And I can't stand jokes made over human tragedy or physical handicaps, or vitriolic jokes about the president. It's as easy to get a laugh by panning the president as it is to get applause by waving the flag. It is the greatest and highest office in the world. We should all remember that and not jest about it."

How long will Benny stick to his comedy schedule?

"Only time can tell," he said. "But I think you can go year after year if you maintain the qualities of sincerity, humility, and a continuing freshness.

"I don't think anyone on the air is too intelligent for the audience. It's deadly to be patronizing. I don't ever want to thank the audience 'for letting me come into your living room.' A lot of them watch me because there's nothing else to do in their town Sunday evenings. And how do I know their set is in the living room. It may be in the den, the bedroom, or the basement.

"Anyway the audience doesn't want to be thanked. They just want to sit back and have fun—and feel free to give you the devil if they think the show wasn't good. Everyone's a critic in television.

"I'll stick around on television as long as the public and the sponsor want me." END

GETTING THE MOST OUT OF YOUR FEET
(Continued from page 51)

weaker neighbors, particularly the second metatarsal, causing strain and pain. Doctor Morton devised a leather insole to prop up the short metatarsal, much as you would prop up a short table leg.

Doctor Schwartz looks to the foot-leg relationship. The weight-bearing axis of the heel is about five-eighths of an inch to the outside of the weight-bearing axis of the leg bone. Two joints connect it to the leg bone, but unless these fit and lock securely, the body's weight coming down the leg bone to the inner side of the heel

The DOUBLE LIFE of Mr. J. Benny

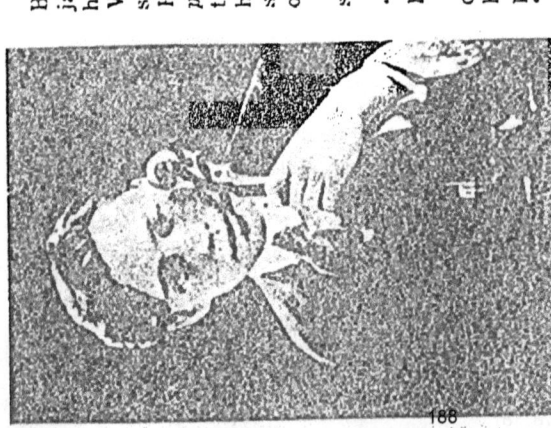

The man who wanted to be Heifetz

A long time ago, when the Jack Benny of today was still little Benjamin Kubelsky, he was minding his father's haberdashery shop in Waukegan one evening when a stranger walked in and handed Benjamin some money. Kubelsky *pere*, seeing the cash in the register later, asked his offspring what he had sold. "Nothing," said his son. "He just gave me some money on his account."

"But what was his name?" insisted Mr. Kubelsky.

"I don't know," said Benjamin.

"Gee whiz, Pop, do you have to have his name, too?"

Not long afterwards a customer came in and purchased some ties, handkerchiefs and shirts and departed without leaving any cash. "But it's all right," Benjamin told his father later, "he told me to charge it to his account. And this time I got his name."

"Name!" the old man screamed. "That fellow has no account in my store!"

Jack Benny, at 53, according to his intimates, is only a little less naive than the youthful Benjamin Kubelsky, who could be flimflammed so easily by a smooth-talking sharper. "Benny," said Ed Beloin, one of his former writers, "is probably the most unsophisticated man I know."

Yet Jack's radio self-portrait of a sport-jacketed, Beverly Hills Simon Legree, who makes Dennis Day mow his lawn as well as sing for his $17.50 a week, is taken as pure gospel by the 25,000,000 people who listen regularly to his Sunday night half-hour over NBC. Benny's mail still bristles with indignant letters demanding that he pay Rochester a living wage. (Rochester gets over $1000 a week.) Even Mr. Whiskers once fell for the Benny myth, when the WPB, a Government war-time agency, sent Jack a business-like letter requesting that he turn in his legendary Maxwell to the scrap drive.

Strangers still turn their heads when Jack lunches or dines in Romanoff's or the Brown Derby, curious to see if he will leave either a nickel or a dime tip. Benny always overtips lavishly, both because that is his nature and because he is almost pathologically sensitive about his penny-squeezing "reputation."

The truth is, no one knows the real Jack Benny—no one, that is, outside of Jack himself, and he is only a shade more voluble than the

One of the secrets of their success is that Jack and his wife Mary have a lot of fun when they work together on the program.

Above, the Sportsmen, give out with "L-S-L-S-M-F-T," and below, Jack catches up on news with Phil Harris and Rochester.

late Calvin Coolidge. Millions of words have already been printed about this man who is the highest-paid comedian in radio. His scrap book, if he kept one, would in sheer stacked-up wordage make the Sears, Roebuck catalog seem like something marked "Reading Time: 10 Seconds," yet Benny still remains one of the most elusive, paradoxical figures in show-business.

Benny is a fabulous personality, not so much because of his stratospheric Hooper rating, or his individual brand of humor or because he virtually revolutionized the pattern of radio comedy. Jack is radio's most intriguing figure because he has for more than 15 years succeeded brilliantly at the business of manufacturing laughter when he himself is anything but a funny man.

To an observer watching Benny prepare his Sunday program, he looks for all the world like a harried, cautious Seventh Avenue garment manufacturer worrying about his next Spring's line.

There is nothing uncomplimentary in this. The creation of a Benny broadcast is an arduous, painful, seven-day-a-week task, worth every penny of the reported $22,500 weekly check Jack gets from the American Tobacco Company. Benny's product comes from the sweat, toil and savvy of The Boss himself, from a quartet of the highest-priced writers in radio and a superlative surrounding cast whose talents all mesh like the jewelled gears of a Naval Observatory chronometer. Jack's competitors — Fred Allen, Danny Kaye, George Burns and others — frankly admit that when it comes to judging comedy material, Ben-

ny tops them all.

People, meeting Jack for the first time, stand around hopefully waiting for him to let loose with a barrage of boffolas. They go away disappointed. Jack gives strangers a limp handshake, a shy, almost distant "Hello" and seems eager to evaporate the next moment. On the other hand, Jack can be the greatest audience in the world during rehearsals, howling with laughter, pounding the floor in glee over a line, while his cast sits there dead-pan.

And yet Benny, as George Burns says, "is the greatest editor of material in the business. He's got the knack of cutting out all the weak slush and keeping in only the strong punchy lines." Because he has made the creation of comedy such a serious business, Jack knows better than any other man in the world what will be funny on his program. "I can't always tell when a line is good," he admits, "but, brother, I can tell when it's lousy."

Despite all this, despite his stature as "Mr. Radio," his consistent standing among the top five on the air, his huge earnings, his talent as a star-maker, the kudos paid him by the public and the trade, Jack Benny is still the "unhappy fiddler." (Why must comedians always want to play "Hamlet"?) Oddly enough, Benny really believes that if he had listened to his father, and practiced more on the fiddle when he was a boy in Waukegan, he would be a fine violinist today. He honestly envies the great virtuosi like Heifetz, Isaac Stern and Szigeti. He still remembers that Heifetz once told him he had a rich tone and that he should have continued with his music. The pre-comedy Benny was actually a soulful fellow with a violin. Unfortunately, it didn't get him any place.

Even Jack realizes this in his less pre-occupied moments. As his wife, Mary Livingstone once told him, "If you had kept up with your fiddle-playing, you would have lost all the humor of being a lousy violinist on your program." (Jack is actually quite proficient.) But he can never seem to forget that he was once a fiddle player. Being no noodle, despite the role he plays on the air, Jack has managed to sublimate his musical yearnings. He has turned his frustration into one of the most riotously funny routines among all the running gags on his program—the "Professor Le Blanc" situation in which Mel Blanc, as the "Professor," gives Jack violin lessons and forever ends up with his buck-fifty unpaid.

Occasionally, however, Jack will rebel against the fate that has made him the comedian with the longest run in radio among the top funny men. He sets out to prove that he has other talents, only to wind up behind the pert pantaloons like Danny Kaye, George, Burns and Georgie Jessel were panic-ing the guests, bouncing ad libs around like so many basket balls. After a couple of hours Jack turned restless. "Everybody gets laughs around here but me," he complained. "And in my own house."

Benny went upstairs, then came down again a short time later, made up like the corniest of gypsy fiddlers. He strolled among the guests, playing as schmaltzy an assortment of *tzardas* ever heard outside of the ineffable Rubinoff. Then he passed around a battered hat.

No one bothered to laugh.

Another time, at a Hollywood benefit for Greek War Relief, Benny, instead of his expected comedy turn, performed an elaborate concerto arrangement of "Love in Bloom." The surprised audience burst into applause, but Jack merely bowed to the conductor, bowed to the audience, then sauntered off the stage, his treasured violin under his arm.

The contradictions in the Benny personality show up in many ways. Take, for instance, his reputed inability to get off a fastie unless his scripting crew is running interference for him. True, Benny is no rapier wit like Fred Allen or Henry Morgan. "Benny," said Harry Conn, his first writer, "couldn't even ad lib a belch at a Hungarian banquet." Yet Jack, when hurt or cornered, can dish it out as well as take it. Radio circles still chuckle over Jack's famed bout with Fred Allen, who had Benny hanging on the ropes with his ad libs. Jack stood it as long as he could, then said, plaintively, "You wouldn't dare do this to me if I had my writers with me."

On another occasion when Benny, Bob Hope, Fred Allen, Jimmy Durante and Jerry Colona were starring on a Christmas "Command Performance" for the Army, the photographer lined up the comedians for a series of pictures. Someone had to say something and Hope started it with a crack about his profile. There was a pause and Durante yelled, "Hey, you ushers, stand erect and give this jernt a little class." Neither Benny nor Allen could think of anything to say. Allen started mugging and Jack jammed his hat on crosswise. "Well, at least I'll *look* funny," he quipped. Then Benny pulled a parking ticket out of his pocket. "I don't mind doing this show for free," he announced, "but who in heck is going to pay for this parking ticket?"

The delighted screams of the audience could have been heard all the way to Anaheim, Azusa and Cucamonga.

His studio audience, watching Jack do a warm-up before a broadcast, see Benny come out with all his own hair, see him tanned, genial and sassy-looking. He looks like a man with a million bucks in his pocket and a phone call from Lana Turner. "Welcome to the Lucky Strike Program," he says, then flips the ashes off his cigar.

But that incredible Benny poise is ersatz. Jack's "deliberately cultivated suavity," said a friend, "conceals an almost irrational terror of an audience. Nobody watching him realizes that he is trembling inside and that every line he speaks and every piece of business he does requires an effort of will power."

Even in the days when he was an unknown vaudevillian, happy to pick up a fast twenty-five dollars with a dog act, Benny had that magnificent poise. Once, Jack tried out a turn at the Academy of Music Theatre in New York—a vaudeville house not particularly

Gould, Dennis Day, Rochester, Phil Harris, Mary Livingstone, Benny, Don Wilson and Mel Blanc, beaming at their boss, Fred Allen.

noted for its polite treatment of entertainers who weren't too well known. Everything went—from boos to over-ripe tomatoes. As Jack came out on the stage with his violin under his arm and his routine "Hello, folks," opening, the Bronx cheers began. When Jack got to the center of the stage the raspberries were deafening. But instead of going into his act, Benny kept on walking obliviously toward the other wing. Just as he reached the wing he turned and faced the customers. There was an ominous silence. "Goodbye, folks," he said. Then he strolled off the stage and out of the theatre.

To his cast—Dennis Day, Mary Livingstone, Rochester, Phil Harris, Don Wilson and the others—Benny is simply The Boss. He is no whip-cracker, but he demands and insists on perfection. Benny is his own producer. He rarely glances at the control booth for cues. He can get together with the sound man and patiently go over a sound effect—the clank of the chains in his "vault," for example—as many as 40 times, until his meticulous ear is happy. Jack himself labors over the hilarious rhymed commercials that his Sportsmen Quartet sings—incidentally, one of the freshest new routines to appear during the last twelve months. All of the painstaking Sunday-to-Sunday writing sessions are master-minded by Benny, though he may not contribute an original line of his own.

The Benny show has almost as many recurring situations and running gags on tap as the objects that fill Fibber McGee's closet. There's the broken-down Maxwell, the violin lessons, the Benny vault with its caretaker who never sees the light of day, the brash telephone operators, Mr. Kitzel and his "peekle-in-the-meedle," the synthetic feud with Fred Allen, the Quartet and a packet of others. On the whole they pay off with laughs. But even so shrewd a judge of material as Benny will occasionally rely too much on strictly local references—things like his "Eastern - Columbia, Broadway and Ninth" routines which at best ring hollowly on the ears of listeners away from Los Angeles.

It's been said of Jack that he lives on a diet of black coffee and fingernails. It's true that he just can't wait to start to work and begin worrying every day. Benny arises at six in the morning, goes out for a couple of rounds of golf, then is ready for work. He is always the first on hand for conferences and rehearsals. Ten minutes before the end of a luncheon break, Benny is back in the studio, hunched up in a corner studying his script. He fumbles nervously with his hair, clamps his teeth on an unlighted pipe, keeps fingering his tie. He is so concerned about the carefully-contrived spontaneity of his show that he keeps the side men in the Phil Harris band away from the final Sunday rehearsals. Jack wants the lines to be as fresh to them as to the audience.

All this is part of the perfection Benny strives for and—usually achieves. Yet Jack's own bedroom at home, where he relaxes before he goes to sleep, has been described as "the worst mish-mash since the cyclone hit Lecompton, Kansas." Old scripts, recordings of broadcasts, books, magazines, newspapers and fan letters are piled high on every table and chair. In this cluttered room Benny the perfectionist finds a certain surcease from the strain. Here he wallows in mystery stories and listens to who-dun-its on the air—rarely to other comedians. "I know they're suffering, just the way I suffer," he once said. "If a gag of theirs doesn't get a laugh, I cringe."

Jack has been known to add $1000 out of his own pocket to boost a guest fee for violinist Isaac Stern. His four writers who have been with him five years—Sam Perrin, Milt Josefsberg, George Balzer and John Tackaberry—together earn around $5,000 a week. Jack keeps Artie Auerbach, the "Mr. Kitzel" of his show, on salary all year round, though he may use him but three or four times a season. Recently, when Sara Berner and Bea Benaduret—"Gladys" and "Mabel," the telephone operators—were written out of two programs at the last moment, because the shows were overboard on time, both girls received their full fees just the same. One year Jack spent more than $100,000 on line charges to put on his broadcasts from remote camps and hospitals. This was Jack's own money, spent without publicity. And when the troupe travels, Rochester stops in the same hotel with Jack and the rest of the cast, or Jack moves the troupe to a hotel where Rochester is welcome.

Yet Jack, abnormally sensitive as he is to the feelings of others, can sometimes reveal a curious naivete. Preoccupied with the problems of his own program,

Benny displays an odd surprise when he is confronted with the fact that there are also other programs on the air. Not long ago he used a couple of 12-year-old radio actors in the roles of "Steve" and "Joey," two neighborhood youngsters who, on the air, play football with Jack, fall for his tall stories and believe he is the superhero he claims to be. After a preliminary script reading, Jack told the boys they could leave, but to be back that afternoon at 2 for another rehearsal. After the boys had scurried out, John Tackaberry, one of Benny's writers, said, "Jack, I don't think that one kid will make it back on time today. He's got a 'conflict'."

"What do you mean?" asked Benny.

"Well," said Tackaberry, "that boy has a show of his own, you know."

"A show of his *own*?" repeated Jack. "Ohh."

Going into his record consecutive 16th year on NBC, Benny is still shrewdly playing to the listener in his living room at home, still using the narrative show with a framework of situations which he developed. Actually, Benny is the great revolutionist of radio. He was, as Fred Allen said, "the first comedian on the air to realize that you can get big laughs by ridiculing yourself, instead of your stooges."

Just where the once-skinny Waukegan kid who was born Benjamin Kubelsky got his superb sense of timing, is unimportant. But not even the most lukewarm can deny that Benny has it. Jack seems able to get more laughs out of a pause, or a simple word like "Well," than other comedians out of a dozen prattfalls. Jack reads a line so that the very inflection makes it funny. He is "a masterly comedian who could wring a laugh out of an executor's report."

Benny is still the only radio artist who has a lifetime option on NBC's choice 7 o'clock spot on Sunday night. Niles Trammel, president of the network, gave Jack that option back in 1941, no matter who sponsored him in the future. And for the next three years, at least, Jack will be toting home around one thousand dollars a minute, just for being the very opposite of himself on the air.

Reprinted from *Radio Best*, March 1948.

JACK BENNY BACK ON THE AIR

with
MARY LIVINGSTON
PHIL HARRIS · ROCHESTER · DON WILSON

Presented by
LUCKY STRIKE
L.S./M.F.T.

Sunday Night Oct. 1
NBC NETWORK

7 P.M. WGY

THE JACK BENNY TIMES

Volume XIV, Numbers 1-6   INTERNATIONAL DISTRIBUTION   1994 Issue

President's Message

Jell-o again, folks! Well, it has been a while since you have heard from me (but you already knew that--the last issue went out on February 14th), and so I have decided to compile the entire year's worth of newsletters into one big extravaganza. In this issue you will get various information that has been in the works for quite a long time (like a complete, updated library list with the length of all special shows/appearances), as well as an update on standards like the Tape Trading List. In an effort to get this issue out before the end of the year, I have not sorted through the mail that has been piling up, so if you requested a Jack Benny Classified, addition to the Tape Trading List, or similar item, keep your eyes on the next issue. I am certain that nearly a year's worth of back correspondence should yield much valuable information for next time.

Now since I have 48 pages (normally 6 issues in a year, at 8 pages per issue) to fill, I want to indulge in something that I make a strict point of not doing; taking a moment to fill you in on my personal life, in an effort to try to explain why I have been delayed so long in publication. Will try to keep it to just a couple of medium-length paragraphs. Firstly, I want to say a tremendous **THANK YOU** to all the members who have been so patient and understanding after not receiving the newsletter for some time. This past year has probably been the most difficult one of my life. After publishing the last issue, I was sent to Los Angeles by my company for the entire month of April, and was scheduled to be there pretty much right up until the date of my wedding, May 15. I was working sometimes up to 18 hours a day, catching sleep and food during my breaks. Then as I was repainting the poles (at home) for our chuppah just eight days prior to the wedding, I received a phone call. It was my father, in a voice I did not recognize at first, telling me that my mother had died.

Now let me digress somewhat for a moment. My mother had been a fan of Jack Benny since she was a young girl. She was born in 1937, and was thus able to enjoy Jack's shows during a good portion of his heyday in radio. One story that she liked to tell people who knew about the fan club was that when I was three, she sat me down in front of the television to watch <u>Jack Benny's Second Farewell Special</u>. "Watch this, Laura. He's a famous comedian," she said. If memory serves me correctly, I believe it was the skit where Jack and George Burns are Roman statues in a fountain. Folks, I couldn't appreciate it one bit, and ran out of the room after a couple minutes. As many of you know, it was actually the Warner Brothers cartoon <u>The Mouse That Jack Built</u> that eventually "turned me on" to Jack. So my mother thought that it was tremendously funny that the little girl who ran out of the room totally bored by Jack Benny eventually started his fan club. My mother was not *fanatic* about Jack, but enjoyed his comedy just like many people did. My interest in Jack was purely coincidental. But Mom (her name was Gayle Armstrong Lee, by the way) and I were very close--best friends as well as mother and daughter. She had a stroke in December of 1988, which took away (or perhaps I should just say changed) a lot of the person I knew; but she still was very high-functioning, although she could not read or drive a car. A few of the last times I spoke with her I started to see a glint of the "old her"--a funny, intelligent, warm, loving, independent individual. Perhaps it was the candle flickering up just before going out; but I thank God for those moments. Her death was completely unexpected--an apparent heart attack. She was 56. I still miss her so much. I love you, Mom.

Dad had been in Pittsburgh. I canceled my week in Los Angeles and flew to Fort Wayne. Somehow we scheduled everything (i.e., memorial service, interment, etc.) together so quickly that we were able to fly back to California three days before the wedding. I barely remember anything between that time and the day of the wedding. By that time, my father and I were so emotionally numb that I, for one, just wanted to go through it and get it over. The wedding went beautifully. **Yes, my name is still Laura Lee.** The honeymoon in New Orleans was splendid. Grieving had to be forcibly delayed until a more "convenient" time; thus I am still having a difficult time dealing with it. My maternal grandmother then passed away in July, which leaves my only relative that I truly know being my father. Dan and I moved at the end of August. **New address:**

**3190 Oak Road, #303
Walnut Creek, California 94596
(510) 933-3879**

Now I know you are asking, "Why did you move AGAIN?" No, we are not escaping bill collectors. My husband, Dan Leff, started at the California Culinary Academy studying to be a professional chef. Our new locale is accessible via mass transit (BART, for those in the know about the Bay Area). Thus, and I will forewarn you, we will be moving again around March of 1996 or so. Then in October Dan's paternal grandfather died. Several people have cracked that we have had "three funerals and a wedding." Please, let's not try for four. So with money being tight because of Danny's school, the move, etc., as well as trying to deal with all the various emotional traumas in our lives, it has been a very difficult year in almost every respect. So now here I am, trying to regroup and get back on track. Thank you again for your patience and understanding.

READ THIS! IT'S VERY IMPORTANT!

Now on to other topics. Since people's dues have been "due" throughout this year, I am sending this issue out to everyone who has paid through last October. I understand that through an error of mine (Yes! I admit it!) some new members did not receive the November-December issue of the Times. Ergo, those members are receiving copies of both newsletters. If anyone has been left out, please contact me. Now, rather than try to tabulate how "past due" everyone is, **EVERYONE'S $6.39 IS DUE NOW FOR THE COMING YEAR.** What this basically means is that due to my own delay in sending out this newsletter, everyone gets at least one (and in many cases, as many as six) free issue. **If you have sent me $6.39 since June of this year, I will credit it toward next year's dues.** I hope that this will make amends for the delay. If anyone is unhappy with this arrangement, please send me a letter and I will make every attempt to rectify the situation to your satisfaction.

Now additionally, considering everything (costs, material, time, etc.) I have decided to reduce the frequency of Times publication to every four months, or three issues per year, with 16 pages per issue. Thus you get the same amount of material you would have received in the six issues, but in different installments. I believe that this is a more realistic schedule than the previous bimonthly publication. Since the overall quantity is the same, so is the subscription price.

Lastly but not leastly, this year celebrates the **tenth anniversary** of the publication of The Jack Benny Times! A few issues went out at the beginning of the fan club, but regular (or as regular as I usually am) publication started in June, 1984. Here's to at least ten more years. Now on with the show!

Jack Benny's 100th Birthday

Every February 14th, the Jack Benny Center for the Arts in Waukegan has an affair, which has been mentioned in previous issues of the Times. This year, the Jack Benny Junior High School got into the act with their own celebration, complete with a banner reading "Hey, Jack Benny HAPPY 39TH BIRTHDAY!" For additional information, I refer you to the three items in the articles section of this newsletter. I should also note that "Spangler and Spangler" are the children of longtime member David Spangler. My heartfelt thanks to David Motley and the Jack Benny Junior High School for supplying me with this information.

"New" Members

It has been so long since I published a New Members list that I hesitate to call it "new." A belated welcome to you all. Any names not previously published that do not appear on this list should appear in the next issue.

****ELTON T. RIDLEY ****SAM RABER ****ELIZABETH TEICHER ****LORETTA ZERBY ****SCOTT SMITH ****GERTRUDE BARDOLPH ****MRS. MARTIN KAPLAN ****RICHARD GOLDFARB ****GORDON HUTTON ****WILLIAM HARWICK (UK) ****MICHAEL MILLS (UK) ****MIKE WARING (UK) ****JOHN POOLE (UK) ****DAN PEAT (UK) ****PAUL RUDDOCK (UK) ****JOHN McGREGOR (UK) ****ALISON GRIMMER (UK) ****J.D. BAIN (UK) ****LOUIS PHILLIPS ****JOSEPH PHILLIPS ****CHARLES MOORE ****AL CATE ****KAREN SIMONIAN ****JIM PROBASCO ****DENNIS BENEDICT ****JIMMIE HICKS ****RICHARD LARSON ****PATRICK CAREY ****KIM CUNNINGHAM ****MEL HOLT ****TROY A. KAIB ****WAYNE SCHULMAN ****LISA MELCOMBE ****EMERSON WILLIAMS, JR. ****CHRIS REALE ****JAMES R. STEWART ****THEODORE RIDLEY ****RICHARD NATHAN ****DAVID Z. JOSEPH ****TERRY HEATH ****MORRIE K. BLUMBERG ****MARIA ROSA PIERAMICO ****RONALD EBERHARD ****DIANE BERKOWITZ ****MYRNA CHARET ****LEV MAILER ****CINDY CHESSER ****A.C. ETTINGER ****DAVID ETTINGER ****RAY DRUIAN ****CHRIS TURNER ****ROBERT NYSTROM ****ALICE RAMSEY ****MARTIN BRAUN ****PALMA CABILES ****TOMMY HOUSOS ****JIM SEITZINGER ****DAN SCHRYVER ****M.T. FISHER ****STEPHEN H. WOODS ****MICHAEL AVEDISSIAN ****STEPHANIE BONIFANT ****TOM WILLIAMS ****DAYTON CRANDALL ****RAY VALADEZ ****KAREN HUGHES ****MIRIAM WILSEN ****JAY WILD ****RICH ADLER ****DAWN ADLER ****DENNIS KANE ****HOWARD SANDS ****DAMON McMANUS ****EDWARD A. LARSEN ****JAMES K. DABNEY ****LARRY SACKS ****STEVE SCHOTTLER ****MARY OPLIGER ****BARRY OPLIGER ****KENNETH KOFTAN ****RUSSELL J. FOLSOM ****P.A. KING ****WARREN DEBENHAM ****GREGG OPPENHEIMER ****REV. FRED G. FOTION ****MYRTLE M. WILKE ****CINDI DAVIS ****PETER LIND ****WILLIAM LUCAS ****JOE VALENTINE ****ROBERT C. FALLIS ****JAMES G. BURKE ****TOM HEATHWOOD ****JOHN TREASURE ****GLORIA HERZOG ****NANCY ZAWADSKI ****CHARLES NOVACK ****YOCHEVED MIRIAM NOVACK ****TZVI HIRSH NOVACK ****SHMUEL ARON NOVACK ****TZIPORA NOVACK ****BRYNA NOVACK ****MENACHEM MENDEL NOVACK ****YOSEF YITZCHAK NOVACK

Jack Bloom Pasadena Chapter

Traditionally in the May-June issue, the list of members of the Jack Bloom Pasadena Chapter is printed. This is an honorary society for IJBFC members who have been active for four or more years. Jack Bloom was one of the most active members of the fan club, contributing greatly to our tape library, <u>39 Forever</u>, and various other archival material and data. Jack and I maintained extensive correspondence, and his letters were always a perfect joy to read. I was going to finally meet Jack when I went to Los Angeles in August of 1990, but he passed away just about a month and a half prior to my trip. We are all indebted to him for his contributions to the fan club. I still think of you often, Jack.

JACK ABIZAID	TOM MASTEL
JACK BLOOM	BILL OLIVER
BRUCE BAKER	ROBERT OLSEN
HAL BOGART	EMILY RIFFLE
FRANCIS W. DALY	PEGGY RIFFLE
WAYNE ENNIS	REX RIFFLE
PHIL EVANS	JOHN SCHLAMP
LE ROY FILLENWARTH	JOYCE SHOOKS
MARILYN FILLENWARTH	BENJAMIN SPANGLER
ALAN GROSSMAN	BONNIE SPANGLER
JAY HICKERSON	DAVID SPANGLER
TIM HOLLIS	STEVE SZEJNA
SAREE KAMINSKY	EVA TINTORRI
LAURA LEE	MARION TINTORRI
GEORGE LILLIE	BARBARA WATKINS
JAMES A. LINK	KEN WEIGEL
PATRICIA LINK	DOUG WOOD

Tape Trading List

Ellen Barker, P.O. Box 1402, Reseda, California 91335

Hal Bogart, 2029 Aldersgate Drive, Lyndhurst, Ohio 44124

Stephanie Bonifant, 1807 West 14th Street, Ashtabula, Ohio 44004

Yosef Braude, 25 Longhorn Road, Providence, Rhode Island 02906

Rob Cohen, 6635 Helm Avenue, Reynoldsburg, Ohio 43068

The Everills, 1558 Knox Drive, New Haven, Indiana 46774

Andrew Haskell, 160 West 39th Avenue, Vancouver, British Columbia V5Y 2P2, Canada

Dick Hill, 1802 Bateman, Hastings, Nebraska 68901

David A. Howell, 1300 Kennedy Boulevard #419, Cuyahoga Falls, Ohio 44221

Wendy Jernigan, P.O. Box 1219, Four Oaks, North Carolina 27524

Tom Kleinschmidt, 26101 Country Club Boulevard #706, North Olmstead, Ohio 44070

Steve Lake, 7780 North Pinesview Drive, Scottsdale, Arizona 85258

John Malone, Rural Route #2, Wee-Ma-Tuk, Cuba, Illinois 61427

Bill Oliver, 516 Third Street NE, Massillon, Ohio 44646

Jack Palmer, 145 North 21st Street, Battle Creek, Michigan 49015

Lewis and Sedalia Pearson, 240 Ridge Drive, Marion, Iowa 52302

Michael Pointon, 11 Kings Court, Kings Road, London SW19 8QP, England

Frank Pozzuoli, 2830 Waterbury Avenue, Bronx, New York 10461

Keith Scott, 4 Bellbird Crescent, Forestville 2087, N.S.W. Australia

Joyce Shooks, 2026 Lafayette NE, Grand Rapids, Michigan 49505

Steve and Kim Smith, 1945 Coit NW, Grand Rapids, Michigan 49505

John Smothers, 22 Townsend Drive, Freehold, New Jersey 07728 (Open reel preferred)

Steve Szejna, 7806 West Waterford Avenue #1, Greenfield, Wisconsin 53220-2275

Peter Tatchell, 40 Bambra Road, Caulfield, Victoria 3161 Australia

James E. Treacy, Jr., 900 Hargrove Road #234, Tuscaloosa, Alabama 35401

Additions to the list will also be noted in the next issue.

Tape Preservation

Speaking of tapes, on December 11th I heard a story on NPR's <u>All Things Considered: Weekend Edition</u> that will be of note to almost all of our members. You probably knew conceptually that your tapes (both audio and video) would not last forever, but they may be dying faster than you think. It seems that depending on the environment in which the tapes are kept and how much they are played, **most tapes will start breaking down in approximately ten years.** Some tapes can even start showing problems after as little as five years. One of the basic problems with this is the decomposition of the tape's binding agent. In short, there are three layers to a tape: 1) a plastic backing, 2) iron oxide that rearranges itself to replicate the recorded sound, and 3) a binding agent to hold the first two together. Tapes may produce squealing noises, give degraded or distorted sound quality, or other various problems.

SO WHAT CAN YOU DO?!?! First of all, store your tapes in a cool, dry place. For tapes that you particularly want to insure remain intact, make two copies of them. Store the copies in two different places, separate from the original. Every five to seven years, make copies of those copies. Handle tapes as little as possible. If a tape is already showing the aforementioned signs, (and I am only reporting what was said on the air, I make no guarantees or claims on these measures) you can actually bake the tape in a **convection oven** at 130° for 6 to 8 hours. This should make the tape playable for up to 30 days, which will give you a chance to make backups.

So what of our tape library? Good question. As you know, your $6.39 covers only the costs of production and publication of the newsletter. If anyone wishes to make a contribution of blank tapes or money to a fund for backing up the tape library, it would be greatly appreciated. We currently have 372 audio tapes of varying lengths (most 60 to 90 minutes). Any contributions would be used to start backing up the tape library starting with tape 1 and working forward. **A contribution of $5 or five tapes from**

everyone should serve to create two full backups of the current tape library. Please enclose a note saying "Library Backup" on any contributions; thank you.

The Tape Library!

Since it is so much easier for me to publish an update here rather than collect you $1 and SASEs, here is the listing of the holdings of the IJBFC audio tape library.

Probs: O = Poor sound   P = Wrong speed   A = Part of show missing

The Jack Benny Program:

Date	Probs	Date	Probs	Date	Probs	Date	Probs
5/2/32		1/6/35		12/19/37		6/18/39	
1/1/33	A	11/3/35		1/2/38		6/25/39	
1/22/33	A	1/19/36		1/9/38		10/8/39	
3/31/33		2/9/36		1/16/38		10/15/39	
4/21/33		2/16/36		1/23/38		12/3/39	
6/2/33		2/23/36		2/6/38		12/10/39	
6/9/33		4/5/36		2/13/38		12/17/39	
6/18/33		10/4/36		2/20/38	P	1/7/40	
6/23/33		10/11/36		2/27/38		1/21/40	
12/10/33		10/18/36		4/3/38	P	1/28/40	
2/11/34		10/25/36		4/17/38		2/4/40	
2/18/34		11/1/36		4/24/38		2/11/40	
2/25/34		11/22/36		5/1/38		2/18/40	
3/4/34		1/10/37		10/2/38		6/16/40	
3/11/34		2/7/37		11/13/38		11/17/40	
3/18/34		2/21/37		11/20/38		11/24/40	
4/6/34	A	2/28/37		11/27/38		12/1/40	
4/13/34		3/7/37		12/11/38		3/2/41	
5/4/34	A	3/21/37		1/1/39		3/9/41	
5/11/34		3/28/37	O	1/8/39		3/16/41	
5/18/34		4/4/37		2/5/39		3/23/41	
8/3/34		4/11/37		2/12/39		4/13/41	
8/10/34		4/18/37		2/19/39		5/18/41	
8/24/34		4/25/37		2/26/39		5/25/41	
8/31/34		5/30/37	P	3/12/39		6/1/41	
9/21/34		6/6/37		3/19/39		10/5/41	
9/28/34		10/3/37		3/26/39		10/12/41	
10/14/34	A	10/10/37		4/2/39		11/2/41	
10/28/34	A	10/31/37		4/16/39		11/30/41	
11/4/34	A	11/7/37		4/30/39		12/9/41	
11/11/34	A	11/21/37		5/21/39		12/12/41	
11/18/34	A	11/28/37		5/28/39		12/14/41	
12/2/34	A	12/5/37		6/4/39		12/21/41	
12/16/34		12/12/37		6/11/39		1/25/42	

Date		Date		Date		Date	
2/1/42		10/24/43		4/6/47		2/6/49	
2/8/42		10/31/43		4/13/47		2/20/49	
2/15/42		11/7/43		4/20/47		3/6/49	
3/1/42		11/21/43		4/27/47		3/13/49	
3/8/42		12/5/43	O	5/4/47		3/20/49	
3/15/42		1/2/44		5/11/47		3/27/49	
3/22/42		1/7/44		5/18/47		4/3/49	
3/29/42		1/16/44		5/25/47		4/10/49	
4/5/42		2/6/44		10/5/47		4/24/49	
4/12/42		2/27/44		10/12/47		5/22/49	
4/19/42		3/5/44		10/19/47		9/11/49	
4/26/42		3/19/44		10/26/47		9/18/49	
5/3/42		4/2/44		11/2/47	O	9/25/49	
5/10/42		4/9/44		11/9/47		10/9/49	
5/17/42		4/23/44		11/23/47		10/16/49	
5/31/42		10/1/44	O	11/30/47		10/23/49	
10/4/42		10/8/44		12/7/47		11/6/49	
10/11/42		10/15/44		12/28/47		11/13/49	
10/18/42		11/5/44		1/4/48		11/27/49	
10/25/42		12/3/44		1/25/48		12/4/49	
11/1/42		12/10/44		2/15/48		12/11/49	
11/8/42		12/24/44		2/22/48		1/1/50	
11/15/42		2/4/45		2/29/48		1/8/50	
11/22/42		2/11/45		3/7/48		2/12/50	
11/29/42		5/13/45		3/14/48		4/2/50	
12/6/42		6/6/45		3/21/48		4/9/50	
12/13/42		10/14/45		3/28/48		5/28/50	
12/20/42		11/4/45		4/4/48		9/10/50	
12/27/42		11/11/45		4/11/48		12/3/50	
1/3/43		11/25/45		4/18/48		12/17/50	
1/10/43		12/9/45		4/25/48		12/31/50	
1/17/43	P	12/15/45		5/2/48		1/28/51	
1/24/43		12/16/45		6/6/48		2/11/51	
1/31/43	P	12/23/45		6/13/48		2/18/51	
2/7/43		12/30/45		6/20/48		3/18/51	
2/14/43		1/20/46		6/27/48		3/25/51	
2/21/43	P	1/27/46		10/3/48		4/1/51	
2/28/43	P	2/10/46		11/7/48		5/27/51	
3/7/43	P	2/17/46	O	11/14/48		9/16/51	P
3/14/43		3/17/46		11/21/48		9/23/51	P
3/21/43		4/14/46		11/28/48		10/28/51	
4/4/43	P	5/19/46		12/5/48		11/4/51	
4/11/43		10/13/46	O	12/12/48		12/1/51	
4/18/43		1/5/47		12/26/48		12/9/51	O
4/25/43	O	2/16/47		1/2/49		12/16/51	
5/2/43		3/9/47		1/9/49		12/23/51	
5/16/43		3/16/47	P	1/16/49		1/20/52	
5/23/43		3/23/47		1/23/49		2/17/52	
10/10/43		3/30/47		1/30/49		2/24/52	

Date		Date		Date		Date	
3/2/52		2/1/53		3/28/54		1/16/55	
3/9/52	P	2/19/53		4/4/54		1/23/55	
3/16/52		3/22/53		5/2/54		1/30/55	
3/23/52		3/29/53		5/23/54		2/13/55	
3/30/52		4/12/53		9/26/54		2/20/55	
4/6/52		4/19/53		10/3/54		2/27/55	
4/12/52		4/26/53		10/10/54		3/6/55	
4/27/52		5/17/53		10/17/54		3/13/55	
5/4/52		5/24/53		10/24/54		3/20/55	
5/11/52		5/31/53		10/31/54		3/27/55	
5/18/52		6/7/53		11/7/54		4/3/55	O
5/25/52		6/14/53		11/14/54		4/10/55	
9/21/52		11/22/53	O	11/21/54		4/17/55	
9/28/52	P	11/29/53		11/28/54		4/24/55	
10/5/52		12/6/53		12/5/54		5/1/55	
10/26/52		12/13/53		12/12/54		5/8/55	
12/14/52	P	12/27/53		12/19/54		5/15/55	
12/21/52		1/10/54		12/26/54		5/22/55	
1/18/53		2/14/54		1/2/55			
1/25/53		3/7/54		1/9/55			

Other Jack Benny appearances, interviews, related items:

Length given in minutes   Date of 00/00/00 means unknown
<u>A Day in the Life of Dennis Day</u> may not include an appearance by Jack

Date	Title	Length	Probs
4/16/72	50th Anniversary of KFI Radio	60	
4/18/46	A Day in the Life of Dennis Day	30	
11/14/46	A Day in the Life of Dennis Day	30	
12/25/46	A Day in the Life of Dennis Day	30	
1/1/47	A Day in the Life of Dennis Day	30	
1/22/47	A Day in the Life of Dennis Day	30	
2/12/47	A Day in the Life of Dennis Day	30	
3/5/47	A Day in the Life of Dennis Day	30	
9/3/47	A Day in the Life of Dennis Day	30	
12/17/47	A Day in the Life of Dennis Day	30	
6/23/48	A Day in the Life of Dennis Day	30	
3/26/49	A Day in the Life of Dennis Day	30	
4/16/49	A Day in the Life of Dennis Day	30	
5/27/49	A Day in the Life of Dennis Day	30	
6/25/49	A Day in the Life of Dennis Day	30	
00/00/81	A Love Letter to Jack Benny	120	
3/2/44	Academy Awards	60	
11/10/44	Amos 'n' Andy	30	
2/14/53	Amos 'n' Andy Life Story	30	
00/00/00	Best of Jack Benny	30	
00/00/00	Best of Jack Benny - Money or Your Life	30	
00/00/47	Bing Crosby Show	30	

Date	Title	Length	
2/12/53	Bing Crosby Show	30	
12/12/53	Bing Crosby Show	30	
5/29/56	Biography in Sound - Fred Allen	60	
11/9/48	Bob Hope Show	30	
12/27/42	Buck Benny Rides Again premiere	30	
11/9/43	Burns and Allen	30	
6/28/45	Camp show	30	
3/24/40	Campbell Playhouse	60	
00/00/00	Christmas in Killarney - Dennis Day	5	
00/00/00	Christmas is for the Family - Dennis Day	60	
00/00/00	Classic Routines	90	
00/00/00	Command Performance #125	30	
00/00/00	Dennis Day 78s	30	
5/28/83	Dennis Day interview	60	
9/15/87	Dennis Day interview - Laura Lee	60	
00/00/00	Don Wilson interview	30	O
00/00/00	Don Wilson tribute	180	
11/25/42	Eddie Cantor Show	30	
1/3/45	Eddie Cantor Show	30	
10/24/91	Eddie Carroll interview - Laura Lee	120	
00/00/00	Famous Comedy Stars of the 30s and 40s	30	
3/4/49	Ford Theatre	60	
9/21/87	Frank Nelson Tribute - KCSN	30	
00/00/00	Frank Nelson interview - Laura Lee	60	
05/00/88	Fred deCordova interview - Larry King	60	
1/21/70	Friar's Club Roast of Jack Benny	60	
01/00/90	Funny That Way - BBC JB Tribute	30	
00/00/00	George Balzer interview - Laura Lee	90	
00/00/00	Golden Moments of Radio	60	
2/17/38	Good News of 1938	60	
2/8/41	Greek War Relief Program	120	
1/8/39	Gulf Screen Guild Theatre	30	
10/20/40	Gulf Screen Guild Theatre	30	
3/29/42	Gulf Screen Guild Theatre	30	
11/18/48	Hallmark Playhouse	30	
00/00/00	Halls of Ivy - AFRS #18	30	
00/00/00	Irving Fein interview - Laura Lee	60	
00/00/83	Itzhak Perlman interview - Laura Lee	10	
00/00/89	Itzhak Perlman interview - Laura Lee	10	
00/00/40s	Jack Benny - Top Ten Records	30	
00/00/00	Jack Benny Classic Routines	90	
00/00/00	Jack Benny Fiddles with the Classics	40	
12/21/56	Jack Benny Program - Christmas Special	60	
00/00/73	Jack Benny Tribute - BBC	30	
12/29/74	Jack Benny Tribute - CBS	60	
00/00/00	Jack Benny Tribute - KCRW	120	
1/5/75	Jack Benny Tribute - KXL p. 1	120	
12/27/74	Jack Benny Tribute - NBC	30	
1/2/75	Jack Benny tribute - NPR	150	
00/00/00	Jack Benny by Max Bygraves	5	

Date	Title	Length	
00/00/73	Jack Benny in Southend, England - BBC	90	
9/24/74	Jack Benny interview	30	O
9/12/69	Jack Benny on The Tonight Show	30	
11/18/69	Jack Benny on The Tonight Show	30	
00/00/00	Jack Benny vs. Fred Allen	120	
00/00/00	Jack Benny's 39th Birthday	60	
6/16/74	Jack introduces George Burns	5	
11/28/46	Jack's 15th year in radio skit - Unknown show	15	
00/00/00	Jack, Bing Crosby, Harpo Marx, Gary Cooper	10	
2/3/91	Joan Benny - Manhattan Radio Club	90	
00/00/00	Joan Benny interview - KNBR	30	
12/15/90	Joan Benny interview - Larry King	120	
00/00/00	Joan Benny on KNBR	15	
00/00/00	Joan Benny on WCAU Philadelphia	30	
00/00/00	Johnny Carson's History of Radio	120	
1/20/47	Kenny Baker Program	30	
12/17/40	Love Thy Neighbor premiere	30	
00/00/00	Love in Bloom - Longines Symphonette	5	
3/10/39	Lum and Abner	30	
2/15/37	Lux Radio Theatre	60	
9/26/38	Lux Radio Theatre	60	
00/00/00	Mail Call	30	
00/00/45	Mail Call	30	
00/00/00	Mail Call #122	30	
00/00/00	Mail Call #72	30	
2/3/91	Manhattan Radio Club - Joan Benny and panel	90	
00/00/00	Mary Livingstone tribute	60	OP
11/21/40	Maxwell House Coffee Time	30	
1/8/48	Maxwell House Coffee Time	30	
3/31/49	Maxwell House Coffee Time	30	
00/00/66	Mel Blanc talk	30	
00/00/00	Mickey Rooney interview - Laura Lee	10	
11/10/90	Modern Times - Phil Harris and Joan Benny	15	
10/3/45	Pabst Blue Ribbon Town	30	
10/26/45	Pabst Blue Ribbon Town	30	
8/15/90	Phil Harris interview - Laura Lee	120	
8/15/90	Phil Harris w/Laura Lee	120	
00/00/00	Phil Harris/Joan Benny interview - Modern Times	10	A
1/28/45	Radio Hall of Fame	60	
00/00/00	Red Cross Show	15	
1/8/39	Screen Guild Show	60	
11/25/43	Soldiers in Greasepaint	90	O
4/5/51	Suspense	30	
2/2/53	Suspense	30	
1/18/54	Suspense	30	
5/9/41	Tenth Anniversary Testimonial	30	
00/00/00	The Best of Jack Benny	30	
00/00/00	The Classic Comedians	60	
00/00/00	The Comedy Show	120	
6/19/83	The Comedy Show - JB tribute	120	O

6/26/83	The Comedy Show - JB tribute	120	O
00/00/56	The Continental Jack Benny - BBC TV	30	
1/30/47	The Eddie Cantor Show	30	
00/00/00	The Jack Benny Story	120	
7/28/38	Tommy Dorsey	20	
00/00/48	Top Ten 78rpm record set	30	
12/22/37	Town Hall Tonight	60	
1/11/48	USO Farewell Program	30	
00/00/49	VFW 50th Anniversary	30	
3/15/40	Waitin' for Jane - Rochester	5	
00/00/00	Wedlock and Snyder Stag Party	10	
00/00/84	Writers at Sperdvac convention	60	
6/11/44	Your All Time Hit Parade	30	

Now I am certain that many of you are saying, "Hey! I want that show! Now what do I do?" The rules of the tape library are as follows:

- Make a list of the items you want, up to ten hours of material (assume all Jack Benny Programs to be 30 minutes long). If something is less than 30 minutes in length, it will be coupled with an/other item/s from the list. Thus in selecting a five-minute item, I will dub the entire side from the tape containing it; therefore, assume no items to be shorter than 30 minutes. (Sorry folks...I've tried it the other way, searching through tapes for hours and hours trying to find all the excerpts, and it just is far too time-consuming for me and too much wear and tear on the tape. Think of it as a surprise grab bag!)
- Send your pick list, an appropriate amount of blank tape, and cash or a check for the service fee ($1.00 an hour for the first five hours, 50 cents for each additional hour, up to ten hours) to: Laura Lee, 3190 Oak Road #303, Walnut Creek, California 94596. (see also note below).
- I will copy your pick list onto the cassettes you send and return them to you. I will I will I will, no matter how long it takes (hopefully not too long).

Note: You may be thinking, "What is that service charge for?" Well, most of it is eaten up by return postage and restorative measures for the dubbing equipment. I encourage those of you placing orders to donate either one additional blank tape or dollar for every hour you order, to be put towards the aforementioned library backup fund.

39 Forever

I still have some copies of my log, 39 Forever, from its sixth printing. For the uninitiated, this is a listing of Jack's radio and television shows, specials, and selected appearances, as well as related books, magazine articles, and discography. All this for only $15.00. What a bargain (insert your own cheap joke here). Is very helpful in dating one's own collection, and determining which shows you want from the library!

You Do Know!

Had an old letter from Vice President Rex Riffle in my "Next Issue" file, and it contained a list of Jack "sightings." Although the letter goes back a ways, the information is still good if shows come around again (as they are wont to do on cable):

1) Jack has been on the Disney Channel on the Classic Comedians, he was included in the TV comedians
2) Jack was briefly on the Discovery Channel's The Way We Were, about the war years. Jack was shown sitting on a table in a mail room reading "I Can't Stand Jack Benny Because..." letters. He says, "Here's a letter from Fred Allen. It says, 'I can't stand Jack Benny because he can't stand me any more than I can't stand him!'"
3) Jack's picture was in U.S. News and World Report connected with an article on how CBS had lured David Letterman away from NBC, like Jack had been lured many years ago.
4) Phil Harris was on a rerun of Ben Casey on Nostalgia Channel, playing a wino, of all things.
5) Alice Faye was interviewed on AMC (American Movie Classics), they showed some really early pictures of Phil, but never mentioned his association with Jack.
6) The Disney Channel, again, had An Evening with George Burns where George was interviewed by members of the audience, and he sang some of his great songs. He also told great stories about Jack, and the tricks he played on him.
7) Jack and Rochester were shown on a health insurance commercial briefly, along with a lot of other classic folks.
8) AMC also had a special Stars and Stripes: Hollywood and WWII, which featured a section on Jack.
9) (You probably know this) The sports teams of Jack Benny Junior High School in Waukegan are called the "39ers."

Jack Benny Classifieds

§§§ Erstwhile Radio, P.O. Box 2284, Peabody, Massachusetts 01960. 72-page catalog is $4, tapes are $4 apiece. Contains four pages of Jack Benny material.

§§§ The Antique Trader Weekly, P.O. Box 1050, Dubuque, Iowa 52004-1050, (800) 482-0147, (800) 531-0880 fax. America's largest antiques and collectibles marketplace.

§§§ Radio Classics Live, Massasoit Community College, One Massasoit Bouelvard, Brockton, Massachusetts 02402, (506) 588-9100, contact: Robert E. Bowers. Look for their sixth annual gathering in April.

§§§ Handbook of Old Time Radio: A Comprehensive Guide to Golden Age Radio Listening and Collecting by Jon D. Swartz and Robert C. Reinehr, Scarecrow Press, Inc., P.O. Box 4167, Metuchen, New Jersey 08840, (800) 537-7107, (908) 548-5767 fax. 825 pp. ISBN 0-8108-2590-2, $92.50. I personally would be interested to hear any reviews on this volume.

§§§ Adventures in Cassettes, 5353 Nathan Lane North, Plymouth, Minnesota 55442-1978, (800) 328-0108. Catalog always has some Jack Benny items.

§§§ The Old Time Radio Gazette, Tom C. Miller, 2004 East 6th Street, Superior, Wisconsin 54880. One year's subscription is $8.50 for 12 issues.

§§§ Christopher McPherson, Box 37214, Phoenix, Arizona 85069. Per Bob Olsen, Christopher is offering a 45-minute documentary to commemorate Jack's 100th birthday. It contains interviews with Joan Benny, Steve Allen, Fred deCordova, three Benny writers and two experts on dramatic radio. Discussed is Jack Benny, the man, how his show was put together, the creation of his famous gags, and Benny's influence today. $9.95 plus postage. I would also be interested in any reviews of this tape.

§§§ Wendy Jernigan, P.O. Box 1219, Four Oaks, North Carolina 27524. Wendy is eager to find sources for Jack Benny movies. She has a few already, but is hungry for more. (She is the first member I know of who was introduced to Jack through his movies rather than radio or television!)

The Tale Piece

Now that the holiday season is upon us, I was reading over a few old letters where people mentioned how much they enjoyed Jack's Christmas shopping shows. **Did anyone ever find the show where Jack buys Don shoelaces?** I've had so many requests for it, but I do not have it. Plastic tips, metal tips, plastic tips, metal tips. Remember the paints-- watercolors versus oil paints? And it goes on. Now considering that Chanukah is over (and my apologies for my belated greetings--almost missed it myself) and Christmas is still coming, I thought I would pose an interesting paradox that was put to me during this past year.

One Jewish family put to me that they did not care for Jack Benny because they felt that he was "too Jewish" (and you thought that was only said about Jackie Mason), in that his stinginess and violin actually played upon Jewish stereotypes. However, another Jewish family (members of the fan club) stated that they often found that Jack was not Jewish *enough*, in that he always mentioned Christmas but not Chanukah, the Easter Parade, food that was obviously trayf (non-kosher, like inventorying a can of pork and beans), etc.

I found it interesting, first of all, because it is a question that had not previously been put to me. As for Jack being "too Jewish", I think that as Jack himself said so many times, he used what got laughs. If it was a cheap joke that got laughs, you played it. If it was Jack being a woman-chaser that got laughs, then you played that. There are so many stereotypes that I think almost any humorous characteristic you could select would be related to one stereotype or another. As for Jack not being Jewish enough, I wonder if it is because Christmas is such a prevailing theme at this time of year, it would seem almost odd to ignore it. Regarding trayf, Jack certainly did not keep kosher (cf, George Burns' story about Jack ordering bacon and eggs versus Cream of Wheat), so perhaps it was just not an issue. I know I am asking a biased audience, but I am interested in hearing your views on this question as well. Please, no political/religious fights over this; just some food for thought.

Ether One

WQEW in New York (1130AM) carries OTR on Saturdays from 7:00 to 7:30 P.M. This includes 39 weeks of shows including Jack Benny and Burns and Allen. (Yah...sounds like the Charles Michelson package. Does anyone know if there are any plans for additional shows to be added to that?)

Dennis Day: Encore! Encore!

Many members ask me why I shy away from reprinting articles. I generally say that I want all the members to get their money's worth from the <u>Times</u>, and the members who have been around for a while have already read the previous articles. However, considering the space we have here, I want to make an exception. The Dennis Day interview received such an overwhelmingly positive response during its first publication, I want to reprint the entire interview in one edition. For those of you who were there the first time, think of it as taking down an old, favorite book and enjoying it again. I will certainly be enjoying it right along with you.

L: Oh, Dennis!
D: Yes, please?
L: Oh that kid drives me nuts!
D: Now cut that out!
L: Well! Say, getting down to it, what were some of your first performances before you actually went on the Jack Benny Show?
D: Well, before I went on the jack Benny show, I had graduated from Manhattan College in New York City about nine months...before the Benny show--before I auditioned for it...I had always loved singing--I was in the glee club--I was President of the college glee club, and I had won a contest in New York among the metropolitan colleges for performing. There were instrumentalists, there were all kinds...I was a singer and I was chosen...The prize was to sing with Larry Clinton and his orchestra, who was then a very popular orchestra. He had written the Dipsy Doodle among other things...and several other classical songs that were adapted from Tchaikovsky, and he had adapted them into a popular mood...It was a great challenge to me, and I got on that program with Bea Wayne, I remember distinctly at the time. I did two songs and I took an air check of it...an acetate, because we didn't have tape at the time. Of course radio was the only thing we had--we didn't have television, it was just radio. I took an aircheck of the two songs, and I suppose that it would be about six months latter--Kenny Baker was my predecessor on the Jack Benny show, [he] left the program, I suppose had a little disagreement with Jack Benny, I think it was about money or something.
L: That figures.
D: Whatever it was, he left the program and jack and his agents were looking for a new singer to replace him, and somebody suggested I send it over to his agent because I was told after I got the program that Jack had auditioned or at least listened to records or people who had said, 'This is a great singer,' and everything. About 500 singers throughout the country, and I sent the record over thinking that nothing would ever happen, and by good fortune--God rest her--Mary Livingstone, Jack Benny's wife, she happened to be in the agent's office one day listening to a lot of audition records, and she heard mine and she was the one. She liked it, she went to Jack, and she persuaded him to audition me in person. Well, I did. I went down, I was called to audition and I nearly went through the floor. I'll never forget when I first went down to the agent's office to meet somebody--they didn't tell me who--and I walked in and there was Jack Benny sitting behind the desk. Now, you remember that Jack Benny was the number one program on radio at that time, and here I'm face to face with jack Benny which I never in my wildest imagination ever dreamed of just meeting the man. So here I walk in and meet him, and he said, 'Dennis, I heard your recording and Mary played it for me, and would you like to audition?' And I said, thinking it was maybe another week or so, I said, 'Oh, sure.' He said, 'Well, how about tomorrow?' There again I nearly went through the floor, too because this meant I had to get hold of someone to accompany me and go over a whole repertoire of songs to sing for him. So I did and after the meeting, I was to go the following day to NBC, up to the eighth floor I believe it was, at Rockefeller Center and they had a studio there. So I rushed over and worked with a man who was a song plugger, really. He worked for Chappell Music Company--Billy Bruce, and Billy was a wonderful, wonderful little man who coached me and

worked with me--I was nobody at the time--and that's the way you got songs. You went around to the publishers, you know, and they had people who played piano, mostly for people who were stars or budding stars on radio who had their own programs. Well, I didn't have my own program, but he took a liking to me and was very kind to me, and he coached me a lot. So I went over to him and I said, 'Would you play for me for my audition?' So we worked for an hour or two or so getting songs together and we then went to the audition the following day...I say for about fifteen minutes--Jack Benny, his director, and a few other agency people, the agent...were all in the control booth, and I was on a stage with a mike and a piano and my pianist. So I sang for about fifteen minutes, then I heard a voice say, 'Dennis take a break,' so I took a break for about a few minutes and I was talking to my accompanist and my back was turned to the control booth, and I was talking about what songs we were going to sing next and everything else...Then I heard a loudspeaker say, 'Oh, Dennis!' and I turned and said, 'Yes, please?' That was the thing that Jack Benny told me months and months later, he said, 'You know, that was one of the things that sold me on you.' and the fact that I was kind of naïve to say...instead of...'Yeah, what do you want?' I turned and I said, 'Yes, please?' In an Irish household, you never were impolite to your parents or your betters. Here he told me this months later, 'You know, that helped me decide that I kind of liked you.' Well, then shortly after that, I guess after I finished the audition a couple days later, Jack Benny gave me a round trip ticket to go out to California to audition for his writers and producer out there. I went out on the train, on the Golden State Limited, I'll never forget, and...my mother and dad came down to see me--I'd never been west of the Mississippi--to me, there were still Indians in Chicago...I was twenty-one, and I got on the train and who was on the train...and I ran into Irene Ryan--God rest her--who was on the Beverly Hillbillies as the grandmother, and Irene was so wonderful to me, knowing I was a scared kid and was going out to Hollywood. She was only going as far as Chicago, because there I had to change trains...and then went on to Hollywood, and then I auditioned for the writers and producers when I got out there...I was told to wait around because Jack Benny hadn't come back from San Francisco. He was up at the World's Fair, which was then being held at Treasure Island--this is in 1939--September of 1939. Well, he came back maybe a week or so later, and I stayed at the Hollywood Athletic club which it was at that time, and I had a lovely time there, but of course I didn't have any money--they didn't give me any money, and I had to wire home to my folks to send me some money so I could eat! So I did stay there, and then I got a call to come down to jack Benny's office after he got back down, and it was at that meeting that I knew I was going to be the new singer on his radio program-- you know it wasn't when I signed the contract, mind you, but when Jack Benny took back the other hand for the train ticket! He did! I kid you not!...But here I signed the contract, and it had a two-week option in it. If I didn't make good in two weeks, he had the option of dismissing me and looking for somebody else. So the I lasted for the first thirteen weeks, because those options came up every thirteen weeks on the first year, and then after that it would be on a yearly basis. So I lasted for the first full year, and then I was picked up again, so I must have been doing something right, because that two-week option and everything else stretched all the way to over twenty-five years with Jack Benny--and they were wonderful, wonderful years, because I owe everything that I ever have...my place with Jack Benny, he gave me my break, my start--everything I have I owe to jack Benny. And I'd say that even if I didn't know it was good for me! Honestly, Jack Benny was a wonderful man...You know, the things that were portrayed about him on radio, newspapers, magazines and the like as being a cheapskate, tightwad and a miser up close with the dollar--that wasn't Benny at all...He only seemed that way...because so many other people spent money. Benny was a generous man.

He had to bend over backwards when he would go anywhere to have a bite to eat or anything like that, he'd have to overtip. Instead of leaving a dime, he'd leave a quarter! But he was a beautiful man. You see, all of that was built up. He got all his laughs on character--not on jokes, out-and-out set-up jokes and then boom. It was all on character, because people could relate to Jack Benny because first of all he was a nice man, he was a gentle man, he was a beautiful man, he had a good heart, and a very sincere man. But everybody could relate because he played the part of a cheapskate. Well, there's one in every family, and also we're all vain. When they'd ask him his age, he'd say, 'Thirty-nine,' and the color of his eyes. He said, 'Blue. Bluer than the lips of a schoolboy at forty below!'

L: And bluer than the thumb of a cross-eyed carpenter!

D: Exactly...These are things that are part of human nature. So here I was the brash...well, silly, naïve kid. But see, there was logic in everything silly or naïve or stupid that I might have said or did, and...the logic was simply to drive Jack Benny nuts, and I used to do this. Of course, I always had to go to his house in the first year or so, and rehearse the song that I'm going to sing on the following Sunday's program so that he would approve it because I couldn't do a song on the show without his approval--'Is this okay?'...and he was always very nice about it. He never would say, 'No, that's no good,' or 'Maybe you could get another song,' or something like that, but I always went over there. Well, this time I went over, and I sang the song I was going to do on the following Sunday's program and after I was through, Jack Benny said to me...'That's very nice, Dennis. That will be fine.' And I said, 'Gee, thanks, Mr. Benny! I gotta go now,' and he showed me to the door, and I was about to leave, and I turned and said 'Goodbye, Mr. Benny! And have a nice trip!' and I left. You know, he went upstairs, he was halfway through packing before he realized he wasn't going anywhere! So that's the way I used to drive Jack Benny, these silly things that they would write for me, and...we stuck pretty much to the scripts. Every once in a while somebody would make a blooper, he was always fast to pick it up. I remember Mary Livingstone in one particular script where she was supposed to say 'the grease rack,'--she saw the car on the grease rack. Instead she said 'grass reek.' And Benny...picked that up and carried that on, and I think we referred to that for about three or four shows then. He could respond to anybody. The only man, I think, that I saw get the better of Jack Benny, and I'll always remember that at the Paramount theatre, Jack Benny and Fred Allen. That was the man. They had made a picture...it might have been <u>Love Thy Neighbor</u>, yes. And this was a premiere, and they were on stage, you know, and here every time Jack would open his mouth, Fred Allen would have some spontaneous answer, and finally Jack Benny turned to him and said, 'You know something, Fred? You wouldn't say that if my writers were here!' He was so great. The man was, to me, I think not only a very human and wonderful friend of mine--a great heart--but you know, the thing about Jack Benny--he was a gentle man, and that's what they have on his tomb where he is buried: Jack Benny, a gentle man...which is true. He would never want to hurt anybody. I remember one instance where we had a bit player on our radio show, and he was reading the line at rehearsals, and Jack would try to correct him. He aid, 'No, that's not the way I want you to read it. Read it this way...', and we'd go over it again, and the fellow would read it wrong...Finally at the dress rehearsal, we went through it and he read it wrong, and Jack flew off. He said, 'No, no, damnit, I told you that's not the way, this is the way!' and the poor fellow was crestfallen. Well you know, twenty seconds later, Jack Benny went over to this many who was probably getting about $150 for his spot on the program, and Jack Benny...said, 'I'm sorry. I apologize. It wasn't you. It was something else that was bothering me.' That's the sign of a man who has...a bigness about him, to go over to a little bit player and apologize. [He] wouldn't want to hurt anybody. See, he never wanted to hurt

L: anybody, and he felt by blowing steam he had hurt this man...and it shows the true character of Jack Benny.
L: [Jack] never really took too many of the lines in the show himself.
D: Well, no, he played straight for all of us. That was the whole secret of Jack Benny's success...Each of us: Phil Harris, Rochester, Don Wilson, myself, Mary Livingstone or anyone, we got a page and a half of dialogue, and he was playing straight for us. We got all the laughs, but it was dynamite material, because he had the best writers anyone could...buy, and that's one thing he insisted upon: good writers. You're only as good as your writers and the material that was given to you. And Benny...had four writers, and he paid them exceptionally well--he paid all of us really very well because we were exclusive to him, we could not work outside of the Jack Benny show unless we got his permission. I know my contract was exclusive, so was Rochester, so was Don Wilson, so was Phil Harris. You could not work outside of the Jack Benny show, on other shows, without his permission on radio...He was always very generous. He never would turn you down, but the reason he did that was to protect the characters that he was building...because lots of other shows would destroy or have you say something that would hurt that character. That's why he was very exclusive. We were exclusive, so he paid us very well. I didn't get the thirty-five dollars a week that was in the script--I got seventy-five! You know, actually I got $250...for the first thirteen weeks I was on with Jack Benny per program...To me I thought that was the end of the world! Remember...my first program was October [8], 1939, and...I remember I rented a house out in Studio City in San Fernando Valley, a furnished house, three-bedroom house and I rented it for $125 a month!
L: That's good!
D: That shows you the difference [with] what's happened with inflation, and what the value at the time was. So $250 was equal perhaps to $1500 today, at least in today's dollars or maybe more. Still in all...before...I went in the Navy after four and a half years with Jack Benny, I was getting then $1000 a week, which was a lot of money then. Then after I came out, I had my own radio show...for Colgate-Palmolive, and then I went back with Jack Benny. My job was there. Larry [Stevens] was the one who took over my place the two years I was in the Navy. So I was given my job back when I got out of the Navy, so I had two programs; my own radio program and the Jack Benny show. On the Benny show I was getting $2500 a week then, that was in 1946. So we stayed on radio through 1954 or 55. So that was quite a thing for us. What a career I had! Here I had a two-week option and it lasted all of those years.
L: Did you ever have a problem breaking out of that character since it was so set by the Benny program?
D: No, it's amazing that people even on the Benny program, being a silly, naïve kid, would separate the fact that I could sing a good song--that I was a good singer--that I was able to sing a legitimate, good song; I could do semi-classics, classics, whatever. So they accepted that. They separated the two characters. Of course, like Benny, the 39, after he was 60 he couldn't say that any more because then it wouldn't be believable. When I did my personal appearances, I was able to refer to the Benny character but not *be* the Benny character, particularly the silly, naïve and...stupid kid. Stupid things would not go, even with somebody else playing against me, and I'd say silly things, they wouldn't be funny. Only with Jack Benny they came to be because he was the perfect straight man for all of us.
L: Are there any particular anecdotes that stand out in your mind from any of the Benny programs?
D: Well, it's awfully difficult to pick out any particular anecdote about Jack Benny that you feel that...this is funny or funnier than the other or anything that may have happened. I know every time I went to a rehearsal when I first went with Jack

Benny for the first five or four and a half years before I went in the Navy, it was always an excitement for me...because you knew it was going to be a funny script and it was going to be <u>really</u> funny just to hear and to listen to that...We always went out to his house or sometimes we would read it in the studio, but normally we would go to his house out on Roxbury Drive in Beverly Hills, and we'd sit around--we'd get the script and we'd read it just once. See, Jack wanted to get a reading and see how the...lines were going to play...We'd go out there, and I always get a tremendous charge out of the reading the first time because you didn't know what was coming, and Benny was the greatest audience because if something was funny, he could see. this man could see humor...this was his whole life; he had an intuitive sense of humor in reading this thing. He'd say, 'Oh!' and fall right down on the floor laughing!...He was the greatest audience and intuitively, too, he knew if something in the script was not right, that it was not good for himself or for any member of the cast. He knew that intuitively, and out it would come. You know, after that first reading we would leave the house...which would be probably on a Thursday we'd have that first reading, Wednesday or Thursday, normally on a Thursday, then we'd come back in on Saturday to the studio and we'd have another reading; and that script would, of course, then have been tightened up, they would have maybe taken out some spots and substituted others for them, and really that script would be fifty times better than the original that we first read...when we went out to his house...He was a great editor...and he knew instinctively what was good for Jack Benny, for each and every one of us in the show for the whole program. He knew instinctively what was good for us, and if anything wasn't, you knew it was out.

L: So you never actually sat in on the <u>writing</u> sessions...

D: No, I never did...I know that in...the first ten years or so that I was with him, Jack used to sit with the writers and they'd discuss what they were going to do on the following Sunday's program...He had four writers, so one set like George Balzer and Sam Perrin would write this part of the program, and Tackaberry and Milt Josefsberg would write the other part of the program, and then they'd get it together...Jack was always the one who sat on top and said, 'No, that's not good,' or...'This is the way we're going to go,' when they'd be editing the particular script, and then after the show was over what they were going to do for the following week. Because jack never liked to reminisce a great deal, he always liked to talk about 'What am I gonna do next? Who am I gonna have on my program?' I just came back from Maui as a matter of fact, I was over there, my wife and I and some of my family, we have a condominium over there, and we just came back and I happened to go into Woolworth's over in Kohoolawe on the east side of the island, and here they have all of these video tapes, and there was a Jack Benny video tape with Humphrey Bogart, and I had to get that tape! I think that was one of the specials he had done in the early 50's for Chrysler [E.N.: or October 25, 1953 for LSMFT], and I bought that tape and ran it on the VCR, and it still holds up great today as it did at that time. That was the beauty of Jack Benny's humor. They show his TV shows now on the Christian network, and they run practically, I think a couple of times a week, and they also run his old radio shows, and that humor, even though it's forty or forty-five years old, is still as funny today as it was then. You see, he didn't have topical humor necessarily...[he] might refer to President Truman or somebody like that, but it was still funny then and it's as funny today. That's why a lot of the college kids and the younger group of people are saying, 'Hey! This is funny stuff!' when they hear it or they happen to see it on video.

L: So which shows do you think were better--the radio shows or the television shows?

D: Well, I think radio had a great deal more to it in the fact that you used your imagination. Each one of you were your own painter in your mind of what that scene and those people [looked like] and what was happening. In your mind--you could hear it over the radio. So that to me was very difficult for many of the people, Bob Hope was able because he was more or less of a stand-up comic, was able to transfer from radio to television, so was Jack Benny. But not to me, it didn't have the impact...I remember, just to give you an example...very famous on radio was Jack Benny's visit to his vault. Down in the cavernous depths, you know, and you could picture in your mind just from the way sound effects were and the dialogue where he was going, and you could picture, there was a moat there when you're dear the chain clanking of raising the moat, and the sharks and then alligators and everything else, and you could all picture that in your mind. I remember the first time it was done on television. It was very funny, believe me. It was very funny when they did it on TV, but I remember after we did it...the next day probably, going down the street the next day going to the Brown Derby and people would come up, friends and just people, and they'd say, talking about the show, 'It was a great show, but uh-uh, that's not the way I saw it.' Each one had their own picture of what it should be like. So this was the thing that's very difficult to do in television what had already been done, or what people's minds in their own imagination thought it was like in radio, because we did not have the boob tube, you know, television. We had only your imagination in radio. So I think that was probably...much better for us and certainly for Jack and for everyone else to do it in radio, although Jack still lasted a long, long time and had a career not only from 1932 to 1955 or so on radio but also on TV. He started in about 1950, and he was doing television right up until the time that he passed away--he was preparing to do a show. He died [December] 26, 1974, and he was going to do a show February 14, 1975 which was his birthday. So he was just a few months short of being 81 years of age, and what a great life--what a beautiful life--and what joy and happiness that he gave to so many people throughout the world.

L: Just to sidestep a little bit away from the Jack Benny Show...I suppose this won't be exactly sidestepping it, but how did <u>A Day in the Life of Dennis Day</u> evolve?

D: Well, when I got out of the Navy, Ted Bates' agency...the advertising agency for Colgate-Palmolive...got hold of Frank Galen who had been a writer with Burns and Allen, and they came up with the idea of the Dennis Day show, where I was living in a boarding house...Bea Benaderet was playing the woman who was married to Dink Trout, of course Mr. and Mrs. Anderson--that was their name, and they had a daughter [Mildred], and I was living at the boarding house there in Weaverville, or whatever you want to call it. So that's how they came up with the idea was Frank Galen, and he had a couple of other writers with him, and they formulated on the basis of a Dennis Day character...that they knew from Jack Benny...I had that program for five years on radio.

L: Right. From '46 to '51 I think.

D: In television I had my own show...RCA Victor were my sponsors, and of course my last year they put me against <u>I Love Lucy</u>. That was 1953. They were then at the height of their popularity, and I could never get any kind of a rating. As a matter of fact, I've had requests now...I'm going to release on video to be shown on TV my Dennis Day show. So even thought it's in black and white...the Lucy show is still on. <u>The Real McCoys</u> are out now...and an awful lot of shows. So I think I'm going to get that out.

L: so was it really kind of an extension of the <u>Day in the Life</u> show?

D: Not really, it was...a little bit, but not really. First I tried, more or less, one with my mother, Verna Felton, just trying to find a format. It was very difficult to do singing in a show--I did three songs in every show, usually, and then have a storyline...Really you only had twenty-six minutes of show because the rest would be commercials. So it was very difficult to try to find a real format. Then...Paul Henning [Petticoat Junction] was my writer, and that's when they had Charley Weaver, Cliff Arquette...and we had little Susie James [who] was the little girl who lived in the apartment [Susie Sterling played by Jeri Lou James] and Ida Moore played one of the older people in it. That's how this thing evolved, so...I guess it was two and a half years I was on TV. But I couldn't get a rating against <u>I Love Lucy</u> and that was it.

L: Well, if it's going to be rereleased, who knows!
D: Yes, a lot of people never saw it then!
L: Jumping ahead to today, what kind of music do you listen to now?
D: Oh, I listen to...[music] mostly in my era. You know my kids all...have the radios when they play...the tapes. They go for all the Madonnas and...things.
L: Heavens, there's rock in the Day household?!
D: Well, they like...the current things. So each generation finds their own. We had our own. There's no Jerome Kerns around or Cole Porters...
L: Or George Gershwin.
D: Or Oscar Hammerstein, and Rogers and Hart and all of those, so it's a little different today...But I think they find their own--what they like...To me, it seems...repetitious, kind of monotonous. It's a beat, really. I can't understand any of the lyrics half the time...
L: I'm sympathetic to that. I still play your records and Al Jolson...[So] you are still performing?
D: I was...As a matter of fact I went back to Holyoke. I performed...over St. Patrick's--that's my big time! And I performed in Cleveland and in Youngstown, Ohio, then I was also in Pittsburgh, then I went to Hiyanis (sp?), I was up in New Hampshire, and then...on the 21st and 22nd, I was given by the city of Holyoke, Massachusetts, the John F. Kennedy memorial award for distinguished Irish-American, and I was very honored to get that...I received that, and I marched in the parade almost three miles! But from that time on, I started having problems with my legs, and I thought it was part of growing old because I'm not 39 anymore! And finally...when I got home and then I went to an orthopedic [doctor]. He x-rayed my back and said I had deterioration of the lower spine and that physical therapy would do me some good. So he sent me to a physical therapist, and then we were leaving May to go to Maui...While I was there I thought...I might get an adjustment. I went to a chiropractor--he did a little adjusting, and he said, 'I don't think you need adjusting--I think you've got a nerve problem...Would you mind if I sent you to a neurologist?' So I went to a neurologist on Maui, and he examined me and gave me certain tests...He said, 'Definitely you have a nerve problem in your neck and probably your back...You better have it attended to.' So I made arrangements...when I got home to go to Scripps Clinic down in San Diego. They ran all the tests on me, the cat scan, the myogram and the electromyogram and everything on me, and they came up with the diagnosis that I had motor-neuron disease and more then likely was ALS or Lou Gehrig's disease...I have a spastic walk, I can hardly walk now. I do walk with the aid of a cane. I'm afraid all my days of performing are in the past. I can still sing, and I love singing, but I'll have to do like Jane Froman used to do. When she was hurt flying on the transatlantic over on one of the clippers going to Portugal I guess it was, World War II, the plane crashed and she was paralyzed so she did all her performing from then on in a wheelchair. So God willing, I might be able to do that. So I hope to continue. I have a recording I did about six months ago--it's a 45...I believe Dick Clark is interested in releasing it...
L: Maybe you could be on <u>American Bandstand</u>!
D: Yeah! Well, all the money...that will come from it will go to the research center ALS, which is USC, Dr. King Engle...I'm now under his care--he's the head of

research at USC for motor-neuron diseases, and he treated the last Senator Javits of...the state of New York, and all the moneys...from the recording would be going to help him and research. I did the Jerry Lewis telethon here this past Sunday...and...I saw one portion of it when I was in Maui, but I understand they ran it three times, first with Sammy Davis, then with Jerry Lewis and also with Ed McMahon...So it was a short spot where I am walking with a cane and telling them what has happened to me, and it could happen to anybody. I never dreamt that it would happen to me. The good Lord had different ways of testing us...so that we can share in some of his glory, that we can share in the fact that He loves us all, He loves us eternally, and He's got an infinite love for us. He must love us an awful lot, when He allows us to share in the suffering of Jesus Christ.

L: Well, you're definitely in all of our prayers...

D: Well, I appreciate that. I know I've had a...wonderful response from people all over the country since this was announced...

L: One last question I must ask out of personal curiosity. Some time ago, there was a Dennis Day bear that came out, wasn't there?...

D: Yes, yes...they did have it. It came out of Illinois...and the first bears were fine. My wife had a gift and antique shop in Santa Monica, and the first bears were made in the United States...They were very good and we sold out all...of what she had, because I had a little song on it about the bear. Then after that, I guess something happened with the American manufacturer...he was too busy to make them, so they went to Korea, and evidently the quality of the bears went down, and I pulled out of the whole thing. I said, 'I'm sorry, I just can't have my name on it.'

L: ...Well thank you so much for your time. It's been quite an honor.

D: Well, it was an honor for me to be able to talk to all of you wonderful fans of the Jack Benny Show, and those wonderful years that I had and was blessed to be able to be associated with a man like Jack Benny, and Mary Livingstone and Rochester and Don Wilson and Phil Harris...Phil and I are the only two left...God knows how long either one of us will still be here.

L: Well, Mel Blanc is still around...

D: Yeah, well he was not one of the original starring cast--he wasn't announced...The Jack Benny Show starring Jack Benny, Mary Livingstone, Phil Harris, Rochester, Dennis Day, and...yours truly, Don Wilson! Actually...a featured player [who] was a wonderful man, too, who passed away not too long ago was Frank Nelson. YESSSS! Oh yes, he was a beautiful man. Mel is still working. He's had about seventeen operations since his automobile accident about twenty-five years ago...But Bea Benaderet used to be on there. I do see Sandra Gould every once in a while, she played one of the telephone operators on the program. There's still a number of them--Elliot Lewis who played...Frank Remley, and...Sheldon Leonard. He was the '[Hey] bub...C'mere. What elevator you takin'? Uh-uh.' Those were funny things.

L: Yeah, there were so many wonderful cast members.

D: ...I appreciate your talking with me, and as I say to be able to talk to you and to all the fans of the Jack Benny shows, and to all my wonderful friends.

L: Believe me, it's been an immense pleasure.

❄❄❄❄❄❄❄❄❄❄❄❄❄❄❄❄❄❄❄❄❄❄❄❄❄❄❄❄❄❄❄❄❄

Please send all questions, comments, additions, and corrections to:
Laura Lee (510) 933-3879
c/o The International Jack Benny Fan Club Offices
3190 Oak Road #303
Walnut Creek, California 94596   Internet: JACKBENNY@DELPHI.COM

Please friends, send no bombs.

TO: GARY CALCYN
FROM: DAVID MOTLEY

Jack Benny's Birthday

ITINERARY

Jack Benny Middle School
Cafeteria
8:30 - 9:15 am
2/14/94

8:30 Mayor introduces himself, then outlines the significance of this day. Next, Mayor makes presentation of a scholarship to the Illinois Summer Youth Music Camp in Champaign-Urbana to an outstanding orchestra student on Behalf of Jack Benny and the City of Waukegan. Mayor introduces Dr. Lynn Shornick Director of the Jack Benny Center for the Arts.

8:35 Dr. Lynn Shornick outlines Jack Benny's accomplishments and his contributions to our community. Dr. Shornick introduces Waukegan Police Chief George Bridges.

8:45 Chief George Bridges gives presentation regarding staying focused and the evils that students of today face. Chief Bridges turns the mic over to the Mayor.

8:55 Mayor Durkin introduces the comedy team of Spangler & Spangler.

8:55 Spangler & Spangler take over and perform.

9:15 Mayor concludes program; students return to class; program ends.

City of Waukegan

410 Robert V. Sabonjian Place
Waukegan, Illinois 60085
(708) 360-9000

William F. Durkin, Mayor
Sam Filippo, City Clerk
Dan Drew, City Treasurer

RESOLUTION
94-R-6

WHEREAS, February 14, 1994 marks the 100th birthday of Waukegan's favorite son, Jack Benny; and

WHEREAS, Jack Benny is an important role model to the youth in our community; and

WHEREAS, Jack Benny is still remembered for the humor and warmth he brought to many people; and

NOW THEREFORE, BE IT RESOLVED, that the Mayor and City Council of the City of Waukegan hereby acknowledge his many contributions to our community and extend our appreciation in his honor.

BE IT FURTHER RESOLVED that the City Clerk be and he is hereby directed, to forward a suitably embossed copy of this Resolution to the Jack Benny Middle School in commemoration of Jack Benny's 100th Birthday.

DATED THIS 7TH DAY OF FEBRUARY, 1994.

_____
MAYOR

ATTEST:

_____
CITY CLERK

Chicago Tribune
MetroLake

MONDAY, FEBRUARY 14, 1994

Waukegan's love for Benny in bloom on comic's 39th birthday... plus 61

By Penny Roberts
TRIBUNE STAFF WRITER

Jack Benny, who fashioned himself into a national comedic treasure by cultivating the image of being irrepressibly cheap and eternally 39, would have loved this.

On an October 1961 trip to his hometown of Waukegan, the comedian announced he would establish trust funds for each child born during his visit. The 10 so-called Benny Babies received $39 accounts and orders not to touch the money until, of course, their 39th birthdays.

Now, nearly 7½ years short of that moment and as Waukegan celebrates what would have been Benny's 100th birthday, it has come to this: At least one of the 10 school's most promising music pupils will receive a band-camp scholarship named for the man whose shtick emphasized mediocre violin virtuosity.

Mayor Bill Durkin will proclaim all residents 39 years old for the day, and one of the middle school's most promising music pupils will receive a band-camp scholarship named for the man whose shtick emphasized mediocre violin virtuosity.

Strike the Pose: placement of the chin in a palm, please, and the exasperated "Well!"

There will be a birthday assembly and a cake at the Benny Middle School and an exhibition of memorabilia at the Benny Center for the Arts.

Not that the comedian is forgotten on any other day in Waukegan—home of Jack Benny Drive, Benny Avenue, the Jack

Tribune photo by Bob Langer

Benjamin Spangler, 12, of Northbrook and his 10-year-old sister, Jamie, will do the "Sj, Sy, Sue" skit during Waukegan's celebration Monday of what would have been Jack Benny's 100th birthday.

Benny Bronze Star on the Walk of Stars (Grand Avenue and Sheridan Road) and the Benny Middle School athletes: the 39ers.

By way of explaining why the city has such a love affair with the native son, Benny memorabilia collector Jack Melcher said,

See **Benny**, PAGE 4

Benny
CONTINUED FROM PAGE 1

"He put Waukegan on the map. That's reason enough to li.e him."

Born Benjamin Kubelsky at Mercy Hospital in Chicago to Meyer and Emma Kubelsky of Waukegan, the comedian grew up in two places, first in an apartment on Genesee Street north of Belvidere Street and later at 518 Clayton St.

Though Benny's example is being touted to students in hopes of keeping them in school and striving for excellence, he was expelled from Central High School at the end of his sophomore year, fired from his father's Genessee Street haberdashery, and flunked at Waukegan Business College.

Nonetheless, he got a job playing pit violin at the Barrison Theater, then one of Waukegan's top vaudeville houses. The rest, they say, is history.

This year's Benny fanfare began

"It was pretty exciting to have Jack Benny leave me something."
Pamela Quinn

Saturday night with the eighth annual Benny Birthday Bash and the presentation of the Jack Benny Arts and Humanities Award.

With such events, Waukegan hopes to introduce Benny to a new generation of residents born long after his death from cancer in 1974.

"Most kids don't know who Benny is, the significance he holds for our city, the nation and the world," said David Motley, Waukegan's special events coordinator.

Perhaps the best Benny lesson will be presented Monday morning by the comedy team of Spangler & Spangler. Benjamin Spangler, a Northbrook 12-year-old who is a seasoned Benny impersonator, and his 10-year-old sister, Jamie, will present updated versions of some of Benny's enduring routines. They'll begin with Benny's traditional "Jell-O, folks!" and end with the "SJ, Sy, Sue" skit.

The Benny Babies need no reminders about who the man was.

One of them is Pamela Quinn, born at Victory Memorial Hospital, who loved the idea of the trust accounts and became a devoted follower of her benefactor.

"It was pretty exciting to have Jack Benny leave me something," recalled Quinn, now 32.

But the excitement of the idea clashed with the dreariness of reality. She closed her account about seven years ago when it became evident the service charges were going to surpass the amount of the trust, then worth about $70.

Well!

Fred Tannenbaum contributed to this article.

JBC ENTERTAINMENT AND ARTS NEWS

FEBRUARY EDITION 1991 — WAUKEGAN PARK DISTRICT — VOL. 2, NO. 8

WHAT A PROGRAM!

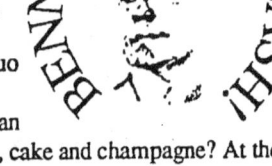

Where can you hear songs from the nineteen-teens, see an eight year old impersonator of Jack Benny, see a nationally recognized dancer perform with his protege, hear and see one of the funniest skits ever to hit the stage, hear duo piano music from the turn of the century, get an historical tour of an era, enjoy popcorn and soda pop, cake and champagne? At the Fifth Annual **Benny Birthday Bash!**, that's where.

Saturday evening, February 9 at 8:00, the Jack Benny Center for the Arts in conjunction with the Friends of the Jack Benny Center for the Arts will host this special event. A fundraiser for the scholarship endowment fund, tickets are $25.00 per person. The 1991 Bash! will be a salute to Vaudeville in Waukegan during the early 1900s. The Waukegan Park District is celebrating its 75th anniversary and the **Benny Birthday Bash!** is a special attraction during the month of February. There's no denying 1916 was a great year for Vaudeville and the Waukegan Park District!

Here are more specifics about what you'll see and hear at the fifth annual **Benny Birthday Bash!** The Divas, starring Jeri Whitson, Lora Hiney, Anna Witt-Kite, and Nancy Sutton; Al and Willie in a classic Doctor Skit starring Egon Schein, Jerry Emerzian, Christi Geidner-Kirby, and Mark Kettner; Mulligan & Schwinn in Duelling Pianos; Ned Fisher, Comedian; Barbershop Quartet featuring Doug Cole, Jim Stiles, Doug Stiles, and Gary Saxvik; Shonfeld & Mulligan in a Moment with Strings and Keys; a Special Appearance by Benjamin Spangler as the Young Jack Benny (of course young, he was always young!); Sally Peterson, Marimbist Extraordinaire; Alexson and Lehman dancing in Fancy Feet; Gretchen Stevenson-Poland in The Voice on Wings; The Benny Sisters in A Dark and Stormy Night, starring Lora Hiney, Dolores Strazer, Bo Carroll, and Janet Cole; Vaudevillian Histrionics with Jim Neal, Birthday Cake and Champagne, AND, the presentation of the **1991 Jack Benny Arts and Humanities Award** to Kenneth W. Smouse!

For more information, contact us at 360-4741!

GIFTED PROGRAM WILL HAPPEN

Meetings with Association Superintendent in charge of Curriculum and Planning, Dr. G. Robert Kurtz, led to the inclusion of a request for program support by the Waukegan Public Schools Board of Trustees at their January meeting. With the backing of the administrative staff of the district, the board agreed to support the program by providing the program with a space in which to operate. The bilingual division of curriculum planning will support the program also. The goal is to provide one hundred hispanic students to the program. Support is being sought for financial aid for all students needing financial assistance. The program is set to run from July 1 though July 19, a three week program.

Run by Joan Smutny and Cheryl Siewers of National-Louis University, the program will feature classes for children from first through the sixth grades, with special explorations in science, math, writing, dance, art, music, and a host of other activity areas. The three week program will cost $195 per child. The program will run in the mornings, Monday through Friday, for the three week period. The Jack Benny Center for the Arts has been asked to help supply instruction in the arts. The teaching staff, all highly motivated and creative individuals, are not only specialists, but have that particular ability to spark interests in new and innovative techniques and ideas. Many children from the Waukegan area have taken advantage of Mrs. Smutny's Worlds of Wisdom and Wonder in surrounding communities. The Friends of the Jack Benny Center for the Arts are particularly interested in seeing that area children have the advantage of these programs. Glowing reports of the success of this program are standard. It certainly is a program that is needed during the summer months. It affords the opportunity for talented and gifted children to find new sources of development for their skills. For more preliminary information about the Waukegan Worlds of Wisdom and Wonder call the Jack Benny Center at 360-4741. Brochures for the program will be distributed through the month of February. Plan now to enroll your children in this extraordinary program. Chances are tremendous that your child will come home the first day and repeat a phrase already heard from hundreds of youngsters, "Mommy, it was great!"

UPCOMING EVENTS

February 4	**Winter Session Begins at JBC**
February 9 8:00 p.m.	**Benny Birthday Bash!** Jack Benny Center for the Arts Vaudeville in Waukegan! Goodfellow Hall
February 22, 23, March 1, 2, 3*, 8, 9 8:00 p.m., *3:00 p.m.	Bowen Park Theatre Company Neil Simon's **The Good Doctor** Goodfellow Hall
March 10 - April 30	**Waukegan Park District 75th Anniversary** Historical Display Jack Benny Center for the Arts
March 29	JBC Closed to observe **Good Friday**
April 8	**Spring Session Begins at JBC**
April 26, 27, May 3, 4, 8:00 p.m.	Bowen Park Opera Company Pergolesi **The Maid Made Mistress**/Bernstein **Trouble in Tahiti** Goodfellow Hall
April 28, May 5 7:00 p.m.	**Maid** and **Trouble** continued
May 27	JBC Closed to observe **Memorial Day**
June 14, 15, 21, 22, 23*, 28, 29 8:00 p.m., *3:00 p.m.	Bowen Park Theatre Company Sam Shepard's **True West** Goodfellow Hall

The Jack Benny Center for the Arts
39 Jack Benny Drive
Bowen Park
Waukegan, Illinois 60087-5145
Call 708-360-4741.

Eleanor Powell in a scene from Broadway Melody of 1936.

MELODY, MISERY, MIRTH

The Films Present a Captivating Musical, a Pungent Child Picture from France, and a Graceful Variation of the Cinderella Theme

by BEVERLY HILLS

READING TIME ● 13 MINUTES 50 SECONDS

★★★ **BROADWAY MELODY OF 1936**

THE PLAYERS: Jack Benny, Robert Taylor, Eleanor Powell, Una Merkel, June Knight, Sid Silvers, Vilma Ebsen, Buddy Ebsen, Nick Long, Jr., Robert Wildhack, Frances Langford, Harry Stockwell. Directed by Roy Del Ruth. Story by Moss Hart.

4 stars—Extraordinary 3 stars—Excellent
2 stars—Good 1 star—Poor
0 star—Very Poor

LONG noted as the studio that could make almost any sort of pictures but musicals, M-G-M, with a somewhat prematurely titled film, Broadway Melody of 1936, breaks its jinx in a captivating array of dancing, singing, beauty and wit.

Rather than rely on the established stars from its long list of world-famous performers, M-G-M has entrusted its lavish extravaganza to new faces. New cinema faces are generally new for the simple reason that they have lacked the ability or the chance to be famous. There is no reason why the public, fooled more than once by ballyhooed debuts, should get unduly excited just because it doesn't know the performers.

The players in Broadway Melody of 1936, however, need only the chance to be seen. Headed by Eleanor Powell, whose really amazing dancing should make her the rhythmic sensation of the year, the entire group is grand. Jack Benny, the radio jester, and Sid Silvers, as his lame-witted stooge, wrap up the acting honors; while Robert Taylor, June Knight, Buddy Ebsen, Nick Long, Jr., Una Merkel, and Robert Wildhack—who is, of all things, an expert on snores—give this delightful film all the comedy, beauty, and music it can use.

Featuring the loveliest ballet ever photographed and Frances Langford's superb rendition of You Are My Lucky Star, the picture is given a plot that would hold the interest even if it had none of its handsome embellishments. The story concerns the feud of a young play producer (Robert Taylor) and a Broadway columnist. Planning to make a chump of the producer, the columnist publicizes an imaginary French actress, and the producer falls for the ruse by announcing that she will appear in his new show. How the boys work themselves out of this spot is told in an amusing, swiftly paced manner that makes this spirited spectacle as entertaining as it is impressive.

Not only a stunning treat to the ear and eye, Broadway Melody of 1936 is, above all, a smartly contrived merger of talent, music, and humor. You don't have to be a tired businessman to enjoy it.

VITAL STATISTICS: M-G-M—Muggum to you—reputed not to have realized bigness of the Melody till after big Chinese Theater preview, at which it killed the people. . . . About a million dollars went into the making of this one. . . . Director Roy Del Ruth—borrowed from Warner Bros.—believes in a fluid camera which flows from place to place and gives pace and that breathless *je ne sais quoi* to entertainment. That is why those Del Ruthian dances move so breezily, and are known as the Del Ruthian wallops. . . . Eleanor Powell isn't related to Bill or Dick. Learned to dance to overcome shyness. Had no intention of making dancing her career, her maw sending her to dancing school at six, when all other means of ditching Ellie's timidity had failed. It wasn't till 1929 that Eleanor learned to tap-dance and in a year she was crowned World's Greatest. Robert Taylor will probably leap into demand after the Melody. A Nebraska

LOOK, MARY A $10 RAISE

...and all because he learned how to put his ideas across

● YOUR boss wants good ideas too. Are you getting full credit for yours? There's one way to make sure. Type them out in clear, understandable form on your own Remington Portable. You'll be surprised how seeing words in clean-cut black and white speeds up your own thinking. Best of all, neat, typewritten ideas command executive attention...make a good impression for you wherever they go.

Only $4 down buys a new Remington

As advertised on "March of Time"

Greatest portable typewriter bargain ever offered...only $4 down buys a brand new, latest model Key-Control Remington. Every essential feature of big machines...standard four-row keyboard, standard width carriage, margin release, back spacer, etc. If your dealer cannot supply you, mail coupon.

10 Day Free Trial Offer

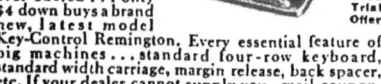

Remington Rand, Inc., Dept. 12-JB, 205 E. 42nd St. New York City.
Please tell me how I can buy a new Remington Portable for only $4 down. Also enclose catalog.

Name_____
Address_____
City_____ State_____

BACKACHES NEED WARMTH

Thousands who suffered miserable backaches, pains in shoulders or hips, now put on Allcock's Porous Plaster and find warm, soothing relief. Muscle pains caused by rheumatism, neuritis, arthritis, sciatica, lumbago and strains, all respond instantly to the glow of warmth that makes you feel good right away. Allcock's Plaster brings blood to the painful spot... treats backache where it is. Allcock's lasts long, comes off easily. Only Allcock's is the original porous plaster... guaranteed to bring instant relief, or money back. 5 million users. 25¢ at druggists, or write "Allcock, Ossining, N. Y." **ALLCOCK'S**

Be a Beauty

make skin Clear..
White..Flawless
Quick, Easy Way!

HAVE dirt and exposure robbed your skin of its youthful charm? Here's thrilling news! *They mar only the outer skin*—a dull mask that can be melted away—safely and gently! Golden Peacock Bleach Creme helps nature flake off that outer skin that makes your complexion unattractive! It dissolves the coarse, invisible particles of surface skin! In five days the supreme thrill is complete—a clear, fresh, satin-soft skin that looks years younger and shades whiter! Surface blemishes and freckles vanish! Relied upon by thousands to keep young-looking and alluring! 55¢ at drug stores.

'small-towner, he's been looking for a break for a long time and deserves it for handsomeness alone, girls. . . . Buddy and Vilma Ebsen are of Orlando, Florida. They debutted professionally in Ziegfeld's Whoopee. Buddy is married to Ruth Cambridge, who is Winchell's Girl Friday; and for his comedy work in the Melody he's been handed a contract as a Muggum comedian actor. Vilma's married to Bobby Dolan, nervous jazz maestro and classico-jazz composer. . . . Una Merkel, than whom there are worse comediennes in higher places, had to practice at a real switchboard for her hello-girl part—think of that! . . . That operation Frances Langford had on her throat to regain a lost voice made her a contralto crooner instead of a silver soprano, if you know what I mean. She can soprano it if necessary, however. . . . Jack Benny is of vodvil, in which I can remember him telling poolroom jokes in the ballroom manner. Radio took Benny to its windy buzzum and put him high in the air waves. Benny is happily married to Mary Livingstone; they live from hotel to hotel; have no kiddie-widdies. Was not too successful in his movie debut in Transatlantic Merry-Go-Round, what with being miscast—his part being too sympathetic for his causticity. The role of the columnist suits him to a sour pickle, so well, indeed, that he was immediately cast by Muggum for the role of a Broadway chiseler in Let Freedom Ring. . . . Sid Silvers, the Jewish gnome, is the answer to a stooge's prayer. Starting as Phil Baker's stooge, he sat in a box and interrupted Baker's act, delivering strong unpleasant remarks that entirely confounded Baker—a happy, happy victory for the Stooge Association, a group never allowed to dish it out. . . . That Happiness Boy writer Moss Hart, who wrote what is laughingly termed the original story of the Melody, will soon take a hand at doing drama.

★ ★ ★ LA MATERNELLE

THE PLAYERS: Paulette Elambert, Madeleine Renaud, Alice Tissot, Henri Debain, Sylvette Fillacier, Mady Berri. Directed by Jean Benoit-Levy and Marie Epstein. Story by Leon Frapie.

A FOREIGN film worth catching if it comes your way is La Maternelle, a realistic mordant yet tender study of homeless waifs. Though the picture is told in French dialogue, there are superimposed English titles and the story itself is simple enough to follow without much trouble.

These grimy, dirty-nosed foundlings are caught in strikingly natural attitudes and their mass appeal for the affection and love that is denied them at home makes for a deeply touching photoplay. Assiduously avoiding the maudlin, La Maternelle centers about a day school for children of the Paris slums, whose parents are the demimondaines, the thieves and drunkards of Montmartre.

The charm of these Gallic youngsters lies in their ability to forget the camera. They have none of the calculated cuteness of the Hollywood infants and their honestly attained effects are something not often sent out from the studios.

Paulette Elambert has the leading role, that of a child whose mother has run away. Starving for affection, she pours out her love on a school maid, beautifully played by Madeleine Renaud, who very nearly breaks the child's heart when she becomes engaged. This tale is told in lean, poetic scenes and, except for a few early bits, is intelligently and objectively directed.

A treat for moviegoers seeking something different in entertainment, La Maternelle is, moreover, a pungent morsel for all serious fans, and quite possibly the truest picture of the prepuberty age yet recorded by the camera and microphone.

VITAL STATISTICS: La Maternelle (Lah Mahtair-nell), the name given to French state orphanage schools for tiny tots, means, actually, "the mother feeling" and, applied to said schools, "the second mother." . . . Book, La Maternelle, is an old-time 2 year jerker. . . . Picture codirected by Jean Benoit-Levy and Marie Epstein, who previously had collaborated on scripts together. They are quite young, being under thirty. . . . La Maternelle cost, when it was made about two years ago, $50,000 to $60,000 or about 1,200,000 francs. . . . French stars short of Chevalier type work for 1,000 francs ($70) per day average, graded up to 3,000 francs. . . . Paulette Elambert was nine when chosen from all comers for part. More the Jane Withers than the Shirley Temple type, she is considered an adult mind. . . . Madeleine Renaud is well known star of La Comédie Française of Paris. She is around forty, unmarried, and one of France's leading exponents of the classics. . . . Mady Berri, no relation to Wallie, resembles him somewhat in heft and comedy capacities. Alice Tissot is an old stage hand who always plays heavy roles. Alice's been around for about thirty years. Sylvette Fillacier is always typed as a country bumpkiness maid. . . . Picture took quite a while in making, a real *maternelle* being used as background as well as real orphans, slow in responding to the megaphone. The Elambert is not an orphan.

★ ★ ★ THE GAY DECEPTION

THE PLAYERS: Francis Lederer, Frances Dee, Benita Hume, Alan Mowbray, Lennox Pawle, Adele St. Maur, Akim Tamiroff, Luis Alberni. Directed by William Wyler. Story by Stephen Avery and Don Hartman.

THE GAY DECEPTION has Frances Dee as a stenographer who wins $5,000 on a sweepstakes ticket and then goes to New York. Posing as a lady of wealth while on the spending spree, Miss Dee falls in with Francis Lederer, who is not the lowly hotel employee he seems but an actual prince learning about the hotel trade.

While it exhibits no startling originality in its conception or plot development, The Gay Deception can be listed as one of the more pleasant pictures of the month. Director William Wyler has handled the situations with a deft and light touch, and Frances Dee, hitherto but a competent leading woman, displays an unsuspected comedy flair. The picture moves with an easy grace, and by the time Miss Dee learns that her bellhop, who manages to work in every hotel she visits, is really a prince, one realizes that one has been having a pretty fine time watching the old story.

Benita Hume, the dark English beauty, gives it all a decorative touch, and Alan Mowbray, Lennox Pawle, and Akim Tamiroff stand out in supporting roles. Mr. Lederer gives his nicest performance since The Pursuit of Happiness.

The screen play by Stephen Avery and Don Hartman contrives to make this fluffy concoction a pleasant respite from the sturdier cinema offerings.

VITAL STATISTICS: This is Jesse Lasky's last for Fox before moving over to United Artists to work for Mary Pickford. . . . Son of a poor leather merchant, Francis (Honeyboy) Lederer was born in Prague, Czechoslovakia. As an impressionable inferiority-ridden lad he got a bellyful of the war, accounting for his passionate crusading for world peace. Within past few months he has delivered a bushel of speeches for self-founded World Peace Federation, before audiences totaling more than 100,000. Lederer maintains entire cost of his organization, 20 per cent of his salary going to the noble purpose, said wages being about $50,000 per picture. He lives in Hollywood, is unmarried; never goes to hot spots. He's hard to suit roles to, being terribly finicky. . . . Picture cost about a half million. . . . Frances Dee colored prettily in Becky Sharp. In private life she's Mrs. Joel McCrae; they have a baby boy and a ranch near Chatsworth, California. She free-lances; began as an extra. Born in Los Angeles but schooled in Chicago, she started in pictures as a co-ed in Her Golden Calf, after which Chevalier cinched it for her. . . . Director William Wyler got himself married and separated in quick spank time from Margaret Sullavan, ex of Henry Fonda, who is now making himself a little Hollywood niche. . . . Benita Hume is dark and teddibly good at the social thing, don't you know. Born in London, she's about twenty-eight. Royal Academy of Arts educated. She's shuttled back

Judy Canova and Ben Blue

Jack Benny

ARTISTS OF MELODY
Hollywood's leading hit writers come through with 6 smash songs!

ARTIST OF WISE CRACKS...BENNY'S THE NAME!

Radio's Number One Entertainer, the biggest laughmaker the screen has ever seen...the one and only Jack Benny at his super-funniest heads the all-star cast of "Artists and Models." Above you see him in an artistic moment, below, at the head of the parade in one of the huge production numbers. At the top right you see Ben Blue teaching Judy Canova how to swing that thing. At the lower right is Martha Raye going to town in blackface, giving you a glimpse of "Public Melody Number One"... just one of the half dozen hit numbers Louis Armstrong and his Band and Andre Kostelanetz and His Orchestra help you to enjoy in "Artists and Models," the biggest gag and gal, yes, and the biggest song and dance show of this or any year.

MARTHA RAYE attacks "Public Melody No. 1"

My Best Friends

featuring **Walt Disney©** Character Merchandise

NOW OPEN in Historic LONG GROVE

My Best Friends has opened a big new store in the charming, historic yesteryear community of Long Grove, Illinois.

COME VISIT US!

We're just a few steps above the Long Grove Confectionery Company... a few steps across the square from the Pine Cone Christmas Shop and the Long Grove Apple Haus.

WE HAVE

- T-SHIRTS • ADULT JACKETS
- STORYBOOKS • COFFEE
- MUGS • TOYS • MUSIC BOXES
- CERAMIC FIGURES
- ORNAMENTS • POSTERS
- SCHOOL SUPPLIES • PLUSH
- LASER ART • WINDSOX

MUCH MORE!

WINTER HOURS
Tuesday thru Saturday
10 a.m. to 4 p.m.
Sunday Noon to 4
Closed Monday

MY BEST FRIENDS
212 Robert Parker Coffin Rd.
Long Grove, IL 60047-9539
PHONE: (708) 634-1022

The FILMS of JACK BENNY

BY BILL OATES

(From *Classic Images*, Number 135. Reprinted by permission of the author.)

"It's the *Jack Benny Show* with Mary Livingstone, Dennis Day, Phil Harris, Rochester, ..."

And as the voice of announcer Don Wilson trails off into the ethereal void, the avid radio listener reminisces on one of the most enduring programs of pre-television during broadcasting's golden age. Whether one recalls countless nights poised before the old Philco or more recently transcribed on record or cassette, *The Jack Benny Show* and its namesake loom over the rest as the epitome of the radio crafter's art.

So successful was Benny that no one else was given his or her own time slot by a network (a place on Sunday nights that was occupied by Benny for the better part of 23 years), and fewer still successfully made the transition into television. Even though Jack Benny seems to typify the art of 1930s-1940s broadcasting, it was the motion picture that first brought American's premiere cheapskate and perennial thirty-nine year old to the masses.

It may seem incongruous to examine the non-radio career of Jack Benny, but his 24 starring and numerous cameo roles in film are often overlooked and moreover the butt of ill-sent (frequently by Benny himself) jokes. Most of Jack Benny's fellow radio performers, like Fibber McGee and Molly, Fred Allen, Lum and Abner, Amos and Andy, Ozzie and Harriet, and many others, made at least one film based on their radio personalities.

No greater example of a transition to film from radio could be exemplified than by that of Orson Welles' *Mercury Theater of the Air* cast's sojourn into the celluloid world in *Citizen Kane*. Usually the references to Welles, Joseph Cotton, Agnes Moorehead, and even orchestra conductor Bernard Hermann's connection to the radio program is but a footnote to the ultimate American film. Jack Benny's film career is often a more minuscule note to the comedian's long tenure in show business.

Jack Benny's movie "career" began in 1929, when he was asked to m.c. the lavish MGM part-Technicolor *Hollywood Review of 1929*. He was rewarded with this role because of his successes as a monologist headlining vaudeville stages in the 1920s.

Benny, born Benny Kubelsky of Jewish immigrants, first made his bow on February 13, 1894, in Waukegan, Illinois, "over a tailor's sign." After paying more attention to playing the violin than to his schooling, Benny worked his way up through the vaudeville ranks to the prestigious Orpheum circuit with pianist Lymann Woods for $200 a week. World War I interrupted his stage career, but provided him with a chance to change his method of entertaining forever. The recruits at the Great Lakes Naval Training Station preferred the young violinist's humorous bit as a juvenile in a review called *Maritime Frolics* to his pizzicato and arco.

Benny realized his potential as a humorous speaker and so, after his discharge, continued on his move up vaudeville's ladder, ultimately playing the famed New York Palace. While changing his name first to Ben K. Benny and later to Jack Benny, MGM noted this talent and brought the monologist out to Hollywood to introduce some of those who were under Leo's care in 1929, including Marion Davies, John Gilbert, Buster Keaton, Norma Shearer, Lionel Barrymore, and many others.

The film is a strange mixture of talent

FILMS OF JACK BENNY

and among the more interesting segments are the magic skit pantomime by Laurel and Hardy and the singing of Charles King and Cliff "Ukulele Ike" Edwards.

Amazingly, this early all-talking, singing and dancing film received a nomination for Best Picture Academy Award of 1929-1930. Jack Benny was on his way.

Benny's next three films are often forgotten. While under contract at MGM, he m.c.'d another film, *The Songwriters' Review* (1929), wherein prominent songwriters, such as Herb Nacio Brown, played their songs on the piano prior to the singing and dancing of same. While at Metro, Jack made *Chasing Rainbows* (1930), a starring vehicle for Charles King and Bessie Love. Finally, just prior to Benny's four-year absence from Hollywood, he starred in a Tiffany Production film, *The Medicine Man* (1930). In this film, Jack has the chance to play a role different from his now stereotyped M.C. role, when he acts as a medicine show barker. He's the love-em-and-leave-em type who falls for a tough grocery store owner's daughter.

Since this B-film was made quickly, Jack was able to accept an offer to return to the New York stage in Earl Carroll's *Vanities of 1930*. Though the show was reviewed as bawdy, Jack received accolades and a chance to appear on Ed Sullivan's Broadway talk and gossip radio show in 1932.

After Benny's radio debut, CBS opened up a spot for him on his own show on May 2, 1932. While starring on radio and television for 32 seasons, Jack Benny was able to star in 18 more films.

Jack's return to films began in 1934 in the Reliance picture *Transatlantic Merry-Go-Round*. Benny plays an ocean liner's m.c. who is in love with Nancy Carroll. One interesting part of the film is the parody of *Grand Hotel*, which is entitled *Grind Hotel*, an idea that was first introduced on Benny's radio program.

Frank Parker was included in the cast of the film after he had been brought West to become Benny's radio show tenor. Jack was noted for his effort in the press and was called soon thereafter to begin his most active movie life. Simultaneous to *Transatlantic*'s opening, a play written by Benny, George S. Kaufman, and Morrie Ryskind opened in Washington, D.C. and closed soon after. The play was a flop despite the talented comedy writers, but in the meantime, the radio program and new sponsor Jell-O were being tested and enjoyed more and more.

Jack Benny returned to MGM in 1935 to appear in two films, *It's in the Air* with Ted Healy, Una Merkle and Nat Pendleton and *Broadway Melody of 1936* with Robert Taylor, Eleanor Powell and Vilma and Buddy Ebsen. The former film is about Benny and Healy (recently divorced from the Three Stooges), who are two con men trying to stay ahead of the feds. This suspense filled comedy once again earned Benny critical praise which increased even more after his next picture. *Melody of '36* had the cast, story by Moss Hart and songs by Herb Nacio Brown and Arthur Freed ("Got a Feelin' You're Foolin'," "You Are My Lucky Star," and "Broadway Rhythm"), to create an early classical MGM musical. Jack plays a Broadway gossip columnist who, in a need to spice up his Walter Winchell-like radio show, invents damaging gossip about producer Taylor. The movie is a delight from Benny and his stooge Sid Silvers' harassment of Taylor to the fine dancing by Powell and the Ebsens. At the film's premier, Jack thanked everyone and announced Jello's six delicious flavors, "strawberry, raspberry, cherry, Metro, Goldwyn, and Mayer."

Though Jack was grateful to MGM, he never starred in another of its productions, but rather began his long association with Paramount. Adolph Zukor's studio was home (at least temporarily) to many of the great comedians of the 1930s, including the Marx Brothers, W.C. Fields, Bob

BUCK BENNY RIDES AGAIN — In this 1940 comedy, Jack teamed up on the screen with radio partners Phil Harris (left) and Andy Devine (right).

Hope, and others, so it was natural for Benny to sign on with the mountain top company. *The Big Broadcast of 1937* is much like *Broadway Melody of 1936* in that a small town girl tries to make good in the big city. Shirley Ross is the would-be star, while Ray Milland is her beau. Though the cast is talent-laden, with the likes of Martha Raye, Bob "Bazooka" Burns, Benny Goodman, Leopold Stokowski's orchestra, and Burns and Allen (in their third *Big Broadcast*), Jack summed up his attitude towards pictures such as these as "stories for song-and-dance" where story lines are secondary.

Nonetheless, it is an entertaining film. Jack starred in seven other films at Paramount from 1935-40. *College Holiday* (1935) with Burns and Allen was another lightly plotted musical wherein Mary Boland plays a scientist interested in heredity and the way some groups of people are smarter than others. Instead of producing offsprings of "superior" intelligence at a gathering of "superior" beings, the student guinea pigs produce a musical.

Artists and Models (1937) found Benny as a financially shaky ad agency owner who struggles to pay his bills while finding

- Nostalgia Digest

FILMS OF JACK BENNY

a queen for the Artists and Models Ball. In the sequel, *Artists and Models Abroad* (1938), Benny tries to get his stranded theatrical troupe back home from Paris after putting the books in the black. Joan Bennett plays a wealthy American abroad employer, opened, as his who might offer the needed capital if Jack follows her whims. Both *Artists* films are fun to watch.

Between these movies, Jack was offered a chance to appear in *Big Broadcast of 1938* but declined the role because it was like those he had disliked before (the m.c. type). He would have likewise felt uncomfortable singing the romantic song of the picture, "Thanks for the Memory," a theme that was readily adopted by young comedian Bob Hope. When Kenny Baker sings the song on the *Benny* radio show shortly after the film's release, Benny mentions that the violinist should not attempt to butcher another good song, alternate to "Love In Bloom," but one cast member says that the song might be a good though he announced that he would try it the next week anyway.

In 1939, Jack began the first of his last three Paramount films, *Man About Town*. This mediocre musical about a producer trying to crash London's high society played on the success of Jack's radio show. Two members of the radio cast, Eddie "Rochester" Anderson and Phil Harris, had parts in the film as did Dorothy Lamour (a last minute replacement for ailing Betty Grable) and Edward Arnold. So positive were the prospects for this movie that Paramount premiered the film at Waukegan's Genessee, Academy and Rialto theaters and broadcast the proceedings on stage as part of the June 25, 1939 radio show. The gala event was attended by regular radio cast members, guest stars Lamour and Andy Devine, and most importantly, a very proud Meyer Kubelsky, the 70-year-old father of the star.

In *Buck Benny Rides Again*, Jack is joined in a screen adaptation of his oft-used radio skit of the late 1930s by sidekick Andy, "Hi ya', Buck" (to be said like a teenage boy's voice vacilating between youth and manhood, but unsure of the course) Devine, Ellen Drew and radio members Anderson and Harris. This western parody, which provided black valet Rochester as many lines as his employer, opened, at Benny's insistence, at Loew's Victoria on East 125th Street in Harlem.

In a poignant introduction, Bill "Bojangles" Robinson related to the audience the three people he thought were color blind in show business: Irving Berlin, who hired Ethel Waters for *As Thousands Cheer*, Shirley Temple's mother for encouraging Fox films to allow "Bojangles" to appear with her daughter, and Jack Benny, the man who often gave the black man in his cast funnier lines than he did for himself

Later in that year, *Love Thy Neighbor* opened for those who wanted to see the famous Benny-Fred Allen feud on the screen. The high point of the movie was Mary Martin's rendition of her hit song "My Heart Belongs to Daddy," because the incredibly funny and long lived radio feud was not effectively transferred to film.

For all the films that Jack Benny made at Paramount, one non-Benny movie gave him one of his trademarks, "Love In Bloom." Bing Crosby introduced the song in *She Loves Me Not* (1934); and after Jack effectively butchered it as a violin solo, hearing it was never quite the same.

Jack did one picture for Twentieth-Century-Fox in 1941, *Charley's Aunt*. Benny's effort is an amusing remake of the 1925 film that starred Sydney Chaplin. In this updated version of the 1892 play about a college aunt impersonator, Benny is somewhat miscast as an Oxford student, but is extremely successful when wooed in drag by the unknowing Edmund Gwenn. During the year of this film's release, Jack Benny became one of the top ten box office attractions while he was in his eighth year

HOLLYWOOD CANTEEN — In 1944 Jack appeared with violinist Efrim Zimbalist, Sr. and an all-star cast.

on radio and on top of that medium's list of most listened to programs.

So important was Jack Benny to comedy in America that renowned director Ernst Lubitsch sought him to play opposite Carole Lombard, the premiere comedienne of the day, in the Alexander Korda production *To Be Or Not To Be* (1942). Clark Gable and Carole Lombard had been close friends of the Bennys so it would be an even greater pleasure for Jack and Carole to work together.

To Be Or Not To Be was completed close to the winter holiday season in 1941. Ernst Lubitsch moved within Jack the actor as Benny had never been directed before, and the result is Jack Benny's best performance on film. With Lombard, he created the Tura's, a Polish husband and wife acting team that was being forced out of business by the invading Nazis. When Meyer Kubelsky saw Jack on screen in a Nazi uniform, the star's father stormed out of the theater and didn't speak to his son for two weeks. After several pleas, Benny got his father back into the theater to prove that it was the Nazis who were being lampooned, and the result was the aged Kubelsky's first of thirty viewings of the complete film.

Unfortunately, audiences who loved Carole Lombard were unable to enjoy this her last picture, unreleased at the time of her death in a plane crash on January 16, 1942. The film that Benny starred in was well crafted but had a pall over it, not only

FILMS OF JACK BENNY

because of the leading lady's death during a war bond promotional tour, but also because the story was about the valiant heroes in a "European conflict" that was more remote when made, but of a subject matter closer to Americans when released after December 7, 1941.

The results of the release of *To Be Or Not To Be* were mixed. Jack was unable to do his radio show on January 18, 1942, out of respect for Carole and also because he had to take time to sort out the reason for the loss of such a vibrant person. Instead of the regular show, Dennis Day presented a program of appropriate musical numbers and Don Wilson invited the audience to join the singers in a chorus of "America The Beautiful."

Critically, the movie was a success; and although it did not receive as many Oscar considerations as one might feel, it did win Best Scoring of a Comedy or Drama. The film was remade in 1982 with Mel Brooks and Anne Bancroft, but the remake was unable to blend poignancy (to a holocaust aware public) and Brooks' wacky humor effectively. As has been the case so often in Hollywood, the original should have been left alone.

From United Artists, Jack Benny journeyed over to Warner Brothers, a stay which was artistically rewarding, but not as long as one might glean from his references to the Brothers' studio on the radio program. In 1942, Jack appeared in the film version of the George S. Kaufman-Moss Hart play *George Washington Slept Here*. Benny plays the husband to Ann Sheridan, a wife who had accompanied her husband from the friendly confines of New York City to the hostile environs of rural Pennsylvania. As the couple adjusts to a back-to-nature experience, humorous circumstances develop around their "quaint" house and neighbors (one played most convincingly by Percy Kilbride).

Jack made a return to Fox films in 1943 to do a remake of George M. Cohan's *The Meanest Man in the World*, the story of a small town lawyer who is convinced by his valet (Rochester, of course) to become nasty towards his business clients. This 1920 story is aptly adapted for Benny, who finds himself coming full circle back to happiness and his lost girlfriend (Priscilla Lane).

Jack returned to Warners for two more films: *Hollywood Canteen* (1944) and *The Horn Blows at Midnight* (1945). The first film was the type that Jack generally balked at doing, but since it was for the War effort, a cause for which the comedian spent many hours and travelled many miles, he consented. *Canteen* was one of those typical star-studded extravaganzas, this time set at the real haven for G.I.'s in southern California. Joan Crawford, John Garfield, Eddie Cantor and many others are among those who play themselves in the movie, while Robert Hutton plays the soldier hopelessly in love with actress Joan Leslie. Jack does have a chance to pose himself and his infamous violin within earshot of conductor Efrin Zimbalist, Sr. The result of this very successful film was that Jack L. Warner turned over forty percent of the gross to the real canteen. Jack's personal support of the war effort included a tour of North Africa and the Mediteranean from late July to September of the previous year.

Jack's last picture at Warners was both his most maligned and most famous film. *The Horn Blows at Midnight* was favorably reviewed and often in the light of another angel-messenger film from 1938, *Here Comes Mr. Jordan*. Jack plays the sent-to-earth character, an unsuccessful seraph, who plays in the celestial orchestra and must signal with his trumpet the end to wicked earth. Athaniel, from the third phalanx, fifteenth cohort, is sent to his old home planet to play his trumpet (Gabriel did not have a violin) at the exact stroke of twelve, but is sidetracked by the personal affairs of a beautiful earthling (Alexis Smith). Directed by Raoul Walsh, the cast also includes Guy Kibbee,

Margaret Dumont, Frank Pangborn and others, who all assist Jack in playing a rather unique role (certainly unlike that of m.c. or radio comedian). The part was recreated in the lavish 1949 *The Ford Theater* production on radio and again in 1953 on the prestigious television show *Omnibus*. The Benny production was the highest rated of that television series during a year which also saw Orson Welles in a production of *King Lear*. Unfortunately, and often at Jack's own ribbing, *The Horn Blows at Midnight* gained more notoriety than fame and is seen today by many as another Benny joke, somewhere after his being thirty-nine years forever and eternally cheap.

Later in 1945, as a favor to his personal friend and radio enemy Fred Allen, Benny made *It's In The Bag*. The parts of the film that are funny involve cheap jokes at Benny's home. Allen is on a search for some chairs that he sold, because the seat of one contains twelve million dollars (much like the Russian seats in Mel Brooks' *Twelve Chairs*). This film reinforces the strength of Benny's radio character portrayed in the poorer Benny films, since the salvation of at least part of the film is based on exchanges between Fred Allen and Jack Benny, reminiscent to some degree of the powerful "playing the dozens." After this film, Jack only appeared in cameo roles including: *Somebody Loves Me* (Paramount, 1952), *Gypsy* (Warner Brothers, 1962), *It's A Mad, Mad, Mad, Mad World* (Twentieth Century Fox, 1962), and *Guide for the Married Man* (Twentieth Century Fox, 1967).

Perhaps one of the greatest films that Jack Benny might have made late in his life was signed, but not shot before the comedian's death in 1974. The original choices for Neil Simon's *The Sunshine Boys* were Jack Benny and Red Skelton, but the latter stepped out and was replaced by Walter Matthau. In September of 1974, Jack was asked to make a screen test.

Director Herbert Ross told Jack that all was fine with the test except that when Benny walked across the room he did so too youthfully. Ross, though half the star's age, showed how it should be done. Jack was 80 at the time but complied and erased a very famous gait with the director's.

Jack had some time before the actual shooting began and was able to do some public speaking and guesting on television before his death on December 28, 1974. If he could have chosen his own replacement, it might well have been his long time friend, George Burns. Not only did Burns take his friend's part, but he also captured the best supporting Oscar, the oldest person to do so. Although it fits into a multitude of Hollywood "what ifs," it is curious to think about how Jack Benny would have portrayed the aged vaudevillian and if Benny's film career might have been rejuvenated. Jack said that he did such roles "every 28 years, that way the pressure won't be on me, and I'll be around forever." It now seems that George Burns, who restarted his movie career after a 40-year absence, will be around forever.

Unless one is a devotee to late night movies, it is more difficult to recognize Jack Benny's career as a Hollywood film star in light of his incredible achievements for 23 years on the radio. Benny did make some very good movies, among them: *To Be or Not To Be*, *Charley's Aunt*, *The Meanest Man in the World*, *Broadway Melody of 1936*, *Buck Benny Rides Again*, or even *The Horn Blows at Midnight*.

If one can find these on late night television, a reward is there for the finder, as well as a display of talent as vibrant as that which endeared Jack Benny to millions of Sunday night listeners. He was not only the man who was so cheap that when asked by a robber, "Your money or your life?" responded, "I'm thinking it over," but also a talented presence on the movie screen.

JACK BENNY SHOW

A FACTUAL PORTRAIT OF JACK BENNY

Sunday will always fill the calendar spot between Saturday and Monday. But for millions of laughter-prone television viewers the traditional day of rest may never be the same.

The reason -- no Jack Benny.

After 30 years of broadcasting via radio and television on Sunday night, the comic legend from Waukegan will air his 1962-63 season of "The Jack Benny Program" on Tuesday night.

And as he segues into his 13th television year for CBS, the indefatigable master of the raised eyebrow school of comedy will continue to appear on a weekly basis -- a feat which astonishes many show business observers who have seen established stars settle for a rare two or three "specials" a year.

But not Jack Benny. He thinks the fast-paced weekly stint keeps him in closer touch with audiences and allows him to sustain a higher level of quality for his program. And in keeping with the tradition of being extremely buck-conscious that he has established he adds:

"I like the idea of being paid once a week rather than just two or three times a year. There's something so comforting about it."

This, then, is Jack Benny, an entertainment wunderkind at the mature age (self-styled, of course) of 39. In addition to his heavy TV schedule he will continue to carry out top night club engagements, charity appearances and the all-important dates with some of the most important symphony orchestras in the nation.

(more)

He will, of course, be violin soloist. Nor will his programs involve minor works as Love in Bloom. He will, rather, choose from such major fiddle fodder as the Mendelssohn Concerto and some bowing excercises by Rimsky-Korsakov.

Despite his almost three decades in broadcasting, audiences still do not know how to accept Benny: is he a virtuoso sidetracked into a career as the classic comedian of this generation, or is he a comic with a musical sideline?

Benny is not about to answer. He prefers to be a man of mystery.

But there is no gainsaying the fact he has done more for fine music than most recognized stars of the concert stage.

Says Isaac Stern, the master violinist: "When Jack walks out in tails in front of 90 musicians he looks like the greatest of soloists. What a shame he has to play!"

Says Leonard Bernstein, conductor of the New York Philharmonic:

"Benny has done more than raise thousands of dollars to erase operating deficits of major orchestras. He has brought multitudes of people who would not otherwise be there into the concert halls to prove that good music can be entertaining and rewarding."

Benny's greatest fans include such bowmen as Jascha Heifetz, Isaac Stern and other distinguished musicians, who count him "one of the boys."

They also include those men whose fiddling is done upon the strings of industry. In a world which talks in terms of penetration, sponsor identification and impressions per dollar spent, Benny is very big. While polls for years have shown many viewers could not tell offhand who sponsored what TV show, the average American has not

Since he first faced a radio microphone as star of his own show 30 years ago, Benny has never been one to feel the entertainment should pause for the commercial. There was, he felt, no reason the commercial itself should not entertain.

Benny is a showbusiness paradox. Not only has he survived 30 years in a sphere where 39 weeks is an eternity, but he has spanned the decades with but little change. He is, of course, not really 39, some time ago confessing he's just turned 40. Since he served in the U.S. Navy during the first World War it is likely he lied about his age.

Age has served him well as the butt of more jokes than he cares to remember. It is but one of the Benny gags which somehow defy all experts on comedy geriatrics. His relationship with Rochester has never paled. There is always a hearty laugh when mention is made of Benny's Maxwell, his vault surrounded by an alligator-filled moat, the way a dollar remains glued to his fingers, the semi-slavery under which he keeps Don Wilson and Dennis Day.

He is Mister Comedy. Vice President Nixon has played piano accompaniment to Jack's violin virtuosity. President Truman played straight man on a Benny show in 1959. Benny's satires on major motion pictures have often been as successful as the films, themselves.

Nor has he spared himself. Millions feel his 1945 picture, "The Horn Blows At Midnight," must have been an all-time dud because of the comedian's merciless razzing of the production. But it was really quite a funny film -- and Benny indicated his true feelings when he hired James Kern, director of the Warner Brothers opus, to direct several of his video shows a few years ago.

Radio and TV combined, Benny has starred in over 1,000 broadcast programs. They contained some classic laughs tied to the portrait of miserliness he has built for himself through the years. There was, for instance, the night he was faced by a gunman who ordered "Your money or your life"...to which Benny replied, after a few seconds silence, "I'm thinking it over." There was his description of Beverly Hills as a suburb so snooty even the police department has an unlisted phone.

But Benny, the man, is constantly embarrassed by the spectre of himself as a penny pincher. He genuinely enjoys the delicious food served at New York's Automat restaurants where nickles or dimes dropped into a slot allow the purchaser to lift a glass window and obtain anything from salads and sandwiches to excellent pastry at very normal cost. Yet he is afraid to be seen in an Automat for fear people, knowing he is a millionaire, will point him out as a miser. He leans over backward to tip generously.

Recently Jack figured a way to eat Automat food in style — he took over the entire restaurant at 45th Street and Fifth Avenue, invited 400 guests including the elite of both theater and newspaper worlds, hired a dance band, installed a couple of bars and hosted a formal black tie affair. To each arriving guest Jack dished out two dollars in nickels with which to purchase a tray full of Automat food.

The effectiveness of this self-portrait was brought home to Benny once more recently when he drove a brand new Rolls Royce over to a friend's home to show him the purchase. The acquaintance's housecleaning woman happened to be leaving as Benny drove up in the magnificent auto with its ultra conservative lines. Her eyes wandered

"With all his money you'd think Mr. Benny wouldn't drive such an old fashioned car," she said.

It was Fred Allen who said Benny couldn't ad lib a belch after a Hungarian dinner. This is not precisely true -- he is a witty conversationalist among friends and Benny does ad lib on the air. However, he has not remained atop the heap nor gained the stature of king of American comedy by relying upon the accidental funny remark.

For every 30-minute program he airs Benny and his crew work a full five days, starting with script reading sessions at his office at which the director, producer, cast members and associates join Jack in frank constructive criticism aimed at improving the script -- no matter how funny it may be to start with.

This session is followed two days later by the first of three days' intense rehearsal at the studio during which the complex movements and camera work is organized. There are no cue cards, no teleprompters on a Benny show. His group of fellow performers has long been indoctrinated in Benny's gospel of thorough preparation, and all dialog is fully memorized.

The evening of the third rehearsal day an audience is admitted to the studio, and the program is either filmed by three motion picture cameras operating simultaneously (the film is later edited and intercut) or it is videotaped.

So strong is Jack's desire for perfection that even his so-called "live" programs are taped an hour or so prior to airtime to avert any possibility of a miscue or slip.

(more)

And this entire five-day operation is preceded by prolonged labor by Benny's writers, two of whom have been with him 20 years, and two 14 years. The oldsters are Sam Perrin and George Balzer, the youngsters Hal Goldman and Al Gordon. Benny provides them a huge boardroom in his Beverly Hills headquarters plus an office at Revue Studios. Contrary to widespread belief, the apples, coffee and cokes are on him.

Benny is probably the greatest living example of pure American comedy. While a humorist makes humorous comments on such factual matters as finance, art and politics, and a stand-up comic tells jokes -- Bob Hope qualifies in either category -- Benny does neither except occasionally briefly in his opening monolog.

His every word, gesture and look is calculated to produce one end result: laughter. He is one of the world's great listeners, frequently preferring to give the funny lines to his supporting or guest players while he evokes audience hysteria with his famed long look and so unfunny a word in itself as a heavily sighed "Well..!"

This further illustrates his firm belief in the necessity of team work. Except as an occasional one-shot, Benny says the one-man show cannot survive today. It had its day when radio was young and blessed with such stars as Jack Pearl (Baron Munchausen) and Ed Wynn (the Firechief).

Always years ahead of the field in anticipating comedy style, Benny's format was so advanced in its initial concept that he has hardly changed it through the years. His jump from radio to TV was really no jump at all -- his cast merely donned makeup and did their chores as usual.

Benny describes himself not as a clown but as a character. The character did not arrive upon the broadcast scene full blown. Benny's first broadcast was as a guest on Ed Sullivan's radio show in 1932. His first words were, "Hello, folks. This is Jack Benny. There will now be a slight pause for everyone to say, 'Who cares?'"

Apparently several million cared, for he was soon back on the air as star of his own show for Canada Dry. His entry into broadcasting was in itself an indication of the man's vision, for Jack had already attained much stature in Broadway musical comedy and in addition to being a vaudeville headliner he was under contract to MGM for motion pictures.

He realized, however, that nothing could penetrate like radio. He gambled. He gave up a highly paid role in an Earl Carroll musical in order to try radio. From the start his concept was to provide a set of characters listeners would come to recognize and like and look for every week. And from the start he was the lovable boob, the walking example of human frailties -- but with dignity always -- the butt of most jokes on his own show.

His first vocalist set the pace for the others. Frank Parker was a tenor -- so were Kenny Baker, Larry Stevens and Dennis Day, and all except Parker were unknown when Benny put them on the air. All have been not only very legitimate singers but highly skilled comedians developed under the Benny tutelage.

Don Wilson has been Benny's announcer 29 years. Benny laughingly says he auditioned for announcers and signed Don because he laughed loudest at the Benny brand of humor. Don is, of course, far more than an announcer. Almost weekly he is placed by Benny in one outlandish situation after another, all geared to cue from-the-pit-of-the-tummy

Early in his radio career a Benny script called for a young fan from Plainsfield, New Jersey, to "crash" his show and insist on reading him her poems. The character was written in for one show only, but Mary Livingstone was such a hit she became a regular. Jack had married her a little earlier when he deserted the stage and movies for broadcasting.

Rochester was another character created originally for one show, but his comedics as a Pullman porter serving the troupe on their trip to Hollywood so ingratiated him to the audience that he has remained in the troupe over a quarter century (26 years).

During the years virtually every top entertainment star able to read a funny line has appeared on the Benny aircasts. Others in war years joined him in entertaining troops around the world. To all echelons of military personnel he brought such luminaries as Ingrid Bergman, Carole Landis, Larry Adler, Phil Harris -- his erstwhile band leader -- Alice Faye and others.

Among the regulars who appear in lesser but frequently hilarious roles on the Jack Benny programs are Frank Nelson, Mel Blanc, the man of many voices and faces, and Benny Rubin.

Jack Benny's family lived in Waukegan but Jack was born in nearby Chicago where his mother had been transported for his birth. The date: February 14, 1894.

"The only reason I conceal it," smiles Jack, "is that if I told it nobody would believe me."

And he's right, for Jack Benny at 68 has the appearance of a man 15 years younger.

(more)

Scarcely out of diapers he began, at his father's behest, taking violin lessons and was soon considered something of a child prodigy. While still in grammar school he became the only knickerbockered member of the pit orchestra at the Barrison Theater in Waukegan. During high school he doubled between the school band and the Barrison pit, and at 16 he teamed up with Cora Salisbury, the Barrison pianist, as a vaudeville duo.

Miss Salisbury left the act when it became necessary for her to care for her sick father, and Jack then teamed with Lyman Woods. The team of Benny and Woods in due time became vaudeville headliners here and abroad.

During the first World War Jack was a sailor in grease paint, his prime duty the raising of funds for Navy relief. Jack's routine in the Great Lakes Revue was almost entirely musical, but one night during his performance electricity failed and the lights went out in the auditorium. To keep the crowd from getting restless Jack and a pianist named Zez Confrey (who later wrote "Kitten On The Keys") started to talk. The audience roared with laughter.

It was this ad libbing in an emergency which first indicated to Benny that he could be funny. It is ironic that an ad lib started him on his phenomenal career as a comedian although once he entered broadcasting -- where he won his greatest fame -- he boycotted the ad lib in favor of carefully prepared material.

Benny's postwar progress was largely as a comedian. He progressed to the top rung of vaudeville, then musical comedy for Earl Carroll and the Shuberts. During the Los Angeles engagement of a Shubert musical he met Mary Livingstone, who was at that time not yet

The "sick" comics leave Benny cold. He is frankly concerned about the state of comedy and the lack of proving ground for new comics. Vaudeville and musical comedy, which taught him pace and timing and gave him an opportunity to perfect his act in small towns before exposing it to metropolitan audiences, are no longer available to the newcomer. Jack is aware that one thing essential in the development of a comedian is exposure.

He knows <u>audiences</u> make the comedian -- an audience is akin to an umbilical cord which tells a comedian how far he can go.

Benny is recognized as a great comedy technician. He is not a gimmick comedian -- gimmicks come and go, and when a gimmick wears thin the gimmick comedian is in trouble.

Benny lives in a fine Beverly Hills home with his wife, Mary, who is no longer active in show business.

"We live economically," says Jack. "Mary is an expert bargain hunter. If she discovered a good cheap toothbrush she'd buy 800 of them."

Jack's prime relaxations are two: golfing -- he has golfed around the world -- and fiddling. He carries his Stradivarius with him to rehearsals and practices in his dressing room when time permits. He still studies the violin and always tunes up seriously for his benefit concert appearances which have thus far raised over $3,500,000 for worthwhile causes.

The Bennys have a daughter, Joan, and two grandchildren. His office walls are decorated with dozens of testimonials and trophies, and his closet holds hundreds more. He is sensitive to criticism but appreciates it when it is constructive. If he ever questions the wisdom of having given up a fiddling career for comedy the doubts fail to mar his sleep. He can always remember his friend, Fred Allen's classic remark:

"Jack's a very funny guy. I love him. But he's the only violinist who makes you feel the strings would sound better back on the cat!"

The fact is they sound pretty good when Benny fiddles with the major orchestras.

But it is obvious that the happiest music to Jack's ears has always been and will remain joyous laughter.

* * *

By Neil McDonald

IT MUST BE JACK BENNY (insert) on the phone, judging by the expressions of The Sportsmen, Jay Meyer, Bill Days, Gurney Bell and (back) Marty Sperzel. Benny, the so-called "Old Tightwad," has featured the song men for six years.

The "Hmmmm" That Jack Built

THROUGH THE years a healthy proportion of radio listeners have been convinced that Jack Benny is a "stingy" man. It is natural, since the basic humor of his CBS show lays considerable emphasis upon that tightwad "eccentricity."

However, today in Hollywood there is irrefutable evidence that such is far from the truth. The proof comes in package form—the Sportsmen Quartet—who are, left to right, Bill Days, Jay Meyer, Marty Sperzel and Gurney Bell.

"Hmmmm" Boys

After listening to Benny's "Hmmm" boys, it becomes immediately apparent that they consider him one of show business's most generous men. It's quite natural they would think this, too, because it was Jack who gave them their first "big-time" break when he signed them to do the Lucky Strike commercials six years ago.

The Sportsmen were a hit overnight and today are ranked the country's top "salesmen" of the singing commercial. They were given the Sponsor Magazine award this year for the "most effective and entertaining commercials." Jack's help, the Sportsmen avow, didn't stop there. Through the years he has been a constant help to them, suggesting new tricks, attending their night-club dates and even doing a recorded phone routine which is a highlight of their night-club act.

Jack's Show

True, the Sportsmen were doing well in radio before Benny signed them, but it wasn't until after they appeared on Jack's show that they suddenly were in demand for personal appearances, records and movies.

With considerable help from Jack, plus the aforementioned routine with radio's "tightwad," the Sportsmen built a night-club act which has broken records at Billy Gray's Band Box here in Hollywood, at the Hotel Fairmount in San Francisco, at Las Vegas' Last Frontier Hotel and many other spots across the country.

Actually, the boys have parlayed a "hmmmm" into a half-million-dollar enterprise. Organized in December, 1946, as The Sportsmen Enterprises, their reputation has grown until now they are rated America's top quartet.

They Were a Hit

In addition to six years with Benny, the Sportsmen now are in their fifth year on the Phil Harris-Alice Faye show. Universal-International has just released their "Sportsmen Short" and they just completed another short at the same studio.

Four years ago they signed a contract with Capitol Records with their most famous discs including "Woody Woodpecker," "You Can't Be True, Dear," "Me and My Shadow" and a barbershop and Christmas album. They recently learned that their version of "Me and My Shadow" hit the number-one record spot in England, selling more than a million copies.

Their Past

Sperzel, Days and Bell are all local boys, Marty graduating from Hollywood High, Days from Los Angeles High, and Bell from Belmont High. Meyer is a native of Webb City, Missouri, but came to California at an early age.

Meyer, the youngest looking member of the group, is called "Dad" by the others for a very humorous reason. It seems that a couple of months ago when they were making a personal appearance at the Last Frontier Hotel in Las Vegas, a cop wouldn't allow Jay to enter the casino, claiming he was "too young."

Actually, Meyer is twenty-seven, served four years with the U. S. Marine Corps and saw some rugged duty in the Pacific!

December 28, 1951

International Jack Benny Fan Club
3190 Oak Road #303
Walnut Creek, California 94596

THE JACK BENNY TIMES

❄❄

January - April 1995   **INTERNATIONAL DISTRUBUTION**   Volume XV, Numbers 1-2

President's Message

Jell-o again, folks. Well, looks like the first of our three-times per year editions will be out on time (someone call Ripley!). I would like to take a moment to thank the many members who not only renewed but sent letters of support and sympathy, particularly in light of my mother's passing. This outpouring took me very much by surprise. I was asked soon after just why I continue with the fan club. I responded that it was partially the obvious, a love of Jack Benny and a desire to see his comedy perpetuated. Yet in addition, when you receive letters from members saying how much they enjoy the club, there is just no way that you can walk away from that. On January 1 we celebrated our 15th anniversary; here's to another 15 years (or more)!

A couple of miscellaneous items, now. Some time back I received a request for club information from Don Brockway, Box 661, Oyster Bay, New York. By the time I got around to responding, the letter was returned as "Box Closed." Anyone have a new address for him? Also earlier today, I listened to a record (for the first time) entitled "George Burns Sings", put out by Buddah Records BDS-5025. There is not a date on the sleeve, but was probably circa 1968 - 1972. The cover is in the style of the Beatles' "Sgt. Pepper" album, with George in a Nehru jacket and beads making a peace sign in front of a collage of photos (including Jack, but not Gracie...interesting). Just a few of the songs included are: "King of the Road", "59th Street Bridge Song", "Satisfaction", "With a Little Help From My Friends", and a handful of older songs such as "Ain't Misbehavin'" and "Grizzly Bear". I found it (appropriately enough) in a used record shop on Haight Street. It is most definitely "different", pure George in singing style, and...well, words defy description. Just envision George singing and Goldie Hawn dancing go-go with sayings painted all over her body, and you'll get the feeling. If you see it, snatch it--I'm told there are very few floating about. A treat for any Burns fan.

Three additions and one update to the tape trading list:

Michael Avedissian, 31 Morris Drive, New Hyde Park, New York 11040

Wendy Jernigan, P.O. Box 1219, Four Oaks, North Carolina 27524

Mark R. Linke, 815 Pine Bluff Road, Morris, Illinois 60450

Rob Cohen, 763 Oaksedge Drive, Gahanna, Ohio 43230 (new address)

Now on with the show!

New Members

**** WENDY JERNIGAN **** RICK SCHECKMAN **** HOOMAN MEHRAN
**** BRIAN THOMAS **** RON HARRIS **** JOE GOFF **** G. W. NICHOLS
**** FRANKLIN HEYNEMANN **** ELLIS HOGUE **** DREW WIEST

**** JOHN DUBUCLET (our first member in Spain!) **** STEPHEN H. LOEB
**** PATRICK H. ADKINS **** JOSEPH E. WRIGHT **** NIK KIERNIESKY
**** GARY LEVINE **** GORDON ERNST **** BILL SLANKARD
**** KEVIN TROTMAN **** CAREY FOSTER **** BRIAN COPELAND
**** MATTHEW MARK DREW

International Jack Benny Fan Club Online

I could not be a self-respecting high-tech employee and not be on the Internet, a.k.a. the information superhighway. Quite a few of our new members came to us via the Internet. If you have access to Internet or the World Wide Web (WWW), here are a few items you might want to check:

OTR Digest, daily electronic newsletter. To subscribe, send email to otr-request@airwaves.com, with SUBSCRIBE in the subject. The body of the email will be ignored. Specific questions can be directed to wdp@airwaves.com or lgenco@crl.com.

Radio Drama, electronic newsletter. To subscribe, send email to radiodrama-request@world.std.com, with SUBSCRIBE in the subject.

OTR Web Page, address: http://www.memst.edu/radio-archive/radio-archive-homepage.html.

Vaudeville newsgroup, alt.comedy.vaudeville. Little traffic at the moment, so let's get on there and generate some. Other newsgroups of related interest are alt.movies.silent, alt.music.big-band, and rec.antiques.radio+phono.

International Jack Benny Fan Club, address JackBenny@delphi.com. If you want a speedy response from me, send an email. I check my account just about every day so the email does not go out of control. I am considering starting our own electronic newsletter, ala OTR Digest, containing posts sent by subscribers. Please email if you would be interested in such a publication.

Do You Know?

Phil Lieberman writes:
"Back when I was a teenager, I met some actors and actresses at a stage party after a summer-stock showing of The King and I. One of the had recently appeared in a Jack Benny Program episode 'Harlow Gets a Date.' As I recall, in the episode, she played the role of Judy, a girl Don Wilson hires to make his bashful son more comfortable with women. It was a hilarious show, but 'Judy,' both in person and in the character, has to be one of the most lovely and winsome gals I've ever seen.

"Could you please provide 'Judy's' real name and whereabouts today? What other TV or movie work has she done? Although I'm happily married to an equally beautiful gal, I'd love to contact 'Judy' to compare notes and let her know what a lasting impression her one appearance on the Benny show made on me."

Also in conjunction with the Internet OTR activity, there has been extensive discussion in the OTR Digest about who won the Jack Benny/Fred Allen feud. Now, admittedly this crowd is biased, but I would like to put this question to you. The gist of the responses were as follows: Jack Benny based his comedy on character humor. Each of the people on the show had their own personality and background, and the jokes were centered around their personal traits. The humor, on the whole, is timeless. Fred Allen did a lot more topical jokes, which frequently can escape a modern listener. However, Fred also had an excellent cast of characters. He was one of the great wits of his time, generating the bulk of the script for his shows. Few were in his ranks as an ad-libber, at least once prompting from Jack the exclamation of, "You wouldn't say that if my writers were here!" Who won? It is a three-way split vote on the net of Jack, Fred, or both. Any thoughts?

Tape Library

Thank you to all the members who donated to the Tape Library Preservation Fund. I will soon start making backup copies of the library with these funds. Have had some ongoing discussion about transferring the shows to digital audio tape (DAT). Does anyone have any experience transferring regular cassettes to DAT tape, and/or running the digital copy through software to remove static and amplify sound? I have access to a piece of software called "SoundEdit" on a Macintosh, which could prove useful (I just have not had the opportunity to test its limits yet). Any information would be appreciated.

There were at least two typographical errors in the library listing in the last issue. 12/9/41 should have been 12/7/41, and 2/19/53 should have been 4/19/53. Also, the 2/3/91 Manhattan Radio Club panel with Joan Benny should have been 45 minutes, not 90.

By popular request, I am reprinting the library practices:

- Make a list of the items you want, up to ten hours of material (assume all Jack Benny Programs to be 30 minutes long). If something is less than 30 minutes in length, it will be coupled with an/other item/s from the list. Thus in selecting a five-minute item, I will dub the entire side from the tape containing it; therefore, assume no items to be shorter than 30 minutes.
- Send your pick list, an appropriate amount of blank tape (send 60-minute cassettes PLEASE), and cash, check, or money order for the service fee ($1.00 an hour for the first five hours, 50 cents for each additional hour, up to ten hours) to: Laura Lee, 3190 Oak Road #303, Walnut Creek, California 94596.
- I will copy your pick list onto the cassettes you send and return them to you.

Back Issue Index - 1984 to 1986

Back issues are available for $1 per number (some multiple issues, like the 1994 edition, contain more than one number).

V. 4, #1: (June, 1984) New Members; Jack Benny Logs; Suggested Reading; Lest We Forget; North American Radio Archives

V. 4, #2: (July, 1984) New Members; Honorary Members; Lest We Forget; Suggested Reading; inserts for Bob Burnham's Technical Guide to Collecting Old Time Radio and Friends of Old Time Radio's 1984 convention

V. 4, #3: (July addition, 1984) Death of Kenny Delmar; Internship at local radio station

V. 4, #4: (August, 1984) President's Message; Suggested Reading; Interview with Itzhak Perlman; Members' Activities; inserts for Bob Burnham's Technical Guide to Collecting Old Time Radio

V. 4, #5: (September-October, 1984) President's Message; New Members; Family Album; Lest We Forget

V. 4, #6: (November-December, 1984) President's Message; Jack Benny TV Show Log; OTRwear; Jack Benny mug; Friends of Old Time Radio; Lest We Forget; articles on Jack Benny TV shows listing (abbreviated), "Jack Benny's Style Makes People Laugh"; inserts for Old Time Radio Digest and Bob Burnham's OTRwear

V. 5, #1: (January-February, 1985) President's Message; New Members; Jack Benny Stamp Committee; Family Album; Lest We Forget; excerpt from The Digest of Chiropractic Economics (Nov/Dec 1984)

V. 5, #2: (March-April, 1985) New Members; Mail Auction; Interview with Mickey Rooney; Letter from Isaac Stern; Members Close-Up; Lest We Forget; articles "'Cheapskate' Jack Benny left us richer" (1/24/85), "Readers are anti-abortion, pro-Benny" (2/1/85), "Jack: 'Good Night, Folks'" (1/6/75), "...and all the gang" (12/74)

V. 5, #3: (May-June, 1985) President's Message; Mail Auction; Family Album; Radio Recordings; Statues; Video Recordings; articles "New mayor old face in Waukegan [Robert Sabonjian]" (5/7/85), "'That's Me, Baby' He Yelled, and Collected His $5 Million" (lottery winner who chose Jack Benny's age, date unknown), "How to Tell a Joke" by Jack (3/26/61)

V. 5, #4: (July-August, 1985) President's Message; New Members; Mail Auction; Video Recordings; article "No joke - they're pals [Jack and George Burns]" (12/22/74); insert for Friends of Old Time Radio's 1985 convention

V. 5, #5: (September-October, 1985) President's Message; History of the IJBFC; Information, Please or The Benny Classified; SPERDVAC; press release for Jack Benny Exhibit at Westwood Savings and Loan headquarters (6/10/85); photo from cover of 1/20/6? TV magazine of <u>The Times</u>; <u>TV Guide</u> ad and close up on "Jack Benny's New Look"

V. 5, #6: (November-December, 1985) President's Message; New Members; Mail Auction; Tape Trading List; Biographies; Friends of Old Time Radio convention tapes; Jay Hickerson's list of OTR publications and organizations; articles "A Hometown Tribute to Jack Benny" (2/21/85), "Jack Benny - nation's best-loved comic" (12/28/74)

V. 6, #1: (January-February, 1986) President's Message; New Members; Jack Benny Stamp; Jack Benny Mugs; Tapes; Back Issues; Mail Auction; first "Please friends, send no bombs"; articles "Funny Business: Vintage radio shows to be syndicated" (85), "Honoring the 'pin-up girls' post haste [Jack Benny Stamp]" (2/6/86), "Jack Benny Changes His Tune" (5/9/64), "A Sentimental Farewell [Jack Benny TV show]" by Benny Rubin (8/3/65)

V. 6, #2: (March-April, 1986) President's Message; Tape Trading List; Smothers Brothers; What Do You Know?; Jack Benny Mugs; Jack Benny Stamp; Lest We Forget; various photos; articles "Coming Up: One Jack Benny - Well Done [Friar's Roast]" (1/17/70), "Jack Benny's Amazing Psychic Experience on His Deathbed" (<u>National Enquirer</u>, 8/31/76)

V. 6, #3: (May-June, 1986) President's Message; New Members; Member Announcements; Vice Presidency; Jack Benny Mugs/Note Cards; Family Album; articles "Benny's Genius payed off [sic]" (2/20/76), "Jack Benny, 80 Talks About Jack Benny, 39" (2/24/74), "It's Bach, Beethoven and Benny" (11/29/85), "Benny's Time-Tested Formula for Success: Know What's Funny, Make Best of It" (2/17/69)

V. 6, #4-5: (July-October, 1986) First cover photo; Obituary for Frank Nelson; President's Message; Mail Auctions; Wanted (Jack Benny Classified); Lending Library; various photos; articles "This Is Jack Benny--Who Cares?" (5/43), "Jack Benny Grills Himself" (33), "The Secret of Jack Benny's Success" (11/10/50), "Benny's Man Sunday [Rochester]" (50s), "Mary vs. Mrs. Jack" (12/21/46)

V. 6, #6: (November-December, 1986) President's Message; Interview with Irving Fein; Wanted (Jack Benny Classifieds); press release and calendar of events for Jack Benny birthday celebration (1/19/87); article "Beyond the deadpan: a comic content" (4/3/77)

The Top 10

By popular request, here is a reprint of an article from the November-December 1989 Times discussing a potential "Top 10" Jack Benny programs:

Recently talked with a member who informed me that he was largely unacquainted with the Jack Benny radio shows. Like me, he had enjoyed Jack through television first, and was now starting to discover his prior years on radio. Requested that I choose ten shows which would give a well-rounded picture of these programs.

What an enjoyable task! Think about it...23 years of shows, narrowed down to ten. Naturally had to amend the original list according to the shows in the library, but thought I would share my original ten with you. If you would like, feel free to send me your list of ten; can publish them occasionally in a separate column, similar to "Favorite Scenes" [E.N.: Now "The Tale Piece"]. These are listed in chronological order.

1-10-37: First show after Fred Allen's comment on the "Bee" by Stuart Canin. The style of this show is rather representative of the early years. It contains the first buds of the Benny-Allen feud, plus a sketch of the famed "Buck Benny Rides Again," naturally preceding the movie of the same name.

1-7-45: Debut of the vault, "Hey, Bud," and "Anaheim, Azusa, and Cuc...amonga" skits.

12-9-45: Dinner at the Colmans'. This was the first appearance of the Colmans on the show; George Baker has also commented that this was the "classiest" radio show they ever did.

3-28-48: Your money or your life. Need I say more?

4-25-48: Guest Dorothy Kirsten. Jack always claimed that this show elicited the longest laugh ever received on the program.

3-13-49: Loses $4.75 at Santa Anita. Along with being a good show, has some historical (hysterical?) significance. The following day many people bet 4-7-5 in the California numbers game. The winner was a combination of those three digits, and it was the biggest losing day for the state.

4-9-50: Gives 50 cents to a panhandler. Have had lots of members tell me that this is their favorite show. Yup, it's good...(crash)!

4-12-53: Jack showers with a peeled potato. Has one of the cimeron roll bits (crumbs?). The last half concerns itself with Jack inheriting [$5000] from a long-lost relative; love that last line!

2-14-54: Jack turns 40 (or 39). Lots of good stuff in this one...you just have to listen to it.

ALSO...any of the Christmas shopping shows. Take your pick.

The Tale Piece

I am cleaning out my file on favorite scenes, etc., so I am counting on all of you to send me your favorite scenes and/or stories about Jack!

In response to the question in the last issue about "Was Jack too Jewish/not Jewish enough?" Paul Wesolowski (of The Freedonia Gazette for Marx Brothers fans) wrote:

"People tend to forget that Jack Benny was a character created by Benjamin Kubelsky. He tried to make the character believable by using that name in real life, and by always staying in that character, but it was, after all, a character. Just like the leering, skirt-chasing Groucho Marx was a character created by husband and father, Julius Henry Marx. Just like the Italian Chico Marx was a character created by Leonard Marx, of German ancestry. Just like the mute, blonde-ogling Harpo Marx was a character created by a devoted family-man named Adolf Marx, who was married to one woman all his life. Just like Pee Wee Herman was a character created by comic actor Paul Reubens. Or Larry 'Bud' Melman a character portrayed by Calvert DeForrest.

"These aren't just stage names; they're well-developed characters which may or may not share common traits with the actors portraying them. It doesn't really matter whether Benny's character was Jewish or Christian; a miser or a spendthrift; an accomplished musician or a rank amateur; married or single; 39 or older. As long as the character was funny, he's a success. When the character is no long funny (e.g., an old man still pretending to be 39) some character traits get changed. But there's no reason to expect the character to have all of the traits of the actor." Well said, Paul...well said!

Bill Oliver wrote:
"The Phil Harris article made me think of a favorite Jack Benny-Phil Harris gag. It was the first show in the fall (I can't pinpoint the date right this second) and the program begins with the Harris band playing Guy Lombardo's theme song. Jack breaks in 'Wait a minute! Stop the music! Phil, you're playing Guy Lombardo's theme song. He was our summer replacement!' Phil: 'Well, why didn't they take their music off the stands?!'"

Ellis Hogue wrote:
"On April 1, 1965, Mr. Benny was in Atlanta for a benefit performance for the Atlanta Symphony Orchestra. I was only 16 years old but I managed to find out the hotel where Mr. Benny was staying. I walked up to the front desk and started to ask the Desk Clerk for Mr. Benny's room or suite number when a gentleman walked up to me and asked me a couple of questions. I later found out the gentleman was Mr. Benny's manager [Irving

Fein]. He told me the room number, so I went up and knocked on the door. Mr. Benny answered the door himself. He autographed a 3x5 index card for me, which I still have in my possession today, along with the program for that night. I also have the book <u>Jack Benny: An Intimate Biography</u> by Irving A. Fein. It is autographed by Mr. Fein, and also by Mr. George Burns."

Ken Weigel wrote several things that I have been stockpiling:
"Enjoyed the Phil Harris interview. The incidental background on Boasberg, Morrow, Perrin, et al is priceless. There ought to be a monument to radio's comedy writers somewhere, like the Rube Goldberg statue for cartoonists. Say, a microphone taking a custard pie. They made life bearable for a lot of people, especially during the war."

"...Speaking of smog, remember the time Benny drove the Maxwell into the service station in Santa Barbara and the mechanic found a hole in one of the tires, and he couldn't understand why the tire still held up? Jack explained that he had filled the tires back in Los Angeles--the air was too thick to leak out."

" [Last December 23]...I can't swear to it Laura, but I think I saw Jack Benny last week in Beverly Hills. I saw a man in a Santa Claus suit with a bell and a pot [E.N.: is that a reflection on his figure?] working the sidewalk in front of a jewelry store on Wilshire Boulevard. He seemed anything but jolly. In fact, he was down on his knees before a fancily dressed woman, bawling real tears and begging for a small donation. She gave him a dime. Immediately his eyes lit up, he stopped crying, stood up straight and tall, thanked the woman--and bit the dime. Hmmmm. Santa's tears had seemed real, but I noticed when he stood up an onion had fallen out of his collar. That made me suspicious that this Kris Kringle character was a gypsy, and a lousy one at that. Sure enough, looking closer, the first dollar he had ever made was still visible under his scalp, where Fred Allen had said the Waukegan comic had it sewn." (A few long-time members may recall the <u>Times</u> series on "Jack Benny Is Alive" during the "Elvis is Alive" escapade. The melody lingers on...)

And finally from Ken, appropriate on the anniversary of the liberation of Buchenwald:
"In <u>Pabst Blue Ribbon Town</u> (10/26/45), Benny, Phil, and Mary go see Danny Kaye's new movie, <u>Wonder Man</u>. Benny resents the talented Kaye, and the jokes are anchored to his jealousy. Later he relaxes at home with a book of ghost stories. As he reads he scoffs, but the ghost of Hitler, among others, pays him a visit just the same. As Hitler, Mel Blanc is *vunderbar*. Here's the skit:

[Sound: hobnailed boots marching. Over the top of it, Hitler is making one of his typically frenzied speeches]
Benny: Wait a minute. Who are you?
Hitler: [filter throughout] I am Adolf Hitler.
Benny: Adolf Hitler? They you <u>are</u> dead.
Hitler: Ja, and I'm lucky I'm dead. If I was alive today, they'd kill me! Hey, <u>Benny</u>, tell me, you vas in Chermany lately, ja?

Benny: Ja. I was in Germany, Adolf, only a couple of months ago. I was in Nuremberg, Frankfurt, Munich, Stuttgart...
Hitler: You vas in Berlin, too?
Benny: Yeah, I was in Berlin too.
Hitler: Tell me, <u>Benny</u>, tings are pretty hot now in Berlin, ja?
Benny: [chuckling] Not as hot as where you are, Adolf. How d'ya like it down there?
Hitler: Not so gudt. Tell me <u>Benny</u>, vat does Berlin look like now?
Benny: You oughta see it, Adolf. Remember how nice the Chancellery looked? The Avlon Hotel? And the Kaiser Hall?
Hitler: Ja! Ja!
Benny: There's nothing left of 'em. Remember how beautiful Unter den Linden was?
Hitler: Ja, Unter den Linden!
Benny: Well, now it's 6 feet <u>unter</u>. Adolf, The Wilhelmstrasse, and the Scala Opera House, and all the other beautiful buildings and streets--there's nothing left of them now, Adolf. It's rubble--all rubble.
Hitler: Schtop, I tell you! [He breaks down and continues raving behind]
Benny: But there's one thing we owe you, Hitler. You taught us that greed and intolerance and lust for power go hand in hand. They all lead to destruction.
Hitler: I tink I go now! [He fades out raving in garbled Deutsche]
Benny: Go ahead, go ahead. Don't bother me, I'm reading. [beat] Whoever saw a ghost with a mustache anyway? [2 beats] ...I wonder what he meant by 'rooten' schuten' tooten"?

Jack Benny Classifieds

§§§ Bob Crump is looking for a copy of Jack's TV show on which Johnny Carson guest starred (10/22/63). This is one in which Jack's "secret" of longevity is revealed. 753 Cypress Drive, Memphis, Tennessee 38112; internet: jcrump@utmem1.utmem.edu

§§§ Looking for a source of information on fan clubs worldwide? Contact The National Association of Fan Clubs, P.O. Box 7487, Burbank, California 91510, phone: (818) 763-3280, fax: (818) 752-4848

§§§ The Early Spring 1995 Wireless catalog contains many OTR-related offerings, including a set of 18 remastered Jack Benny broadcasts. Wireless Audio Collection, Minnesota Public Radio, P.O. Box 64454, St. Paul, Minnesota 55164-0454

§§§ Tony Hyman's <u>Where to Sell</u> guide offers guides to individuals looking to purchase various items. 2141 Shoreline Drive, Shell Beach, California 93449, (805) 773-6777

❊❊❊❊❊❊❊❊❊❊❊❊❊❊❊❊❊❊❊❊❊❊❊❊❊❊❊❊❊❊❊❊❊❊❊❊❊

Please send all questions, comments, additions, and corrections to:
Laura Lee (510) 933-3879
c/o The International Jack Benny Fan Club Offices
3190 Oak Road #303
Walnut Creek, California 94596   Internet: JACKBENNY@DELPHI.COM
Please friends, send no bombs.

National Cyclopedia of American Biography Vol. 60 (1981)

ANDERSON, Eddie [Edmund Lincoln], comedian, was born in Oakland, Calif., Sept. 18, 1905, son of Edmund Lincoln and Maude (Williams) Anderson. His father was a minstrel performer. Eddie Anderson, best known as Rochester, received his education at public schools in Oakland and San Francisco. As a boy he sold newspapers on the street and at the age of fourteen began his theatrical career, working in an all-black revue. He joined his brother, Cornelius, in a vaudeville act and toured for six years before winning the part of Noah in the motion picture "Green Pastures" in 1936. The next year he made his radio debut as Rochester, Jack Benny's gravel-voiced valet and chauffeur, on Benny's regular show, following this with regular appearances until 1954 and continuing after that date, when the radio show was discontinued, on Benny's television series, which lasted until 1964. He was then in several of Benny's television specials. Anderson's professional trademark was his hoarse, rasping voice, the result of strain during his newsboy days. The Rochester character was originally a Pullman porter and was such an immediate success that the writers for the Benny show had to create a situation in which Benny hired Rochester away from the railroad to work in the Benny household. Thereafter Rochester's famous line "What's that, boss?" always produced laughter from audiences who recognized the skepticism in Rochester's tone of voice as an indication that Benny's servant knew that his boss was a vain, parsimonious fraud. In addition to his radio and television work, Anderson played in several motion pictures with Jack Benny and by himself in other films, including "Three Men on a Horse" and "Transient Lady" (both 1936); "Rainbow on the River" (1937); "Melody for Two," "White Bondage," "Jezebel," "You Can't Take It With You," and "Thanks for the Memory" (all 1938); "Gone With the Wind" (1939); "Tales of Manhattan" (1942); "Cabin in the Sky" and "Meanest Man in the World" (both 1943); "Broadway Rhythm" (1944); "The Sailor Takes a Wife," "Brewster's Millions," and "I Love a Bandleader" (1945); "The Show-Off" (1946); and "It's a Mad Mad Mad Mad World" (1963). He repeated his role in "Green Pastures" with a television portrayal on the Hallmark Hall of Fame. Other television programs on which he appeared were Bachelor Father; "The Last of the Private Eyes;" a segment of Dick Powell Theater; and Love American Style. His nightclub work included performances at the Moulin Rouge in Las Vegas, Nev. Outside of the entertainment world, Anderson had several other interests. From 1942 to 1945 he operated the Pacific Parachute Co., San Diego, Calif., and he built a sports car, the Rochester Roadster, in 1950. In addition he owned and operated the Eddie Anderson Stable in Compton, Calif., from 1942 to 1953 and became the first black man to have a horse at the Kentucky Derby when his Burnt Cork ran there in the 1940s. He belonged to the Screen Actors' Guild, the Actors Guild of Variety Artists, and the Motion Picture Academy of Arts and Sciences. In religion he was a Baptist and in politics a Republican. His hobbies included model railroads, gun collecting, classical music, hunting, and fishing. He was married twice: (1) in Kingman, Ariz., in 1932 to Mamie Sophie Wiggins; his first wife died in 1954; (2) in Kingman, Ariz., Feb. 8, 1956, to Eva Simon, and had three children: Stephanie Amber, who married Jim Gilchrist; Evangela Rochelle, who married Richard Johnson; and Edmund Lincoln. Eddie Anderson died in Woodland Hills, Calif., Feb. 28, 1977.

SWAN, Thomas Walter, judge, was born in Norwich, Conn., Dec. 20, 1877, son of Thomas Walter and Jane Adelaide (Maynard) Swan. His father was a lawyer. Thomas W. Swan received his preliminary education at the Williston Academy, Easthampton, Mass., and was graduated B.A. in 1900 at Yale University and LL.B. in 1903 at Harvard University. Admitted to the Illinois bar in that latter year, he began law practice in Chicago with the firm of Bentley & Burling, and during 1907-16 was a partner in the firm, which became known as Bentley, Burling & Swan. He assisted in the basic organization of the

law department of the University of Chicago where he subsequently was a lecturer on conflict of laws in 1903-04 and again in 1908. In 1916 he was appointed dean and professor of law at Yale University Law School. He led the school through a period of intensive growth and increasing scholarship and was credited with transforming American thought about law in the process, also having introduced the case system of teaching. He saved the Yale Law Journal in a period of financial difficulty by lending it $6000 of his own funds. In 1927 he left Yale when he was appointed by President Calvin Coolidge to the bench of the United States Court of Appeals, Second Circuit (New York, Connecticut, and Vermont) and assigned to the court in New Haven, Conn. He served on the bench, in association with Learned and Augustus N. Hand, until his retirement in 1953, having been chief judge of the court during 1951-53. In his last decade on that bench he was involved in many decisions on cases pertaining to national security. In 1950 he was part of the three-man bench which affirmed the convictions of eleven Communist Party leaders for conspiracy to teach and advocate violent overthrow of

WHY JACK BENNY ENTERTAINER

The Surprising Story of a Young Man from Waukegan and a $400,000-a-Year Trick

[E.N.: Lots of errors in this article, but fun reading.]

READING TIME ● 8 MINUTES 55 SECONDS

Liberty 3/28/36

by FREDERICK L

WHO would have thought that Mayer Kubelsky's little boy Benny would become the world's highest salaried entertainer?

Not Mayer! He was a haberdasher himself, and a jolly earnest one. But he was broad-minded. He didn't insist on Benny's taking up haberdashery. In fact, when son Kubelsky—left to mind the store—fell asleep and let a phony customer steal eleven pairs of pants, he handed the boy a monkey wrench.

"Plumbing," he said, "is a good business too."

Certainly the pedagogues of Waukegan, Illinois, saw no promising future for Benny, for they fired him before he had completed his second year in high school. He was more interested in the theater, they said, than he was in the pursuit of learning.

Nor was the Waukegan theater manager especially impressed when little Benny came looking for a job. He had taken violin lessons since he was six. At fourteen, his rendition of Home, Sweet Home was a knockout. But when he applied at the local theater for a job, the best he could get was doorman. It was weeks before he reached the orchestra pit. Then the theater folded up. "I didn't have anything to do with it," Benny still insists.

When Benny—both he and Mayer insist the name was Jack, Jack Kubelsky, but I like Benny Kubelsky better!—suggested going on the vaudeville stage with his fiddle, Mayer's blood got up. All actors, he insisted, were bums, and all actresses were immoral.

But Benny or Jack—or Jack Benny, as he now called himself—formed an orchestra of his own, played for dances all over Lake County, and finally landed a week's booking with his boys in the Opera House at Racine. They stayed twenty weeks. Then that theater folded up too.

Undismayed, Jack formed a partnership with a piano thumper named Woods. Benny and Woods toured the small time for four years. High point was an engagement at the old Kedzie Theater in Chicago.

When the war came along, Jack enlisted in the navy—and landed in the entertainment department, with headquarters in Illinois. There he was expected to play Love in Bloom, or whatever his favorite tune was at that time, to a lot of gobs in training at the Great Lakes Naval Station. The idea was to get contributions to something or other. Jack played. Faint applause but no coins. Pat O'Brien, out in front, said, "For God's sake, *talk!*"

Benny didn't throw away his fiddle, but he did stick it under his arm instead of under his chin.

"I was having an argument with Pat O'Brien this morning," he began, "about the Irish navy—"

The coins began to fall. The violin, with a few notable and chiefly private exceptions, has stayed under the arm ever since. Jack still feels that this was a major calamity—but for the last three years he has been voted the most popular comedian of the air.

For the last two years his program has been chosen the outstanding radio program of the country.

The 1936 vote wasn't close enough to be a contest. Two hundred and thirty-nine radio editors throughout the United States and Canada took part in the voting under the auspices of the New York World-Telegram. Counting three points for first choice, two for second, and one for third, the results were:

Jack Benny	240
Rudy Vallee & Co.	91
Fred Allen	90
Major Bowes's Amateur Hour	85
Fred Waring's Pennsylvanians	53

Benny's weekly pay envelope for his Sunday-evening half-hour on the air is admittedly more than $6,000; probably $7,500. He gets $100,000 every time he makes a motion picture. Whenever he wants to pick up a little extra change, he can make personal appearances indefinitely at $5,000 a week.

The combined weekly take sometimes exceeds $20,000.

It isn't all profit, of course. But even two years ago he is said to have turned down extra work because it would take him out of the $400,000 *net* income class.

But why should all this happen to Benny? What has he got that others haven't got?

Well, the answer didn't stand out during his first years of trouping as a vaudeville single act. He found the road to the Palace in New York a fairly rough one. And once he had arrived there, he died the death. In a week he was back in Scranton, Wilkes-Barre, and Altoona. Then he met the champion of champions.

"Why don't you try New York?" asked Dempsey.

"I did!" he said. "And flopped all over Broadway."

"So did I," said Dempsey, "twice. But I went back and licked 'em. And so can you."

Benny tried it again. He was a wow. It wasn't long before he was heading the bill at the Palace. With Lou Holtz, he established a record for vaudeville longevity at one house.

Even so, Jack Benny was just another vaudeville headliner. Meanwhile, however, he had formed a nontheatrical alliance. In Vancouver, about 1923, the Marx Brothers came into his life. They and he were playing the same theater. One night after the show, Zeppo Marx, who was always the promoter—he is now a Hollywood agent—invited Jack to visit some people named Marks, who had a marriageable daughter named Florence and a twelve-year-old child named Sadye. The latter, under the name of Mary Livingstone, is now Jack's wife and favorite stooge.

Seven years passed, and Sadye had become a lingerie buyer for a Los Angeles emporium. She had also become engaged to a local youth, and was leisurely shopping for her trousseau when an invitation for a visit came from her sister, who had married and was living in Chicago.

Sister met her at the train. So did Benny. He quickly persuaded her that she was too young to marry anybody but him. That was Monday. They were married Friday, in Waukegan.

Meanwhile, in 1928, when Benny was master-of-ceremonying at the Orpheum in Los Angeles, Louis B. Mayer saw him, and decided he was just what Metro needed for The Hollywood Revue of 1929. He was. Directly after the preview, Mayer signed him to a long-time contract.

IS THE HIGHEST-PAID in the WORLD

COLLINS

Under this contract Benny made Chasing Rainbows, with Bessie Love and Charlie King; then, about a year later, The Medicine Man. He might have loafed around Hollywood, making a picture now and then, for another couple of years at $1,500 a week, but he was getting restless. He was used to working every day. So he went back to Broadway as head man in Earl Carroll's Vanities, and afterward took a try at radio.

It was a very tentative try, that first experience on the air in 1932. Columnist Ed Sullivan needed a "voice" in his act. Jack volunteered "for one night only." A sponsor heard the voice and liked it. Within a week Jack signed his first thirteen weeks' contract as a radio star. And that's what he has been ever since.

He has never wholly given up his first love, the stage. And the movies continue to fascinate him. He went out to Hollywood a couple of years ago, and did Transatlantic Merry-Go-Round with Nancy Carroll. Last year he tried again as the keyhole-peeking Broadway columnist in Broadway Melody of 1936. Dramatically, this was the best role he had yet had —but the sparkling feet of Eleanor Powell danced away with the picture.

M-G-M was delighted, however, with Benny's work. But after making one more picture, In the Air, he took to the road, and made more money in a few weeks than most movie stars make in a year.

The first—and Mary, his wife, thinks the greatest—thing that radio did for Jack Benny was to give him a chance to have a home of his own. Mary—whom her husband calls Doll—hated trouping, and still does. Her main interest is in a home; and Jack seized the first opportunity to give her what she wanted, in New York. They took a three-room-and-kitchenette apartment overlooking Central Park; and, in spite of their mounting fortune, they're in it yet.

IN Hollywood the Bennys rented Bill Powell's old house on Walden Drive. But there were no real signs of "going Hollywood." Jack liked the place—especially the climate. He called it "June in January." But he is glad to be home. So is Mary. So, presumably, is adopted daughter Joan, who is at the age when she prefers New York styles in bibs.

Mornings, Jack works over his scripts. Afternoons in the summer, he plays golf; afternoons in winter, he goes down to the Friars and talks about it. Mornings, afternoons, *and* evenings, he smokes the longest and fattest ten-cent cigars he can buy.

In short, Jack Benny is folksy. When he says, "Hello, folks," we know he means it. When he has finished, he isn't going out to a uniformed chauffeur in an elegant limousine and say, "The Ritz, James." He is going to say, "Come on, Doll, let's go home."

This genuineness is a primary reason for his hold on his public and for his amazing earning power. A Benny broadcast is, after all, a triumph of personality. Although the glibbest of gagsters, he doesn't depend for his laughs wholly on gags. He deals in human situations. And he knows that an audience's sympathy always goes out to the underdog.

N.B.C. photo

Jack Benny and Mary Livingstone, his wife and favorite stooge.

Most radio comedians are always on top, always riding the boys below them. They ask all the questions, and know all the answers. Benny lets the other fellow tell the answers—and nine times out of ten they leave him, the star, out on the limb. Jack seems to suffer when the joke turns against him, and we suffer with him—and he is the only radio comedian about whom we feel that way.

He is much more subtle than other comedians in many of his appeals for sympathy. That Love in Bloom sequence, for example, when Jack would try to play his favorite tune on his violin, and Mary and Don and Frank wouldn't let him. Knowing Benny's thwarted ambition to be a violin virtuoso, which had been played up plenty in the ballyhoo, strong men and brave women broke down and wept. Thousands of Americans will go to their graves sorry for Jack Benny because he wasn't allowed to play Love in Bloom.

That's it—the sympathy gag. And Benny is its master.

Flo Ziegfeld glorified the American girl, but it remained for Jack Benny to glorify the American stooge.

It's a great trick, a $400,000-a-year trick. Nobody has topped it yet.

THE END

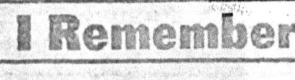
I Remember

The Last of the Big Tippers

BY HAL GOLDMAN

Contrary to his stage persona, the real Jack Benny was a supportive boss, a loyal friend and a generous guy.

It was 45 years ago, but I can still feel the excitement of that day. My new partner, Al Gordon, and I had just been added to Jack Benny's four-man writing staff. Now, after his morning cast rehearsal at the CBS Radio studios in Los Angeles, we were finally going to meet our new boss and comedy idol. He was already half an hour late, but rather than barge into the rehearsal hall, we decided to stay in the lobby, getting more nervous by the minute.

Suddenly, there he was, coming toward us with that loping, arm-swinging stride that once prompted his bandleader, Phil Harris, to remark, "Put a dress on him and you can take him anywhere."

His first words to us were, "Shmucks, I was waiting for you in the rehearsal hall." That put us at ease. Somehow you knew that, with him, the derogatory appellation was reserved for friends.

During lunch at the restaurant next door, I kept thinking that the Jack Benny we were sitting with was a carbon copy of his radio character. That is, until the check came and he paid for our lunch. He then compounded our surprise with a 40 percent tip. "I'm not sick," he assured us. "That's what I have to do because of all those stingy jokes everyone believes." He told us that just the week before, a waitress had pocketed his generous tip and said to him, "You won't believe this, but I could have sworn you were Jack Benny."

Benny, the radio character, used to say: "I don't under-

▲ Mel Blanc sarcastically offers Benny some money for autographing his cast.

stand the Writers Guild. They set minimums and then they get mad at me when I pay them." The real Benny paid his writers very well, was a soft touch for anyone he'd ever known who was down on his luck, and kept his wife Mary supplied with shoes second only to the collection owned by Imelda Marcos. He also had a generosity of spirit that allowed him to genuinely enjoy other comedians. The belly laughs his old buddy George Burns could elicit from Jack were legendary in the industry. It got so the slightest thing Burns said or did would have Jack rolling on the floor. One time they were sitting in a restaurant waiting to order and Jack started to break up. George said: "Why are you laughing? I didn't say anything." Barely able to get the words out, Jack said, "But you didn't say anything on purpose."

It wasn't just George. Ask any of the funnymen Jack hung around with and they'll tell you he was their greatest audience. More important for us and for the success of his show, Jack was also a great audience for his writers. Al and I found that out when we went to his house to show him our first completed assignment, four pages of monologue for an upcoming performance at the London Palladium. It was morning and Jack was still in his pajamas, relaxing upstairs in his bed. So that's where he received us. As he read our material he roared and pounded the pillow at so many of our lines that then and there I fell in love with him.

Apparently the feeling was mutual. He raved to everyone about the "new writers," which is what he always called us. We were the "new writers" through the entire run of the half-hour TV series, and in 1974, 24 years after we

▲ Benny and his stable of writers, circa 1956, observe a rehearsal of Benny's TV show. Back row, left to right: Hal Goldman and Al Gordon. In the front row: Sam Perrin, Benny and George Balzer.

joined his staff, we were still the "new writers" as we wrote the script for his final special. Not that we minded; Jack got a kick out of it, and it could have been worse. He could have called us "the boys."

What a dream job. You didn't work *for* Jack Benny, you worked *with* him. Although his specialty was script editing, he *thought* like a writer. Knowing what it meant to sweat over a line or a scene, he always looked for ways to save the material, not throw it out. Never once did we hear, "Fellas, this script doesn't work. Let's forget it and start over." Nor did we ever hear, "I'm the boss – we'll do it my way."

Once, Jack had been uncharacteristically stubborn about a particular routine, and after a long discussion, insisted we take it out of the script, period. One of Jack's "old" writers, George Balzer, said: "Fine, Jack. After all, the *four* of us could be wrong." Jack broke up, the routine stayed in, played great and Jack couldn't wait to admit he'd been wrong.

Is it any wonder that in his 42 years of radio and television, Jack Benny had only 12 writers? He was incapable of being mean — or pretentious. He could dine at the White House one night and spend the next night with his boyhood pal Julius Synikan. You've never heard of Julius Synikan? That didn't matter to Jack; he was his friend.

In 1959, when Jack's voice-and-sound-effects man and all-purpose performer Mel Blanc lay in a coma at the hospital following the car crash that shattered almost every bone in his body, Jack was a daily visitor. As the weeks went by and Mel slowly improved, Jack's visits continued. Finally, one morning, when Mel was still in traction, completely immobile and bandaged from head to foot, he was nevertheless allowed to go home. Jack watched as the three orderlies carefully inched him out of the room. Mel's wife later told me that she answered the door the next night and "There, God bless him, was Jack. And when he said, 'Hi Estelle, is Mel home?' he gave me my first laugh in months."

There are lots of show business legends around, and I've found that most of them come off best when viewed at a distance. All but one. You can't get much closer than his writers were to Jack. No one saw more of him, except possibly his masseur. Yet today, 21 years after his last 40 percent tip, Jack Benny remains for me the legend of legends. ★

International Jack Benny Fan Club
3190 Oak Road #303
Walnut Creek, California 94596

The Jack Benny Times

May-August 1995 INTERNATIONAL DISTRIBUTION Volume XV, Number 3-4

★ ★ ★ ★ Sunday, August 13, 1995

A section of the San Francisco Sunday Examiner and Chronicle

OBITUARIES

ASSOCIATED PRESS/1950

Phil Harris, *singer, bandleader and Jack Benny cohort, was the voice of Baloo the bear in Walt Disney's "The Jungle Book."*

President's Message

Jell-o again, folks...Am certain that you've all heard by now that Phil Harris passed away on August 11, 1995 at 11:00 P.M. at his home in Palm Springs. No services were held, per Phil's own wishes. A public memorial may be arranged some time after October 1. Anyone interested in attending this service is invited to send a SASE or email to me; when I have any definite information, I will send notification. This issue was originally to be focused on Jack's Waukegan roots, and I would like to thank all the individuals who have been so helpful to me over the past few months. I anticipate that the January-April issue next year will be dedicated to all things Waukegan.

Hey! Milt Josefsberg's The Jack Benny Show is being reprinted! Received word from Monologue Publications that the book is due out by the end of this year. The original is very difficult to find (I've only found three copies in fifteen years), and for sincere Benny fans such as yourselves, it's well worth almost any price. For those of you who have not had the opportunity to read this book, run, do not walk, to the nearest location that you can lay your hands on it. Keep an eye on your bookstores, or write to Monologue Publications at: 7130 Harrison Avenue, Pittsburgh, Pennsylvania 15218.

Nu, so what have I been doing for the past four months? Well, I've been out of town probably about 50% of the time (mainly on business), fighting a bad case of bronchitis, and working like crazy. The usual suspects. And fortunately, I've been able to combine my business traveling with Benny-searching. While in Los Angeles in May, I was fortunate enough to interview Frederick deCordova, director of many of Jack's television shows (and presently producer of The Tonight Show). The transcript of that interview will be coming next year. Then while in Boston, I was staying next to the Boston Public Library, where I spoke with one of the women who had assisted in cataloging the Fred Allen collection. The BPL had been notorious for many years for not allowing public access to Fred's collection, but it is fully cataloged and available for review. I am hoping to have a spare day or two there at some point when I can fully review the contents.

Further, my thanks to Bruce Kalver of WBSM radio, who did a phone interview with me in June. The funny thing was that I was spending the weekend with my father in Ft. Wayne (another business trip), and we were determined to go fishing that morning. So we took the cellular phone, and I was interviewed in the middle of the lake! This caused much comment (and some static and drop-outs), so my thanks to Bruce for both his time and patience. Finally, while on business in Chicago, I found in my dial-flipping an appearance of Don Wilson in the Danny Kaye film The Kid from Brooklyn. Don shows up in the oddest places, like his role in the Marilyn Monroe film Niagara. So look sharp!

Now on with the show!

© Copyright 1995, Laura Lee

Jack Bloom Pasadena Chapter

Previously in our May-June issue, we would publish the list of members of the Jack Bloom Pasadena Chapter. For those of you just tuning in, Jack Bloom was a very dedicated member of the IJBFC. He did extensive research on Jack, as well as making very large donations to our archives and tape library. Jack's contributions to our log, 39 Forever, were invaluable. Additionally, Jack and I kept a running correspondence for a great deal of time, discussing Jack Benny and all other related topics. His passing in June of 1990 was a great loss for all IJBFC members; his humor and kindness will never be forgotten, and we are all indebted to him for his great generosity. (For the full story, see the May-June 1990 Times.) I still miss you, Jack.

The Jack Bloom Pasadena Chapter is an honorary society for IJBFC members who have been active for four or more years. Scott Severson called to my attention that I had inadvertently omitted some individuals, and for this I give my sincerest apologies. Below is the full JBPC membership, with members added this year indicated by 3 asterisks.

JACK ABIZAID	ALAN GROSSMAN	EMILY RIFFLE
JACK BLOOM	JAY HICKERSON	PEGGY RIFFLE
BRUCE BAKER	TIM HOLLIS	REX RIFFLE
NEIL J. BASKIN ***	MARGIE JONES ***	JOHN SCHLAMP
BERNARD BECKERT ***	SAREE KAMINSKY	SCOTT SEVERSON ***
HAL BOGART	LAURA LEE	JOYCE SHOOKS
ROB COHEN ***	GEORGE LILLIE	W. ROBERT SMITH ***
FRANCIS W. DALY	JAMES A. LINK	BENJAMIN SPANGLER
STEVE DILLIE ***	PATRICIA LINK	BONNIE SPANGLER
WAYNE ENNIS	TOM MASTEL	DAVID SPANGLER
PHIL EVANS	BILL OLIVER	STEVE SZEJNA
CHARLES FAIR ***	ROBERT OLSEN	EVA TINTORRI
LE ROY FILLENWARTH	JACK PALMER ***	MARION TINTORRI
MARILYN FILLENWARTH	PAUL PINCH ***	BARBARA WATKINS
ROBERT L. GARLAND ***	FRANK POZZUOLI ***	KEN WEIGEL
		DOUG WOOD

Jack Benny Classifieds

§§§ Ted Ridley is seeking: "1) Jack and Mary as guests of the Jimmy Stewarts in which he throws expensive wine glasses into the fireplace, and 2) his overreactions to his sponsors 'rep' in re: renewal of his contract, place: a restaurant." 1011 Beechtree Court, Muskegon, Michigan 49441

§§§ Gail Moore is seeking Jack Benny shows with the Lettermen, Kingston Trio, and the Limelighters. 670 Lola Lane, Mountain View, California 94040

§§§ Bruce Rudesill is seeking a copy of the Dennis Day Christmas tape that I produced in 1987 as a fundraiser for the ALS Association (I wouldn't mind a copy myself). 3940 Washington Avenue, Cheviot, Ohio 45211-3420

THE INCOMPARABLE PHIL HARRIS

This interview was originally published in the September/October 1992, January/February 1993, and March/April 1993 Times.

On August 15, 1990, I had accidentally passed the address where I was to see Phil Harris. As I was doubling back, a familiar figure, deeply tanned and clad in a purple-and-white print top and black shorts, appeared from a house and waved at me. I sat there stunned for a moment, just looking at him. I had been waiting for this moment for *years*. He motioned for me to park at the side of the house, which I recovered my senses enough to do. Phil greeted me as warmly as an old friend, and I immediately felt comfortable and welcome. As I sat in a huge rocking chair (feeling almost a bit like Lily Tomlin's "Edith Ann"), I regarded the walls, covered almost to capacity with photos, mementos, a gold record, and other memorabilia. Yes, there were several bottles of wine and spirits scattered around, but many appeared to be more for decoration than consumption. One of the first things that Phil said to me was (this is from memory, not tape), "You know, I don't drink nearly as much as they said I did on the show! If I drank that much, I couldn't stand up." I queried that he wasn't a complete teetotaler, though. "No," he replied, "but that was one of the keys to the show to take the person's characteristics and just make them 'larger than life', exaggerate them."

The interview did not have a formal beginning, in fact, I would not even call it an interview per se. It was more just spending a couple hours talking about this and that. As always, I will transcribe my tape verbatim; just know that this is a more casual, free-flowing chat, which is probably all to the good! The tape starts with Phil talking about his practice of saving the show scripts, which were later donated:

PH: Well, you were supposed to throw the script up on the desk. For some reason or another, don't ask me why, it isn't my habit, but I'd stick mine in my pocket. And I gave them sixteen years, all leather bound, of 39 shows in each year. Sixteen years, and I gave them to the Bing Crosby Library quite a few years ago.

L: Where is that?

PH: Gonzaga University. It's in Spokane, and they have a beautiful library for Bing in there. Then for seven years that Alice and I had our program, I have those and also have the acetates you know, we eventually put them on tape because there was no tape then, and I have those in our library that we have in my hometown of Linton, Indiana. So I'm very proud of that, because...if they were left, if Jack kept all the scripts, I imagine that he did...

L: Yes, he donated them to UCLA in 1968...

PH: Have you talked to Irving Fein?

L: ...Yes, I've talked with him several times...I was hoping to get together with him when I came out here, but he was having an operation on his eye [E.N.: The operation went very well, and Irving is...well...fine!]...

PH: Well, he's about the only one alive now...He's with George Burns now...George is a very nice fellow...Now what are you collecting this material for?...

L: I'll transcribe the interview in our newsletter, and the tapes will go into the tape library.
PH: You have a library, too?

L: Yes, it's exclusively audio tapes, but we're trying to branch out into video...Oh before I forget, George Balzer has been trying to reach you. I was at his house yesterday.

PH: ...Well, I'm here everyday. Of course I've been in the hospital, I had a little problem, but I'm all right now. But I think, you know, when I first met Jack Benny was in 1933. I was staying at the Essex House, and he was staying there. And I had my own program then, too, I was on for Cutex nail polish, I was with J. Walter Thompson. In fact, I was on it for something like 78 weeks, and he was kind of in between shows because it had been when he was on for [Canada Dry], and they didn't like the idea of his format, which was kidding the product. [E.N.: This bears breaking for a moment to refresh your memories as to the commercial that sparked the ire of Canada Dry, and produced one of the very first funny commercials: "While walking through the desert, I came across a caravan of explorers who had been lost in the Sahara for six weeks. Their water supply had been exhausted a long time ago, and they were all dying of thirst. Quickly, I rushed to them and gave each one a bottle of Canada Dry, *and not one of them said it was a BAD drink!*"] And then I think he went from there to Chevrolet, and then [after a brief time with General Tire]...naturally he went to Jell-o. And what happened was that I was on a circuit at that time, and my contract ran out with J. Walter Thompson, so I was playing like the national hotel chain, which, at that time, was run by a man by the name of Ralph Pitts. In other words, he had the New Yorker in New York, the Netherland Plaza in Cincinnati, the Adolphus in Dallas, the Roosevelt in New Orleans, and then the Hollywood in Galveston, and right back around. I'm in New Orleans, and I get a call from George Burns, and George Burns wanted to know if I had a program. I said "No, my program, I just finished with it." And he said, "How would you like to go on with me?" I said, "Well, I'm under contract, but I'll see if I can get away." So I managed to get away, but in the meantime, by the time I brought my band and got out here, Music Corporation, for some reason or other, had kind of messed around some kind of way and they'd given it to Wayne King. So I found myself back on the coast without a job. Mary and Jack and I had become very good friends, in fact I was there when they adopted Joanie, their little baby...I was invited to the Trocadero, which was one of our top spots at that time, by Jack and Mary and during the conversation, he said to me..."What program have you got this year?" I said, "I don't have one." He said, "Well, you're with me." That's the way it happened....[E.N.: Phil's first appearance on Jack's show was October 4, 1936.]....When we were in New York, Mary happened to [hear a record] of Dennis, so I went over to the Bronx, or wherever it was, and I had dinner with the McNulty's, and that's when Dennis came with us [E.N.: Dennis' debut was on October 8, 1939]. Now as far as Eddie Anderson [goes], Eddie Anderson was working in a place called Sebastian's Cotton Club, and a very good friend of mine because we musicians all used to hang out there because they had a great band there called Les Hite. That's where Armstrong, Louie, and all the top black people used to come to play. So naturally, we musicians hung out there. Well, Rochester had an act with a guy, if I remember correctly, it was a comedy act, something like Anderson and Bloomfield, or something of that order. But anyway, Jack was looking for this black comedian, you know, that was supposed to have been a porter on the Chief. But I told Rochester, because we had two or three people try out, and naturally they were well-educated, they were all pronouncing their "ing"s and "*cahn't*"s and "*shan't*"s and I told Eddie, I said, "Look, that's not what Mr. Benny wants. Mr. Benny wants a real good Southern black man that talks that way." So Rochester tried out and he got the job, and...he and I were very close, and I think that I was the first one, I'm *sure* that we were the first ones that got him into a white hotel, and that was in St. Louis, Missouri, and...we took him in with us, and the week after that we heard that Marian Anderson, the big opera star, came in and tried to get in the hotel and they wouldn't let her. She had to sleep in the Pullman or something, and she blew the whistle on Rochester. She said that Rochester got in, and you don't let me in...but that's how tough it was for those people that far back. And I can remember when I first took Eddie, Rochester, into a top restaurant. I was in Seattle in a place called Ripley's or something, because in those days, I mean, it was kind of tough. They went mostly to Chinese restaurants in those days. So all those things, but I think one of the most amazing things that happened, it'll never happen again, is that on Sunday, if you didn't stop the picture in the movie house and put on Jack Benny, they wouldn't have anybody. Or Amos 'n' Andy. Just those two. And I think one of the most interesting events that ever happened was when he left [General Foods] and went to Lucky Strike. Now in those days, when you went to a cigarette program, it was a market death because all cigarette programs were using whoever was hot, even bands or anybody that was hot, they'd use them for 13 weeks, and then maybe 26 weeks, you know. So at that time, we were broadcasting from Sunset and Vine--that's before Burbank--and Jack and I were very close because, like I said, he didn't find me, I had a job before and we became very close. And he came in one morning and I met him in the parking lot, and he says, "We're leaving Jell-o." Well, now, that's like leaving your mother, you know...because it was like Pablum, you know Pablum had never advertised. I wrote a letter one time asking about Pablum, and you'd never heard Pablum advertised on the air--they don't have to. Well, Jell-o's a household word, you know what I mean...So he said, "We're leaving Jell-o." I said, "Jack, please, please...where are you going?" He said, "We're going on for Lucky Strike." I said, "Oh my God! How can this happen? How can you possibly?" He looked at me and said, "We have to." I said, "What do you mean we have to?" He said, "They can't make Jell-o fast enough now!" Can you imagine?

L: It also was during the war. [E.N.: General Foods moved Jack off Jell-o in 1942 due to a combination of sugar rationing and high demand for Jell-o. The following October, Jack started for Grape Nuts, also under the General Foods banner. Jack did his last show for General Foods on June 4, 1944, and moved to the American Tobacco Company (Lucky

Strike) on October 1, 1944. In his biography of Jack, Irving Fein attributed the impetus of this change to Jack himself, seeing that five different sponsors had made him offers of more money (as Phil indicates below). The ATC was chosen because their President, George Washington Hill, had "agreed to hire the Steve Hannagan publicity office to publicize the program", and that "Jack felt [they] would be instrumental in bringing his show back to the number one spot again in the Hooper ratings." OK...enough of my aside.]

PH: He said, "I have no chance of ever getting any more money." You know what I mean?...However, that's another smart move, or was a great move of Jack Benny, you know. We were all exclusive. We couldn't work anywhere else without his permission. Like I say, he was very, exactly the opposite of what he played, his character, because he was very generous, and the fact of the matter, when somebody he knew would pass away, it would take him two or three days to get over it. I never will forget, *many* times we had a place across the street on Vine where we used to go to get a sandwich or something, you know...before the Derby, you know. And he'd come over...Myrt Blum's the manager [E.N.: Mary's sister Babe's second husband, and became Jack's business manager in 1936], and he'd come over and he'd say to me, "Go to Myrt and tell him to give you a little raise." You know, maybe every six months or so, because I had all three- or four-year contracts. And I never had a home before, you know, I'd always been on the road, you know, in a bus. I put sixteen years in a bus. So I said, "What for? I'm very happy, Jack. All I'm saying is, 'Hello Mary! Here comes Rochester!' That's all I got to say, and you're paying me pretty good." He said, "Well, go ahead. Go ahead and tell him I said give you some more." And he said, "By the way, have you got a quarter? I want to get a couple of cigars." He never carried any money, you know what I mean. At that time, he smoked, I think it was White Owls or something, and then when Burns started using his cigar, Benny quit smoking. See, he used to use it as a prop, you know what I mean? And the minute that Burns started, he stopped. He just didn't use it any more. I don't know why...

L: He still smoked, though, didn't he?

PH: No, he stopped smoking entirely. Oh yeah. He quit smoking for years before he even went into television, I mean, but he used to carry them, you know, when he talked, like Burns did. I guess he thought that there was some kind of similarity, because they were like brothers anyway. But he was something else, you know. He liked me. I used to go in the writing room...of course, you know, all the credit goes to Morrow and Beloin [E.N.: Bill Morrow and Ed Beloin worked with Jack from 1936 to 1943.]. You see, they did the bear [Carmichael], they did the guy in the safe, you know, down in the basement [E.N.: I assume this means the gas man who was eaten by Carmichael, as the vault did not debut until 1945.], they did the cheap bit, they did the Rochester bit, everybody else played off of that. Beloin and Josefsberg and Tackaberry and those guys. The only guy that he used to bring in right at the first when Morrow and Beloin were the only writers, he used to bring in Boasberg [E.N.: Al Boasberg had supplied Jack with some jokes for vaudeville starting in 1926, and had written many one-liners for Jack during his very early radio days when his character was more of an emcee. Boasberg went on to also write for the Marx Brothers.], and Boasberg would sit with his raincoat on...and he used to bring him in on Sunday, and all he would do is sit there and listen to us run through the program, and then he'd punch it up, two or three gags, that's all.

This man [Jack], as I started to say a few moments ago...they had office hours. They'd go to work when **he** was there. It's not like it is now. Two writers took this piece home, and two writers took that piece home. They all sat around a desk, and they worked like office hours. They'd work till maybe 1:00, then they'd go and they could go to the health club and take a rub or a steam and have lunch and come back and work till five. Jack would sit right at the head of the table while all this was being written, and I've heard gags for me that would break the building down, and Jack says, "No, that spends too much time." In other words, he protected his characters, but he had to find something to magnify. There had to be something he overdid...if I drank that much, I couldn't lift 20 pounds. It was just so exaggerated. The thing that put Dennis on right away was at the first rehearsal, Jack said to him, "Dennis!" and he [Dennis] said "Yes please!" And that was it. But he had to find something to magnify...Like I say, he paid you so well that you didn't have to worry about a thing. Like I said before, I'm repeating myself because we were all under contract to him, but he was very lenient. In other words, if we wanted to go on another show as a guest, all we had to do was ask him...Fact of the matter is, to show you what kind of man [he was]...why didn't I go to CBS? What actually happened was when they made that move, when Edgar Bergen and Jack and Amos 'n Andy and all of them made the move to CBS, which in fact was only one block down the street from NBC, I was supposed to go with them, but I was still supposed to follow Jack Benny. So something came up--who knows--you know, I mean all of a sudden "No" they were going to let Amos 'n Andy follow him. So it just hit me wrong--you know what I mean? I mean because we would go so well, and everything was working, and I knew that it had to be a piece of conniving because you know when you follow Jack Benny you already had a ready-made audience. You didn't have to worry about the Nielsens, you know. You had it. So it was, you know, I mean it was too tough to give up. So in other words, and then I manipulated--or I got--a ten-year contract with NBC because I was the only thing left on Sunday night! Everybody else left! And now they were in a terrible fix had I gone, they had nothing whatsoever. But I had a legitimate reason that to show you what kind of guy Jack was, he used to put me on the first 15 minutes on his show, and I'd run through the alley then and warm my audience up, because I was going on in my 4:30 time [7:30 Eastern time]. So that's what kind of guy he was. Nobody else would have done that, because here I am doing a family show with two children and Alice, and on his show I'm loaded! You know, playing pool and chasing women!

L: I do remember hearing some shows where you are talking on the phone to your daughter, though. How was the transition made from the "loaded and shooting pool" to more of a family man?

P: Well, people...they know it isn't true. You know, they know it's just to make a joke. And then we had Frankie on our program, and it worked. And the only reason that I just had had enough and I didn't want to go into television, I didn't want to dress up in funny clothes and you know, I mean, as far as I was concerned [if I had done] Ozzie and Harriet and Desi and Lucy had done, I could have made a fortune I guess. But I don't know, I just...I was making a few pictures at the time and Alice didn't want to work. She wanted to raise her children. Of course we didn't use our girls [on the shows], those were two little actresses that we had on the program. But it all worked out, and it worked out beautifully. It was **the** most memorable [time] and the epitome of my life was the time I spent with Jack Benny. There's only one.

L: You were on the television show just a couple of times...

P: I went on the anniversary show.

L: That's right; you did "That's What I Like About the South" and Jack brought out a map. [I'm fairly certain that this was done on Jack Benny's Twentieth Anniversary.]

P: Yeah, and the other time on his anniversary, he says, "What do you think of my anniversary?" I said, "I'd spend more on a rabbit hunt than you did on your anniversary!" He didn't know I was going to say that. He used to let me [ad lib] once in a while...I was pretty cozy about it because...I was born in show business and I've been around it all my life. My mother and father were in the circuses...But he used to let me ad lib a little bit, you know, I mean that I never abused it. When the time came and I had a pretty good [line]...that I figure it's gonna play, you know. Course that's hard to do. That's one thing you can never do, and I learned it with Jack Benny--you can never tell whether a gag is going to play or not. If anybody tells you it is, because I can't tell you, I'd have a roomful of nuts! Especially seeing we were getting our audiences from off of the street, and it got so bad that we didn't know what to do because the same people were there every week. They've got nowhere else to go, and they knew more about us than **we** did! And we tried to mix it up--we even got to the point where we were taking tickets to the colleges and everything because these same people, every Sunday, they're **there**!...And they might as well have reserved seats!...They could make the Maxwell motor themselves!

L: Give Mel a run for his money!

P: That's right! It was tough, but we couldn't do anything about it. We loved them, they were terrific fans. I mean, they knew what a gag was going to be before we got to it. But it was fun. It was great. Those were the great days.

L: I should know this, but I don't. How did the "That's What I Like About the South" start?

P: Well, I tell you, it started in Cincinnati. I never used to call a set. In other words, I'd call one tune, and while we were playing it, the people would come by and I'd say, "What do you want to hear? You got a tune you want to hear?" So in the meantime, when the tune had stopped, while we were looking for that [requested] tune, I'd see people standing on one foot, one leg, and you know, kinda awkward and they didn't know what to make of it. They'd dance together just the first time and all. So I started what we call a little eight-bar turnaround, just a little vamp, you know what I mean? [E.N.: For the uninitiated, a "vamp" is generally a very short piece of music that can be repeated as many times as needed before going into the actual musical piece. If you look at sheet music of many vaudeville songs, you will see a couple bars marked "vamp" just at the end of the introduction, but before the verse.] And truthfully, we started making up lyrics in the band, and they were risqué, you know. We were doing it just ourselves, you know what I mean? So finally, these people started gathering all around. They wanted to hear this. So I said to myself, "Well, if they want to hear it, we'll do something about it." So me coming from the South [E.N.: Southern Indiana, to be exact. But if you've lived there, you'd agree it's pretty much the South.], the first thing I thought about was food. But that's why I never had it published because I don't remember who, but I put in three or four verses, maybe five, maybe the drummer did one about cornbread or something, and somebody else...so actually it was kind of a [mix of authors], and in that way, see, when we'd stop a tune, we'd start this vamp. And then I'd get a tune and play it in the same tempo, and that would keep the music from stopping, and keep the people from feeling uncomfortable. But I wouldn't keep it too long--I'd keep it equivalent maybe to four tunes, and then when I'd play my one-nighters, I would never stop the music, because in the towns and all where I was going, they had to be 175 miles apart. And people drove that far just to go to a dance. But if you stop, then they wanted to get familiar with you, you know, and I mean this and that's pretty rough, Texas and all, panhandle and all down in where I was. So I would keep five men, I'd start with my full band and then after they'd played a while I'd put on the dixieland group. Take five out of it. Then I always had a bar set up in the back, my guys never overdid it [E.N.: Sorry to be smashing so many of your long-standing impressions here!], they could have Coke or they could have a drink if they wanted to, smoke a cigarette, and then when we came back with the full band again, then I'd take the five that didn't do it, and I'd put on a waltz set. So consequently I had music on all the time, cause in those days we had to go from like nine to one. Then you get in the bus, and drive till you got to the next town because you couldn't stop and eat, because there was only one restaurant. So if you'd eat in a town where you'd [played], you'd never get finished. So it looked like the Safeway [grocery store] when you'd walk on the bus. Everyone had their special kind of food up on the bus. But it was fun. I'd like to do it again.

L: How many from the band are still around?

P: ...Only one that might be is, and I doubt it, is the bass player. You know it's kind of...I don't like to talk about that, you know. I don't mind, but you know it's kind of frightening that I'm the only one left...

[E.N.: I had mentioned before the interview started that George Balzer wanted to get in touch with Phil, since they had not been in touch for quite some time--I had talked with George the day before. I gave Phil his phone number, and I was rather surprised that Phil immediately picked up the phone and called him. Well, no time like the present!]

P: Mr. Balzer?...Well, when they find a safe place to bury my liver, I'm gonna call you!...I'm fine, and I'm sitting here with Laura Lee and she say's you've been trying to get hold of me...Well, I'll tell you, I just got back. I went fishing in Alaska, and I went from there to the Bohemian Grove, and I was feeling kind of lousy, and I go to the infirmary and the guy gives me the wrong medication, so I just spent five days here in intensive care. He almost knocked my roof in, but I'm all right. They gave me a thing called [], way, way too much, and I was terribly...Oh yeah, so...Oh, he's got to be just about 60!...I'll be darned...What ever happened to Tackaberry?...Is that right?...[E.N.: John Tackaberry passed away in the 60s or so; cannot find an exact date at the moment. Help!]...Listen, let me ask you again, what happened to the kid, what was the name of the kid who was in Russian and was friends with Jack and me and was in a couple of shows in New York...He was like Nelson, or like Sheldon Leonard, or like Elliott...only he was...no, no not a writer. An actor...You know him well. He was studying Chinese some time, and sometimes Russian...[E.N.: Anyone have any ideas on this? I'm stumped.] You knew this guy well. Everybody liked him. He was real tall and skinny and he looked Russian...no, he lived out here. He was part of the staff. He worked a whole lot with you...No, not the Jewish guy...He used to do like if you were doing Russian or something like that...I can't think. How about Perrin, is he gone? Are you the only one left? [E.N.: Happily, Sam Perrin is still around!]...That was too bad too about Dennis, you know...Just happened all of a sudden, didn't it?...I was telling this young lady about Boasberg, you know, about how he used to come in at maybe the last reading and sit down with the raincoat on, and put maybe in a couple of gags you know...Well, yeah, but then he had two writers before you guys, friends of his from vaudeville. What were their names? [E.N.: I assume he means Hugh Wedlock and Howard Snyder, who at times worked in conjunction with Bill Morrow and Ed Beloin. Wedlock and Snyder were preceded briefly by Sam Perrin and Arthur Phillips, who wrote for three weeks following the dismissal of Jack's first writer, Harry Conn. Ed Beloin was recommended by Fred Allen, and Bill Morrow came from Chicago. Wedlock and Snyder were previously columnists, and Sam Perrin and Arthur Phillips were loaned to Jack by Phil Baker. Harry Conn was recommended by George Burns. Sam had written a few lines for Jack in vaudeville, and my memory says that Harry Conn had written some for Jack on stage also. Most of this info comes from Irving Fein's book. OK...enough of me.]....Yeah, he was one of the first writers. And then they had two guys that came around once in a while, I think, when you guys were there...That's it! Wedlock and Snyder [E.N.: Ah. Well, I'll leave my comment in for your information.]...And then they had that young little kid. What was his name? A little short guy--he worked with you guys. Goodman or something?...Al Gordon! Wasn't he a kind of a little short guy?...Yeah...That's right...I never will forget when we picked that guy up in New York, and coming out on the train he was asking me all the questions and all this and "What kind of a girl is Mary?" and "What kind of a guy is Jack?" and he said he couldn't write with anybody. You remember?...Cy Howard! Right! I don't think he wrote a thing, did he?...Twenty minutes or something...[E.N.: Cy Howard was hired for the season beginning in the fall of 1943. Three other writers began with him: George Balzer, Milt Josefsberg, and John Tackaberry. Sam Perrin joined a couple weeks later. Cy had met Jack in Chicago, and Jack hired him. Cy Howard left the show after thirteen weeks, and went on to write <u>My Friend Irma</u>, <u>Life With Luigi</u>, and Martin and Lewis' <u>That's My Boy</u>. He also directed <u>Lovers and Other Strangers</u>. All this info is taken from Milt's book, page 124.]...Hey listen, do you ever get down this way?...I'll tell you what you do. You've got my number, haven't you? And now I just got yours. So here's what's gonna happen. I had it, but I don't know what. But here's what's gonna happen. The next time maybe that they have one of those things at [], maybe we get together...Maybe I can get my guy, you know Audrey's friend...From <u>Green Acres</u>...One of my best pals...Pat Buttram....All right, it's sure nice talking to you...Well I'm glad I got you. Now I won't let you get away. I'll check in once in a while...All right, partner. Right. [Hangs up.] Nice guy!

L: [During the call I had been looking at the pictures and mementos which leave very little of the wall uncovered. Several times, my eyes had set upon a gold record hanging up near the ceiling.] I must ask, which record went gold?

P: Oh, I had...four, I think. I think that one is "The Thing". [E.N.: If you don't know about the song "The Thing", run--do not walk--to your nearest rare/used record store and look for it. It's great.]...We just needed something to put on the other side, and it was an old English sailing song that...we dressed up the lyrics....The things I'm proud of, they're in my library, are the albums, the big things are from like Jungle Book and The Aristocats and Robin Hood [E.N.: Disney movies]. I just finished one that will be out in November called Rock-a-Doodle, and it's gonna be pretty good.

L: Animated Disney?

P: Animated, yeah. But they're fun to do because they can make you clever. Make you dance and do everything...So you live in from Fort Wayne? [E.N.: I did at the time.]...Yeah, I played Fort Wayne 14 years....[E.N.: I mention a friend of his in Fort Wayne, for whom he leaves a phone message.]

L: You were mentioning about the song "The Thing".

P: Oh yeah, then we just changed the lyrics, but everybody says "What was it about?" But nobody knows what it was about.

L: It was about a percussion section!

P: Yeah, that's it. We just stomped our feet. Everybody stomped their feet. Then "That's What I Like About the South" and "Poker Club" and "The Preacher and the Bear". We start talking about people, my God, Gene Autry's got a roomful of them. I think he got more gold records than anybody living. Course in those days, you know, there were very few. One tune. I can remember when a tune would stay popular for a year. The same way if you'll notice with a picture. It will be on top for one week, and then the next thing you know it'll be fourth, fifth, and then out of the first ten. Got new cream coming on all the time....The girl that had my fan club for years and years, passed away last year, from Allentown, Pennsylvania...I met her in the Earl Theatre in Pittsburgh. She was in Allentown, Pennsylvania. Nice lady...She gave me all the stuff for the library that she had collected. Scrapbooks, you know...Alice's biggest fan club is in England...She has a couple of them. They get together in London and show one of her pictures...[E.N.: Phil asks if I am going to college at Indiana University. I am.]...See, I'm right near there. I'm in Litton, and Litton is halfway between Terre Haute and Bloomington. Southern Indiana, down around Vincennes...It's right near the Tennessee border, you know...

L: Actually, one of the Maxwells is in that vicinity. By the way, would you have any idea how many Maxwells there were?

P: I think about two or three. [E.N.: Think that three is right, as the first one was purchased to be donated to the scrap drive for World War II, and I have seen publicity photos of Jack in two different Maxwells. A member once told me that one was a 1916 Maxwell, and the other was about a 1924 Maxwell, but I am not positive of this info.] It was the sound, you see, Mel Blanc. Mel Blanc together with our sound department, two or three other guys. He was doing all the belching, I mean. So I actually don't know...When we'd go someplace, they get one. But I'll tell you, when Mark Sanders made the picture--with all due respect to Mark because he was a great genius, he did all the Fred Astaire/Ginger Rogers pictures later--but when he showed the bear, I mean, Carmichael, when he showed the Maxwell and the [vault] down where they kept the money, we never got the laughs that we got [on radio] because, see, people had a different [vision]. That's one good thing about radio, you know, you can draw your own pictures....Does he have anything at all in the library in Waukegan?

L: There's the Jack Benny Junior High School, but just about the only major thing that's related to him is the Genessee Theatre, where you did a number of broadcasts when you were in Waukegan. [There is also a display in the Waukegan Historical Society, and the Waukegan Public Library has some selected holdings.] Also Am Echad [the synagogue co-founded by Jack's father, Meyer]...

P: Where they planted the tree that died. [E.N.: Regarding the tree that was planted in Jack's honor that died, Fred Allen said, "How can a tree live in Waukegan when the sap is in Hollywood?"]

L: ...What are your recollections of Fred Allen?

P: Oh, I like him. Oh, and that feud was one of the greatest things that ever happened. Course they used to do that, you know, when the ratings would get low or something. Bernie had a feud, too. Ben Bernie had a feud with somebody [E.N.: Walter Winchell]. But the feud with Allen and, of course they were very close friends. But they were all vaudevillians, they were all vaudevillians, you know, like Burns and Allen....

L: [The phone rings again, this time with someone inviting him to a golf tournament. He notes that he does many of those.] About how many golf tournaments do you do per year?

P: I do too many. I'm cutting down. I do a lot of them.

L: Just want to spend more time here at home?

P: No, just too much to do.

L: [Phil hands me a glass of iced tea] There's no vodka in here, is there?

P: No, you want some in there?

L: No, no...I'm always curious if people have favorite episodes of the Benny shows.

P: One show? Oh, no--we did 39 a year. I can never know, because that's what's most amazing about it. I could hardly pick a bad one. We didn't have any bad ones. You know what you call "bad", I can't ever remember when we came off of there on a Sunday saying, "Hey, wait a minute. We didn't get too many laughs." I can't remember that, because the show was so well-written. We were so fortunate, I'm telling you, Beloin and Morrow, regardless of what anybody tells you, they never improved on their basis...The whole foundation was their idea. Rochester, Kenny Baker, all of those people--with all due respect--they were all good writers, but they didn't create it...And Beloin, they tell me, this is just heresay, but back in Massachusetts he was a typewriter salesman. With all that talent. And this [where the interview took place] was Morrow's house. This is who I bought it from. Course he was a bachelor, and it was nothing like this...it was many years ago, and nobody lived up here. This was just a little hideaway in the desert, and fact of the matter is that room you came through there was a breezeway, and it had one bedroom because he was single. I planted all this stuff [E.N.: There was a lot of beautiful vegetation around the place]...but this is where he used to come to from L.A. to relax.

L: [Tape ran out, so there is a jump here] Exactly how did the Fitch Bandwagon start?

P: That started by using a different band every week. That's way before me...I just went on with my band like everybody else, and they liked it. And that's when Jack gave me permission to do that, too.

L: So basically now you're working in the golf tournaments and with Disney...

P: That's it. I do quite a few benefits...I do as far as nightclubs are concerned or any of that kind of work no more. I spent 25 years in Vegas, and I was very proud of the fact that I only worked for one man, Moe Dalens [sp?], most of the time, and I worked only in two places, and they were both owned by the same people: the Desert Inn and the Frontier.

L: Also, I know I saw you once on a hunting show with Bing Crosby.

P: Oh, I made a lot of American Sportsman.

L: One other thing, a friend of mine said that he thought he had seen a movie from the thirties where there was a fellow who was trying to impersonate you to impress a girl, and you were playing the impersonator.

P: Oh yeah, well that was a Gold picture that was made years ago at RKO, where [in the movie] I owned...an escort service, and so I saw this girl and I liked her. It was a cheap picture. And so I posed as somebody that I'd sent, but I went myself. Very cheap.

Phil had another appointment and I had taken up plenty of his time, so here we ended. You can make up your own jokes about the interview focused so much on Jack ending with the words "Very cheap."

☺ ☺

Please send all questions, comments, additions, and corrections to:
Laura Lee   (510) 933-3879
c/o The International Jack Benny Fan Club Offices
3190 Oak Road, #303
Walnut Creek, California 94596   Internet: JackBenny@Delphi.com

Please friends, send no bombs.

Bandleader Phil Harris dies at 89

By Robert McG. Thomas Jr.
NEW YORK TIMES

Phil Harris, the brash, bourbon-swigging, fast-drawling band leader who became a comic radio star in the 1930s and then enchanted new generations of fans as the unlikely voice of Baloo the Bear in Walt Disney's "Jungle Book," died Friday night at his home at the Thunderbird Country Club in Rancho Mirage. He was 89.

Whether as part of the famous Jack Benny radio ensemble from 1936 to 1952 or as the star of his own show with his wife, Alice Faye, from 1946 to 1954, Mr. Harris, with his black curly hair, toothy grin and trademark "Hi ya, Jackson," was the epitome of the slang-slinging, wise-cracking slacker, a drummer given to one-liners and two fingers of bourbon.

Although he grew up in Nashville, the guitar-strumming capital of country music, he played the drums, not the guitar, and the touring 25-piece orchestra he led was known for its sophisticated big band sound.

And while he had a distinct Southern accent and affected down-home humor with such songs as "That's What I Like About the South," "Is It True What They Say About Dixie?" and "Smoke, Smoke That Cigarette," he delivered the lines with a rapid-fire staccato. His biggest hit was "The Thing."

For all his Tennessee affectations, Mr. Harris was born in a coal mining camp outside the small town of Linton, Ind. His father, a circus bandmaster and vaudeville musician, moved the family to Nashville when his son was young, and later hired him as a drummer.

He was retired and largely forgotten in 1967 when Walt Disney picked him for the voice of Baloo the Bear in his animated cartoon version of Kipling's "Jungle Book."

When Harris did his first reading, he found his lines too plain for his style. As he later recalled it, after a wooden reading of a line like, "Now, Mowgli, you be careful because you're in this bad jungle," he asked if he could do a bit of improvising and was told to go ahead.

"I came out with something like, 'You keep foolin' around in the jungle like this, man, you gonna run across some cats that'll knock the roof in'."

The Disney staff was so impressed that the entire script was rewritten, incorporating the personalities of the actors into the cartoon characters they portrayed.

Mr. Harris, whose song in the film, "The Bare Necessities," was nominated for an Academy Award, became famous all over again, much to his surprise and delight.

In addition to his wife, he is survived by two daughters, Alice Regan of New Orleans and Phyllis Harris of St. Louis and Rancho Mirage; four grandchildren, and two great-grandchildren.

BENNY HAPPY RETURNS

Aside from the obvious physical similarities between Kelsey Grammer and his comedic idol Jack Benny (as displayed in the picture, below), the *Frasier* star and his mentor share a similar intellectual approach to humor. "Jack was instrumental in my life," says the host of **Kelsey Grammer Salutes Jack Benny** (*NBC, Thanksgiving*). "I remember being 16 years old and hearing him say that the key to his success was that he never talked down to his audience. That became my credo for *Frasier*, and the kind of comedy I do." Grammer went to NBC West Coast President Don Ohlmeyer with the idea of doing the special and claims it was the quickest meeting he ever had. "He said, 'Kelsey Grammer, Jack Benny. Let's do it.' It was under two minutes." Thanks to a bit of techno-wizardry, Grammer will get to appear side by side with Benny in vintage clips from *The Jack Benny Show*. The special will also include classic Benny routines from TV and film, and personal tributes from the likes of such famous fans as Jay Leno, Phil Hartman, and Dan Aykroyd.

J. DELVALLE/NBC

The International Jack Benny Fan Club
3190 Oak Road, #303
Walnut Creek, California 94596
JackBenny@Delphi.Com

To:

Address Correction Requested

THE JACK BENNY TIMES

September-December 1995   INTERNATIONAL DISTRIBUTION   Volume XV, Numbers 5-6

🕮 President's Message 📖

Jell-o again, folks...normally I take this opportunity to apologize for the newsletter being late and give excuses relating to work and family. This issue is an exception. I had long planned for this issue to be a tribute to the friendship between Jack and George Burns, and have it come out on George's 100th birthday. In light of George's health, I believed that it would be most wise to delay publication rather than do a birthday issue and likely follow it up with a memorial issue.

Additionally, I have been trying to get caught up on my correspondence and tape orders. I hope to have that all done by the end of March because...yet again...**WE'RE MOVING!** Contrary to the popular belief that we are running from bill collectors, we are finally moving back into a house (although still renting...I get my own garden again). **As of April 6, please send all correspondence to:**

4749 Wilkie
Oakland, California 94619
(510) 530-1243

Internet address (JackBenny@delphi.com) remains the same, of course. Which reminds me--a virtual "hello" to the many members who have recently contacted me via the Internet. If you have the option to contact me by email or snail mail (post office mail), I do recommend that you try the email route first. It's much easier and faster for me to keep up with my email, and you're certain to get a more timely response.

As always, Jack pops up in the most interesting places. Seems that during this past year, Chicagoland Cadillac Dealers have had television ads for their Cadillac deVilles featuring clips of Jack, including the one where Jack is stranded in the rain outside of Don's house and recreates the "Money or your Life" bit.

Now on with the show!

⇨ Do You Know? ⇦

Barbara Fisher sent me an interesting article from the October 7, 1995 New York Times about a composer by the name of John Moran. Moran had just opened a "science-fiction techno-opera" entitled "Matthew in the School of Life" at the Ridge Theatre. So what does this have to do with Jack Benny, you ask? Well, as per the article, "As in his earlier operas, 'Jack Benny!,' 'The Manson Family' and 'Everyday Newt Berman,' all of the music and dialogue in 'Matthew' is 'found sound.' What comes out of the actors' mouths is expertly lip-synched." An opera entitled "Jack Benny!"? Now that's a new one on me. Does anyone know about this, or have any information on Moran?

© Copyright 1996, Laura Lee

Also stumbled across something on the World Wide Web that mentioned a movie entitled The Man from 1972. Says that it was shot in black and white, directed by Joseph Sargent, starred (among others) James Earl Jones, Martin Balsam, Burgess Meredith, and Lew Ayers. Jack allegedly appeared "as himself." I am wondering if anyone has seen this movie and can shed any light on it or Jack's role.

Also had been told by a few of you that you had special ordered the reprint of Milt Josefsberg's The Jack Benny Show from Monologue Publications. I have not heard of anyone actually receiving a copy, nor have I heard from Monologue lately. Has anyone gotten anything? I would like to follow up with them if there has been any delay. If you would like to contact them directly, their address is: 7130 Harrison Avenue, Pittsburgh, Pennsylvania 15218; (412) 731-8639.

❧ Burns and Benny: Together Again ☙

Well, since this issue is a combination birthday salute and memorial, I will start with the birthday information. George Burns was born Nathan Birnbaum on January 20, 1896 in New York City. To tell how George met Jack, I really have to tell about how George met Gracie. George had gone through a number of acts (including one with a trained seal) and stage names. In 1923, he was working with Billy Lorraine as Burns and Lorraine at a theatre in Union City, New Jersey. There's a story that I have often heard told about Billy Lorraine: he had a terrible stammer, but not when he sang. One time George was in the lobby of their hotel (or somewhere), and Lorraine came rushing up to him, stammering unintelligibly. George tried to make out what he was saying, and finally said "Billy, sing it!" At this, Lorraine sang "We were just robbed!"

Gracie had also gone through a few acts, and was in the process of searching for a new partner. When Burns and Lorraine had decided to break up, one of Gracie's roommates, Rena Arnold (who was on the same bill with Burns and Lorraine), encouraged her to come to the theatre to see their act. She came backstage, Rena introduced her to George, and they agreed to team. Their first show was at the Hill Street Theatre in Newark, New Jersey. It is now legendary how initially George had all the comedy lines and Gracie the straight lines; the audience laughed at Gracie's straight lines. So by the end of the run in Newark, Gracie had most of the jokes.

At this time, Gracie was rooming with Rena Arnold and Mary Kelly, both vaudeville performers. To celebrate their first show, George and Gracie had gone to dinner with friends, including Mary Kelly and her boyfriend...Jack Benny. And that is how George and Jack first met. As George himself said, "I liked Benny right away, he had something I enjoyed very much--a worse singing voice than mine."

George and Gracie married on January 7, 1926 in Cleveland. On their wedding night at...well, I'll just let George tell it: "At two-thirty in the morning on our wedding night the phone in our hotel room rang. When I answered, I heard a gruff voice say, 'Hello, George?' Jack Benny trying to disguise his voice sounded exactly like Jack Benny trying to disguise his voice. 'Listen,' I said, 'send up two orders of ham and eggs.' Then I hung up. About a half hour later he called again, 'George, I just...' 'The eggs were cold,' I interrupted, 'now send up some hot coffee.' And I hung up again. Actually, I hung up on Jack only to make him happy. Even then he loved it when I played practical jokes on him. After hanging up for the second time I imagined him sitting in his hotel room in California laughing hysterically. I figured he'd probably keep laughing until he realized he had to pay for two long-distance telephone calls."

Such was typical of the fifty-one year friendship between George Burns and Jack Benny. There are many stories that George has told over the years of making Jack laugh. I will recall these from memory, so if some of the details are incorrect, please forgive me. The one I have heard most often (and had the good fortune to hear George tell it in person) was about George and Jack eating together. Jack says to George that he wants to order bacon and eggs. "So order bacon and eggs," says George. "No, Mary says that I should eat Cream of Wheat. It's good for me." "So let Mary eat Cream of Wheat," replies George, "If you want bacon and eggs, order bacon and eggs." The waiter comes over. George says, "I'll have bacon and eggs." Jack says, "I will, too." When the check comes, George says, "Give it to Jack Benny." Jack says, "Why should I pay the check?" George replies, "If you don't pay it, I'll tell Mary you had the bacon and eggs."

Which reminds me of another story about George and Jack dining out. I think they were at Chasen's, when George says, "Jack, let's see if we can get Chasen to pick up the tab." Jack asks how they could do that. George replies, "Well, when the bill comes, you insist on paying it, saying that if George Burns pays the bill, you'll never eat here again. Then I'll insist on paying the bill, because if you pay it, I'll never eat here again. Chasen will then offer to settle it by picking up the tab himself." Jack says that it is a great idea, and agrees to it. The check comes, and Jack proclaims, "I'll take that--if George Burns pays for this dinner, I'll never eat here again!" The dumbfounded waiter looks over at George, who looks back and shrugs his shoulders. I think this may also have been the time that Jack crawled under the next table, pounding the floor and laughing.

And speaking of falling down laughing, there was the time that George and Jack were at a gathering where, I think it was Jeanette MacDonald who had been asked to sing. George leaned over to Jack and said, "If when Jeanette MacDonald begins to sing you were to laugh, it would be very inappropriate." When MacDonald opened her mouth and the first note came out, Jack completely broke up.

One night George and Jack were ready to go to a gathering, and Jack had a little piece of white thread on his lapel. George commented, "That white thread is very impressive. May I borrow it?" George then took the white thread from Jack's lapel and placed it on his own. This broke Jack up in itself. Then occasionally during the evening, George would catch Jack's eye, point to the thread, and wave or wink, breaking Jack up at every instance. The next day George took the thread, put it in a box, and enclosed a note thanking Jack for loaning it to him, and that he had received many compliments on it.

After the box arrived at Jack's house, Mary phoned George saying that Jack had been on the floor laughing for an hour.

Of course, Jack sometimes tried (unsuccessfully) to make George laugh. One time Jack was in a hotel, and asked George to come up to his room. Deciding that he would try again to break up George, Jack removed all his clothing, put a lampshade on his head, held a rose in his hand, and posed on a table ala a Grecian statue (which makes me think of the routine they did on Jack's Second Farewell Special with the two of them as a fountain, but I digress). So here's Jack posing and waiting for George. Naturally, George had the last laugh--he sent the maid in first.

In spite of this, during one of George's Las Vegas shows he paid Jack a high compliment. George announced that Jack was in the audience, and asked Jack to come up on stage. George quoted the old adage that a "comic says funny things, but a comedian says things funny," and that a good comedian can get laughs reading the yellow pages (geez, I think Jack did that on one of his specials, didn't he?). So in that spirit, George invited Jack to drink a glass of water on stage. Jack complied, doing his initmitable pauses between sips. The audience was roaring by the time the water was gone.

The story that's been noted as a favorite by many people occurred during a party at Jack's house. Jack approaches George and says, "The party's not moving." George says, "The party's moving--people are talking and eating and having a good time. It's fine." "No, the party's just not moving," replies Jack. George then says, "Jack, if you want to get the party moving, I'll tell you what to do. Go upstairs, take off your pants, put on one of Mary's big hats, and come downstairs playing your violin." Jack quickly goes off to do just that. George then announces to the party guests, "In a few minutes, Jack Benny will come downstairs with his pants off and playing the violin. Pay no attention to him." So shortly, here comes Jack just as suggested, parading and playing his violin. No one bats an eye, or even turns. At this Jack falls on the floor laughing and proclaims, "NOW the party's moving!"

I have frequently been asked about the story where Jack and George were arrested for smuggling. It all began when George and Gracie were dining at 21 with another couple. The man was named Albert Chaperau. Chaperau's wife was wearing a very wide diamond bracelet. At this moment, I should digress and mention that when Gracie was very small, she had pulled a pot off of a hot stove and badly scalded her arm, leaving her permanently scarred. For the rest of her life, she always kept this scar covered by long sleeves or gloves. George admired the diamond bracelet, and thought that Gracie could wear it to cover her scar. They struck up a deal right there, and George presented the bracelet to Gracie.

Jack later bought a pin from Chaperau for Mary. It seems that the jewelry had been smuggled into the country, and the fact that Jack and George now owned it (although they were unaware that it had been smuggled) made them guilty. They pleaded guilty to a misdemeanor, and George was given a suspended sentence of one year and one day. George paid $15,000 in fines, and Jack paid $10,000. Gracie ended up giving away the bracelet because she din't want to be "reminded of [George's] criminal career." (Specifics of this story taken from Gracie: A Love Story.)

୶ ୰

So let us now jump ahead in time to George's recent 100th birthday. The following are excerpts from Internet stories:

("Comedian George Burns to mark 100th Birthday" by Steve James)
January 11 - Wise-cracking, cigar-puffing comedian George Burns, who has entertained audiences in every form of show business this century from vaudeville to television and movies, turns 100 years old this month too frail to fulfill his dream of playing the London Palladium or Caesar's Palace in Las Vegas one more time.

"Physically, he's just not able to do the show," said his long-time manager and producer Irving Fein.

"He's very frail. I understand he's not been feeling too well recently but at 100 years old he's entitled to feel that way," said Irving Feintech [E.N.: ironic similarity], past chairman of the board of the Cedars-Sinai Medical Centre, a charity close to Burns' heart. But Feintech added, "I saw him a couple of weeks ago and he still enjoys playing bridge and two-martini lunches."

About 18 months ago, a fall forced Burns to cancel plans to appear on the Palladium stage to celebrate his centennial on January 20. And last year his frailty prompted him to drop a scheduled appearance at Caesar's, the casino-hotel, where he had sold out five nights a year in advance, Fein said. He said Burns' book A Hundred Years, a Hundred Stories was scheduled to be published on January 26. "He writes about the greats, Al Jolson, Fanny Brice, Danny Kaye. It's very funny."

Los Angeles Mayor Richard Riordan has proclaimed January 20 "George Burns Day" in the city known as "the Entertainment Capitol of the World"--an honor for a man born on Manhattan's poor lower East Side as Nathan Birnbaum, the ninth of twelve children. The city already has renamed two streets, which intersect at Cedars-Sinai, for Burns and his longtime wife and partner Gracie Allen, and Riordan's proclamation calls Burns a "national treasure" for bringing happiness to people. In addition, the mayor said, "many have benefited as a result of George's philanthropy." Feintech said Burns was a "very substantial major donor" to the medical centre.

Fein said Burns, who launched his career in vaudeville at the age of seven, was expected to attend a party on January 16 at the Four Seasons Hotel in Beverly Hills. The bash is for donors, such as movie star Ann-Margaret, to a new research institute at Cedars-Sinai to be named for Burns and Allen. Burns, who won an Oscar for best supporting actor at the age of 80 -- two years after undergoing open-heart surgery -- is not expected to perform at the party, however. Four days later, Feintech said, Burns probably will celebrate his landmark birthday quietly at home with family and friends such as fellow comics Milton Berle and Don Rickles.

Over the years, Burns has made much of his increasing age, and he once said, "Audiences were afraid that if they didn't applaud I'd drop dead on stage." He escorted a host of beautiful women, but said he could never marry again after Allen's death at the age of 58. "I was with Gracie for 24 hours a day. There can be no replacement," he said. "I take girls to restaurants and sit them in dark corners so they can do their homework," he laughed. "Some of my suits are older than the girls."

Still smoking 10 cigars a day -- "I also drink martinis and dance very close" -- Burns gave this recipe for stage success: "When the people laugh, I smoke. When they stop laughing, I stop smoking and start to talk." Feintech, who has known Burns for many years, described him as "A man who enjoys life and cares about people."

For 19 years Burns and Allen appeared on radio and television, with Allen playing a daffy, scatterbrained wife and Burns the bemused, tolerant husband and straight man, philosophically puffing on his cigar. "All I had to do was listen," Burns once said. "I'd throw in a 'Your brother did what?' or 'You don't say,' and Gracie would take it from there." When Allen died, Burns decided he had to start working again. "My talent up to that point was in marrying Gracie," said Burns, who is known for his quick wit and a mastery of timing on stage.

But it was the death in 1974 of his best friend, comedian Jack Benny, that made Burns a celebrity all over again, bringing him to the attention of a whole new generation. Benny was slated for the role of a retired comedian opposite Walter Matthau in the film version of Neil Simon's The Sunshine Boys. Burns landed the part instead, despite undergoing open heart surgery two years earlier, and won the Academy Award for Best Supporting Actor.

His career soared after that. He went on to make more films, including playing God in 1978 in Oh, God! and its two sequels during the 1980s, as well as Just You and Me, Kid with Brooke Shields and Going in Style [E.N.: with Art Carney and Lee Strasberg]. His books include How to Live to Be 100 - or More and Dr. Burns' Prescription for Happiness. He even made a country and western album, with a hit song "I Wish I was Eighteen Again". [E.N.: This isn't right..."I Wish I..." was on the album that preceded the country/western album.] And at age 95, he became the oldest-ever Grammy award nominee, in the spoken-word category for Gracie: A Love Story.

("George Burns turns 100 Quietly" by Bob Tourtellotte)
January 20 - George Burns, the cigar smoking grand ol' man of comedy, celebrated his 100th birthday quietly on Saturday, resting at his Beverly Hills home with his family.

Hollywood had scheduled a series of parties to honor Burns, but a flu he caught two weeks ago caused him to cancel. A celebrity dinner set for the evening of his birthday had to be scrapped. "He spent the day with his children," said manager and producer Irving Fein. "He's really too weak to get out."

Burns' health didn't stop the entertainment world and its capitol city from paying tribute to the master of the punch line, who rose during 93 years of entertaining from singing on vaudeville stages to playing God in the movies. Saturday was proclaimed "George Burns Day" in Los Angeles by Mayor Richard Riordan, and at Planet Hollywood restaurant in Beverly Hills, employees sported limited edition T-shirts with Burns' trademark cigar and eyeglasses. Burns' book <u>A Hundred Years, a Hundred Stories</u> will hit bookstores in the United States on Wednesday, Fein said.

All week around Hollywood, celebrities have been praising and even poking some friendly fun at the century-old comedian. Screenwriter Larry Gelbart said if the 89-year-old entertainment magazine "Daily Variety" had been publishing when Burns was born, his arrival would have been listed in the "New Acts" section. "(Burns) is truly a legend in his own time-and-a-half...who did not become wise because he got old, but got old because he was wise," Gelbart said at a gala celebration. Although Burns missed that event, he sent a video message, "What do you give a man who has been so lucky? Another 100 years? A night with (sex symbol) Sharon Stone?" Burns asked.

Though he never remarried after his wife, comedienne Gracie Allen, died of a heart attack in 1964, Burns liked being accompanied by attractive young women. Comedian Bill Cosby said he met Burns, a gorgeous woman on each arm, four years ago at a book signing. "I said, 'George, why do you always have two young girls with you?' He said, 'They're hipper than canes'," Cosby told "Daily Variety".

But he remained devoted to Allen, whom he met on the vaudeville stage. They married and formed a comedy team that would become a huge hit in radio and on television, Allen playing zany wife to Burns' straight-arrow husband. He "was the greatest straight man in the business," Dan Aykroyd told Variety. "I did it for a long time, playing straight to John (Belushi), Billy (Murray) and Eddie (Murphy) on 'Saturday Night Live'. If not for George, I wouldn't have known how to do it."

For those interested in reading George's many books, they are:
<u>I Love Her, That's Why</u>
<u>Living It Up, or They Still Love Me in Altoona</u> - 1976, ISBN 0-425-04811-X
<u>The Third Time Around</u> - 1980, ISBN 0-425-04732-6
<u>How to Live to Be 100 - or More</u> - 1983, ISBN 0-399-12787-9
<u>Dr. Burns' Prescription for Happiness</u> - 1984, ISBN 0-399-12964-2
<u>Dear George</u> - 1985, ISBN 0-399-13105-1
<u>Gracie: A Love Story</u> - 1988, ISBN 0-399-13384-4

All My Best Friends - 1989, ISBN 0-399-13483-2
Wisdom of the 90s - 1991, ISBN 0-399-13695-9
A Hundred Years, a Hundred Stories - 1996

I've read all of George's books (except the first and last) and recommend them all, most particularly Gracie: A Love Story. The love that they had just comes off the pages and envelops you. Other books about George are:

Say Goodnight, Gracie!, Cheryl Blythe and Susan Sackett, 1989, ISBN 1-55958-019-4
George Burns and the Hundred Year Dash, Martin Gottfried, 1996, ISBN 0-684-81483-8

Have not read these books and thus cannot critique them. Some of the above are out of print; check your local used book store for them.

⍋ The Tale Piece ⍋

Apologies that I don't have an actual name to attribute this comment to:
"I had once found a Sunday Magazine Supplement to the Portland Oregonian, late 30's--featuring the top money-winners in Hollywood. Shirley Temple, #1 with $500,000 for the year; and Jack Benny had come in as #2. The newspaper page was of special interest to me at the time, for JB was seated at a backgammon board (I was a player--and a collector of such paper ephemera). A very strange juxtaposition from his screen persona; as the game itself is more associated with images of riverboat gambling, lightning-fast calculations of patterns and permutations, and steely nerves." I personally never had heard of Jack being into playing backgammon, but it may have just been a publicity shot. Does anyone know otherwise?

This from Jim Reid:
"I had to take some relatives to Union Station last night in downtown Los Angeles. It was so fun to imagine Jack and the gang roaming around waiting for the train even though none of them were really there during the show. I saw the information booth where Frank Nelson would've been working. The magazine stand where the tout, Sheldon Leonard, would hang out. We didn't take a taxi there, so we didn't have to worry about the driver not wanting us to leave. I was really hoping for the announcement: 'Train leaving on track five for Anaheim, Azusa, and Cuc...amonga' but of course it never came. The station still has a lot of class, although it looks like they're doing some modernization. Too bad. I thought it looked fine the way it was."

In response to the section a few issues ago about comments on Jack being too Jewish or not Jewish enough, Steve Dillie said:
"I never really associated Jack with being Jewish from listening to his shows. When I found out he was Jewish I wondered how he felt about doing Christmas shows. Did he tire of them, did he just consider it business, or not a big deal since the shows were secular. In Sunday Nights at Seven Joan told about having a Christmas tree when a child,

that Jack would buy. I realized it was another good example how tolerant Jack was of other people and different ways."

From John Jensen, in response to a discussion about NBC:
"I got a kick out of Fred Berney's comments on being asked by NBC for material they supposedly already own. I had a similar occurrence when I ran KMPX in San Francisco. On the day Jack Benny died, I was called by their CBS all news O&O, KCBS, if they could have some excerpts of some Benny shows to run on their obit segments. I sent over three bits, and they sent them down the line so that the whole network could run them on the network news at the top of the hour. I heard the bits all through the day. Postscript: I didn't tell them that all three bits were off of programs from when he was at NBC."

From Bruce Reznick:
"I was at a Christmas party with my father in LA, and talking to Stan Chase, who wrote for many sitcoms in the 60s and 70s. Stan said: 'You know Jack Benny was a lovely man, but he had one weakness as a comedian--he could not tell a line and do a bit of physical business at the same time. Once, NBC (possibly CBS, I don't remember which) asked me to shoot the annual promotion of the fall schedule with all the stars. We asked Jack to do a line and switch on a light. After 10 takes, we gave up.'"

And finally, from Kathy O'Connell:
"...the story Fred Foy told at the FOTR announcer's panel. Basically, it started when Fred Foy filled in for Don Wilson many, many years earlier (perhaps as early as 1938? that date sticks in my mind). Many, many years later, Fred Foy had a chance to work with Jack Benny again. He approached Mr. Benny and said, "I don't suppose you remember me, but..." Jack Benny not only remembered Fred Foy, but he remembered everyone connected with that particular show. Fred Foy used that anecdote to go off on what an incredibly kind man Jack Benny was. And I never saw so many people nod in agreement at once!!!"

§§§ Jack Benny Classifieds §§§

§§§ Clair Schulz is seeking an audio copy of the September 30, 1945 show, having obtained a copy of the script at an auction (I'm jealous!). P.O. Box 659, Stevens Point, WI 54481

§§§ Eric Rhoads has published Blast from the Past: A Pictorial History of Radio's First 75 Years. It is a coffee table book, with over 900 photos. The press package alone contains photos of Jack that I have not previously seen. It is available from Streamline Press, 1-800-226-7857.

§§§ Thrilling Days of Yesteryear is a bimonthly publication on all facets of old time radio performers and shows. Enjoyed the writing style of the issue I received. Carol T. Rayburn, P.O. Box 36106, Denver, CO 80236

§§§ The Old-Time Radio Gazette is published by Tom C. Miller, and also deals with all facets of old radio. 2004 East 6th Street, Superior, WI 54880-3632

§§§ George Fowler of The Great Radio Shows is in his 27th year of old time radio taping. Shows are available on 7-inch reels ($5.50 per hour) or cassettes ($6.50 per hour). Their catalog is $4.00 and over 600 pages. 304 Eunice Street, Sequim, WA 98382

§§§ Bob Burnham of BRC Productions has another installment of his catalog out for old time radio tapes. BRC Productions, P.O. Box 2645, Livonia, MI 48151-0645

§§§ John A. Barber of Golden Age Productions also has a catalog of old radio shows and scripts available. Box 70711, New Orleans, LA 70172, 504-943-6091

§§§ Bill Oliver sent me information on a reissue of Phil Harris' musical material. Includes "That's What I Like About the South", "The Thing", "Smoke! Smoke! Smoke! (that Cigarette)", "The Preacher and the Bear", "Goofus", and many others. 2 cassettes for $12.98, or CD for $16.98. Available from the Good Music Record Company, 1-800-538-4200, P.O. Box 1935, Ridgely, MD 21681-1935

§§§ MC Productions offers 30,000 titles from 1900 on of many vintage artists. Neat offerings for anyone with a love for vintage music. Richard Savill, #330 10637 150th Street, Surrey, British Columbia, Canada V3R 4B8, Internet: rsavill@direct.ca

§§§ McFarland & Company's Performing Arts catalog contains a variety of interesting and unusual titles on all facets of entertainment. Fun just to look through the catalog. Box 611, Jefferson, North Carolina 28640, 910-246-4460

Please send all questions, comments, additions, and corrections to:
Laura Lee
c/o The International Jack Benny Fan Club Offices

Pre 4/6/96:
3190 Oak Road, #303
Walnut Creek, California 94596

(510) 933-3879
Internet: JackBenny@Delphi.com

Post 4/6/96:
4749 Wilkie
Oakland, CA 94619

(510) 530-1243
Internet: JackBenny@Delphi.com

Please friends, send no bombs.

George Burns, who turns 100 Saturday, says, 'I didn't quit'

1/14/96

BY DAVID LYMAN
Free Press Staff Writer

George Burns describes himself as a late bloomer. He trod the vaudeville stage for 15 years before trying his hand at comedy. He made movies at 33, but he didn't win an Oscar until he was 80. And though he had been a notable singer in his youth, he didn't make a hit record until he was 84.

So there's no telling what he may come up with when he turns 100 on Saturday.

"There were only about six or seven great radio comedy shows," recalls Tom Wilson, host of a Detroit-based syndicated radio show called "Somewhere in Time." "And George Burns and Gracie Allen were right up at the top. They were ahead of Bob Hope. They were ahead of Jack Benny."

That George Burns should have been ahead of anyone in show biz would have shocked those who knew him as a child. The ninth of 12 kids growing up in Manhattan's lower east side, Burns — born Nathan Birnbaum on Jan. 20, 1896 — was a spunky, tenacious kid. His father died when he was 7. And since school had never been his strength anyway, he went to work to support the family.

He had several odd jobs, but when an acquaintance heard the crooning of Burns and his pals in the candy store where they worked, it was the birth of Burns' first stage act: "The Peewee Quartet." They weren't great, but by age 14 he was a stage veteran. By 18, he was a high-stepping theatrical dandy. He'd performed in animal acts — nameless sidekick in the notable seal act, Flipper and Friend — as part of several song-and-dance teams and even as a featured roller skater.

But his career was decidedly forgettable until, in 1923, he crossed paths with Grace Ethel Cecile Rosalie Allen — Gracie, as we came to know her. They were a smash, first in vaudeville, later on radio and television.

"Gracie was a gracious woman — audiences adored her," recalls Detroit television legend Bill Kennedy, host for 27 years of "Bill Kennedy at the Movies." Kennedy worked briefly as an actor on television's "The George Burns and Gracie

BURNS, from Page 1F

Allen Show" in the early 1950s. "It was George who was in complete charge. He made all the decisions with the show.

"What I remember most about him is how generous he was. When we went in for rehearsals in the morning, we had tea and crumpets. And we all had our own dressing rooms, which was unheard of in television in those days."

Burns' onscreen persona was a different one. With an ever-present stogie perched in his pinkie-ringed left hand, he was the savvy one, the skeptic who was sure he knew more than his ditsy wife.

"They had a standard routine," says Wilson. "George would try to push Gracie into some odd situations. It always seemed like she would fall for it, but then at the end, there would be a little twist and Gracie would come through in the end. You knew it would end that way no matter what."

The formula was the same as that in several other shows, the most notable being television's "I Love Lucy," which debuted just a year after the Burns and Allen show. But somehow, it worked better with George and Gracie.

"Their popularity was far above 'Lucy,'" says Wilson, "because they created situations that you could actually find yourself in. Lucy and Desi were funny, but there you were looking in from the outside. With Burns and Allen, you were in the middle of it."

But in 1958, at the height of their television fame, it all ended. Gracie, troubled by a bad heart, retired. George tried to resurrect the show on his own, but it was canceled after a single season. And when Gracie died unexpectedly in 1964, Burns virtually disappeared from public life. There were a few abortive attempts to resuscitate his career, but it took another personal tragedy to jump-start it: the 1974 death of his best friend, Jack Benny.

Burns and Benny had been friends for more than 50 years. Predictably, Burns was devastated. But unbeknownst to him, Benny, who had contracted to perform in the film version of "The Sunshine Boys," had asked director Herbert Ross to use Burns instead.

At the age of 79, Burns was an up-and-coming star. He won an Oscar for

George Burns, turning 100, has a new book

George Burns and Gracie Allen in their Christmas show for 1953.

his performance. Suddenly, he was everywhere. He played the title role in 'Oh, God!' and was the darling of the Las Vegas stage and TV talk shows.

"I didn't quit," he told an interviewer at the time. "I stayed in there and I finally got so old I became new again."

And according to Kennedy, Burns was still performing the same shtick that had made him a success in the first place.

"He was one of the greatest of all straight men," says Kennedy. "And the irony is that when he first started working with Gracie, she was supposed to play the straight man. But when people laughed at her lines, they just reversed everything. They found that it worked. And when you've got a great formula like that, why change it?"

Burns has been in failing health since a fall and resultant surgery in 1994. Night club performances scheduled for his birthday have been canceled.

Public appearances are increasingly infrequent, though there are two new books — one by Burns himself — scheduled for a Jan. 20 release — "George Burns and The Hundred-Year Dash," by Martin Gottfried (Simon and Schuster, $23) and "100 Years, 100 Stories," by George Burns (G.P. Putnam's Sons, $15.95).

But as Burns cautioned a reporter several years ago, one should never count him out.

"I'm not afraid to die," he said. "I come from a family of 12. They're all dead. So what are you going to do? When the guy knocks on your door, he knocks.

"Of course, I may not answer. I may keep him waiting. Who knows?"

GEORGE BURNS ON ...

He may have played the straight man during his partnership with Gracie Allen, but George Burns was always good for a pithy — or sometimes very touching — remark:

"You know, all you needed in vaudeville was 17 good minutes. If you had 17 good minutes you would work for 17 years. There were so many good theaters, you wouldn't come back to the same one for four years and who would remember what you did the last time you were there?"

On his marriage to Gracie: "It was a great marriage. I was never a great lover, but marriage is what you do out of bed, not in bed. The marriage was a by-product of what we were doing for a living: show business. We never worked at our marriage. We were married, we stayed married. If the soup was hot, it was a great marriage. If the audiences were good, it was a great marriage."

"Let me tell you what my philosophy of life is: Don't believe everything they tell you. I use salt. I smoke 15 cigars a day. I have three or four martinis a day. If I don't like the food, I send for ketchup. And I'm almost 93."

"The truth is simple. I haven't said good-bye to Gracie. I'll never say good-bye. When I die, I'm going to be with Gracie again. I know that for sure."

"I was very fortunate that I met Gracie. I was with Gracie for 40 years. I was retired when I was working with Gracie — I did nothing. I said to Gracie, 'How's your brother?' and she talked for 40 years. And then when she retired, I went into show business. I learned a lot from Gracie."

LIVELY ARTS

"There were some routines that you were sure of, like when Gracie kissed me and asked, 'Who was that?'"

George Burns

No joke –

By BOB THOMAS
The Associated Press

In a town where friendship is as fleeting as a starlet's fame, the 50-year association of Jack Benny and George Burns is legendary.

They are legends themselves.

Benny, 80, entertainer of three generations, was one of vaudeville's smoothest funnymen. He starred in radio — ever stingy, ever 39. His films ranged from "To Be or Not to Be" to "The Horn Blows at Midnight." One of the few radio comics to succeed in television, he continues to appear in his own specials.

Burns, 78, is best known for his cigar and rakish humor. For 36 years he played the patient straight man for scatterbrained Gracie Allen. They, too, starred in vaudeville, radio, films, and television. But Gracie retired in 1958 and died in 1964. And Burns created a new role as a successful stand-up comedian.

The Benny-Burns friendship has flourished in the often competitive world of show business.

Nearly every day when they're in town, they meet for lunch at the Hillcrest Country Club, joining a comedian's roundtable for the latest jokes and gossip. Recently they lunched with a reporter for a session of reminiscence.

Both hospitalized

Both seemed fit considering their recent hospitalizations. Burns underwent open-heart surgery two months ago. Benny canceled a performance in Dallas because of stomach pains but was declared well after hospital tests here.

Benny didn't remember how he met Burns.

"Well, I do, Jack," Burns said. "Gracie and Mary Kelly and Renee Arnold shared an apartment at the Coolidge Hotel in New York. I was going with Gracie, and you were serious about Mary Kelly, who was thin and beautiful. . . . So we met at the girls' apartment, then we went out on double dates. That had to be 55 years ago."

Benny: "The Coolidge Hotel! You know something, I was moving offices recently and I came across a poem I had written called, 'The Little Old Coolidge Hotel.' It was on 47th Street — still is, in fact — just a block from the Palace Theater."

Was it fun playing vaudeville — or just work?

Benny: "Oh, it was fun. I'll tell you why: You didn't have to worry about writing all the time. If you got a good act together, you could play it for seven years. Because you were in a different town every week, you know."

Stealing jokes

Burns: "And another thing: nobody could steal your jokes, the way they do today. If you caught somebody using your material, you could send your original act to Pat Casey [labor executive for the theater owners] and he'd make the guy stop. Nowadays if other comics don't steal your jokes, you fire your writers."

Benny: "But they never stole from George and me. We don't use one-liners. We're story tellers; we start talking and one line leads into another."

Was vaudeville really as good as people's memories of it?

Benny: "Sure it was. Every city in America had a big-time vaudeville house, and they had top performers. Of course there were small-time houses too, and that's where the talent had a chance to train. You know, George Jessel is always saying that there's no place for talent to be lousy any more. It's true. All of us had a chance to be lousy in small-time vaudeville and gradually we learned how to be good."

Burns: "That's right. We all built our acts gradually, learning what would get laughs and what wouldn't."

Benny: "You learned what were things you did best, and bit by bit you developed your own style. You ended up with 17 minutes of surefire material."

Minute by minute

Burns: "That was how you determined how successful an act was. The smaller acts did 10-12 minutes. You'd ask a vaudevillian how he was doing, and he'd answer 'Seventeen minutes.' That meant he was playing next to closing [the star's position on the bill]."

Were there times when that "surefire material" didn't get laughs?

Burns: "Sometimes. There were some routines that you were sure of, like when Gracie kissed me and asked, 'Who was that?' And sometimes you'd do your act at Monday matinees and nothing happened. Then Monday night you'd get big laughs. Why? I don't know."

Benny: "The only time I found when my act wouldn't work was when I was following another comedy act, particularly knockabout comedy. One time I had to follow the Marx Brothers for 13 weeks in

"... they never stole from George and me. We don't use one-liners. We're story tellers; we start talking and one line leads into another."

— Jack Benny

they're pals

a row. It was just murder. The bad thing is that the minute you lay an egg it hurts your timing."

Burns: "You've got to find your own capability and stick to it. Now Jack and I work much the same: we both talk slowly."

Benny: "Some comedians talk fast, and that's their own style. Like Bob Hope. Bob has told me more than once that he admired the way I talk slowly, and he tried to do it himself. But he just couldn't talk that way."

In the sticks

Did you change your material when you played "the sticks?"

Burns: "Never. We never knew what 'the sticks' were. Audiences were the same everywhere."

Benny: "Every town had its sophisticated audience, whether it was New York City or South Bend."

"They could tell, Benny added, when vaudeville started dying.

"Gradually the audiences got smaller. The people just weren't coming in," Benny said.

Burns: "Vaudeville couldn't compete with talking movies. For a dollar you could go to the Roxy Theater in New York and see 70 musicians, 60 Rockettes kicking in unison, a feature movie. And the way out they pressed your pants and did your income tax for you! Vaudeville never changed."

Benny: "And radio killed vaudeville. People stayed home to hear it. Here's a funny thing. In theaters all over the country they would stop the movie and play the Amos 'n' Andy radio show!"

When vaudeville died, Benny and Burns changed gracefully to radio, worrying initially if they could produce enough material for a weekly show. They were successful.

Grinding 'em out

Burns: "We were blessed with some great writers. They'd come to you with four-five pages of jokes. If you didn't like them, they'd go into the next room and write four-five more pages. In vaudeville, we'd go to Altoona to try out one joke."

Benny added that he enjoys the company of other comedians.

Burns: "I do, too. Oh, there are some comics who are always 'on,' but they're just breaking in new material."

What got them into comedy?

Burns: "I had seven sisters and five brothers, and I was the only one in the family that went into show business. I liked it because I could be somebody. For the first 27 year of my life I was a failure — I never got out of small-time vaudeville. But bad as I was, I liked it. Because I was somebody."

Lately more risque

Benny: "The same with me. I started out playing the fiddle in the orchestra pit of the Waukegan vaudeville house. We were all lucky in those years that we had a place to learn our craft."

Comedy, the pair agrees, has changed over the years.

Benny: "Well, we're all more sophisticated than we used to be. In the last five or six years I have been telling risque stories that I would never have done before. People expect it nowadays. But George and I would never use four-letter words."

Will they ever retire?

"Never," said Burns.

"Well," said Benny, "It's tough not to retire. Sometimes I think . . ."

Burns: "What would you do — stay home with Mary? How long have you been with her?"

Benny: "Almost 50 years."

Burns: "Well isn't it nice to get out of town?"

Box office opens for new comedy

Tickets to Murray Schisgal's comedy, "All Over Town" are available now at the Booth Theatre box office for the preview performances through opening night Dec. 29.

Dustin Hoffman, making his professional directorial debut, has staged the two-act play which stars Cleavon Little and Barnard Hughes.

Opening night originally was scheduled for Sunday.

Gracious Dining

The International Jack Benny Fan Club
3190 Oak Road, #303
Walnut Creek, California 94596
JackBenny@Delphi.Com

To:

Address Correction Requested

www.ingramcontent.com/pod-product-compliance
Lightning Source LLC
Chambersburg PA
CBHW080358170426
43193CB00016B/2753